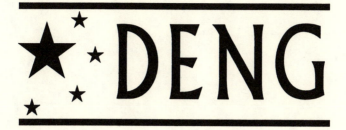

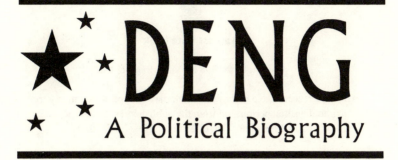

DENG
A Political Biography

Benjamin Yang

With a Foreword by Ross Terrill

An East Gate Book

M.E. Sharpe
Armonk, New York
London, England

An East Gate Book

Copyright © 1998 by M. E. Sharpe, Inc.

Library of Congress Cataloging-in-Publication Data

Yang, Benjamin.
Deng : a political biography / Benjamin Yang.
p. cm.
"An East gate book."
Includes bibliographical references.
ISBN 1-56324-721-6.—
ISBN 1-56324-722-4 (pbk.)
1. Teng, Hsiao-p'ing, 1904-
2. Heads of state—China—Biography.
3. China—Politics and government—1949-
I. Title.
DS778.T39Y33   1997
951.05'092—dc21
[B]   97-23950
CIP
Printed in the United States of America

For Shang Yang

With Deep Love and High Hope

Contents

Foreword

Barely five-feet high, a chain-smoker for sixty years, Deng Xiaoping became the un-Maoist giant of post-Mao China. His little eyes were set far apart on a round face and his bullet head sat on wide shoulders with virtually no neck. As a presence, he could not compare with the imposing Mao Zedong or the handsome Zhou Enlai. Yet he changed China, enormously, mostly for the better.

Mao brought communist rule to China. Deng tried to save communism with one hand and bury it with the other. His career paralleled the rise, crisis of faith, and decline of the revolution which Mao made—and the birth of a different China, economically minded at home and nationalistic abroad.

Deng planted seeds that will continue to show fruits well into China's twenty-first century. In foreign policy, he basically replaced "revolution" as the key value with "nation." Has this change ushered in a period during which China will be to Asia what Bismarck's Germany was to Europe? Deng dismantled Maoism, but did he also dismantle the essentials of the Leninist system?

China during most of the twentieth century has clung to single, over-simplified solutions to its post-dynastic problems. "Mr. Science and Mr. Democracy" were supposed to rejuvenate China after World War One. Chiang Kai-shek in the 1940s thought he found a panacea in reliance on the United States. In the 1950s, Beijing said "the Soviet Union's today is China's tomorrow." By the 1980s, a certain amount of blind pro-Westernism returned as the presumed key to China's salvation.

By contrast, Deng, to his credit, spurned single, over-simplified solutions. His bent was for eclecticism. In this respect he was less akin to Mao than to Sun Yat-sen, the Honolulu-educated patriot who helped overthrow the last dynasty in 1911. He benefited from being regarded as a political man within the army, yet as a military man in the eyes of the Party Center. Despite his reputation, he was less an economic thinker than a skillful manager, choosing good people, and trusting them somewhat more than Mao did. All this we find analyzed in Benjamin Yang's important biographical study.

Born into a rich landed family in Sichuan Province in the southwest in 1904, Deng went to France and the Soviet Union to study in the progressive fashion of the time. Back in China in 1927, he advanced by doing concrete work and avoiding large conflicts in which others fell. Two marriages were cut short by betrayal and political turmoil. A note-taker at many Communist Party meetings, a shrewd organizer and balancer, Deng spent a decade building up credit as an efficient secretary of the revolution.

He made the Long March in the mid-1930s and afterwards married Zhuo Lin, his longtime wife and mother of his two sons and three daughters. From 1937, as Japan attacked China, Deng rose by learning how to make himself helpful to Mao. He proved good at coordinating talent, knowing whom to please and whom to be wary of, making a decision without regrets, and summing up a situation in a single concept. "Who has food, has all," he declared during a critical period of the Sino-Japanese War.

After the Communists won power in 1949, Deng's political acumen and military experience made him an effective boss of his native southwest, and by the mid-1950s he was secretary-general of the Communist Party. In the 1940s and 1950s, he essentially made himself indispensable to Mao.

When Mao launched the utopian Great Leap Forward in 1958, Deng for the first time realized that his great mentor could be terribly wrong. But Deng kept quiet and in the early 1960s he helped pick up the pieces as Mao brooded on the sidelines. Again in the Cultural Revolution of the 1960s, the quixotic Mao, aided by his wife Jiang Qing and the defense minister Lin Biao, struck out in a leftist direction that left Deng uncomprehending and exposed. He tried to appease Mao by joining in the denunciation of head of state Liu Shaoqi, but Deng himself was being marinated as the next goose for the oven ("the Number Two person in power taking the Capitalist Road").

It is not an easy task to write a biography of Deng. His private demons were kept private indeed. As one of his daughters remarked, "Father has never talked a lot." He did not try hard to stuff and embroider the historical record with details that would make his career look good to posterity. None of the existing biographies is fully satisfying on both Deng's life and his career. As David Goodman has said of books on Deng, "In examining the man and his times, they often have no choice but to write about the times."* One generally must rely on works which illuminate particular aspects of Deng, such as Ruan Ming's *Deng Xiaoping: Chronicle of an Empire*, or Deng Maomao's account of some episodes in her father's early career in *My Father Deng Xiaoping*.

Benjamin Yang, too, has a particular angle of approach. He is the author of *From Revolution to Politics: Chinese Communists on the Long March* and acute studies of the Zunyi Conference and other events in the CCP's climb towards power. He contributed substantially to Tony Saich's *The Rise to Power of the Chinese Communist Party*. Of all the Chinese scholars of his generation who came to the West and wrote in English (as well as Chinese), none has contributed a body of work as substantial as Yang's. The great virtues of his book on Deng are his immersion in Chinese party history, his reflective mind, and his understanding of Chinese political motivations. His revealing chapter titles reflect his understanding of Chinese political ways. Yang's eye and ear for politics were sharpened by his family background and his chastening experiences as a young man in the Cultural Revolution. His book is spare, witty, skeptical. Yet it also reflects a fascination with Chinese Communist politics and a passionate concern for a "way out" for the Chinese nation.

The single greatest contribution of *Deng: A Political Biography* is to lay bare the political mind of Deng. Nowhere has the relation between Mao and Deng been limned so profoundly; Yang shows us that Deng's closeness to Mao from the 1930s to the 1950s is inseparable from the breathtaking yet subtly handled departures from Mao that Deng wrought after Mao's death. Compared with Mao, Deng lacked original ideas, preferred unobtrusive methods, and eschewed extremes. Perhaps he understood himself better than Mao understood himself. With Deng, whose upbringing was more tranquil than Mao's, issues were short term, and decisions seldom caused him sleepless nights.

---

*David Goodman, "The Definitive Deng: Biography, Memoirs, Speeches and Writings," *The Pacific Review*, vol. 7, no. 2.

There came a time when he was willing to let a matter rest and go play with his grandchildren.

Yang skillfully traces how Deng won political points by knowing when to be absent, by keeping his mouth shut when others were eager to speak. All in all, *Deng: A Political Biography* enhances Deng's reputation as a political strategist. Deng's way was to achieve a desired result without regard to images, theories, or the opinions of others. Rising three times like a phoenix from the ashes of disgrace, he was seen by some Chinese as a superhuman post-Mao hero, by others as a compromiser whose ruling passion was to hold on to power.

Yang sees a certain political rationale in every phase of Deng's story, even in the clashes between Mao and Deng. He does not view Chinese Communist history as divided into periods of "excesses" and "errors" on the one hand, and a supposed normalcy of advance toward reasonable goals on the other hand. He indeed shows us the political man Deng Xiaoping. He finds him clever and quick, but not always wise.

In *Deng: A Political Biography* the reader learns not only about Deng but about the enduring ways of the Chinese Communist Party, and, beneath them, the sense of history and the stratagems of power politics that far predate the twentieth century.

Even the non-political man Deng emerges to a degree from Yang's book. He was kind enough to have bathed his crippled son daily during the harsh years of rural exile, stubborn enough to have refused a phone call from President Bush during the Tiananmen Square crisis, suspicious enough to have knocked two appointed Number Two figures from their waiting perch (just as Mao did), and good-humored enough to crawl under a table as the agreed penalty for losing a round of bridge.

The Deng era brought four momentous improvements to China, all with limits or side effects. Deng put dramatically less stress on class struggle than Mao did, yet the values of the revolutionary road proved re-usable when convenient. The mood became one of seeking efficiency and prosperity by almost any means; at the same time, there also came higher expectations, as the government encouraged people to be money-minded, and there arose increased inequality, crime, and corruption. The role of law generally was enhanced, and more predictability came to public policy, but words could still be crimes, as many a priest, democrat, and poet found out. Deng not only tilted to the West, as Mao had done, but looked economically and even spiritually to the West; yet the police and security officials still often viewed foreigners as spies.

The ambiguity of Deng's domestic achievements boils down to the ultimate futility of trying to combine a market economy with a Leninist political system. The revolution brought to office a Communist Party which monopolized political power, and Deng's reform opened the economy to market forces. But political paternalism and economic autonomy are not easy to mix. Probably Deng will be more famous for his courage in dismantling Maoism than for the distinctiveness of what he built in its place.

As the twenty-first century approaches, the Deng Xiaoping era is over for better and for worse. Yet gaining a perspective on this second ruler of the Communist period in China's history is essential to mapping China's future. Benjamin Yang expertly provides that perspective. If communism only lasts a few more years in China, Deng may be seen as a Gorbachev, the one who pulled essential planks from under the structure, causing the resulting collapse. If Communist rule persists, Deng will for a time be viewed as its savior, who kept communism going by undermining it. Yet eventually he will be criticized, even by those who try to remain Communists, for failing to match his economic reform with political reform. "If while you are living you receive no criticism," Mao once said, "after you're dead, people nonetheless will criticize you." It was true of Mao. It may also be true of Deng.

Ross Terrill
Cambridge, Massachusetts

Preface

In a scholarly work of the kind presented here, the preface is normally a place for the author to discuss some personal experiences and express some personal sentiments. This is no exception. Here I attempt to use, and even abuse, this custom a bit. This biography of Deng Xiaoping may be regarded as my farewell speech or swan song: for various reasons, personal as well as intellectual, I think it is time for me to retire from studying and writing about Chinese Communist Party history.

I arrived in the United States from mainland China shortly after the establishment of diplomatic relations between the two countries, making me among the earliest of the mainlanders who came to study in America. I was also among the luckiest, thanks, in my case, to a generous scholarship from Harvard University. Somewhat in return, I chose Chinese communist history and politics as the subject of my doctoral research, under the guidance of Professors Benjamin Schwartz and Roderick MacFarquhar. It seems a bit ironic, though not unheard of, for someone to study Western affairs while in China but Chinese affairs while in the West.

Historical research is a tedious and life-consuming business. For me, it meant spending about ten years probing through several thousand historical records to finish a doctoral thesis and then revising it into a book on the Long March of the 1930s. I started working on this Deng biography in 1986 and finished a preliminary draft in 1992. Reading, thinking, and writing about Deng will have been an integral part of my everyday life for more than ten years by the time it is finally published.

Sometimes, after working long hours to check out a couple of dates and names, or quotes and notes, I could not help muttering to myself, What for?! Then I would remember a conversation I once had with

Professor John Fairbank about an article in the *Harvard Crimson* some years ago. The article's author believed that most Asian affairs majors at Harvard must be exhibiting some kind of obsession or mental perversion. Apparently somewhat in agreement, Professor Fairbank told me that, when he was a college student in London in the late 1920s, several opportunities for his future career then became apparent, the least profitable of which from a practical perspective was China, the one on which he eventually embarked.

Carma Hinton, the producer of the documentary film *The Gate of Heavenly Peace* and a schoolmate of mine at Beijing's Summer Palace High School, lamented recently that Partisan approaches to Chinese communist history and politics may offend just one party, while non-partisan approaches may offend two parties. I agree with her. I expect both my Western colleagues and my Chinese compatriots to offer criticisms of this book, some of which I may understand and yet may not be ready to accept. In this preface, as well as in the text that follows, I also offer them my criticisms, likewise without anticipating their immediate acceptance.

"Criticism is one thing, and unfairness is another," to quote Paul Cohen of Wellesley College. But beyond fairness and unfairness is truthfulness. We are scholars and intellectuals, dealing with something impersonal, and above all, we search for truth, the fairness or usefulness of which is not instantly apparent like pure, sparkling water served at the dinner table but whose value ultimately becomes evident like a diamond unearthed from a deep subterranean deposit.

Deng was a member of my father's generation, and thus one whom I should piously respect. Actually, one of the accusations made against me during the Cultural Revolution in the late 1960s was my sympathy for Deng against Madame Mao. His two sons had been my schoolmates at Beijing University: Deng Pufang and I belonged to the same Red Guard faction, and we both suffered a great deal in the late 1960s. Deng Zhifang and I lived in the same graduate dormitory for two years before our departures for the United States—he to Rochester, New York, in 1980 and I to Cambridge, Massachusetts, in 1981.

As a matter of fact, I do highly respect Deng; otherwise, I would not have written this biography. But I do not think the Dengs will be pleased with it, nor do I intend that they be. Its general approach and content differ significantly from official Chinese positions. After all, a biography is a biography, not a funeral eulogy. In covering its subject, it should, as Deng himself suggested, present not only the good but also the bad—as long as, together, they both make the true.

What I expect from my Western colleagues might be termed "criticism of criticism." In spite of—or perhaps owing to—my indebtedness to all the previous authors and my acquaintance with some of them, I feel obliged to bring to their attention some basic drawbacks in the profession of Sinology in general and Dengology in particular. It is not that I wish to present myself as an agent of enlightenment for the ignorant heathens but that, if I must choose between the sins of incivility and pretentiousness, I would pick the former.

I am convinced, correctly or incorrectly, that some Western biographers of Deng have perpetuated many factual errors, regardless of fresh discoveries in the primary and secondary literature. Thirty years ago, an eminent biographer of the Chinese leadership believed that Deng had been with Peng Dehuai as the chief of staff of the Third Red Army Corps in the early 1930s; this was an obvious instance of mistaking Deng Xiaoping for another Red Army leader, Deng Ping. I have pointed this out in a number of articles and feel somewhat wronged to find today's authors still repeating the same error.

The study of history is somewhat analogous to the study of mathematics and physics, in that once an issue, major or minor, is settled, we should realize it and not keep repeating past errors; otherwise, we can hardly make progress. As long as we have to argue over basic facts, we cannot move forward. In this regard, less apparent but more important than the need to clarify basic facts is the need to achieve an appropriate understanding of Deng's involvement or noninvolvement in some key historical and political events. There are a few such events, just a dozen or so, that require a biographer's careful attention but almost never receive it.

It should be pointed out, furthermore, that the problem involves more than just an individual biography. It is my observation that China is growing ever more important, while China studies are lagging ever further behind, at least in the United States. As compared to their Chinese counterparts in general, I believe that American scholars have a less solid knowledge of China and American politicians have a less firm policy toward China.

President Bill Clinton once mistook the People's Republic of China for the Republic of China (what's the difference?!), and House

Speaker Newt Gingrich once called for admitting both Taiwan and the mainland to the United Nations (why not?!). Inadequate knowledge of China and lack of due respect for it have been costly and may become even more so. Of course, America can well afford such costs—which, in most cases and for most individuals, do not seem so burdensome anyhow. General Douglas MacArthur was dismissed from his Korean War command not because of his ignorance of Chairman Mao Zedong but because of his disobedience to President Harry Truman—although the opposite rationale might have been equally valid.

Flexible engagement or resolute containment? American politicians are calling loudly for both China policies but seem capable of opting for neither. As a result, they tend on the whole merely to reflect on and react to current events. Nevertheless, the United States does have a decisive advantage—namely, its vastly superior position in the world economy and in global politics, which gives it the luxury of not having to take China as seriously as China must take the United States, at least at this moment.

As for American experts on China, their publications are not always held to strict standards of intellectual accountability—as they ought to be—as long as their colleagues and readers in general adhere to equally lax standards. But every once in a while, dramatic events such as the Cultural Revolution in 1966 and the Tiananmen incident in 1989, and recently the Taiwan Strait crisis, occur that demand their expertise. If they follow public emotions and commotions or vice versa, inaccurate information and inappropriate judgment may result, thereby disturbing their comfort and complacency.

My attempt at writing this biography of Deng was prompted in the summer of 1984 during my trip to Sichuan with Ross Terrill, who had just published his *Madame Mao* at the time, and who has ever since provided me with advice and assistance. In a special forum on Deng held by *The China Quarterly* in London in 1993, I learned much from other participants, particularly David Shambaugh and Dick Wilson. Martin Revlin of Columbia University helped check the entire manuscript. I also benefited from David Goodman's publications as much as from our direct communications. Mark Selden offered warm encouragement at a critical juncture, and the admonishments of an anonymous reviewer for M.E. Sharpe prevented me from making a variety of methodological and technical errors. I owe them all my deep thanks.

But to be honest, I do not lean on others, such as my professors and advisers, as much this time as previously. For better or for worse, I am no longer a young student. All else aside, this volume is an expression of my own hope and wish that China and the United States, which will presumably be the dominant nations in the coming century, should have a better understanding of each other and better relations with each other!

Cambridge, Massachusetts
August 1997

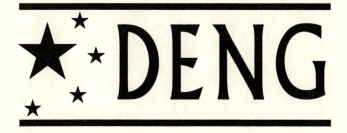

— 1 —

Prologue: Why Deng?

Presented here for English-speaking readers is another biographic study of Deng Xiaoping, the paramount leader of communist China. I assume—and I am sure most readers would agree—that a good political biography should fulfill at least two fundamental requirements: its subject should be important enough to be worth notice, and particularly, its author's presentation should be interesting enough to be worth attention. This short prologue largely focuses on these two issues.

Deng was a man of many years, many names, and also many controversies. During the course of his long life—he was ninety-two years old at the time of his death in February 1997—Deng adopted a number of names, some official and others less so, but the one he chose for himself when he joined the communist revolution in the late 1920s is now the one by which China and the entire world recognize him. Literally translated from Chinese, "Deng Xiaoping" means "Deng the Small and Plain."

He was small indeed, even by Asian standards—barely five feet tall and normally weighing no more than 120 pounds. He was also rather plain in his appearance and manner. With dark eyes set far apart on a flat, round, chubby face and with a miniature figure wrapped loosely in ordinary Chinese clothes, Deng Xiaoping could hardly, even in his younger days, equal the stature of some of his colleagues, such as the imposing Chairman Mao Zedong or the handsome Premier Zhou Enlai.

By no means unaware of his own physical shortcomings, Deng was occasionally heard to make himself the butt of jokes. Once, in response to the concern expressed by a group of foreign visitors that his reform

3

policy might bring unpredictable consequences to both China and his own political fortunes, Deng laughed and stated, "I am a short and small man, as you can see. If the heavens were indeed to fall down, I would not be held as responsible for shouldering them up as those tall folks."[1]

Hence arises a simple question: Why Deng? The answer is also quite simple, but very crucial. Deng would not be so important if he had not been the dominant leader of the Chinese Communist Party (CCP). But he was. The Communist Party would not be so important if it were not the governing party of China. But it is. And China, in turn, would not be so important if it did not possess one-tenth of the land mass, one-fifth of the population, and three-fourths of the organized communists in the world. But once again, it actually does!

There should be little doubt about Deng's political importance and achievements. For more than six decades, he assumed various active roles in the Chinese communist movement, enjoying a political career longer than that of any other Chinese communist leader and, in terms of influence, and he was, perhaps, second only to Mao in shaping communist China's cause. Mao brought the rule of communism to China, whereas Deng saved it in one sense and simultaneously buried it in another.

Mao has by now become *history,* whereas, until quite recently, Deng remained alive as *politics.* This constitutes another significant difference, as far as we are presently concerned. The last two decades in communist China are commonly called the Deng epoch, character- ized by its dual policies of "economic reform" and "openness to the world." Thanks to these Dengist policies, among other factors, China's national economy has grown with staggering speed and is rapidly catching up with the economies of Japan and the United States.

"Good for them! So what?" some people may say with a shrug. But we must realize that China's economic expansion is in large part based on its international trade and commerce, which, like Japan's, has quite a lot to do with us, directly or otherwise, for better or for worse. We must also realize that in connection with changes in the world economy come changes in world politics. China, not quite like Japan, is a politi- cal nation, and subsequent to its economic growth will be its expansion in world politics and confrontation with America, as Deng told his comrades.[2] After the dissolution of the Soviet Union, Deng told his com- rades in 1991, China's confrontation with the United States becomes more inevitable. It is a question not of if it exists, but how to handle it.

More than a dozen biographies have thus far been published on Deng, mostly outside China, as have thousands of articles and essays, mostly inside China. We can easily find such Deng biographies as those by David Bonavia (1989), David Goodman (1994), Richard Evans (1993), and Deng Rong (1993). These are among the latest and most serious works.[3] The authors are well-known China experts or, in the last case, Deng's own daughter, and their writings are all available in good English. Why bother with yet another Deng biography?

Errors and flaws, I must say, remain fairly common in almost all of these earlier works. There are still numerous factual inaccuracies and ambiguities, and above all, there are still inadequate understandings of numerous historical and political episodes in which Deng was personally involved. In short, there are many points of fact and analyses that I think are mistaken and misleading. A scholarly work is not supposed to be misleading, nor are intelligent readers to be misled. That, at least, should go without saying.

Just a few examples: Bonavia says that Deng returned to China in September 1926 to attend a historical event called "the Wuyuan pledge," whereas Deng was actually studying in Moscow at the time. Goodman believes that Deng led the Seventh Red Army to arrive in the Jiangxi Soviet in March 1931, whereas Deng actually left the troops on his flight to Shanghai. Evans asserts that Deng assumed the political commissarship of the 129th Division after his predecessor died in January 1938, whereas Deng was actually appointed to that position by Mao owing to some delicate political concerns.[4]

Deng Rong's problems are of quite a different nature. Somewhat contrary to the position expressed by her own father, who suggested that a biography should present both the positive and negative sides to make a comprehensive whole, Deng Rong—actually, this is true of Chinese official historians in general—tries just to include the former but exclude the latter. Did Deng join the Communist Party in 1924? Did Deng become the chief secretary of the Party Center in 1928? Did Deng oppose the Li Lisan adventure in 1930? Did the Front Committee permit Deng to leave the Seventh Red Army for Shanghai in 1931? Was Deng a participant at the Zunyi Conference in 1935?[5]

Few of the available biographies seem to achieve a true sense of Deng's delicate mind and complex role in the Gao–Rao purge in 1953, the antirightist campaign in 1957, the Great Leap Forward in 1958, the

Sino-Soviet debate in 1963, the Cultural Revolution in 1966, the arrest of the "Gang of Four" in 1976, the decision on the Tiananmen incident in 1989, and so forth. Fully grasping Deng's participation in these events entails considerations not only of specific factual accuracy but mainly of general knowledge and approach. More bluntly, these biographers tend to regard Deng and Chinese communist politics too simplistically and too straightforwardly, more or less the same way American teenagers interpret kung-fu movies.

Time magazine chose Deng for the second time as its "Man of the Year" in 1985, praising his role as a pragmatist in reversing Mao's radicalism and placing China's feet on the capitalist road. Ironically, Deng was not at all grateful for this praise, and that issue of *Time*—featuring a cover photo of Deng's bright image emerging from Mao's shadow—was forbidden to circulate in China.[6] Deng described himself as a true disciple of Mao and a faithful follower of Maoism. Yet to remain true to Maoism, he also argued, some of Mao's own words and deeds had to be undone and redone. Isn't it doubly ironic that Mao didn't seem to understand himself as well as did Deng, nor did Deng understand himself as well as did *Time*'s editors?!

U.S. President George Bush was angered by Deng's refusal to take a phone call from him during the June 1989 massacre in and around Tiananmen Square. But this refusal reflected more than Deng's personal animosity toward Bush—actually, the two men liked each other personally—for Deng later instructed his friends and colleagues: "We don't mind what they say and what they do now, and we aren't afraid of their sanction. As long as we can get through this situation and remain in control of this country, they will come back to us."[7]

Deng proved quite correct. After offering a few excuses and apologies once the domestic crisis was under control, Deng indeed won back President Bush's sympathy. Special envoys were secretly dispatched twice to Beijing in late 1989. Subsequently, Japanese Prime Minister Kaifu Toshiki, British Prime Minister John Major, and U.S. Secretary of State James Baker visited China. In this episode, Deng appeared to be a more resourceful leader of a less governable country, whereas Bush appeared to be just the opposite—a less resourceful leader of a more governable country.

To those readers who open this biography expecting to find a glamorous personality who accomplished miraculous deeds, I honestly suggest that they close the book now. Deng's life contained few such moments, nor do I intend to describe him in that manner. He was a politician, and this is a political biography. To the best of my understanding, Deng was an ordinary person who did some extraordinary things.

This biography attempts to provide readers with, on the one hand, inductive facts as accurate and comprehensive as possible and, on the other hand, deductive interpretations as appropriately imaginative as possible: facts based upon my specific documentary research and discoveries, and interpretations based upon my general historical knowledge and political experiences.

There are so many things about Deng that we do not know and cannot easily learn. In the past two decades alone, for instance, Deng received several hundred foreign guests and spoke at several hundred conferences—almost all of which were officially recorded by hand or on tape. What can we outside observers do—break into the safes of the CCP central archives? Nonetheless, to overcome this technically insurmountable gap, we can and must depend upon our professional knowledge and painstaking research, together with a serious, impartial attitude. As China experts, that is not only what we are trained for, but please don't forget, that is also what most of us live on!

In this particular regard, I have always appreciated the recommendation of Harvard's Professor Benjamin Schwartz that Chinese communist history and politics be approached with "humble agnosticism." Didn't the ancient Greek philosopher Socrates say, "I know that I don't know," and didn't the ancient Chinese philosopher Confucius say, "Knowledge is to know what we know and also what we don't know"?[8]

The same humble yet noble approach ought to be adopted in treating Deng. It is not so easy to write well on Deng and communist China, for a variety of practical reasons—and I hope that readers can somehow understand that. I would be satisfied just to shed some fresh light on this subject and a little beyond. Nor is it so easy to *read* well on Deng and communist China, so I also hope that readers are mentally prepared for the effort that will be required. If not, how about dropping this unpalatable volume and putting another entertaining kung-fu movie in the VCR?

2

Like Father, Like Son, 1904-1918

Until recently, there have been a variety of inaccurate allegations regarding Deng's childhood, some of which have persisted to the present day—allegations involving such matters as his birthplace, his birth date, his name or names, his family origins, and his schooling. Whereas some of these inaccuracies are more excusable, others can hardly be excused. We outside observers tend to blame the Chinese communists, who seem to keep everything a state secret, even the simplest biographical facts regarding their party and government leaders. Nonetheless, to be fair to them as well as to ourselves, it must be said that, although we authors may well be justified in blaming the Chinese when they fail to provide correct information, we must also be held responsible when we disseminate incorrect information. After all, we alone are responsible for the accuracy of our writings![1]

Let's start with a few simple facts: Deng Xiaoping was born on August 22, 1904, in the small village of Paifang, Guang'an County, Sichuan Province. In the Chinese lunar calendar of that time, Deng's birth date was July 12, and 1904 was the year of the dragon. His father first named him "Deng Xiansheng"—a name later changed to "Deng Xixian" at the recommendation of his preschool tutor. He might have had a nickname or baby name, "Xianwa," which literally means "Nice Boy" and would have been used by his parents and older relatives, as was quite common among Sichuanese farmers. The Dengs had by then resided in Sichuan for more than a dozen generations. His father was not born and brought up in Guangdong, nor could his grandfather possibly have served with the Qianlong emperor. Also, please don't believe any tales of a connection between Deng's revolutionary career and his supposed Hakka or immigrant family background.[2]

Anything before the most recent dozen generations must be regarded as too distant and too vague to have been recorded with accuracy, although the Deng family tree can be traced back some six or seven hundred years. The intense warfare between the Mongolian rulers (1271–1368) and Chinese peasant rebellions in the middle of the fourteenth century killed or scared off millions of Sichuanese, leaving the province a demographic vacuum and in a state of administrative disorder. As the new Ming dynasty (1368–1644) came into existence, Deng Xiaoping's earliest known ancestor, presumably a minor army officer, joined an immigration trend by leaving his hometown of Luling in Jiangxi Province to trek to Guang'an in Sichuan Province.

The Dengs' early years as strangers in a strange land must have been rather tough, but they seemed to have adapted themselves to the new environment well enough to have propagated a single family into a thriving clan of several hundred households. There were in the Ming Dynasty nine generations of Dengs, among whom two individuals were recorded as having passed the *jinshi,* or national civil service examination, and consequently served the government as county and prefecture magistrates.[3]

Another eight generations passed during the Qing dynasty of the Manchus (1644–1911), bringing the Deng lineage down to Deng Xiaoping's own father. According to its genealogical book, which was aimed particularly at showing off its previous glory and pride, the Deng clan in this period even produced a high-ranking official with a reputation well known throughout the country and a prestige felt throughout northern Sichuan.

In the heyday of the Manchu dynasty in the early eighteenth century, one of Deng Xiaoping's ancestors, Deng Shimin, passed the civil service examinations successively at the regional (*xiucai*), provincial (*juren*), and national (*jinshi*) levels and was subsequently appointed a member of the royal Hanlin Academy in the capital city. During his approximately forty-year-long service with the Manchu court, Deng Shimin apparently held a number of central government positions such as supervisor of the civil service examination and chief justice of the supreme court.

Nonetheless, aside from providing a role model for later generations to follow, Deng Shimin could hardly have left a heritage of wealth and power large enough for his descendants to dwell on a century and a half later. He was not Deng Xiaoping's grandfather, as commonly believed, nor even his direct lineal ancestor. In any event, seven generations separated Deng Shimin from Deng Xiaoping, so the former's influences upon the latter could only have been spiritual rather than practical.[4]

Deng's father, named Deng Wenming, or "Deng the Civilized," was born in 1886 to a farming and handicraft family. He grew up just as China entered a period of decline. In the wake of the humiliating Sino-Japanese War of 1895, the aborted "One-Hundred-Day Reform" of 1898, the desperate Boxer Movement of 1900, and the terrifying "Eight-Country Joint Assault" in 1901, the Manchu Empire fell into an appalling state. It was a case of "a watermelon carved up among imperialist invaders" according to Chinese patriots and a case of an "open door and equal opportunity" according to U.S. Secretary of State John Hay in President William McKinley's administration.

Nevertheless, in the countryside of a hinterland province like Sichuan, where the Dengs lived, Confucian traditions still prevailed over modern influences in the first decade of this century. Men wore pigtails, women had bound feet, and children's marriages were arranged while they were still toddlers. The Paifang villagers were less interested in national politics than in their families, economic activities, and rural community affairs.

Great controversies have arisen among local folk over Deng Wenming's moral and ethical character. One version is, "He was a rascal, indulging himself in wine and sex throughout his criminal life, a cruel landlord, who lived the life of a parasite sucking the sweat and blood of poor peasants, and a reactionary element who had brutally suppressed revolutionary people." But according to another version, "He was a good man, hard-working by himself and sympathetic to others. He loved and was loved by his fellow villagers."[5] These two extremes of condemnation and approbation are a reflection less of Deng Wenming's true character than of his son Deng Xiaoping's tortuous political fortunes: the former was recorded by the Red Guards in the late 1960s, when Deng was under political criticism, whereas the latter was presented by local government officials in the early 1980s, when Deng was rehabilitated as the undisputed leader of all China. The truth probably lies somewhere between these two extremes.

It may be too much to characterize Deng Wenming's household as the "trinity of hereditary bureaucracy, local despotism, and superstitious religion," as the Red Guards once did. But there is no doubt that, thanks less to his family fortune than to his own efforts, Deng Wenming was among the most affluent and wealthy individuals in Paifang. He was a big landlord—a title not as bad during his lifetime as it later became under communist rule after his death. He had more than twenty acres of arable land, of which two-thirds was rented out permanently to tenant farmers (*dian hu*), and the rest was managed by Deng Wenming himself and tilled by temporary hired laborers (*duan gong*). The annual yield of grain, mainly rice and corn, from his land totaled about two hundred barrels, or thirteen thousand kilograms. A small part of this amount was consumed by his own family, and the rest was sold for cash. In connection with his farming business, Deng Wenming also raised mules, donkeys, and cows for field work and set up a vegetable garden and a stone mill for family use. He seldom performed any manual labor himself but was the brains behind all operations of the Deng household.[6]

The composition of Deng Wenming's family changed naturally during the course of his lifetime. His father died when he was quite young. Then, his sister "married out," and his wife "married in." For a while in his late teens, his house contained only his mother, his wife, himself, and a couple of servants. Since this wife was from a family named Zhang, she came to be called—in accordance with the rural custom of that time—Deng Zhang. A few years after the wedding, as his economic status grew and yet no child was born to Deng Zhang, Deng Wenming decided to take another wife or concubine and was able to acquire one from a family named Dan. Deng Dan proved able to give birth to a girl and a boy in two years. The boy was Deng Xiaoping, called Deng Xiansheng at the time. The birth of Xiansheng brought to Wenming a "perfect family" according to traditional standards: himself as the master, two wives, a daughter, and above all, a son as his heir.

Attentive as he was to his own family affairs, Deng Wenming was not the type of person who was concerned merely with bread and butter, with wives and kids. He might be said to have been a full-fledged member of the local elite. Within the limited structure of his rural community, he pursued a more vigorous social and spiritual life than almost anybody else in the village. Soon after he reached adulthood, he became a member and later a chief of the "Society of Elder

Brothers" (*Gelao hui*) and was at the same time a devout follower of the "Religion of Five Sons" (*Wuzi jiao*).[7]

Originally a nationwide secret society formed to launch peasant rebellions against the Manchu invasion a few centuries earlier, the Society of Elder Brothers had evolved into a grass-roots organization of rural folk whose purpose was to protect local interests and provide its members with mutual assistance. The rich and powerful would in all likelihood be made chiefs of the society, and chiefs of the society would, in turn, become the rich and powerful. This general formula applied perfectly in the case of Deng Wenming.

The Religion of Five Sons, on the other hand, was a phenomenon peculiar to northern Sichuan at the turn of this century, although some of its basic doctrines were rooted in national history and culture. The religion took its name from a historical figure named Xun Jihe, a gentleman of an ancient dynasty who had supposedly done all the good deeds there were to do, from feeding beggars on the street to burning sticks of incense before statues of Confucius and Buddha. Xun did not achieve much in his own lifetime, but he did father five sons. As a reward from God, Buddha, the Heavenly Emperor, or whomever for his good behavior, and also because of his persistent attention to his sons' education and cultivation, all five of Xun Jihe's sons grew up to be distinguished scholars or prominent government officials.

This religion, if it can be called that, represented an eclectic hybrid of various theories and practices from Taoism, Buddhism, Confucianism, and other religious-cultural beliefs—all blended with the aim of bettering one's own or one's family's secular life. In the year 1904, Deng Wenming could easily find in his Five Sons faith an explanation for his having been granted a baby boy; had he lived to the 1980s, he would have had no difficulty in finding the same explanation for his son's achievements in the national political limelight.

If government means specific offices and formally dressed officials, there was no government in the countryside until the omnipresent communists took over China. As long as the peasants paid their taxes and avoided conspicuous violence, such as murder or rebellion, nominal village heads seemed more than enough to handle everything in rural areas. On the basis of his wealth as a landlord, his power as a chief of the peasant society, and his reputation as a leader of the local religion, Deng Wenming was naturally selected as head of Paifang village—a part-time governmental position whose responsibilities included urging peasants to pay their taxes and reporting to the county *yamen* any grave crimes committed in the village.

A giant basin surrounded by high mountains on all sides and blessed with abundant agricultural products and natural resources, Sichuan has historically been known as the "State of Heaven." The county of Guang'an, in which Paifang is located, lies slightly north of the basin's center, covering a territory of fifteen hundred square kilometers, with a population of more than one million at present—roughly a quarter million in Deng Wenming's time.

Range after range of flat-topped hills offer the Sichuanese plenty of arable land, with crops of corn and wheat raised on their slopes and rice paddies planted in the valleys between them. Nearly everywhere can be seen groves of bamboo, which is used for almost every purpose in rural life—houses, gates, fences, tables, chairs, and more. Some people even go so far as to posit a relationship between bamboo and both the slender bodies of Sichuanese women and the clever minds of Sichuanese men.

The village of Paifang is actually an assemblage of a hundred or so households loosely spread out over about a quarter of a mile along a stream. The stream, too small to have a formal name, runs under a wooden bridge in the middle of the village and meanders westward to join the Qu River at the county seat of Guang'an, while the narrow path over the bridge heads in a slightly different direction toward the adjacent town of Xiexing, where it joins a much wider road also leading toward Guang'an.

Unlike the overwhelming majority of the houses in Paifang, which clung to both banks of the little stream, the Deng residence was set back a few hundred yards from the stream. It was rooted in seclusion on the flat top of a little hill at the far southeastern tip of the village, connected to the main body of the village only by a narrow sand and gravel path, which crawled down the northern slope of the hill.

Unique not only in its location, the Deng house was also the most elaborate one in the whole village. Whereas a typical village house consisted of three to five rooms under a rice-stalk-thatched roof and was either directly open to the fields or streets or surrounded just by a rickety wooden fence, the Deng house was a tightly enclosed brick compound. It had a main structure of a dozen rooms, flanked by two wings, each of which had five rooms, all shielded behind a tall frontal wall with an even taller gate. In the eyes of the local villagers eight decades ago, the Deng residence looked very much like the "Forbidden City" in Beijing, an obvious symbol of the family's wealth and prestige.[8]

This is where Deng grew up. As a healthy boy and the only male heir, he was the darling of the entire family. He was raised in the most privileged manner that a rural landlord could afford to offer. He had his own bedroom at the left rear corner of the house—obviously a luxury, given the fact that, in a normal peasant family, several members of different generations might share a single bedroom. Yet next to Deng's room were the kitchen on one side and the pigsty on the other so that both kitchen waste and baby waste could conveniently feed the pigs through a joint line of wooden troughs—certainly not a comfort by any modern urban standard.

Deng's early childhood was confined to the village of Paifang, primarily the world enclosed by the Deng residence's tall brick walls. Occasionally, his nannies would take him outside the house to the open space on top of the hill, pointing up to the singing birds in the trees or gazing down at the distant horizon, where the earthly hills touched the heavenly clouds, and where the legendary cities of Chongqing and Chengdu should be. When he was old enough to toddle along on his own legs, he would occasionally be taken to the banks of the stream or to the pond, counting ducks and drakes or watching buffalo splash in the shallow water.

When Deng reached the age of four or five, his father hired a private tutor to teach the boy at home to read and write some basic Chinese characters. At that tutor's suggestion, Deng's father changed his given name, "Xiansheng," or "Ahead of the Saint," to "Xixian," or "Aspiring for Sagehood." It was customary in rural Sichuan for parents to express good wishes and high hopes in naming their children. Although Deng's father certainly held high hopes for his son and heir apparent, it was perhaps too bold to be "Ahead of the Saint," and therefore, "Aspiring for Sagehood" should be good enough.[9]

The private tutorship was not a regular program of education but rather a kind of "preschool enlightenment." The tutor and the pupil met a few times each week. After going through several clusters of simple words such as the words for *one* and *two, big* and *small,* and *heaven* and *earth,* Deng advanced to the level of reciting and transcribing the standard children's textbooks, *Three Character Classic* and *Article of One Thousand Words.* Both books were embodiments of Confucian doctrines set forth in nursery rhymes. The young Deng could not digest the texts' full meaning, but he did learn to recite the words and remember the characters.

The year 1910 bore a special significance for Deng and touched his young life in a variety of ways—some obvious even at the time, others subtle yet full of portents for the years to come. It was the time when a massive revolution took place throughout his native province and also when Deng was joined by a baby brother and Deng himself started attending a regular school outside Paifang village.

Beijing was too far away, and to Paifang folk, Sichuan represented almost the whole world. Without post offices or newspapers, peddlers and travelers were the information carriers. Some news turned out to be false rumors, and other rumors turned out to be real news. In the summer of 1910, one piece of real news swept through the Sichuan basin like a brush fire: a mass movement had arisen all over the province to resist the central government's takeover of the ownership of the regional railroad. This was the historically prominent "Railroad Protection Movement" of Sichuan, which would become the trigger for a nationwide revolution the very next year.

After an interval of six years, Deng's mother, Deng Dan, gave birth to another boy, Deng Xianxiu. As far as Deng Xiaoping was concerned, the arrival of this younger brother had mixed implications. On the one hand, he was displaced from his favored position, but on the other hand, he was released from his pressing responsibility as the sole male heir of the family. Had Deng Xiaoping been the family's only son, his father could hardly have allowed him to leave home, let alone go abroad, as he would do a few years later.

More directly related to Deng personally, the year 1910 marked his sixth birthday, the minimum age for attending regular school—that is, a primary school in Xiexing, a much larger village about half a mile northwest of Paifang. Deng spent the next five years in the Xiexing primary school. At the very least, his physical horizons were somewhat broadened. Every day, he had to go to Xiexing and return to Paifang, hiking by several village houses, trudging across the bridge over the pond, hopping many a step on the muddy road between the two villages, and hurrying through a few lanes and streets to finally arrive in the schoolyard.

The schoolhouse, a former ancestor-worship hall, offered a curriculum of reformed Confucian teachings. The small children—all boys but no girls—sat on rows of wooden benches, black pigtails bobbing, repeating and reciting the age-old *Four Books* and *Five Classics* sentence by sentence. The nature of the curriculum was dictated not only by diehard traditions but also by practical considerations: in the teaching profession, there could be found few if any individuals capable of teaching anything else. As time passed and Deng entered higher grades, a couple of courses such as mathematics and Chinese language were introduced, thus bringing in some "modern flavor."

Young Deng was nicely dressed, often in silks and satins, and he brought good lunches, such as fried rice and steamed wheat buns packed by his nannies. Other than that, Deng was an ordinary schoolboy. "He was a good pupil in the school and always handed in his homework on time; the teachers liked him very much," one cousin of Deng told me. According to another interviewee, however, "He was just OK in his studies—not too good, nor too bad. He was too young and small to play with other kids."[10] Today, there are also stories, legends almost, about Deng's sympathy and generosity with poor classmates, such as how he helped them with food and money—stories somewhat comparable to the tale of George Washington and the cherry tree.

After young Deng graduated from the Xiexing primary school in the summer of 1915, his father wanted his eldest son to further his education. To the best of Deng Wenming's knowledge, that would mean sending Deng Xiaoping to attend a secondary school in the county seat of Guang'an, despite the long distance and considerable expense that would be involved.

Compared to the primary school in Xiexing, the Guang'an secondary school was fairly modern. Housed in a Western-style two-story concrete building, the school offered courses in mathematics, geography, history, natural sciences, music, painting, and physical training—more or less the same as nowadays. Confucian textbooks were no longer used, and vernacular Chinese was taught instead of classical Chinese. Even the Chinese language course had a fresh new title: "National Language and Literature." Close to the school campus was a Catholic church operated by a few French priests, adding an even more modern and exotic ingredient to the educational environment.

The county seat of Guang'an is about ten kilometers from Paifang, and normally, it would take Deng and a few other schoolboys from the same village half a day to walk that distance. Fortunately, the Guang'an higher primary school was a boarding school, so Deng could stay in its dormitory and eat in its dining hall. While studying and lodging there on weekdays, he visited home in Paifang once every weekend or two.

The adjacent Catholic church attracted the students. The Western priests—with colored hair and eyes and large noses—and the strange music and singing emanating from the church hall were to them both a mystery and a fascination. Some of his friends were impressed, but young Deng was mainly puzzled by the idea that these neatly dressed and gently behaved people had come all the way from the other side of the earth just to persuade every Chinese to believe that the whole universe was created by somebody with the strange name of Jesus Christ.[11]

Although certain historical events had occurred quite a few years earlier, young Deng began to learn of them only in the city of Guang'an. The county government was located there, as was a post office, and people there tended to be better informed about political affairs than the folk in Paifang. Besides, this was also the time when Deng grew mature enough to become more interested in contemporary social and political issues than he had been before.

In the wake of Sichuan's Railroad Protection Movement in 1910 came China's national revolution in 1911. The Manchu monarchy crumbled and was replaced by the Republic of China. But it soon became clear that republicanism fared no better, and all its seemingly good features—constitution, cabinet, parliament, and provincial autonomy—were corrupted, with various negative consequences. In 1915, President Yuan Shikai tried to restore monarchical rule, establishing himself as a new emperor. The "Yuan Empire" collapsed even before its birth. There followed a period of warlordism, when the whole country was divided into several regional spheres of military influence. In less than a decade, China had experimented with three or four systems of national politics, and none of them seemed workable. As a result, a "New Culture Movement" arose, especially among Chinese intellectuals. It seemed to them that China's was a problem less of government than of people and that what China needed was a change less in political form than in basic cultural substance.

Back at home in Paifang, Deng's mother, Dan, gave birth to yet another boy, Deng Shuping, eight years Deng Xiaoping's junior. Father Wenming was himself neither a saint nor a sage, as he expected his children to be. He brought into his household two more young concubines, respectively from the Xiao and Xia families—the younger being sixteen years old. His previous logical excuse of seeking a male heir was not as relevant this time—he already had three sons—as was his explicit sexual purpose. Other explanations might have included the dual function of concubines as housekeepers and babysitters. To be sure, it was neither illegal nor immoral at the time for a man to have more than one wife or concubine. On the contrary, it was a satisfactory way of displaying one's wealth and power, of which Deng Wenming had both.[12]

It was the summer of 1918, and as Deng's graduation was approaching, both Deng and his father began to ponder what his next step should be. A secondary school was for basic education, not for professional training. Most of his classmates would return home to their native villages; the knowledge and skills they had acquired in school would assuredly be of some practical use. Their literacy would enable them to write letters and make notes, and their mathematical skills would enable them to help keep household or business accounts. Deng could do the same, if he chose.

A fourteen-year-old boy, Deng had yet no firm mind, and for a while, he wavered from one choice to another. He knew that some older boys would like to continue their studies but could not because of economic constraints: many of them were already engaged, and some were even married. This made Deng consider it somewhat undesirable to go back after graduation. The starry-eyed ideas he had learned from his teachers—"Serve the nation and save the people" and "Pursue a noble career and live a worthy life"—also had some bearing on his decision. Furthermore, one of his intimate schoolmates, Deng Shaosheng, who happened to be his uncle from the same clan, favored attending high school rather than returning to the village.[13]

Because ideas were merely ideas and could not be put into practice without paternal approval, Deng consulted his father. Surprisingly or not, his father listened attentively and agreed to his further schooling shortly afterward. As a father, Deng Wenming hoped his son would grow to be more advanced than he himself was, so that he could find in his heir a fulfillment of his own aspirations. What the father wished from the son was for him to become a sage, but no sage could be produced in the village of Paifang or even in the county of Guang'an. In Deng Wenming's mind, moreover, sagehood was defined not only in a moral or subjective sense but mainly in a social or an objective sense—which meant accomplishing or establishing something to win public acknowledgment, just as his forefather Deng Shimin and the five sons of Xun Jihe had done.

In the past, the civil service examination had served as an obvious ladder to success. Parents made all possible sacrifices to support their children in their studies. Once a child was good enough or lucky enough to pass the civil service examinations—regardless of the contents of those exams—immediate wealth and fame would accrue to the whole family. But the civil service examination system was abolished in 1905, and even the emperor was dethroned in 1911. Nevertheless, it still seemed to Deng Wenming that his eldest son should pursue higher education instead of returning home, where his best prospects would be to become a local strongman like himself, far from the sage he wanted his son to become.

Given the consensus among his peers that pursuing further studies would be better than undertaking a farming business at home, and with his best friend taking the initiative and his father offering firm support, Deng was set to continue his education in high school. That meant moving farther away from his native village to Chongqing, the nearest cosmopolitan city that possessed some high schools at that time.

Ever since Edgar Snow's report fifty years ago, it has been well known that Mao Zedong's life of rebellion started within his own family in the form of defiance of his rich peasant father. The elder Mao wanted his son to work in the fields, whereas the younger Mao wanted to read books; the father wanted the son to stay at home pursuing a practical job, whereas the son wanted to leave home for a better education and a more interesting career.[14]

The case of Deng Xiaoping was just the opposite. The relations between Deng and his father appeared to have been neither so intimate nor so intense as those between the Maos. It was his mother and nurses who took care of Deng's daily needs, unlike in an ordinary peasant family, where the father would coddle his baby while the mother cooked. Ostensibly, Deng's relationship with his father seemed much more distant. Unlike Mao, Deng did not talk much to his father when they lived together, nor did he talk much about his father later when they lived apart.

Deng Wenming did not need or want his eldest son to help with manual labor or household chores. What he wanted from Deng was for him to achieve something loftier than Wenming's own local businesses and activities. He therefore arranged for Deng to go as far as his own world outlook could reach and perhaps a little beyond. In this respect, Deng's father certainly exerted a more decisive influence upon his son's future than did Mao's father on his son. In other words, Deng's future career started more as an objective arrangement, whereas Mao's started more as a subjective creation.

Even more important, albeit less apparent, was the personal disposition and philosophy of life that the father conveyed to his son. Deng Wenming's philosophy of life, or his Five Sons faith, was a combination of various religious doctrines and ethical creeds that stressed the gradual improvement of one's and one's own family's secular life and then, if possible, the improvement of society and all humanity through one's own persistent and resourceful practices. What was shared between the father and the son was indeed a kind of pragmatism or utilitarianism, despite its different applications in their respective lives and careers.

The son would leave home for an unusual life, which constitutes the subject matter of the following chapters. The father stayed on. While sending his son out to search for sagehood and to achieve pride and glory that would be reflected from the top down to his family, Deng Wenming worked at home with a less ambitious goal and also in a different way—from the bottom up. Applying his influence as one of the village elite, he gradually achieved prominent social status on the local level, which eventually translated into a position of political power on the regional level. In the late 1920s, Deng Wenming became chief of the Guang'an security regiment in charge of six hundred militiamen, and in the early 1930s, he was promoted to coordinator of the joint security forces of eight counties. "Whenever he went out," the Guang'an folk recalled later, "Deng Wenming sat in a big sedan chair shouldered by four men, with his bodyguards and servants running about and yelling at the watching crowds. What an awesome sight!"[15]

His official position as chief of the security forces would necessarily have involved Deng Wenming with quite a few schemes and intrigues, gaining him friends as well as enemies. Accidentally or otherwise, he was eventually assassinated by unknown individuals in 1938, while his eldest son, Deng Xiaoping, also pursued a military career, although in quite a different locale and for quite a different cause.

While digging a grave for Deng Wenming, local peasants were said to have been shocked to find a golden snake wriggling out of the ground and making its way to the edge of the grave. A young boy began to chase the snake, but an old man shouted for him to stop. The golden snake supposedly symbolized the glory and prominence that some Deng family descendant of the deceased individual was destined to achieve. If he still had consciousness in heaven, Deng Wenming, as a devout believer in the Religion of Five Sons, would certainly—and perhaps legitimately—have made a connection between his own religious beliefs and his son's political achievements. Communist or not, Deng Xiaoping remained his son and heir![16]

— 3 —

Bound for Abroad, 1918-1920

The nameless little stream at Paifang village, with its bubbles and ripples, runs down into the Qu River at the county seat of Guang'an, then rolls on to meet the Jialing River at Daxian, the prefectural capital, and finally proceeds with all its mighty currents to join the Yangtze River at the cosmopolitan city of Chongqing. Deng and his uncle Deng Shaosheng followed almost exactly the same route. They left their home village of Paifang in the summer of 1918, a few days after Deng's fourteenth birthday. They walked to Guang'an as they had in the past; then they hired a cart in which to ride to Daxian; and from there, they proceeded to Chongqing by boat. The entire journey took four days and covered about three hundred kilometers.

Recalling this episode nowadays, Paifang folk would say, "Xixian did not leave home alone. He followed his uncle to Chongqing." This is surely true, as the uncle was three years older than the nephew, which was a big difference for teenagers. In addition to good wishes from their parents and relatives, they each carried a few hundred silver dollars and some names and addresses of family acquaintances for future contacts. Deng's father was said to have been in Chongqing a couple of times before. One person known to the elder Deng did take the trouble to meet the pair at Facing Heaven Harbor and bring them back to his own house in a downtown district by means of a filthy rickshaw pulled by a sweating coolie. By the time he finally got to bed after one day's hustle and bustle, Deng had a clear sense that gone were the days at home, where he as a big (actually, small) boy would be taken care of by his mummies and nannies; now, all of a sudden, he as a small (actually, big) man had been thrown into the big, wide world and become one of its anonymous teeming thousands![1]

The city of Chongqing is located at the intersection of the Yangtze River and its biggest tributary, the Jialing, at the bottom of the Sichuan Basin. This crucial geographic location made it the capital of a number of states and kingdoms in ancient times. It received its present name some eight hundred years ago from a prince of the Song dynasty. While governor there, celebrating his thirtieth birthday, the prince received an edict from the royal court designating him heir to his aging father's imperial throne. The city was therefore renamed Chongqing, or literally, "Double Celebration."

Important as Chongqing was in ancient times as the hub of transportation and communication for southwest China, it was mainly during the last fifty years or so that the city's development had picked up to a dazzling pace. Chongqing was selected as one of the few ports for international business and trade by the Treaty of Nanjing in 1862. By 1918, it had grown to be the largest city in southwest China, with more than half a million permanent residents.[2]

In the two years after their arrival at Chongqing, Deng and his uncle remained together like a body and its shadow. They stayed in a relative's home for a few days before enrolling for the fall term at a Chongqing high school, as planned. It was also a boarding school, where they could sleep and eat three meals a day. The curriculum was more or less the same as that in the Guang'an secondary school, only at a more advanced level and more difficult to cope with, particularly for the Dengs, who came from the countryside. The tuition and living expenses were more costly than in Guang'an, and the pair—especially Shaosheng, whose family was not as wealthy as Xixian's—began to worry about the rapid depletion of their monetary resources.

In addition to attending classes on weekdays, Deng and his schoolmates sometimes toured the city after school in the evenings or on weekends. Major Western countries like France, England, and the United States all had consulates there. Various commercial enterprises and industries, especially in manufacturing and textiles, were sprouting up like "bamboo shoots after a spring rain." Foreign steamers with colorful flags frequently came and went on the Yangtze. Graven in Deng's young heart was the sharp contrast between rich and poor and between Chinese and Westerners. Leaving his family had matured him, and leaving his home village had broadened his insights, producing a great change for Deng in terms of both time and space.

Deng studied his textbooks and reviewed his lessons as required by his teachers but did no extracurricular reading. He seldom read other books, either theoretical or fictional, only occasionally glancing at headlines and advertisements in the *Chongqing Daily*. To Deng, 1918 seemed the most chaotic year that had ever occurred. Maybe it was true, or maybe it was simply because he had not cared much about current events before, but from what he read and heard, he was inclined to think that everything, both in the nation and in his province, was in flux. There were wars everywhere: wars between the southern revolutionaries and the northern warlords; wars among the various cliques within the southern government as well as within the northern government; wars between Sichuan and other provinces such as Yunnan and Shaanxi; and wars within Sichuan among various military factions; not to mention World War I, which was still under way, albeit nearing its conclusion. All in all, the entire world seemed overwhelmed with horrible confusion, and young Deng had to look for explanations, if not solutions.[3]

Deng and his uncle stuck with the Chongqing high school from September 1918 to January 1919. During this period, they began to have increasingly strong doubts about the value of attending such a school. Although they had been there for more than three months, they doubted that they would be able to complete the school's three-year program, and even if they did, they would still have no assurances regarding their future. It was a high school for general education, not a business or technology school or a military academy, where students received specific training and would enter a certain profession after graduation. This three-year high school might be fine for the kids of Chongqing residents, but as country boys coming from afar, the Dengs could hardly afford such leisure, mentally or practically.

Just as the Dengs were wondering whether to stick to their original plan or change direction, a piece of news came that helped them make their decision. They became aware—first through friends and then through newspapers—of a notice for a "preparatory school for work and study in France," which was accepting applicants. The uncle thought they should check into it, and the nephew was immediately convinced. To have a job and study, too, both in an exotic and wonderful land, was not a bad idea at all![4]

Gone with the Manchu monarchy were the remnants of Chinese

false dignity as well as most of the constraints of central bureaucracy. Progressive intellectuals and officials such as Cai Yuanpei and Wu Yuzhang realized the necessity of Western education for Chinese youth and managed to have some eighty of them sent to study in European countries, especially France, in the years between 1912 and 1918. More could have been dispatched but for the high costs of travel and tuition. A round-trip ticket and a four-year college program abroad cost several thousand dollars, which even many wealthy Chinese families could hardly afford.[5]

During and shortly after World War I, France was badly in need of labor. China was well known for its big population and low standard of living. After carefully weighing productive profits against transportation and other expenses, some French business entrepreneurs decided to import Chinese workers with the assistance of Chinese community leaders already in France, such as Li Shizeng and Wu Zhihui, as their agents. From 1915 to 1918, more than ten thousand Chinese laborers were thus brought to France.

The problem with exporting and importing Chinese labor was that it lacked moral justification and cultural appeal. While the French wanted "work," the Chinese wanted "study." Finally, a combined program of "diligent work and thrifty study" was devised to satisfy their mutual interests. In 1919 and 1920, the heyday of the "work and study program" (WSP), twenty groups of more than 1,500 WSP participants, among whom 378 were Sichuanese, left China for France—a historical phenomenon overshadowed perhaps only by the "going to America craze" of Chinese youngsters in the 1980s.

The first preparatory school for overseas studies in Sichuan was founded in the provincial capital of Chengdu in March 1918 under the joint sponsorship of the municipal government and some members of the local elite. After passing a qualifying examination at the conclusion of the course of study, approximately sixty students, notable among whom was Chen Yi, communist China's future minister of foreign affairs, were accepted into the work–study program and departed for France at the end of June 1919.

In regard to his own decision to join the work–study movement, Chen Yi recalled a few years later, "In the summer of 1918, I did some thinking about the WSP advertising. The program sounded like a worthwhile human life. Diligent work meant to produce and to enrich society with material resources; thrifty study meant to search for spiritual life and creative culture; to work and study at the same time meant to carry out theory and practice simultaneously. All this seemed far better than just sitting at home and idling away my breath."[6]

The Chongqing preparatory school opened in January 1919 and operated in a more or less similar manner. Deng's own decision to attend was similar to Chen's, only with a bit less personal emotion and ambition. "I grew interested in national affairs at the age of fifteen," Deng later recalled. "I had at the time much curiosity but little knowledge of Western affairs and therefore entered the Chongqing preparatory school for going abroad to study in France."[7]

Owing perhaps to the lack of timely information or his own hesitation or the need to wait for his father's approval or for whatever reasons, Deng came to the preparatory school a little late, but not too late—as he would at some other important junctures in his subsequent political life. The prep school formally began its courses sometime in January 1919, and Deng and his uncle did not enroll in the program until sometime in early February.

Like the primary school in Xiexing, the prep school in Chongqing also utilized an old establishment—this time, a former Confucian temple—for its campus. It was indeed a combination of ancient and modern, Chinese and foreign. On the walls of the main classroom, where French was taught, Deng and his classmates could still recognize the remnants of Confucius's portrait and classical scriptures. Since there was no dormitory or dining hall, the students had to solve their own room and board problems. The hundred or so students were divided into two classes, both at the same grade level. The entire course would take a year and a half, with three or four subjects, all very practical: Chinese, as some students could not yet read and write their native language well; mathematics, which could be taken as a basic requirement for other subjects; French, for the obvious purpose of living and studying in France; and industrial technology, in order to enable the students to find a job in a factory or workshop upon their arrival there.[8]

Three months after Deng came to the Chongqing preparatory school, a mass student protest erupted in Beijing in early 1919. The May Fourth Movement, as it was later called, was prompted by a secret agreement between the Beijing warlord government and Japan that would allow the latter to take over all of Germany's prewar privileges in Shandong as a condition for its supporting the warlords' authority. The students called the agreement a betrayal of Chinese sovereignty. This patriotic movement immediately won nationwide sympathy and spread throughout the country.

In response to the May Fourth Movement, students of the Chongqing preparatory school joined a demonstration at the municipal garrison headquarters and submitted an appeal to its commander in chief, denouncing the Beijing government as traitorous and demanding Japanese withdrawal from the city of Qingdao and all of Shandong Province. As they could not possibly get any direct result from their protest, the students were at least able to express their patriotic anger after returning to school by destroying all the Japanese goods they had bought and pledging to boycott any such purchases in the future. Though not playing any leading role, Deng participated in these activities. Fortunately or unfortunately, he did not have many belongings labeled "Made in Japan." Thus, his personal sacrifice consisted of throwing into the bonfire merely a toothbrush and a tube of toothpaste.

Deng remained a mediocre student at the prep school, as he had been in Xiexing and Guang'an. He made no significant or lasting impression on others. Only one of his schoolmates has a vague recollection of his very existence: "Comrade Deng Xiaoping was somehow late in arriving at the Chongqing preparatory school. But he showed himself to be an energetic, robust person even at that time. He did not talk much but was very serious and diligent in his class studies."9

These remarks, made when Deng was already a national leader, sounded flattering enough. Deng might indeed have studied seriously and diligently in the Chongqing preparatory school, but just as in Xiexing and Guang'an, he did not earn outstanding marks in any subject, especially not in French. After eighteen months of study, he could say no more than a few simple French phrases, such as "Stand up" and "Sit down."

A final examination was held to determine whether each student was qualified to go to France and, if so, in which category. Despite Deng's considerable efforts, his scores were not entirely satisfactory. He did well enough to participate in the program but not well enough to receive full financial support, as his uncle did. Deng Shaosheng and thirty other boys were provided with three hundred dollars to cover the minimum expenses of their trip, whereas Deng himself was among sixty or so students who each received one-hundred-dollar subsidies from the program organizer and had to come up with the two-hundred-dollar balance on their own.

Since he could get that sum from his father without much difficulty, Deng thought he was still lucky to have met the minimum requirements for admission. It was only a few weeks later that he learned that almost anybody who could afford to pay two hundred dollars could join the program, regardless of how well he had fared in the qualifying examination. Some WSP participants, like Nie Rongzhen, who would later become the minister of military industry in communist China, did not even attend the preparatory school at all.[10]

In the few weeks between the announcement of the qualifying exam results and the group's departure for France, Deng went home to Paifang to bid farewell to his family and get the necessary funds for his journey. He found his father as busy as ever in handling family and village affairs and his two younger brothers in the good care of his stepmothers. For the first time, Deng felt that his father treated him like an adult, not like a child. After the dinner party for his sixteenth birthday, he was called into his father's bedroom for a private conversation. Deng Wenming wanted to know a little more about his son's future plans abroad.

The young Deng tried to answer his father with the words he had pedantically learned from his teachers and schoolmates in the Chongqing preparatory school: "To learn knowledge and truth from the West in order to save China."

The father nodded in agreement and yet did not seem completely satisfied. He then asked his son whether he still remembered a certain quotation from Confucius. Deng said yes and began to recite, "To take good care of the state, one should first of all take good care of himself—" when his father suddenly interrupted him by finishing the quotation: "He would be a sage who could fulfill both objectives."[11]

With the necessary money in his pocket and the farewell of his family in his heart, Deng returned to Chongqing at the end of August 1920, just a few days before departure time. Everything had been well organized by the Sino-French Society of Education (SFSE), and all Deng needed to do in order to go was grab his luggage and follow the crowd, which he did with no problem. The visas had been collectively issued through the French consulate in Chongqing, as had the tickets been collectively purchased for the trip from Chongqing to Shanghai and thence to Marseilles.

A steamer blew its whistle off Facing Heaven Harbor on a bright autumn day in early September and began carrying the hundred-odd youngsters eastward down the Yangtze River. It was a five-day voyage, pleasant, exciting, and also, for these malleable young minds, a kind of schooling in itself. The various places the steamer passed along the Yangtze provided them with various courses: geography—when they went through the Three Gorges, they could not but admire the natural beauty of Mother China; history—watching the City of the White Emperor on top of the mountains brought them back to the age of the Three Kingdoms, seventeen centuries earlier, when Emperor Liu Bei of Sichuan was fighting his competitors in northern and eastern China for supreme state power; politics—while stopping overnight at the city of Wuhan, they visited the location of the 1911 uprising, which had toppled the Manchu Empire; and sociology and economics— glancing over the rows upon rows of slums along the riverbanks, where Shanghai industrial workers dwelled, in contrast with the distant skyscrapers occupied by foreign merchants or Chinese officials, they lost their hearts but gained so many ideas. Given all that they saw for themselves and heard from each other, they were more determined than ever to work hard and study well in France.[12]

Deng and his Sichuanese group arrived in Shanghai a bit ahead of schedule and stayed in the Hotel of Wealth and Fame at 56 Songshan Road for five days, waiting to board the French passenger ship *André Lepon*. Amid farewell shouts and waves, this vessel eventually weighed anchor off Whampoa Harbor and set out for the East China Sea at 11:00 A.M., September 11, 1920.

Deng was the youngest in this group of WSP students, too young to take any initiative on his own but old enough to keep up with his peers' coming and going, and laughing and crying. During their short stay in Shanghai, they had visited the foreign concessions in the Outer Shore district. They felt humiliated at having to submit to a physical search by the Indian gatekeeper at the British Concession. It made them even more indignant to read the notice in the park there: "Chinese and Dogs Not Allowed." One boy wanted to tear the notice down. "This is Chinese territory," he yelled, "yet they treat us like dogs!" Young Deng thought that these remarks were quite correct. But the boy who uttered them was promptly stopped by another: "Don't be so foolish! The problem is more than just one of tearing off that damned piece of wood." Young Deng thought that these remarks, too, were quite correct.[13]

Deng left no written record at the time, so we cannot precisely know his personal feelings at the moment of his departure from China for

France. A prose poem written by Zhou Enlai in June 1920 to a female friend might well reflect the common sentiment of WSP students at the time. Zhou embarked on the same route to France a few months later. Entitled "Farewell Words" and preceded by some romantic lines, Zhou's poem goes on to declare:

> I admire your lofty spirit,
> your determination,
> and your courage.
> Relying on your own effort and struggle,
> you gladly strive forward!
>
> Just leave China, and over you go
> the Eastern Sea,
> the Southern Sea,
> the Red Sea,
> and the Mediterranean Sea!
>
> Gusty winds and roaring tides
> will surge on and on,
> sending you all the way
> to the coast of France
> and the Motherland of Freedom![14]

The voyage was not as pleasant as everybody had expected. After the first few hours of excitement and curiosity, some began to feel bored and tired. In fact, it was more than simply boredom and weariness. The conditions were physically unbearable. This passenger ship normally had three classes: first class was mostly for French diplomats and merchants on business trips; second class was for Western tourists and wealthy overseas Chinese; and third class was filled with poor Chinese workers. But even the third class was judged too expensive for the WSP students. The Sino-French Society of Education had bargained with the travel company and gotten a bulk-rate deal for some spare space on the bottom deck, normally used for the storage of luggage and cargo. There were no berths or beds, and the students had to sleep on the bare wooden floor. It was damp and hot and stuffy, especially at night, when they were shut up beneath sea level. There were fleas, bedbugs, and mosquitoes, and they could hardly sleep at night.

While Deng quietly endured the nuisances, some elder boys began complaining. Several left the group when the ship reached Hong Kong; more dropouts at Saigon reduced the number from more than one hundred to fewer than ninety. From Hong Kong or Saigon, the dropouts could still manage to get back home by land or sea. But once the *André Lepon* passed Singapore via the Strait of Malacca and entered the vast Indian Ocean, any idea of retreat had to be abandoned, and everybody grew more determined to look forward.[15]

The next stops included Colombo in Ceylon, Djibouti under French rule, and Bombay in India. It was about a week's voyage from one stop to another. Deng and his companions would go to the upper deck on fine days to watch the endless ocean around them, the giant clouds of seagulls, and the magnificent sunrises and sunsets, or they would huddle on their bottom deck, terrified by the wind, rain, and thunder on stormy nights. At each stop along the way, Deng and the other boys would go ashore to see the exotic scenery and peoples. They were extremely embarrassed in Bombay to find poor Indian females totally nude, and they were fascinated by the networks of flashing lighthouses in the evening darkness along the Suez Canal.

Once they entered the Mediterranean Sea, memories of China were overshadowed by future prospects of France. Some boys began talking about the "three beautifuls" in France—"beautiful wines," "beautiful arts," and "beautiful ladies"—but they were promptly interrupted by others who solemnly admonished, "Don't forget who we are and what we have come here for! Don't forget diligent work and thrifty study!"[16]

On October 20, 1920, the *André Lepon* sailed into Marseilles harbor. After passing through the customs office, the group of Sichuanese students was received by Li Huang and another staff member of the Sino-French Society of Education. Everybody realized that they had finally arrived in the "Motherland of Freedom." During forty days and nights, they had covered more than fifteen thousand kilometers from Shanghai on the other side of the world to Marseilles on this side. Including the travel between Chongqing and Shanghai, the journey had taken Deng and company almost two months.[17] Of the hundred-odd who had started from Chongqing, eighty-five arrived in Marseilles. It was the kind of extraordinary experience in life that felt awful at the time but would later be remembered as especially precious.

Several decades later, when he attempted to recall for foreign guests his own motive for going to France, Deng sought to make the issue simple and clear, less personal than political, both perhaps too much so: "China was weak and we wanted to make her stronger, and China was poor and we wanted to make her richer. We went to the West in order to study and find a way to save China."[18]

Striding out of the Marseilles customs office, holding his little bundle of luggage tightly and looking to his uncle and other bigger boys for direction, this sixteen-year-old youngster from Sichuan could not have realized how significant a step he had taken by the very act of arriving in France. Pompous sentiments like "Save China" and even his work and/or study plans aside, we must assume that what really mattered was the historical trend that Deng had joined.

Some simple statistics, which Deng did not know or care about at the time, indicate that, of the fifteen hundred or so Chinese students who went to France in 1919 and 1920, approximately two hundred were to take active roles in the nationalist and communist revolutions, and more than twenty were to become the most prominent communist leaders. For those who had gone to France for educational purposes but would eventually turn to Chinese political leadership, the odds were terrific indeed!

Since only a small proportion of Deng's generation could leave their rural homes for the city, and even fewer could go abroad, what Deng did at the time seemed to be going "against the general trend," so to speak. But once such an aberrant trend became fashionable, it became popular in itself. In this sense, by going to France, Deng was following a countertrend to the general trend. The effect of this countertrend was especially apparent in the case of young Deng, whose eventual destiny was dictated not so much by his own decisions or discretion as by other elements and factors.

Among the various reasons why Sichuan sent more WSP students than any other province, two seemed to stand out: the influence of the Railroad Protection Movement and the role of Wu Yuzhang. The Railroad Protection Movement had involved tens of thousands of Sichuanese, both rich and poor, in defiance of the national government, thus creating a sentiment of "provincial patriotism," and the movement concluded with the central government's taking over the railroad's ownership while the provincial private stocks were redeemed in cash, thus creating a solid monetary reserve that could be used for a variety of purposes. Thanks to these conditions, the preparatory schools had been founded quickly in Chengdu and Chongqing and the work–study program had been funded easily in Sichuan.

From 1916 to 1920, Wu Yuzhang worked as accountant and secretary for the Sino-French Society of Education, under the auspices of which the work–study program was organized. Wu happened to be a native Sichuanese. Although he could hardly be credited with sponsorship of the WSP movement on the national level, Wu had played a decisive role in promoting the movement in his native province through his energetic efforts and organizational skills.

Well-organized and well-financed by the provincial government and local luminaries, WSP participants from Sichuan were more numerous than those from any other city or province. For the very same reason, it should be noted, they were generally not as independent-minded and politically oriented as those from other places, such as the province of Hunan and the cities of Beijing and Tianjin—at least not at first.

By the way, Mao Zedong, truly idiosyncratic, sent some close friends off to France but decided not to go abroad himself because, as he told Edgar Snow, "I felt that I did not know enough about my own country, and that my time could be spent more profitably in China." Mao believed, correctly we must say, that the key to the problems of China—and to the success of his own career—could be found only in China, not in France.[19]

The WSP students from Sichuan were generally short on political experience. They joined the program more as individuals, with fewer political and organizational motives. Among them, furthermore, Deng was the youngest, with the least political awareness. He left no writings, no personal letters or messages, nor even clear impressions upon his companions that indicated any bold motives or strong sentiments that would explain his having opted to go abroad, as did some others like Chen Yi and Nie Rongzhen. Perhaps Deng had no such reasons in the first place. The diminutive Sichuanese teenager may just have been following the popular trend—but he followed it nimbly and swiftly!

— 4 —

French Capitalists
Make Chinese Communists,
1921-1925

In 1919 and 1920, more than fifteen hundred Chinese students went to "work and study" in France: roughly six hundred in seven groups in the first year and nine hundred in ten groups in the second year. Most of them were assigned by the Sino-French Society of Education (SFSE) either to study in French schools or to work in factories. Among the six hundred arrivals in 1919, four hundred were sent to work and two hundred to study. A great majority of those who arrived in early 1920 were also assigned quickly; only a few were left with the SFSE, living on its subsistence stipends and awaiting assignment. As time passed, however, the situation became tougher and the arrangement ever more difficult.

Despite all the noble ideas and altruistic sentiments—some were indeed sincere and impressive—on both sides, France and its Chinese agents needed the Chinese students, not just for "international friendship" or "cultural exchange," but for practical purposes. In other words, the economic need of French capitalists constituted the basic foundation of the "diligent work and thrifty study" movement.

During and shortly after World War I (1914–18), France was especially short of labor in several of its heavy industries, including steel-making, coal mining, and transportation. This situation had prompted sponsorship of the work–study program (WSP) in the first place. After a few years of postwar recovery, however, France and the rest of

Europe slid into an economic recession in 1920, which resulted in millions of people losing their jobs. In Paris in 1921, for instance, there were reportedly as many as two hundred thousand unemployed, thus making it practically impossible for Chinese students to find decent work opportunities.

Enrollment in the work–study program had to be stopped in China, but the WSP students already in France could not be called back. Those who came in the latter months of 1920 could hardly find jobs, while those who had come earlier were at risk of losing their jobs. By early 1921, the situation had become so serious that, according to a news report in the *Shanghai Daily,* of the fifteen hundred or so WSP students in France, only slightly more than three hundred were lucky enough to "diligently work" on and off; the remaining three-fourths had to wait for months without any work. As for the "thrifty study" part, it had changed from an organized aspect of the program to an activity undertaken only at the discretion of individual participants, depending on their own wishes and financial resources.[1]

He Changgong, a WSP student from Hunan who later became communist China's minister of coal industry, vividly recalled his "diligent work" experience in Paris in 1921:

> Just like toilers, we would pick up any kind of job—light job, heavy job, filthy job, temporary job—whatever job was available. We got up in the middle of the night to help with the market, pulling vegetable carts, pushing milk bottles, and getting everything ready for daytime sales. We went to railway stations or harbors, loading or unloading goods, and carrying luggage or babies for customers. We went to restaurants to peel potatoes and to hotels to polish shoes. We went to construction sites, laying tiles and bricks, fetching water and cement, and cleaning up garbage. There used to be many horse carts, and we were hired to collect and remove horse and mule dung.[2]

Chen Yi, who had been so optimistic about the work–study adventure in 1919, had become extremely pessimistic by 1921:

> I feel totally disappointed with my original idea. Diligent work cannot support thrifty study at all. If I keep on toiling for another eight or ten years, it will be nothing but a pitiful waste of my time, nothing to do with my intellectual evolution. It is ridiculous to regard this work and study program as a noble cause. A noble cause should have a noble

purpose. What is the purpose of this program? To make a fortune for these French capitalists? It is even more ridiculous to think that the work–study program can transform human society. How can one say that he is transforming the society while he buries himself in heavy loads up to his neck and is barely able to breathe to keep alive?[3]

Even this kind of temporary and burdensome job was hard to obtain. Those who were waiting for an assignment stayed on the bare wooden floor of the entrance hall of the SFSE building or in the large tent set up in its courtyard. The tent, about thirteen meters long and five meters wide, normally accommodated between forty and fifty WSP students at a time. Each of them received five francs a day as a subsistence stipend from the Chinese Embassy through the association to meet his or her basic living expenses.

Li Huang, then an SFSE staff member and later a founder of the Chinese Youth Party, offered a grim picture of the WSP students sheltered in the SFSE building under his responsibility:

> Since so many people were put in such a limited space, I had to ask the building manager, Liu Dabei, to consider the advent of summer with its infectious diseases. Liu answered that many had died already. Then he handed me a file book that shocked me immensely. In less than two years, 61 students had died of illness, 5 had died of violence, and more than 80 had checked into public hospitals. These numbers pertained only to the students in Paris and its suburbs. In other words, out of the 1,000 or so students in factories, schools, and this SFSE building, about 140, or 20 percent, had either died or become seriously ill![4]

Given the situation, it was no wonder that several WSP student protests broke out in 1921. In February of that year, the Chinese Embassy in France circulated a call to those students who could not support themselves in France to return to China; otherwise, their financial assistance would be cut off. On February 28, 1921, some three hundred students, shouting the slogan "For Life and for Study," marched to the Chinese Embassy to protest. Ambassador Chen Lu explained, "This embassy has not received any funds from the government for its staff's salaries in the past two months. How can I take care of you people?" Student representatives replied, "Then why and how could you promise to provide those who wished to return to China with travel tickets?"[5]

During this protest demonstration, one Chinese student reportedly lost his life in a traffic accident, and four were arrested by the Paris police. Nevertheless, the demonstrators did succeed in obtaining from Ambassador Chen a written pledge to continue remitting the five francs per capita per day "subsistence fee" to all unemployed WSP students.

Another mass riot took place in September 1921 in the city of Lyons, when WSP students complained about the admissions policy of the newly founded "French-Chinese University" there. The university had been established by Wu Zhihui and Li Shizeng, who were also the organizers of the work–study program. Their admissions policy stressed the academic qualifications and financial resources of the applicants, without giving any special priority to those students already in France. In practice, the university had already accepted some 120 students from China, most of whom were from rich families and had high school diplomas.

Wu and Li had their good reasons: the Lyons university would be an institution of higher education, not a shelter for the poor and illiterate. But the WSP students also had their viewpoint: since the university was funded with donations solicited in China under the WSP students' name, why could no special provision be made for recruiting them? Why were applications accepted only from "those cubs of wealthy capitalists, rich landlords, and powerful bureaucrats"?[6]

Some 125 Chinese students gathered in Paris and took a train to Lyons. They attempted to occupy the university campus and dormitory but were immediately arrested by French police. They were subsequently detained in an army barracks for nearly two months, before 104 of them were eventually deported to China on October 14, 1921. Among the deportees were Cai Hesen, Li Lisan, Chen Yi, and some others who would soon join the Communist Party and would later become prominent communist leaders.

Deng did not participate in any of the early student political movements in 1921 and 1922—or at least, there are no records or memoirs that document his participation. He did sign the 242–signature petition to the Chinese Embassy requesting that the Lyons university be opened to WSP students already in France; that seemed natural because Deng also wanted to enroll in the university for educational purposes. But he did not participate in the Lyons demonstration once it became something political and extraordinary, although he did reside in Paris at the time.[7]

Thanks to Chinese historians' documentary study of the WSP movement and Nora Wang's pioneering work on the French archives, we are now able to reconstruct a clear itinerary of Deng's five-year sojourn in France. According to the *News Bulletin of Overseas Chinese in Europe,* published in October 1920, "On the 19th of this month, another group of 90 work–study students arrived at Marseilles. Among them 83 were Sichuanese students from the Chongqing Preparatory School for study in France."[8] That being the case, Wang is inaccurate in saying that Deng arrived in France on December 13, 1920. She probably mistook Zhou Enlai—whose group left China on another French ship, the *Porthos,* on November 7, 1920, and arrived on the date Wang mentioned above—for Deng Xiaoping.

Upon their arrival in Marseilles, Deng and his peers were greeted by staff members of the SFSE and took a train to the association's headquarters, in la Garenne-Colombes in the western suburbs of Paris. A few days later, on October 22, 1920, Deng left Paris for his assignment, a middle school in the town of Bayeux in Normandy, in northwestern France. He lived and studied there until March 13, 1921, when he had to return to la Garenne-Colombes. Clearly, the four-month period of study had consumed all his financial resources, and he could no longer continue his schooling.

Deng left Paris shortly afterward to begin working in the armaments factory of Schheider-Creusot in the city of Le Creusot, Burgundy, on April 1. However, he quit that job three weeks later, on April 23, 1921, and returned to la Garenne-Colombes, for reasons unrecorded but apparent. The heavy work in the steel plant was too much for this diminutive teenager. That was the same factory Chen Yi had worked for and complained about. After the February 28 incident, moreover, the resumed payment of 150 francs per month "subsistence fee" seemed sufficient to attract Deng to live in the SFSE building in Paris for the next few months.

The stipend given by the Chinese Embassy continued for a few more months before it finally stopped in September 1921. As a result, Deng had to join the others hunting for any available jobs merely to survive. It was a very difficult moment, and he had to write home for financial assistance. As soon as Deng Wenming received his son's request, he sold a piece of land and sent all the proceeds to Paris.

On February 13, 1922, Deng moved south to the city of Montargis and started work there as an unskilled laborer in the Hutchinson rubber factory, making rubber shoes and bicycle tires. He gave up the job on October 17, 1922, and left the city on November 3. It seemed quite apparent that, with some money earned through his "diligent work," Deng would attempt once again to fulfill his "thrifty study" dream, this time in the Collège de Chatillon-sur-Seine.

After another period of study, Deng resumed his paying job at Hutchinson on February 1, 1923, but was fired slightly more than a month later, on March 7. The available factory record shows that he "refused to work and will not be rehired." He remained in the Montargis region for three more months, presumably attending the night school at the Collège de Montargis, before he had to move back to his familiar la Garenne-Colombes residence on June 11, 1923. Deng's initial objective of "diligent work and thrifty study" in France had now reached a dead end.

In the Communist Party, seniority is such an important matter that many of its members claimed an earlier-than-accurate year for their initial membership. Even Chairman Mao Zedong seemed no exception. In registering for the Eighth Congress in 1956, Mao preferred to have his party membership dated back to 1920, despite the fact that the CCP was not founded until 1921.

Both official Chinese historians and Deng himself say that he joined the Communist League in 1922 and the Communist Party in 1924.[9] Neither of these dates seems probable, or even possible. No historical records show Deng taking part in any political movements or joining any political organizations, communist or otherwise, until the year 1924. More probably and logically, Deng joined the Communist Youth League in late 1923 or early 1924, when he began working with Zhou at the league's organ *Red Lights,* and joined the Communist Party in early 1926, upon his arrival in Moscow, in Soviet Russia.

On June 11, 1923, Deng moved from Montargis back to Paris. He had just missed the Second Congress of the Communist Youth League, which had convened in Paris a few days before. There is no indication that he had had any formal contact with the Communist Youth League previously, but it seems quite plausible that he might have been quickly moving closer to the league's activities in the latter months of 1923. Deng's residence in the SFSE building at 39 Rue de la Pointe, la Garenne-Colombes, had also served as the official address of the league's publishing organs *Youth* in 1922–23 and *Red Lights* in 1924–25.

Uli Franz begins his description of the start of Chinese communist activities in France with Chen Duxiu's two sons and their "revolution-ary bookshop" in Paris in the early 1920s. A quick look at one of the many works on CCP history or the WSP movement shows that in fact, at the time, the Chen brothers were both anarchists rather than commu-nists, despite their later deeds and despite their famous communist father.[10]

The WSP students included Zhou Enlai, from Tianjin; Zhao Shiyan, from Beijing; and Cai Hesen, Li Weihan, and Li Lisan, from Hunan—all of whom had been social and political activists even before they went abroad. They started to form new organizations almost as soon as they arrived in France. Cai Hesen, Li Weihan, and some other mem-bers of the former "New People's Society" established the "Work and Study Society" in late 1920, with about thirty members. Zhao Shiyan and Li Lisan organized the "Labor Association" in early 1921, with about twenty members. In March 1921, a secret five-person commu-nist group, including Zhou Enlai and Zhao Shiyan, was formed in Paris. Their memberships were approved by the newly founded Chi-nese Communist Party in late 1921. According to Chen Duxiu, in his CCP general secretary's report to the Communist International in Mos-cow on June 23, 1922, "Presently, the party has two members in France and eight members in Germany."[11]

On June 3, 1922, the Communist Youth League was founded in Paris with eighteen representatives. Zhao was elected its secretary, Zhou was put in charge of propaganda, and Li Fuchun was put in charge of organization. By the time the Youth League held another con-ference, in February 1923, its membership had increased to seventy-two. As Zhao was about to leave France for the Soviet Union, Zhou took over his post as secretary. The conference passed a resolution for the league to join the Communist Youth League back home as its Euro-pean branch. At the Second Congress of the Youth League, chaired by Zhou on June 11, 1923, all the members voted to join the Kuomintang (KMT) branch in Europe; they also passed a resolution to publish *Red Lights* as the league's organ in place of the earlier *Youth*.

The period from late 1923 to early 1924 indeed marked a turning point in Deng's whole life and career. After his failure to obtain a good education as his father had hoped for, he took part in the communist movement by working with Zhou at *Red Lights*. Such a change from pursuing education to joining a political movement was by no means too great a departure from his father's instructions, which were merely an abstract wish of happiness and success for Deng personally and for the Deng family as a whole. Education was but one practical means to achieve such an objective; politics could be another.

Deng's five-year experience in France—from October 1920, when he arrived in Paris, to January 1926, when he left for Moscow—can be roughly divided into two phases. During the first period, Deng adhered to the original objective of the WSP program of work as the means and study as the end. He moved from one place to another for three years to fulfill this objective, until he found it practically impossible to continue. As Deng's educational prospects diminished, his political career took off.

For the second part of his stay in France, from late 1923 to early 1926, Deng lived mostly in Paris, working in a Renault factory, and became increasingly involved in political activities. While working to earn his own living constituted his "physical infrastructure," his "spiritual suprastructure" had gradually changed from pursuing education to making revolution. Simply put, the first phase was work plus study, and the second phase was work plus politics.

Deng himself explained the change a few years later in Moscow: "The bitterness of life and the humiliating treatment by foremen or capitalist running dogs had exerted a deep impact upon me. Although I felt the crime and ugliness of capitalist society at the very beginning, I could not have any more profound consciousness because of my own romantic style. Later on, I accepted socialist and especially communist knowledge, because of the propaganda of more conscious people and also because of my personal hardship."[12]

In January 1924, Deng started working for *Red Light,* with Zhou as its founder and editor in chief. Deng's initial duties included typing, copying, transcribing, and typesetting—for which, he earned from his comrades the amiable nickname "Docteur du Duplication." Among the *Red Light* staff, Zhou was the only person who worked full-time and received a full stipend—small as it was—whereas Deng had to support himself through other jobs and only worked for the journal at night and on weekends, almost without pay.

Back home in China during 1922–24, the communists collaborated with the nationalists and gradually built up a revolutionary base centered in Canton, with the support of the Communist International and the Soviet Union. The CCP decided to join the KMT formally in 1922 to form a united revolutionary front. Dictated by that domestic policy, the communists in France also joined the nationalists in 1923. Although it still kept its own organizations and activities, the Communist Youth League became a formal part of the KMT branch in Europe.

As a matter of fact, the majority of Communist Youth League members in Europe in the 1920s were also KMT members, and a few, like Zhou and Zhao, were CCP members as well. Who cared? Although the question may sound odd in retrospect, it was not contradictory then. In Europe at the time, few of those young communist revolutionaries, presumably including Deng, regarded the difference between the Communist Party and the Communist Youth League as such a big deal, as they would nonetheless find that it was in 1926 in Soviet Russia.[13]

After Zhou left France to take part in the nationalist revolution at home in July 1924, veteran members of the Youth League such as Liu Bojian, Li Fuchun, Ren Huanwu, Xiao Puchu, and Fu Zhong assumed its collective leadership. Deng was as yet an unknown figure. But as more veterans went either to Moscow or directly back to China, and also by dint of his enthusiastic work, Deng stepped into the de facto circle of leaders. He started writing short articles for *Red Light* by the end of 1924 and became one of the most active and conspicuous organizers of the Youth League in 1925. The communist tide in France ebbed, but Deng's role gradually increased—a pattern that would repeat itself in a similar way in China in the 1980s.

The earliest and most valuable documentary record of Deng's political opinions and activities consists of three articles he wrote for *Red Light* between late 1924 and early 1925, entitled "Look at the Scheme of the International Imperialists," "Look at the News of the *Herald Weekly*," and "Look at the Second Slandering of the *Herald Weekly*."[14]

These three "Look at" articles were all very short, very harsh in tone, and undistinguished in their grammar and wording. The author appeared less interested in theoretical arguments or national affairs than in partisan criticism and critique of another Chinese organization, the Youth Party, and its organ, the *Herald Weekly*. The articles were in sharp contrast to the more sophisticated writings of Zhou Enlai, Li Fuchun, and Xiao Puchu in the same journal during the same period.

The Chinese Youth Party, whose members were largely young anarchists, became the major rival and foe of the Communist Youth League in France. One of the drawbacks of the Youth Party was that it had no Russian background—hence, no monetary or organizational support for its individualistic doctrines. After working with the anarchists in their "Leisure Society" for some time, the Chen brothers—Yannian and Qiaonian—realized that "[a]narchism ignores social reality and is therefore hopeless." They both shifted to communism in late 1922.

On October 10, 1924, the Youth Party organized a banquet to celebrate National Day, which seemed to infuriate Deng and his Youth League comrades. Deng wrote:

> The Youth Party says more than four hundred Chinese and French attended their so-called National Day celebration. The truth is that half of the French guests were prostitutes and girlfriends and landladies acquainted with Youth Party folk. They pretend that dancing with those prostitutes is establishing friendship between the Chinese and French peoples, and that playing a few pieces of rotten music is informing the French people of Chinese culture. Only a three-year-old toddler would believe that! While civil war is running amok in China, these folk are singing and dancing here in Paris. They are simply exhibiting the ugliness of China and the Chinese![15]

As can be seen from the preceding quotation, Deng did not participate in communist activities with a particularly strong ideological or theoretical consciousness. In Paris in the 1920s—and perhaps throughout his entire political career—Deng was noted as an individual who neither read much nor wrote extensively, but who, once involved in action, would show extraordinary determination and enthusiasm.

In the spring of 1925, Deng evidently left Paris for Lyons and stayed there for several months, taking a temporary job and also disseminating Youth League propaganda among Chinese students and workers there. He came back to Paris in the late summer to resume his work as a fitter in the Renault factory during the daytime and take part in Youth League activities at night and on weekends as before.

On May 30, 1925, Chinese workers in the Shanghai Textile Plant went on strike to protest their horrible treatment and arbitrary dismissal by the Japanese owner. About ten thousand Shanghai students and citizens joined the strike in the foreign concession. The British police opened fire on the strikers, killing thirteen of them. The incident, called the May 30 massacre, gave rise to a nationwide, even worldwide, protest movement of Chinese patriots against foreign imperialists.

All the Chinese community organizations in Paris—among which, the Communist Youth League was the most active—took part in this patriotic movement. They applied for permission to hold a mass demonstration in Paris on June 14, 1925, but their request was denied by French authorities. A large group of Chinese gathered on June 21, 1925, in defiance of a French police order. The riotous crowd rushed into the Chinese Embassy and forced Ambassador Chen to sign several papers, directed to the French government, protesting the Shanghai massacre and demanding that French troops withdraw from Chinese territory.[16]

In the wake of this demonstration, French police searched and questioned about one hundred Chinese residents in the la Garenne-Colombes district. Without much difficulty, they managed to discover a number of issues of *Red Light* and other radical journals and pamphlets. The correspondence address of *Red Light* was publicly listed as 39 Rue de Pointe, which was also the location of the SFSE headquarters.

It appears that, under French police questioning, one of the SFSE secretaries, He Luzhi, who was also a leader of the Youth Party, revealed the names and addresses of several *Red Light* editors and contributors. This resulted in the arrest of a number of communists, among whom were Youth League leaders Ren Zhuoxuan, Li Dazhang, and Lin Wei. The confrontation between the Youth League and the Youth Party consequently escalated to a level of "Punish the traitors!" Their struggle became so intense that each side resorted to appealing to the Paris police for intervention on its behalf and also to threatening the other with violent assault and even assassination.

Because of the June 1925 incident and its aftermath, Deng, who had previously resided at 3 Rue Casteja in Boulogne-Billancourt, where many Chinese workers and students lived, had to move to a new residence at 27 Rue Traversiere in the same district. The new neighborhood was less crowded and more secluded. Deng, together with Fu Zhong and a third comrade, shared a small rented room on the third story of an old brick building.

The leadership of the Youth League had gradually shrunk to four or five people by the later months of 1925, with Fu Zhong taking charge of its general operations. By that time, the small, energetic, vivacious Deng had also advanced to the front ranks. He was not very good at writing or talking about subtle theory but proved his mettle in stage quarrels and street fights.

The French police began close surveillance of Chinese communist activities, not just because they were communist but because they were anti-Western. It was also feared that the Chinese communists would cause social troubles in Paris, as they had done over the June 1925 incident. The Paris police therefore enlisted informers, both French and Chinese, to watch and report on the Communist Youth League's activities. In response, Deng and his comrades had to change their public operations into secret or semisecret ones.

Deng played an increasingly important role in the Youth League in late 1925, although he did not hold formal leadership positions to the extent claimed nowadays by official historians in China. One Paris police report indicated that on October 25, 1925, Deng and forty-seven Chinese gathered at 23 Rue Boyer for a meeting, which Deng chaired and at which he was also the concluding speaker. The police were aware of his name "Teng Hi Hien" but did not know his exact address until another report of a second meeting on January 3, 1926, specified that Deng lived at 3 Rue Casteja. The police report further noted that he had not broken any alien-control laws—an indication that his case was not yet serious, as far as the Paris police were concerned.

The Paris police eventually decided to search Deng and Fu's residence at 3 Rue Casteja in Boulogne-Billancourt. They arrived on January 8, 1926, only to find a lot of books and papers scattered on the floor of the just-vacated bedroom.[17] There were revolutionary leaflets in French and Chinese as well as booklets such as "The ABCs of Communism" and "The Testament of Premier Sun." One circular dated January 7, 1926, read as follows: "Twenty-one of our comrades are scheduled to leave Paris for Moscow this very night. They will soon return to the motherland, comrades! On watching one group of our fighters after another marching off to the battlefront of the revolution, we should always keep in our mind the slogan 'Go Back Home as Early as Possible!' "

Partly, but not mainly, because of the French police harassment—it was doubtful that the Paris police had anything like a warrant to arrest Deng before his departure—Deng's group left Paris for Moscow via Berlin on January 7, 1926. They had planned to do so for a long time. To return to China was their constant slogan, if not the only way out for them as a political group. They followed their predecessors' steps to Moscow, with a lingering idea of further study in Russia and of Russia as a convenient transit point back to China—not to mention the fact that so many of their old comrades were already there, their fascination with the birthplace of world communist revolution, and so forth.

Before leaving from Paris for Moscow, Deng did not neglect to terminate his employment with the Renault factory formally, presumably receiving some severance pay. Now available in the factory's file in Paris is his discharge certificate, with a few routine remarks by a factory manager: "Cause of Departure—return to China"; "Assessment of Work Performance—acceptable"; and "General Behavior—fine."

There is still more evidence to refute the simplistic assertion that Deng and his comrades fled France to Soviet Russia just because of the raid by the Paris police. According to a December 14, 1925, letter from Fu Zhong, the Youth League leader at the time, "A great number of Chinese students have recently gone to Russia from Belgium and Germany. We in France have also decided to send some twenty comrades northward around the end of this year."[18]

By late 1925 and early 1926, the communist circle in Paris, which had once claimed a total of several hundred members and followers, had been reduced to about one hundred or so sympathizers. After the departure of Deng and his group, the Chinese communist movement practically died out in France. Although some Communist Youth League members remained there and others also went to Soviet Russia in the latter months of 1926, the movement had by and large turned into an individual rather than an organizational phenomenon.

— 5 —

Russia and Beyond,
1926–1929

The October Revolution of 1917 in Russia was followed by three years of fierce military struggle against domestic rebellions coupled with foreign invasions. It was not until the end of 1920 that the Red Army expelled the White rebels, first from the western frontier and then from Siberia. In June 1921, the Soviet government founded the "Communist University of Toilers of the East," or simply the "Eastern University," in Moscow—a party school for training officials and cadres to control its eastern minority regions. The deputy minister of minority affairs of Soviet Russia concurrently served as president of the university.

From 1922 onward, as the Russian Revolution gradually shifted from domestic defense to international offense, the definition of "East" was somewhat broadened, and the Eastern University was formally put under the supervision of the Communist International rather than the Soviet government. Its objective was henceforth to train party cadres not only of the eastern minorities of Soviet Russia but also of the eastern countries of Asia to make communist revolutions in their own motherlands. In the final analysis, of course, that was also to protect Soviet interests. This double purpose was designated by Joseph Stalin as "both to cultivate leading communist cadres for the eastern minorities in the Soviet Union in order to serve the socialist construction, and to cultivate leading communist cadres for the colonial or semicolonial countries in the eastern world in order to serve the world revolution."[1]

The Eastern University differed from an ordinary educational institution in various ways. Its only criterion for admitting students was recommendations from Russian or other communist organizations, and its departments were divided according to geographic origins rather than academic subjects. There were actually only two departments: the Domestic Department, whose students were all minorities from the eastern provinces or republics of Soviet Russia; and the Foreign Department, whose students were from a dozen Asian countries. The Foreign Department offered classes designated for students from specific countries, such as Japan, Iran, Turkey, Korea, Indonesia, and China.

From 1923 to 1926, a few hundred Chinese youngsters, either in groups or individually, came to study in the Eastern University. Among them, the most notable communists were Liu Shaoqi, Ren Bishi, and Luo Yinong, who had come directly from China; and Zhao Shiyan, Wang Ruofei, Liu Bojian, Nie Rongzhen, Zhu De, Fu Zhong, and Deng Xiaoping, who had come from Western Europe. All were to become important communist leaders after returning to China.

Deng and his Youth League comrades, twenty of them altogether, with Fu Zhong as leader, left Paris by train on January 7, 1926, and arrived in Berlin the next day. They stayed there for a few days, not in a hotel but in some private homes carefully arranged by German communists. They proceeded from Berlin via Warsaw to Moscow, where they received a warm welcome from their Chinese communist friends and were admitted to the Eastern University shortly afterward.

Among the members of the Communist Youth League coming from Western Europe to Moscow in the 1920s, only a few well-known and well-connected individuals, such as Zhao Shiyan and Wang Ruofei, might have concurrently been members of the Chinese Communist Party (CCP). There had been no formal CCP organization in Europe, and it was against Youth League policy for its members to join the Communist Party without specific permission. Deng could hardly be regarded as one of the few exceptions. To reiterate, the current official claim that Deng became a Communist Youth League member in 1922 and a Communist Party member in 1924 is questionable at best. In all likelihood, Deng joined the Youth League in late 1923 or early 1924, when he started working at *Red Light;* he could not have been formally accepted as a Communist Party member until after entering the Eastern University in Moscow in January 1926.

"There were very few CCP members among our students who returned from Europe," recalled Nie Rongzhen, who left Belgium for Russia in 1925 and later became a Red Army leader in the 1930s and

1940s. "Later, in Moscow, when the comrades coming from home got to know that situation, they told us, 'Your party enrollment was too rigid, and in fact, most of your league members were well qualified to be party members.' Therefore, while we were in Moscow, the party organization decided to accept all the Youth League members who had returned from Europe as Communist Party members."[2]

When Deng entered the Eastern University in early 1926, there was a Chinese class of thirty or forty students, which was, in turn, divided into two study groups: the "Workers Group," consisting of industrial workers from Shanghai, Canton, and a few other cities; and the "Common Group," consisting primarily of young students and intellectuals. The general curriculum for all Chinese students in the Eastern University included courses in Marxist-Leninist principles, history of the Russian Communist Party, Soviet government and law, international labor movements, political economics, history of social development, dialectical materialism and historical materialism, and particularly for newcomers like Deng, the Russian language.

When commemorating Feng Yuxiang's one hundredth birthday on September 14, 1983, Deng received Feng's relatives, saying, "Feng Fonong and I were classmates at the Eastern University in the Soviet Union. She was the youngest student in our class, only fifteen or sixteen years old, and the second youngest was Chiang Ching-kuo."[3] Feng Fonong was Feng Yuxiang's daughter, while Chiang Ching-kuo was Chiang Kai-shek's son. Based on their family backgrounds and personal dispositions, we can assume that Deng, Feng, and Chiang all belonged to the Common Group, not the Workers Group.

Through learning Marxist-Leninist doctrines in the classroom, as well as taking part in CCP organizational activities, Deng quickly changed from a romantic youth in Paris to a professional revolutionary in Moscow. Deng himself acknowledged such a basic change at the time: "After I arrived in Moscow, I became firmly determined to devote my whole body to our party and to our class. Ever since that time, I have been absolutely willing to accept the party's training, to follow the party's orders, and to struggle for the interests of the proletarian class throughout my life."[4]

All Chinese students arriving in Russia before 1926 studied at the Eastern University, whereas all those arriving after 1926 were enrolled in Sun Yat-sen University. Deng came just at a transitional period. He entered the Eastern University first, studied there for a few months, and then—together with Fu Zhong, Li Zhuoran, and others—trans-ferred to Sun Yat-sen University, an institution established exclusively for Chinese students.

Formally called Sun Yat-sen University of Chinese Workers, the university was founded in September 1925 in memory of the recently deceased founder of the Republic of China and leader of the Chinese Nationalist Party. It was presumably administered by the Far Eastern Bureau of the Comintern but was actually operated by the Russian Communist Party and the Soviet government. Both communists and nationalists were trained there as revolutionary cadres for the CCP–KMT united front against the warlords and imperialists.

When Fu Zhong and Deng Xiaoping entered Sun Yat-sen Univer-sity in the early summer of 1926, there were about three hundred students divided into ten classes, according to their educational back-grounds and professional interests. Both Fu and Deng were assigned to "Class No. 7 of Theoreticians." Meanwhile, Fu worked as the secretary of the university's CCP branch, and Deng was the head of his class's CCP group. Like all his schoolmates, Deng adopted a Russian name, Dozorov.

In addition to the kinds of courses offered at the Eastern University, Sun Yat-sen University taught its students the history of the Chinese and East Asian revolutions and provided military training—all to en-able them to cope in practical terms with the situation in China. Be-tween lectures, the teachers would lead seminars and encourage their students to participate in free discussion. The Russian language was taught almost every day, either separately or in connection with other subjects. Veteran leaders of the October Revolution, such as Nikolai Bukharin and Leon Trotsky, were invited to give lectures and speeches.[5]

The living conditions and social atmosphere for the Chinese stu-dents in Moscow were far better than they had been in Paris. Here, they were treated equally as revolutionary comrades, whereas in France, they had been regarded as inferior laborers. The university in Moscow provided them with sufficient room and board, year-round clothing, full medical care, and even cultural entertainment, such as opera and ballet. During the few vacations, winter tours and summer camps were arranged free of charge around Moscow and Leningrad.

Deng, short but robust, was nicknamed the "Little Cannon" by his fellow students. One of them recalled that Deng still behaved like a

Parisian and would spend a lot of time drinking coffee and chatting with his peers in the university cafeteria. His political experience in Paris seemed to have provided him with an advantage over the other students, so that he, along with Fu, was assigned to the leadership of the CCP organization at the university.[6]

Chinese students at Sun Yat-sen University did not have to take any tests from their Russian lecturers; instead, they had to undergo periodic assessments by their own party organizations. According to the university CCP branch's "assessment of party members" dated June 16, 1926, Deng "behaved well up to the standard of party membership and did not show any nonparty tendencies." He never missed any party conferences and meetings, and he was further assessed as "most suitable for propagandistic and organizational duties."[7]

Neither the Eastern University nor Sun Yat-sen University was as academic as their names implied. But they did provide Deng with a period of time during which he could uninterruptedly pursue an education outside China. He learned Marxist and Leninist phrases, if not real theories, which would prove necessary for his future political career; he also acquired some basic knowledge of communist revolutions—in terms of both individuals and organizational structures—which would also prove necessary for his future activities. In retrospect, nevertheless, it seemed good rather than bad that Deng did not stay in Moscow as long, or study Marx and Lenin as much, as others like Wang Ming and Bo Gu. Deng studied just enough to be a communist politician, but not so much as to become a Stalinist dogmatist, as had Wang and Bo!

The Chinese students in the Soviet Union were normally supposed to undertake a two- or three-year program. But the exception often became the norm in contemporary Chinese history and politics. The widespread revolution and civil war in China would either draw some of them back home before they finished their educational program, as in the case of Deng Xiaoping, or prevent others from returning to China after completing their education, as in the case of Chiang Ching-kuo.

Back home in China during 1924–26, the united front of nationalists and communists surged forward, with direct assistance from the Soviet Union. The two parties gradually consolidated their southern base and enthusiastically prepared for a military expedition against the warlord regime in northern China. What would later be called the Northern Expedition or the Grand Revolution was just about to be launched.

Despite the various ideological overtones, many episodes in modern

Chinese history can be explained better and more simply in terms of sheer power relations. Under ever-growing pressure from the revolutionary south, the northern warlord regime broke apart, as the "Christian general," Feng Yuxiang, staged a coup d'état to expel his superior, the "Confucian general," Wu Peifu, from Beijing in early 1925. Renewed power struggles, however, caused another civil war between Feng and the Manchurian warlord Zhang Zuolin, resulting in Feng's withdrawal from the capital city in April 1926. It was only after his defeat that Feng realized the need for a possible alliance with Russia. In view of its diplomatic interest in East Asia, Soviet Russia would have liked to draw Feng into the nationalist revolution from the north. In short, Feng needed support from Stalin as much as Stalin needed assistance from Feng.[8]

Owing to such mutually expedient interests, Feng accepted Stalin's invitation and departed for the Soviet Union in May 1926. On his second day in Moscow, Feng announced his intention to join the Nationalist Party and support the nationalist revolution. He remained in Moscow for more than three months; spoke to Chinese students at Sun Yat-sen University; received CCP visitors, notably Liu Bojian; and met with a few Soviet politicians and generals. On August 15, 1926, as the Northern Expedition pushed forward, Feng left Moscow for China secretly with a small group of five or six people. Among Feng's companions were a communist agent, Lin Bojian, and a Russian adviser named Yumanov.

Soon after his return to China, in Wuyuan—a small town in Inner Mongolia—on September 17, 1926, Feng publicly pledged to participate in the nationalist revolution and proclaimed a reorganization of his troops into the Allied Nationalist Army, with himself as its general commander. Liu Bojian was appointed director of the political department, and Yumanov was appointed Feng's political and military adviser. This episode was the historically famous "Wuyuan pledge."

Besides the constant supply of ammunition from Russia, which was no doubt welcome, Feng also fancied that his troops needed political and organizational reforms in order to be as strong as the Red Army he had seen in Moscow. Through the CCP Northern Bureau, headed by Li Dazhao, Feng passed on a request to the Comintern that more communist cadres be sent to his army to help raise its political discipline and militant spirit.

Quite a number of previous Deng biographers are basically mistaken in describing Deng's return from the Soviet Union to China. Lee Ching-Hua, by far the most careful author, for instance, writes the following: "In August 1926, when Feng started back to China, he was accompanied by Teng, Liu Bo-chien, Shih K'o-hsuan, Chang Mu-t'ao, Hsiao Ming and 98 Russian advisers. On September 16, Feng swore an oath at Wu-yuan in the presence of Teng and other communists."[9]

In fact, Deng could not possibly have participated in the Wuyuan pledge in September 1926—he came back to Xi'an via Ulan Bator sometime in March 1927—nor could ninety-eight Russian advisers possibly have accompanied Feng. As General Feng's own diary clearly indicates, only a small group of five or six people were with him on his trip from Moscow back to northwest China under strict security precautions.

At Feng's request in late 1926, the CCP leadership in Moscow assigned some twenty communists, including Deng Xiaoping, as the first group to work in Feng's army. Deng himself recalls: "Mr. Huanzhang asked our party to send some people to his Northwestern Army. More than twenty comrades were selected to come from Moscow. The vanguard squad of three, including me, set off first. I was then only twenty-two years old. I remember that we rode across the Mongolian desert, in a Soviet truck carrying ammunition. The journey was very difficult. We stayed in Kulun for more than a month and eventually arrived in Inner Mongolia."[10]

To be more accurate, Deng's group left Moscow at the end of 1926 and arrived at Kulun or Ulan Bator in early 1927. Then Deng and two other men were chosen to form a vanguard squad to proceed ahead of the others. To enter China, they rode in a Russian truck carrying ammunition for Feng's army; to reach Yinchuan, they changed to riding camels; finally, they switched to horses and arrived at Xi'an in early March 1927. It should thus be clear that Deng did not participate in the Wuyuan pledge with Feng in September 1926, as almost all previous Deng biographers have stated.

There are also numerous exaggerations about Deng's position and functions in Feng's Northwestern Army, with various claims that he was the deputy director of the political department, director of education in the Zhongshan Military Academy, political commissar of the Seventh Army Corps, and so forth. Once Deng became famous, there were those who deliberately or negligently chose to attach conspicuous titles to his past activities.[11]

Feng's diary gives no indication that Deng ever knew him personally or even met him, or that Deng played any significant role in his Northwestern Army. Actually, Deng served with Feng's troops as a political instructor for only three or four months, from March to July 1927. Like the other fifty-odd communist agents present, Deng worked in political propaganda and ideological agitation, teaching Feng's troops what he was taught in Moscow, and played no prominent military role. His position was not important enough to be mentioned in Feng's diary, which records all personal, official, and institutional details of the Northwestern Army at the time.[12] As an old warlord, Feng was more interested in Soviet weapons than communist propaganda. He did not entrust the communists with military commands, nor did the communists seem particularly interested in military power at that time.

But even offering communist lectures would soon become a problem. By the time Deng arrived at Feng's headquarters, the CCP–KMT united front was falling apart. As the Northern Expedition advanced and the northern warlord regime retreated, dissension within the united front intensified and eventually resulted in the Shanghai coup of April 12, 1927. The nationalist troops under Chiang's command crushed the Shanghai workers militia sponsored by the communists. For a while, the KMT leftists and the communists stood together in Wuhan in defiance of Chiang's Nanjing government, while Feng's troops remained temporarily neutral.

Political relations were incredibly complex at that juncture: Comintern agents, Soviet diplomats, KMT left and right wings, CCP right and left wings, old and new warlords—all appeared to make their bids. Feng first consulted with Wang Jingwei in Zhengzhou from June 3 to 6, 1927, and then conferred with Chiang at Xuzhou from June 20 to June 21, 1927. Consequently, Feng would opt for the more powerful Chiang rather than the more eloquent Wang and the communists.

Returning from Xuzhou to Xi'an, Feng decided to dismiss all communist agents from his forces or, to use his own words, "politely dispatch them away." Each communist was offered a few silver dollars for travel expenses. On July 8, 1927, more than fifty communists, Deng included, were thus forced to leave the city of Xi'an. Many of those from the north just quit the Communist Party and returned to their native towns and villages. The southerner Deng, for better or worse, found no easier way to travel than by train to Wuhan, where the CCP Center was located at the time.

Several decades later, when recalling his personal experience in the Northwestern Army in 1927, Deng did not forget to express his profound gratitude toward General Feng. "Mr. Huanzhang had a long friendship with our party," Deng once stated, respectfully referring to Feng by his literary name, "During the 1927 purge, while Chiang Kai-shek was mercilessly killing communists in the south, Mr. Huanzhang instead just politely dispatched us away."[13]

Deng arrived at Wuhan in late July 1927, only to find the CCP Center in chaos. The left wing of the KMT had also turned against the communists. Chen Duxiu, the former Beijing University professor, resigned as the CCP's general secretary, and the party leadership temporarily fell into the hands of a newly formed "five-man standing committee" of the Politburo. Among the five, Zhou Enlai, Li Lisan, and Li Weihan were all Deng's old acquaintances from France. He was assigned to work at the Party Center as a staff member. For security reasons, Deng changed his given name from "Xixian" to "Xiaoping" at this time.

On August 1, 1927, the communists staged an armed uprising in Nanchang, by using their political and organizational influence within the KMT garrison. An emergency meeting of the CCP Center—held in Wuhan on August 7, 1927, under the auspices of the Comintern representative Lev Lominadze—formally decided to retaliate against the nationalists with military rebellions. Participating in the August 7 conference were twenty-one communist cadres from various departments. Because of his junior position, Deng was not among the formal participants, but he did attend the conference as its record keeper.[14]

Although Deng and Mao Zedong met for the first time at Wuhan, neither seemed to pay much attention to the other at that point. Mao, the arrogant party veteran, paid no heed to this small, junior Sichuanese, nor did Deng, the student returned from abroad, stand in awe of the rustic Hunanese. Mao was a formal participant and became an alternate Politburo member at the conference. Immediately afterward, Mao left for Changsha to instigate the "Autumn Harvest Uprising" in the Hunan and Hubei countryside, while Deng followed the Party Center as it moved to Shanghai for security reasons the next month.

From October 1927 to September 1929, Deng worked as a staff member or secretary for the underground Party Center in Shanghai. Chinese official historians and Deng himself nevertheless claim that he held the position of *mishuzhang,* or chief secretary of the Party Center.

Sometime in early 1928, Deng got married for the first time, to Chang Xiyuan, who also worked as a staff member at the Party Center and whom Deng had known as a schoolmate at Sun Yat-sen University in Moscow. The couple rented a small flat in the concession area and lived together for the next two years. While secretly working for the underground Party Center, they had to take public jobs such as grocery store owners and sellers of antiques.

In the Party Center at Shanghai, Deng's duties involved office chores, preparing papers, drawing up conference minutes, conveying directives, communicating messages, and so forth. The Party Center's new boss, Qu Qiubai, was a sentimental intellectual who, to use his own words, was thrown into communist politics by "a certain mistake of history."[15] However, this good-looking and gentle-tempered scholar proved even more enthusiastic in carrying out the radical line of nationwide armed rebellion than perhaps anybody else.

The Nanchang Uprising failed, with almost all of its leaders fleeing to Hong Kong or Shanghai and most of its troops killed or dispersed. The Autumn Harvest Uprising also failed, ending up with Mao leading a few hundred survivors in retreat to the Jinggang Mountains. In November 1927, another enlarged conference of the CCP Politburo was convened shortly after the Party Center moved to Shanghai. Deng once again attended the conference as a record keeper and to take down the minutes. There, Zhou and Mao were harshly punished for their military defeats as a result of having, ironically, executed a "right opportunist line."

The Qu center subsequently ordered even more radical actions, resulting in the Canton Uprising, which took place in December 1927. The uprising started with the establishment of the Canton Commune—a reference to the Paris Commune in 1871—but ended in an even more appalling disaster. Thousands of communists and sympathizers were killed in the uprising or executed shortly afterward. Thus, in a few months in late 1927, CCP membership dropped from fifty-nine thousand to ten thousand. A general party congress was urgently convened in Moscow in the summer of 1928 to review the situation. During the Sixth Congress, most of the party's leading figures went to Moscow, leaving only Li Weihan and Ren Bishi in Shanghai to handle the Party Center's daily affairs at home. Not yet senior enough to participate in the Moscow congress, Deng stayed in Shanghai working under Li and Ren's leadership.

In Li Weihan's memoirs, we find the following description of Deng Xiaoping's function in the Shanghai Party Center in 1928: "While the Sixth Congress was taking place, Ren Bishi and I were entrusted to stay in Shanghai and handle the center's affairs at home. From April 1928 to September of the same year, when the newly appointed party leaders came back, the center often held its meetings in a suite of two rooms in the Tianchan Theater on Shanghai's Fourth Street. There was a small table under the western window of the suite. As the meeting went on, Xiaoping would sit at the table to jot down notes."[16]

On quite a number of public occasions, Deng seemed to make fun of himself by bragging about his own "revolutionary seniority," which caused a lot of confusion for official historians. On one such occasion, Deng told an overseas Chinese scholar, "In 1927, I became the chief secretary of the Party Center for the first time. I was only twenty-three years old. Oh, it was a pretty high position, wasn't it? But actually, I didn't know anything at the time."[17]

No documentary evidence shows that Deng had ever in the 1930s been the Party Center's *mishuzhang,* or chief secretary—even further from its English translation "general secretary" or "secretary general." The official title of chief secretary did exist at some periods in party history, and such a position was normally held by a Politburo member, such as Zhou Enlai or Li Lisan. Deng was not yet a Central Committee member. In his memoirs, as cited above, Li Weihan was obviously trying his best to flatter Deng, but without distorting the historical fact that Deng worked merely as a staff member in the Party Center.

At the Sixth Congress, both Chen Duxiu's rightism and Qu Qiubai's leftism were criticized. Xiang Zhongfa, a proletarian figurehead, became the new general secretary, and the real power of the Party Center was divided between the moderate Zhou Enlai and the radical Li Lisan, both students who had returned from France. Deng was starting to play a more important role, but he was hardly the chief secretary—a key position held by Zhou in 1929 and then Li in 1930.

From 1928 to 1929, when Deng was in Shanghai, the Communist Party underwent drastic changes in its policies and personnel. Thousands of communists were arrested and executed by the nationalists. The party also lost hundreds to suicide or desertion as traitors. During these two horrible years of underground activities, "white terror" over-whelmed the communists everywhere. Many of the slain were individuals whom Deng personally knew and highly respected: Zhao Shiyan and Chen Yannian, leaders of the Youth League in France, were killed in Shanghai; Zhang Tailei, whom Deng had seen in Wuhan only a few months earlier, died in Canton; Luo Yinong, formerly the party secretary at the Eastern University, was arrested and executed; and so forth.

There were internal struggles as well as external ones. Within the Party Center in these years, Zhou Enlai was for Deng a model communist and comrade, yet Zhou seemed not to be trusted by the Comintern; Li Lisan seemed personally wrong but politically correct; Xiang Zhongfa was nothing but a proletarian figurehead, and yet he was the general secretary. Arguments and quarrels among these three bosses became routine affairs. All these events took place before Deng's eyes and made a deep impression on his maturing mind.[18]

His two years' experience working with the underground Party Center had an indelible impact upon Deng's later political career. Although not yet holding important positions, as he later claimed, Deng did become familiar with the mechanisms of central leadership. The good thing about Shanghai was that it contained the "imperialist concession"—making it more secure than many other locations without foreign imperialists. Deng seemed fortunate to have survived the long spell of "white terror" and remained safe and sound without suffering any fatal injuries—physical or political.

We may surmise that, once Deng arrived in Soviet Russia as a student, he was almost predestined to return to his homeland and join the Chinese revolution. His education in Moscow gave him a basic knowledge of communist doctrines, and his experience in Shanghai acquainted him with the organizational functions and personal relations of the central leadership. Nevertheless, Deng had thus far been a follower or an observer rather than a true participant in Chinese communist politics—until the next phase of his political career took off.

6

The Unfortunate Royal Commissioner, 1929-1931

The Nationalist Party and its leader, Chiang Kai-shek, seemed to have achieved a grand victory during and shortly after the Northern Expedition of 1926–28. By the end of 1928, the nationalists had either defeated or reformed or appeased all the major warlords in China. The Nanjing government was legitimately established throughout the country, and its military forces swelled to approximately two million troops.

But the abrupt unification of the country proved little more than a superficial phenomenon and created for the Nanjing government many substantial problems, which quickly flared up in the late 1920s. Although the pacification of warlords through expedient negotiations had helped Chiang to take over national power smoothly, it had also left intact numerous autonomous domains all over China, such as those of Li Zongren in Guangxi, Yan Xishan in Shanxi, Feng Yuxiang in the northwest, and Zhang Xueliang in the northeast. As a result, Chiang had to face one civil war after another between 1929 and 1930.

At the social level, the shift in the nationalists' attention from mobilizing the worker–peasant masses to cooperating with the capitalist–landlord elite in order to bring the state under normal rule alienated the Nanjing government from the grass roots. Particularly in the vast countryside, the nationalists never succeeded in establishing a regular administration below the county level or achieving significant agrarian reform, as they had promised. The communists thereby became the spokespersons for workers and poor peasants and the nationalist regime's most potent challengers.[1]

With incessant civil wars between the Nanjing government and local warlords as its "external conditions," and with the agrarian reforms among the peasants as its "internal substance," the communist rebellion in the countryside grew by leaps and bounds in southern China from the late 1920s onward. This rural insurrection or soviet movement had turned into the major feature of the communist revolution, replacing the urban workers' movement of the early 1920s.

In March 1929, Li Zongren, the military leader of Guangxi Province, and once Chiang Kai-shek's ally during the Northern Expedition, revolted against the Nanjing government. To deal with the situation, Chiang succeeded in bribing several generals within the Li clique, such as Yu Zuobo and Li Mingrui, to refuse to obey Li's orders. These defections contributed decisively to Li Zongren's defeat and resignation in May 1929. Consequently, Yu Zuobo took over as Guangxi's new governor and Li Mingrui as its new military chief.

While Yu Zuobo and Li Mingrui were earnestly reconstructing the provincial government and army, the Communist Party took this opportunity to infiltrate Guangxi. A score of communist secret agents were dispatched to Nanning from July to September 1929; they had little difficulty in quickly gaining various official positions. It turned out later that Governor Yu's own younger brother, Yu Zuoyu, was also a Communist Party member.[2]

In early October 1929, Yu and Li took their turn at rebelling against Chiang. It seemed equally necessary for the communists to attempt to extend their own political and military influence, regardless of the likelihood of Yu and Li's failure. The Chinese Communist Party Center therefore decided to send two special envoys, Gong Yinbing and Deng Xiaoping, to Guangxi to coordinate the local communist agents in an armed uprising. Under the pseudonym of "Deng Bin," Deng left Shanghai via Hong Kong and Canton to arrive at Nanning sometime in mid-October 1929. Because previously dispatched communists such as Chen Haoren, Zhang Yunyi, and Yu Zuoyu had already exerted considerable influence, Gong and Deng's role was mainly to implement the Party Center's order in principle and thus did not involve much performance in a practical sense.

Throughout 1929, executive power at the CCP Center was shared between Zhou Enlai as director of its organizational department and Li Lisan as director of its propaganda department. In September 1929, Li became the chief secretary and Zhou the director of the military department—as a result of the death of the previous director, Yang Yin. In all likelihood, Gong and Deng were personally appointed by Zhou and Li to Guangxi, with Gong acting as liaison between the Party Center and the Guangxi party agents and Deng acting as local representative of the Party Center working among the Guangxi party agents. Their general purpose was to instigate a military uprising from within Yu and Li's troops.

Some biographers hypothesize that Deng went to Hong Kong and Nanning with the assistance of Ho Chi Minh, the Vietnamese communist leader, who was supposedly an old friend of Deng from their Paris days. There is no documentary evidence, nor much logical basis, for such an idea. The basic historical fact is that the Communist Party had maintained strong organizational influences in Hong Kong and Canton ever since the massive Canton–Hong Kong strike of the early 1920s and had no need of a Vietnamese comrade to help smuggle a Party Center envoy like Deng from Shanghai via Hong Kong to Nanning.[3]

Deng Rong and official historians in China must face their own dilemma: On the one hand, they attempt to enlarge Deng's role in the Guangxi Uprising—such as by suggesting that he arrived in Guangxi in June 1929 as the Party Center representative in charge of the whole province's communist affairs, that he was the political commissar of both the Seventh and Eighth Red Armies in 1930, and so on. On the other hand, they try to downplay Deng's role in the Guangxi Uprising, as it ended in obvious failure. Thus, they had to attribute blame to people like the fallen Li Lisan, the deceased Deng Gang, and the deserter Gong Chu. Careful discretion is required in treating this historical period.[4]

The earliest documentary source regarding Deng's Guangxi mission is an appointment notice of the CCP Guangdong Provincial Committee, sent to the CCP Guangxi Special Committee, dated October 30, 1929: "This Provincial Committee has decided to found the Guangxi Front Committee with Deng Bin as its secretary. The Front Committee will be in charge of the Left and Right River areas. It is the Special Committee's obligation to provide the Front Committee with all necessary information and transportation to Longzhou. In case the Special Committee is destroyed, you may ask the Front Committee for work assignments."[5]

Gong and Deng carried with them the Party Center's directives as well as communication equipment and codes. As the Party Center messenger, Gong would travel back and forth; as the local representative, Deng would stay on the spot. Gong and Deng arrived in Nanning just as Chiang defeated Yu and Li's revolt. Yu had fled to Hong Kong, while Li was directing his surviving troops to retreat westward to the Right and Left Rivers. Gong returned to Shanghai from Nanning, and Deng followed Li to the Right River. There, at the town of Baise, Deng met for the first time with Zhang Yunyi, Chen Haoren, and other communist agents working within Li's troops.

Gong rushed back to Guangxi. In the name of the Party Center, he ordered an armed rebellion in no more than ten days; then he left for Hong Kong and Shanghai. The Party Center's order was practically impossible to implement, and the uprising had to be postponed until December 12, 1929. Deng did not personally participate in this Baise Uprising—he left Baise a few days before the uprising took place—nor did Deng participate in the subsequent Longzhou Uprising. After making general arrangements for the latter event, Deng hurried off to Hong Kong, where he attended a special conference of the central military council in January 1930. To report the party and army work in Guangxi at the conference, Gong stood as chief speaker, with Deng as supplementary speaker. From Hong Kong, Deng went on to Shanghai and received further directives from Zhou and Li at the Party Center about future strategies in Guangxi. Since the Guangxi Uprisings had already taken place, Gong's mission was fulfilled. Deng returned alone to the Left River on February 5, 1930, to pass on the Party Center's latest directives and assume the general leadership of the newly formed Red Army and soviet base.[6]

Contemporary communist documents indicate that Deng was not the political commissar at the time of the Guangxi Uprisings, as almost all previous biographers have believed. As a matter of fact, there was no such title as "political commissar" in either the Seventh Army of the Right River or the Eighth Army of the Left River when they were formed on December 12, 1929 and February 1, 1930, respectively. What they did have at the time was the position of "director of the political department," assumed by Chen Haoren in the Seventh Army and Yu Zuoyu in the Eighth Army.

As soon as he returned to Guangxi, nevertheless, Deng indeed behaved like a royal commissioner and took authoritative actions promptly. He lost no time in communicating the Party Center's directives, which sounded entirely correct, and criticizing the incumbent local leaders' policies, which seemed entirely incorrect! Deng pointed out that "the leadership in the Left River lacks any focus, totally fails to carry out mass work, and keeps busy just with bureaucratic matters." After several meetings, it was finally decided that labor union movements and agrarian reforms would be the focal point of work. Deng also regarded it as a blunder for the Seventh and Eighth Armies to attack Nanning and ordered by telephone that the attack be stopped and the troops be recalled promptly. He further urged that the two armies be combined, thereby to "concentrate all the troops to move toward the Hunan–Guangdong border and proceed to join the Fourth Army in order to expand the CCP's nationwide political influence."[7]

In reading through Deng's own words at the time and reviewing his deeds, we get the sense that he cared more about the Party Center's general line than about local circumstances. Besides, the twenty-five-year-old royal commissioner seemed quite eloquent in communicating political slogans yet rather short on expertise and experience in conducting military operations, which would contribute to the defeats of the Seventh and Eighth Red Armies in February 1930 and, to a lesser degree, afterward.

For the purpose of combining with the Seventh Army, Deng himself led the First Brigade of the Eighth Army north toward the Right River. On their way, the troops were intercepted at the little town of Qingxi for a couple of weeks, making no progress and suffering a substantial number of casualties. Deng lost patience and decided to lead a small company ahead, leaving the main body behind. The end result was that both brigades of the Eighth Army quickly collapsed in late February 1930.[8]

By the time Deng reached Donglan on the Right River, the Seventh Army had moved away as a result of its failure on the battlefield. It did not return until mid-May 1930, when Deng met Li Mingrui and Zhang Yunyi in Hechi. Although Deng formally assumed the titles of secretary of the Front Committee and political commissar of the Seventh Army in June 1930, he remained either uninterested in or unsuited for military leadership. Instead, he stayed in the Donglan area experimenting with agrarian reform and soviet construction, while Li Mingrui and Zhang Yunyi took charge of military affairs. Deng had insisted on directing the troops outward, but few army leaders seemed to listen until October 2, 1930, when another Party Center envoy, Deng Baqi, came to his support. Deng himself recalled the events as follows:

> The Front Committee held a conference in Pingma on October 2, which Comrade Baqi attended. He gave a report on the June 11 Politburo resolution. We accepted that line. Then Comrade Baqi and I went to Donglan to arrange the work at the Right River and also to summon the Third Brigade to Hechi. There in Hechi, all the troops were gathered for a reception by Baqi as the National Soviet representative to raise their morale. Also held in Hechi later, on the anniversary of the October Revolution, was a conference of all party members, which totally accepted the Li Lisan line and resolved that the Seventh Army's priority tasks at the present time should be "Go attack Liuzhou!" "Go attack Guilin!" and "Go attack Canton!"[9]

The preceding is a direct quotation from Deng's own report to the Party Center at the time. There seems to be no reason to argue otherwise on Deng's behalf, nor does there seem to be any doubt that he accepted the Li Lisan line at the Hechi Conference on November 7, 1930. He did so not just for ideological and disciplinary reasons, but also for personal reasons, because the Hechi Conference had greatly enhanced his political authority over the military leaders.

The Seventh Red Army departed the Guangxi Base Area and, in November 1930, kept rolling northeastward along the Hunan–Guangxi border. During that period, Li Mingrui and Zhang Yunyi were primarily responsible for the troops' military operations, while Deng Baqi and Deng Xiaoping were joint political leaders, respectively holding the posts of representative of the Party Center's South Bureau and secretary of the Seventh Red Army's Front Committee.

From the very beginning, the slogans "Attack Canton" and "Attack Guilin" were too bold to be militarily achievable. The troops did indeed try to take Liuzhou but failed miserably, incurring a few thousand casualties in the process. As a result, the troops halted and eventually had to quit. Further losses in three smaller clashes with local Kuomintang forces in late November and early December further dampened their previous ambitions.

Even in his early years, Deng proved quick to learn lessons from experience. On January 2, 1931, the Quanzhou Conference of the Front Committee decided to abandon the goal of attacking large cities because of the Seventh Army's heavy losses and the fall of the Li Lisan center. The conference decided to move to the Hunan–Guangxi border and join the Jiangxi Central Soviet. The Seventh Army's two divisions were also reduced to three regiments, for more efficient operations. Deng Baqi and Chen Haoren left the troops, presumably to report to the Party Center after the Quanzhou Conference.[10]

The farther north the troops moved, the colder the weather became. Regardless of the political line and the military strategy, their primary struggle was merely to survive. Since the Seventh Army was originally supposed to attack Guilin and Canton in the warm south, nobody had thought of equipping the soldiers with insulated clothing or heavy shoes—until the sudden advent of winter cold in the north reminded them.

Yan Heng, a staff member working with Deng in the Seventh Red Army at the time, later submitted a report to the Party Center that vividly described the troops' ordeal, roving along the Guizhou–Hunan border in January 1931: "We started at midnight. It was raining. But the rain turned to heavy snow at daybreak. About 110 li [55 kilometers] lay between Daozhou and Jianghua. Marching over such a long distance in snow and ice, the soldiers wore only sleeveless vests. Few even wore straw sandals. The Fifty-eighth Regiment brought up the rear and arrived at the camp rather late. Seven or eight of its soldiers had died of the cold. This truly represented the most tragic page in Seventh Red Army history!"[11]

As a result of the drastic reduction in the number of its troops, the Seventh Army had to downgrade its structure further to two regiments, the Fifty-fifth and Fifty-eighth, on January 14, 1931. Another disastrous battle with the KMT local militia on February 3 resulted in the death or serious injury of half of all the Seventh Army's battalion and regiment commanders. As Deng later reported on that horrible situation to the Party Center, "At this very juncture, all I wanted was to cry wildly!"[12]

On February 5, 1931, the Fifty-fifth and Fifty-eighth Regiments were separated while crossing the Lechang River on the Hunan–Guangdong border. Zhang Yunyi and the Fifty-eighth Regiment under his command were left behind at the Hunan–Guangdong border, while Li Mingrui and Deng Xiaoping directed the Fifty-fifth Regiment to enter southern Jiangxi, where they suffered further losses in fighting local KMT forces. Sometime in early March 1931, Deng left the troops at Chongyi and led a small squad to contact some local party agents at Jiaba. On his return, Deng found that the troops had retreated after another fierce battle. He thereupon wrote a note for his bodyguard to carry to Li Mingrui, which read: "I assumed you have just engaged the enemy and are currently in retreat. As it is impossible for me to catch up with you, please fight your own way through to the Jinggang Mountains and meet the Red Army there. I am going to take this opportunity to report to the Party Center about the Seventh Army affairs."[13]

Perhaps the preceding description, based on Red Guard investigations in 1966, may not be considered entirely accurate. Here is Deng's own contemporary account of the event:

> I and Li Mingrui crossed the river, but Comrade Zhang Yunyi couldn't. After the split at Lechang, our Fifty-fifth Regiment went through the Renhua border to Neiliang in Dayu County and arrived at Chongyi, Jiangxi. We stayed in Chongyi for about twenty days. Then we got information that the enemy was approaching and decided to move to Xinfeng. We were to leave the next day, but two enemy regiments and some local militia had already begun their attack on Chongyi. Lacking adequate intelligence reports, we were unaware of this until the enemy reached the city walls. Our troops had to retreat toward Gefu without putting up much resistance. It was at that juncture that I left for the Party Center in early March.[14]

Despite their differences in approach and detail, these documents all confirm the basic fact that Deng left the troops at his own impromptu discretion, not because he was authorized to do so in advance by any collective resolution of the party and army leadership, as Deng Rong and official historians have argued. This fact is clear, although whether it can simply be called "desertion of the troops" or "betrayal of the revolution"—a claim that was made by the Red Guards but with which I don't quite agree—is an entirely different matter. But some Western biographers simply declare, "Once the Seventh Army arrived in Jiangxi, Deng left Zhang Yunyi in command and headed for Shanghai," and, "He had in any case been authorized by the army's front committee to make his way to Shanghai."[15]

A resourceful politician, Deng knew that self-protection was the very foundation of his political life and career. That was why he left the troops at his own urgent discretion, without collective sanction—a situation rather different from that of Deng Baqi and Chen Haoren after the Quanzhou Conference. If Deng had learned any lessons from the Seventh Army tragedy, one of them must have been that war was an arduous and dangerous matter, as was revolution, and that telling others what to do was far easier than doing it oneself. He carried this bitter lesson with him to good effect throughout his later political life, especially in his cooperation with Liu Bocheng during the wartime period of 1937–49. Deng's Seventh Army experience also showed him to be a politician who was better at personal relations than at tough practical duties.

Leaving Chongyi in early March 1931, Deng exchanged his army uniform for plain clothes and, with the assistance of local communist agents, traveled by way of Canton and Hong Kong back to Shanghai by late March. After a few days' careful effort, Deng managed to contact the Shanghai underground communist organization. Unfortunately, he learned that his wife had died a year earlier, and that the Party Center was in utter shambles.

A few months before Deng's arrival, Li Lisan was summoned to Moscow for trial, and Zhou Enlai's functions were also greatly reduced. Wang Ming and Bo Gu, both students who had returned from Russia, had taken over control of the Party Center. A few days after Deng's arrival, Gu Shunzhang, a Politburo member in charge of secret intelligence and underground networks, was apprehended by the KMT government. Gu betrayed party secrets. Consequently, the general secretary, Xiang Zhongfa, was arrested and immediately executed, despite his pitiful confession and petition for pardon.

The period following the downfall of Li Lisan was one of fierce intraparty struggle, which further facilitated the KMT's apprehension of communist agents, particularly in Shanghai. Some were killed, and others defected. The CCP's failure in urban work left the Party Center in Shanghai as simply a liaison office relaying instructions from the Comintern to the Chinese soviets. It gradually degenerated into a cumbersome bureaucracy with little leadership capability. The Party Center's leaders began considering a general transfer to the soviet base areas in the southern countryside.

Deng's wife, Zhang Xiyuan, had died in a small hospital while giving birth to a baby. The baby girl survived a few days under the care of Zhang's sister. Upon his belated return, all Deng could do was to pay a visit to his wife's grave to express his final respects. Evidently, Deng Xiaoping went to the graveyard with his younger brother, Deng Ken (formerly, Deng Xianxiu), who happened to be in Shanghai applying for admission to college.[16]

On April 29, 1931, Deng submitted to the Party Center a lengthy report on the Seventh Army's affairs. In that historically valuable document, Deng admitted some mistakes and yet blamed the Li Lisan center from above and also the "reactionary elements" within the Seventh Red Army's ranks for its tragic defeat. Specifically, he concluded, "The failure of the Seventh Army constituted a failure in its general line, the focal indication of which lay in the fact that everything had been decided entirely on a military basis instead of according to work on the masses."[17]

The Party Center took no immediate disciplinary action against Deng, nor did it show him much sympathy. He remained idle in Shanghai for several months with no job assignment. He kept asking permission to return to the Seventh Army, but his requests met with only cold indifference. It was a very difficult period in his political life, as Deng himself said; but it could have been even worse, as Deng himself should have known. It was not merely a matter of Wang Ming and Bo Gu being the new leaders. Deng had just failed in a party mission. What else but coldness could he expect from the Party Center, with or without Wang or Bo in charge?

Fortunately for Deng, as a matter of fact, Zhou remained at the Party Center and on the Military Council; otherwise, Deng might have been treated far worse. Nonetheless, nobody could avoid a stern criticism of Deng and the Seventh Army leadership, as can be seen from the Party Center's letter dated May 14, 1931:

> After several defeats because of its military adventurism, the Seventh Army became overwhelmed with pessimism and passivism. Once the enemy was heard to be approaching, regardless of whether the report was true or false, they would run away immediately. Weeds and woods all seemed like enemy troops! We believe that the true nature of rightist opportunism and a rich peasant line, under the disguise of leftist Lisan slogans, cannot be better illustrated than in the behavior of the Front Committee leader at the time.[18]

The May 14, 1931, letter from the Party Center obviously singled out Deng, or "the Front Committee leader at the time," as the target of criticism. For various practical reasons, ironically, this letter was addressed to the Seventh Red Army in Jiangxi, but not to Deng Xiaoping in Shanghai; its immediate effect was the reform of the Seventh Army's incumbent leadership rather than Deng's punishment.

During the Cultural Revolution in the late 1960s, the Red Guards condemned Deng's departure from the Seventh Army at Chongyi as "deserting the troops to save his own life," and Deng himself also confessed that "[i]t was a grave mistake in my life." But at that time, Deng's political opponents within the party leadership, such as Kang Sheng and Jiang Qing, who made every effort to attack him, remained silent about this obviously interesting matter. Why?

The answer lies in some historical background known to the older Kang and Jiang but not to the teenage Red Guards. In fact, during the Rectification Movement at Yan'an in the 1940s, Chen Yi and Mo Wenhua, who were reviewing the Seventh Red Army history, had already raised the issue and concluded, "It was really inappropriate for Deng to have left the troops at such a crucial juncture."[19] But because of Deng's intimate relations with Mao Zedong, as well as his position as military leader at the battlefront, Mao would not allow any formal criticism of Deng. Since Mao's previous instructions were still in effect, unknown to the Red Guards but well known to Kang and Jiang, the latter did not want to involve themselves in this matter, despite their own hatred of Deng.

Finally, in July 1931, Deng was dispatched, together with a female communist agent, Ah Jin, from Shanghai to the Jiangxi Central Soviet. The two arrived in Ruijin, the soviet's red capital, the next month, but Deng did not return to the Seventh Red Army as originally planned. The Seventh Army was then engaged in breaking the KMT's "third encirclement" at the front and would soon find itself in even more serious trouble because of the CCP's intraparty struggle.

Under the slogans of antireformist and antireactionary officers, a political purge took place in the Seventh Army in October 1931. Scores of high-ranking officers, including Li Mingrui, were executed by the "state defense and security agency." There are several documents suggesting that Deng sided with the security agency—rather than standing against it, as his own daughter claims—in attempting to eliminate Li and other former KMT officers from October 1929 up to June 1930. In his April 29, 1931, report to the Party Center, Deng strongly blamed the "old foundations of KMT soldiers" for the failure of the Seventh Army. In all likelihood, Deng himself was involved, supportively if not directly, in the purge of Li Mingrui. Half a century later, in 1984, when this case was brought up for rehabilitation, Deng instructed apologetically, "It would be appropriate to say that Li Mingrui had been one of the founders of the Left and Right River Soviet."[20]

There is little doubt that Deng's first independent performance in connection with the Seventh Red Army turned into a tragic failure and a dark period in his political life. First, he followed the Party Center's adventurous line; then, he left his troops for rather debatable reasons; and finally, he played quite an ambiguous role in the subsequent intraparty clashes. Deng always avoided discussing this period in his life. As a bitter lesson permanently buried in his own heart, however, the Seventh Army experience perhaps marked an important step in Deng's political maturation.

Chinese official biographers now claim that, immediately after his arrival in the Jiangxi Soviet in August 1931, Deng was appointed party secretary of Ruijin County. Such a claim is unsubstantiated and improbable. Had he been in such a prominent position, Deng would have been included in the long list of representatives for the First National Soviet Congress, which was convened in Ruijin in November 1931 to proclaim the establishment of the Soviet Republic of China.

Barring the discovery of any fresh historical records to indicate otherwise, I tend to believe that Deng might have become the party secretary of Ruijin County sometime in December 1931 or January 1932. But that must have been after, not before, the completion of the Seventh Red Army investigation and the arrival of Zhou Enlai as secretary of the Central Soviet Bureau. In other words, Deng's cooperative attitude toward the security agency in purging the "old officers" within the Seventh Army and his intimate relationship with Zhou as the top authority at the time both helped Deng recover from his previous political predicament.

7

Bad Luck Turns into Good Fortune, 1932–1936

Communist history is the history of the communists, and we cannot but listen to them. A Deng biography is the biography of Deng, and we cannot but listen to him. But what about the fact that the communists have offered so many different and contradictory versions of their own historical events, as did Deng with the events of his own life? Generally speaking, it should be noted that almost all, if not all, the official posts ascribed to Deng—by Chinese official historians, by Western China hands, by Deng himself, and by me as well—before the year 1937 are questionable. Some of these "facts" may be true, some may be false, and others may be doubtful. Since 1937, as Deng ascended to the central leadership, at least his official titles are better recorded and less problematic.

Because of the prejudice of Chinese communist official historians, and also because of the ignorance of Western China experts, our writings on Deng's positions and deeds, especially before 1937, have become a matter not only of what Deng was and had done, but also of what Deng was not and had not done. Personally, I have the general impression that the problem with the Chinese historians is a political one (i.e., they know that what they say is not quite right) and the problem with the Western China experts is an academic one (i.e., they do not know that what they say is not quite right). It seems no easy task to tell which is better and which is worse.[1]

Presumably, in May 1932, Deng left his position as party secretary of Ruijin County to become party secretary of the Hui-Xun-An Central

County in the southern part of the Central Soviet. It is hard to determine whether this new appointment was a promotion for Deng or a demotion. Although the latter position had a much broader jurisdiction over three counties, they were all newly occupied territory on the distant southern frontier, where no solid communist organizations except local guerrilla activities yet existed.

For Deng, the main comfort, albeit bittersweet, was perhaps that, in the Huichang area in the summer of 1932, he got married again, to Ah Jin, who had gone with Deng from Shanghai to Jiangxi a year earlier and again went from Ruijin to Huichang with him now. Of course, it was less a formal marriage than a simple cohabitational relationship—a fairly common phenomenon among the communists at the time. The communists were all "criminal bandits," at least as far as the KMT (Kuomintang) government and law were concerned. How could one expect everything about them to be perfectly legitimate? In point of fact, the marriages of Zhu De and Mao Zedong and even Zhou Enlai were of the same nature.[2]

There in southern Jiangxi, Deng became acquainted with Mao's younger brother, Mao Zetan, who was Deng's age and worked as party secretary of a neighboring central county, and with some other local party cadres and army officers. They occasionally indulged in chatting, not always in a positive tone, about current affairs and party policies. They used to gather together crabbing about the newly arrived Party Center leaders' ever-increasing demands on them for grain supplies and troop recruitment. It was also there that Deng for the first time got to know Hu Yaobang, a sixteen-year-old "little red devil" working with the Communist Youth League in the same region.

The entire Party Center, headed by Bo Gu and Zhang Wentian, entered the Jiangxi Soviet in late 1932 and early 1933. It was just at the time of the KMT's Fourth Encirclement Campaign against the Jiangxi Soviet Base Area. Although these "students returned from Russia" were outspoken about the civil war, they had no solid, suitable plans for military affairs in general and combat strategy in particular. Instead, they simply imposed one army recruitment drive after another, which proved impossible to fulfill due to their ever-increasing quotas, such as "one million iron and steel red soldiers," and instead placed unbearable pressures on local party and soviet cadres like Luo Ming, Deng Xiaoping, and Mao Zetan.

Luo Ming was the acting party secretary of Fujian from March 1932 to January 1933. At the early stages of the Fourth Antiencirclement Campaign in late 1932, Luo expressed his opinion on the current situation and the party's work in two articles. "The party has been too mechanistic in its military leadership," Luo argued. "It does not make sense to develop the same plan and apply the same method to different counties and districts." Luo also opposed the Party Center's blind call for "all-around offensive operations" and "all-out military recruitment." For local red armies and new soviet bases like those in his western Fujian region, he suggested that policies different from those stipulated by the Party Center be implemented. He did not think that he could fulfill the troop recruitment quotas demanded for his jurisdiction.[3]

Luo Ming expressed his opinions mainly from a local point of view, with no clear intention of challenging the Party Center's authority and its general political and military line. Nevertheless, Luo was quickly castigated as a "rightist pessimist" by the newly arrived Party Center leaders in the most militant terms. In the wake of the successful Fourth Campaign, furthermore, the anti–Luo Ming repercussions spread from the Fujian Provincial Committee to the Jiangxi Provincial Committee, in which Deng Xiaoping and Mao Zetan were singled out as "Luo Ming liners" and targets of attack.

Excessive and ridiculous as many intraparty struggles might be, there was normally some kind of catalyst or event that triggered their occurrence in the first place. Apart from the Luo Ming issue as a general background, the particular trigger for Deng's becoming a target of intraparty struggle in 1933 was the Xunwu incident in 1932. Xunwu was the name of a county and also of its county seat, under Deng's territorial jurisdiction. During the Fourth Antisuppression Campaign, in which the communists won a general victory, Xunwu was, by contrast, lost to KMT forces in November 1932. That was inexcusable in the eyes of the Party Center leaders, who had consistently supported a militant position: "Never lose one inch of soviet land to the enemy."

On March 12, 1933, the Jiangxi Provincial Committee delivered a letter to the Hui-Xun-An Central County Committee, blaming the latter for the loss of Xunwu and labeling it as "an opportunist mistake similar to the Luo Ming line." Several days later, on March 23, 1933, a conference of party activists in that central county was convened, in which Deng was harshly criticized. The chairman of the conference was Li Weihan, an old acquaintance from Deng's Paris days, with whom Deng had also worked in Shanghai during the Sixth Party Congress. But party principles did not spare personal friendships. As an active follower of the Li Lisan line who had just been released from Moscow back to China, Li Weihan was eager to show his allegiance to the new party leadership. Harsh attacks on Deng seemed a convenient way to do so.[4]

On April 15, 1933, Zhang Wentian, one of the leaders returned from Russia who had recently been promoted to a post in charge of the Party Center's propaganda and ideology, published in the Soviet organ *Red China* an article entitled "The Luo Ming Line in Jiangxi." For the first time, the article publicly linked Deng Xiaoping with Mao Zetan, Xie Weizun, and Gu Bo as an antiparty alliance to be relentlessly denounced.[5]

In order to reach a more formal decision on this matter, a "conference on party work in Jiangxi" was held from April 16 to 22, 1933. The conference passed a resolution relentlessly accusing the "Deng–Mao–Xie–Gu clique" of "having politically embarked on an anti-Comintern line and pessimistic abortionism, and organizationally conducted activities of antiparty factionalism and double-faceism." Deng was compelled to submit one paper of confession and self-criticism after another, each one increasing the seriousness of his mistakes. Despite his repeated confessions, however, neither pardon nor leniency was lightly granted.

It is interesting to note that, while criticizing himself harshly, Deng carefully kept within certain limits or bounds, as he would do later under similar circumstances. He would admit to practical wrongdoing, but not to any inexcusable motives. Thus, he stated in his second confession, "On the one hand, I do realize that I have committed serious mistakes—there is no question about that. Yet on the other hand, I do not, or I did not, think that I was intentionally acting against the Comintern and the party, and I thought that was not a serious problem."[6]

Deng was shrewd enough not to admit to anything like "antiparty motives" or "factionalist plots." He might indeed have been accurate in this regard. Far from forming a confidential antiparty clique with the other three, Deng in fact did not know them very well. Like many other intraparty struggles—the Peng–Huang–Zhang–Zhou clique in 1959 and the Peng–Luo–Lu–Yang clique in 1966, for example—the foursome were arbitrarily lumped together as one "antiparty group." Of course, they might have shared some common opinions as local cadres and were unhappy about being dispatched from central leadership to local areas after the returned students came to the Jiangxi Soviet. Nor did they feel comfortable with the strict orders for food and recruitment from their jurisdictions. Under their existing geographic circumstances, they certainly favored guerrilla activities rather than the conventional warfare requested by the Party Center leaders.

It is also too far-fetched to connect Deng Xiaoping and Mao Zedong directly in this incident, as many Deng biographers have done. That connection may be true—actually very true—in a final analytical sense, but not in a real empirical sense. Such a subtle discrepancy should not be lightly ignored or neglected. Deng had thus far had little personal contact with Mao, as both would recall later, and Deng's own ordeal had little direct impact on Mao's fortunes. Oddly enough, in fact, even the fraternal relations between Mao Zedong and Mao Zetan should not simply be taken at face value as also reflecting their political relations, especially in those earlier fanciful revolutionary years![7]

It must have been particularly painful for Deng to see his own wife (or to be more accurate, his girlfriend) rush up to the podium to expose his crimes and publicly declare herself to be to "cut[ting] off relations" with him. Soon afterward, Ah Jin did leave Deng and fall into the arms of Luo Mai, or Li Weihan, who had chaired several anti-Deng conferences and mass rallies at that time. From late 1933 until early 1938, Ah Jin was formally Li Weihan's spouse.

On May 5, 1933, the Chinese Communist Party Provincial Committee of Jiangxi passed a resolution regarding disciplinary actions against Deng and his three associates. Deng was given a "most serious warning within the party"; he was removed from all his leadership positions, effective immediately; his pistol was publicly confiscated; and he was subsequently dispatched to a remote southern village in Le'an County as a "circular inspector."

The intraparty struggle during that period somewhat resembled young siblings' arguments in front of their parents—snapping at each other, calling each other bad names, fighting, and even hurting each other. But once it was over, it was over! Owing to various circumstances in the Jiangxi Central Soviet, the struggle could not get as violent as in some other base areas, such as the Eyuwan and Xiangexi Soviets, where thousands of communists were executed by their own comrades. Sometime later, thanks once again to his having Zhou as his patron, and also to his own typing and editing skills, Deng was called back to Ruijin to work in the Red Army's General Political Department, first as a staff member and later as editor of *Red Star,* a biweekly Red Army journal.[8]

There were altogether only two or three persons working for *Red Star;* Deng was assisted by one or two youngsters. Hence, his position could be called *Red Star's* editor in chief, as he himself later stated. The journal carried Red Army leaders' articles on military strategy and tactics, as well as military correspondents' news reports on the current civil war. The contents were decided or approved by higher leaders like Zhou, the Red Army's general commissar, and Wang Jiaxiang, the director of the General Political Department. Deng himself did most of the editing and transcribing. He did not seem to care much about the contents, which for the most part consisted of reports of the victories of Red Army troops in the Fifth Antisuppression Campaign. Deng worked with *Red Star* in Ruijin quietly and obediently for more than a year, without bothering, or being bothered by, others.

Chiang Kai-shek started the Fifth Suppression Campaign against the Jiangxi Soviet in November 1933, and on the communist side, Otto Braun and Bo Gu assumed the general command. Braun knew military textbooks too well, just as Bo Gu knew Marxist and Leninist classics, but none of these references seemed applicable to the actual military operations. The foreign dogma led to the final defeat in the Fifth Campaign, as Braun's positional defense failed against the one million KMT troops, who successfully adopted a "blockhouse plus highway policy." After a year's fierce engagement, the communists had to evacuate the Jiangxi Central Soviet and embark on a flight westward in October 1934, which eventually turned into the historic Long March.

In retrospect, Deng was fortunate to have been chosen for the Long March. Many of those left in the Jiangxi Soviet, like Mao Zetan, would soon be killed. One official account says that, as the Long March began, Deng was replaced by Lu Dingyi as the chief editor of *Red Star* and assigned to the central command column under Zhou's leadership. In December 1934, when Zhou's wife was sick, Deng took over her position as chief secretary of the Party Center. His duties included dispatching and receiving telegrams, and taking notes and minutes for meetings of the central leaders—as he used to do in the Shanghai years. Another account says that Deng kept working at *Red Star* until January 1935, when he was elected chief secretary of the Party Center during or shortly before the Zunyi Conference.[9]

From late October to early December, the Red Army succeeded in breaking through the KMT's four blockade lines, but its troop strength was drastically reduced, from eighty-five thousand to forty thousand. And even those who survived had to struggle to continue surviving. As they were forced to move farther away from the soviet base and enter the unknown territory of the southwestern highlands, complaints and protests grew among the troops over the party and army leadership.

A now famous enlarged Politburo conference was held at Zunyi in January 1935, to review the experiences and lessons of the Fifth Campaign. As it turned out, the Zunyi Conference became a fierce power struggle between the incumbent Bo and Braun leadership and the opposition, represented by Mao. Since I have dealt with the factual details of this conference elsewhere, only its direct connection with Deng will be discussed here.

There has been great controversy over whether Deng participated in the Zunyi Conference and, if so, in what position and capacity. The current official version portrays Deng as a participant at the conference, and some Western China experts readily accept that official line even now! As a matter of fact, Deng was at the time neither a Politburo member nor a senior military leader, and therefore, he could not have been considered qualified to participate. He did attend the conference, but as one of the service staff. A participant with a right to speak and vote should not be confused with a minute taker or a security guard. This official error can easily be explained by the fact that Deng himself, the paramount party leader, claimed to have been a participant, and Chinese official historians seemed not to be above deferring to political concerns in their current historical studies.[10]

Too much superficial argument over whether Deng was a participant sometimes overshadows his substantial role at the Zunyi Conference. He was recommended by Zhou, with Bo's approval and Mao's agreement, to attend the conference and exert technical influence in his informal and yet important position as minute taker and record keeper. In other words, although Deng himself did not speak, nor was he entitled to, as minute taker and record keeper, he could dictate who would speak and certify what had been said!

With his head buried in his papers and his hand busily writing, but without uttering a word or showing any emotion—as was normally expected from a note keeper—Deng functioned somewhat like a referee in a boxing match or a reviewer of a dramatic performance. Watching Bo Gu eloquently citing all possible excuses for his failures, Zhou Enlai gracefully admitting his own errors, and Mao Zedong sarcastically attacking them, and seeing military men like Zhu De and Peng Dehuai stand up against Otto Braun, who sat in the corner quietly chain-smoking, Deng could not help having a sense of judgment on the past and strong aspirations for the future.

The most important aspect of the Zunyi Conference for Deng as an individual was perhaps that it marked a decisive advance in his personal relations with Mao. Deng had first met Mao at the August 7 conference in 1927, but this diminutive clerk made no lasting impression upon that veteran leader. After the incident of the Deng–Mao–Xie–Gu clique, however, Deng's name entered and remained in Mao's mind. As the note taker at the Zunyi Conference, Deng must undoubtedly have caught Mao's personal attention even more.

The conference was far more important for Deng than vice versa. In the case of military leaders like Peng Dehuai and Lin Biao, despite their status as full participants, their actual functions were not so substantive at all. They were called from the front to attend the conference, during which they remained silent most of the time, and then they were sent back to the front after its conclusion. This was a political occasion, and they had very little to offer in the first place. Only when a clear consensus appeared to emerge regarding the end result of the conference did they begin to show their support for the position taken by the majority of the Party Center. No matter who became the new party leader, they would remain with their troops as commanders or political commissars. However, for Deng as a political cadre in the Party Center, any change in central leadership would matter a great deal. He had been disliked by the Bo Gu center, and new leadership might be more favorable to him. There was no hope for him with Bo, but with Mao and Zhou, he might have a chance to advance.

During the latter part of the Long March, from June to October 1935, Deng left the party and army headquarters to work in the First Army Corps as either chief or deputy chief of its Propaganda Department. A major part of his duties seemed to consist of running a song-and-dance troupe consisting of a number of mostly young women, including his former wife or girlfriend, Ah Jin. The couple thus met again. Apologies were formally offered by neither but informally accepted by both. In the next six months, they marched together, he as the propaganda chief and she as a propaganda activist. This dramatic rendezvous, in my own judgment, resulted in the birth of Li Tieying—presently a CCP Politburo member and the state commissioner of culture and education—shortly after the Long March ended in 1936.[11]

After engaging the KMT troops in Guizhou and Yunnan for several months in early 1935 with no strategic success, the Central Red Army or the First Front Army had to move north across the Yangtze River to appeal to a subordinate group, the Fourth Front Army in western Sichuan, for support. Along the way, the troops climbed precipitous peaks and crossed swiftly flowing rivers along the western Sichuan–Xikang border. It was not until June 1935 that they finally joined the Fourth Front Army. The journey was rough and resulted in huge casualties. Deng's horse died at the foot of the Snowy Mountain, and he had to proceed on foot for the next several weeks. Upon the union of the two Red Army forces, Deng was delighted to find Fu Zhong, who was working as deputy director of the Political Department in the Fourth Front Army. This old friend from his Paris years presented Deng with "three treasures": a horse, a fur jacket, and a packet of dried beef. "These were really a big deal!" Deng later recalled.[12]

The period from June to September 1935 witnessed first the joyous union and then the acrimonious split of the two major communist forces, Mao Zedong's First Front Army and Zhang Guotao's Fourth Front Army on the highlands of western China. Among the many issues wrangled over, a fundamental distinction can be made between, on the one hand, the struggles between Mao and Bo at the Zunyi Conference, and on the other hand, between Mao and Zhang at the Shawo Conference. The Mao–Bo conflict was basically over revolutionary policies and had strong theoretical overtones. Although it involved the question of internal leadership, their debate was mainly over external relations—that is, how to fight the KMT regime and carry out the revolution. The struggle between Mao and Zhang, on the other hand, constituted what might be termed a pure power clash. It was essentially a struggle for party and army clout, however much overlaid by its rhetorical dispute over Marxist-Leninist doctrines, over policies in fighting the nationalist enemy, and over strategies in conducting the communist revolution.

The service personnel for the Shawo and Maoergai Conferences, which highlighted the Mao–Zhang conflict, were arranged not by Zhou, as at Zunyi, but by Mao himself as the new holder of power.

Deng had nothing to do with these conferences. To keep the conference records, Mao seemed to have more confidence in Wang Shoudao, an old disciple of his Jinggang Mountains years, than in Deng, his new acquaintance. Needless to say, Deng and official Chinese historians had a different explanation for his absence from Party Center affairs during this period.[13]

Zhang Guotao's lengthy memoirs, published in Hong Kong and the United States several decades ago, remain one of the uniquely valuable sources on CCP political history. At one point, nonetheless, Zhang was not quite accurate in describing Deng as deputy director of the Political Department of the First Front Army on the Long March. I assume that might be Zhang's inadvertent recollection of his reunion with Deng in October 1936 rather than of the situation in August 1935.[14]

The struggle at Shawo and Maoergai was of quite a different nature from that at Zunyi. It involved more political plots, factional intrigues, and power clashes than at the earlier conference. Neither Zhang Guotao nor Mao Zedong was like Bo Gu in believing in regal Comintern principles or sacred Marxist doctrines. Zhang applied his superior military force in order to usurp the party leadership, while Mao relied on the legitimacy of the Party Center to defy Zhang's military power. The end result was that, in September 1935, Zhang attempted to use his army to force Mao to go south, and Mao ordered his own troops to sneak north out of Zhang's control. They split, with Mao leading the First Front Army to northern Shaanxi while Zhang and his Fourth Front Army turned south to the Sichuan–Xikang border.

Asked by his daughter what he did on the Long March, Deng shook his head and replied modestly, "I just followed its course."[15] That was easier said than done! The course of the Long March represented a tough experience at the time but a glorious record afterward. In CCP officialdom, it was so good, but not so easy, to win the title of "a cadre of the Long March." Tens of thousands of Deng's comrades could not follow the course. They dropped dead of hunger, cold, sickness, or wounds before Deng's very eyes. They slipped off the snowy mountains, drowned in the swampy grasslands, or were slain on the battlefield. Thanks to his robust physique as well as good fortune, Deng survived the whole course of seven thousand miles without injury or illness.

With his sharp eyes and clear mind, Deng observed the bitter internecine struggles between Mao and Bo at Zunyi and between Mao and

Zhang at Shawo. Furthermore, although Zhou Enlai had for many years been Deng's idol, that image changed a bit, or a lot, after Deng observed the gentle Zhou as a pitiful target of attack at Zunyi and as a physically and spiritually wrecked personality dealing with Zhang at Shawo—all of which constituted a clear contrast with the rougher and tougher Mao.

Gradually but steadily, Deng's appreciation of Zhou's tireless work, careful organization, gentlemanly behavior, conciliatory nature, cool obedience to his superiors, and warm concern for his subordinates was eclipsed by his admiration for Mao as an imposing, authoritative figure and a charismatic personality. The problem, however, remained whether the tall and senior Hunanese shared the same growing respect for the short and junior Sichuanese.

Great changes took place in the party's central leadership as well as the party's general policy after its arrival in northern China in October 1935. Mao's authority was firmly established, with Zhou Enlai as his chief assistant, Zhang Wentian as his party spokesperson, and Peng Dehaui as his army operator. Based on all the information available, we find that Deng was still far from being an important political element at that juncture.

As resolved at the Politburo conference at Wayaobao in December 1935, the communists' policy of waging rebellious war against the nationalists was replaced by a policy of forming a second united front with the nationalists against the Japanese invaders. The CCP's first step in implementing the new policy was to ask the local KMT army leaders, Zhang Xueliang and Yang Hucheng, for a mutual cessation of military confrontations, to which both sides agreed during the early months of 1936.[16]

The Wayaobao Conference was not a formal meeting with opening and closing ceremonies; instead, it was just a series of sessions among party and army leaders. Deng attended several of those sessions, obviously with Mao's approval, if not through his personal choice—but again, as a member of the service staff, not yet as a formal participant.

The year 1936 was less eventful for Deng than it was for the Communist Party. He remained the director of the Propaganda Department of the First Army Corps—a marginal position in the central leadership. Under Mao's resourceful management and driven by the new united-front policy, the communist troops became more firmly settled in the new base area, and Deng in the meantime got more firmly settled in the party and army leadership. He followed Mao in the Eastern Expedition in March 1936, which resulted in a military success but also exposed factional problems among the Red Army troops. In May of that year, Deng was promoted to deputy director of the Political Department of the First Army Corps, shortly after the Eastern Expedition was successfully completed and then reviewed in a meeting at the Premier Temple.[17]

In October 1936, Mao chose Deng to accompany Zhou to eastern Gansu to welcome the Second and Fourth Front Armies, which had just finished their own Long March. Before their departure, Zhou and Deng were received privately by Mao in his cave house in Wayaobao. After offering some directives for their mission, Mao suddenly turned the conversation to Deng and Zhou's experiences in France: "What did you guys learn in France?" Deng replied modestly, "Well, I learned to work. I toiled in one factory after another for those five years." Mao seemed happy with Deng's answer and grew a bit excited: "French women are said to be beautiful, aren't they?" While Zhou was at a loss as to how to cope with Mao's black humor, Deng responded, "Perhaps not. Women are all the same, especially in the dark." Both Mao and Deng burst into hearty laugher, while Zhou grinned uncomfortably.[18]

Deng was a darling—his amiable name, his youth, his small figure, his boyish face, and his witty words seemed to delight everybody, melting away the tensions among the reunited communist leaders. Zhou, together with Zhu and Zhang of the Red Army headquarters, returned to northern Shaanxi, while Deng remained in eastern Gansu working at the front headquarters as Ren Bishi's deputy. Deng had worked under Ren before in Shanghai in 1928, but the difference now was that Deng was entrusted by Mao and Zhou with a position as de facto representative on behalf of the Central Red Army in the newly merged unit.

Japan's large-scale invasion of China and the CCP's united-front policy eventually led to the spectacular Xi'an incident. Deng was in the western front army headquarters in Huiyuan, Gansu, when the Xi'an incident began on December 12, 1936. Chiang Kai-shek was kidnapped at a hot-spring resort outside Xi'an by his own generals Zhang Xueliang and Yang Hucheng, who demanded that the civil war be ended so that Chinese forces could concentrate on national resistance against the Japanese invasion. To cope with the urgent situation, the western front army was immediately called back east, and so was

Deng. Suffering from typhoid fever at the time, he had to be carried on a stretcher.[19]

With his expertise and rich experience accumulated throughout the preceding years and, above all, with Mao's newly granted trust in him, surely Deng could now expect improved political fortunes. In the army reshuffle after the grand reunion of the three major communist forces, he was promoted to director of the Political Department of the First Army Corps in January 1937. This was an important position in itself, but even more important ones lay ahead. Old soldiers of the Jinggang Mountain years, such as Wang Shoudao, might want to be more loyal to Mao than Deng, but the problem was that they proved less politically capable than Deng of knowing exactly how to be more loyal!

— 8 —

Battlefield as "Safe Haven," 1937-1945

Politics entails complexity and paradox and is not always subject to simple laws of causality as contemporary politicians claim and later political observers believe. If we can say that the military confrontation between the Chinese Communist Party (CCP) and the Kuomintang (KMT) in the early 1930s invited the Japanese invasion of China, we can also say that the Japanese invasion promoted the CCP–KMT collaboration in the late 1930s. Unexpectedly—and yet logically, in retrospect—the Xi'an incident resulted in the temporary suspension of their civil war, and the Marco Polo Bridge incident in July 1937 prompted the commencement of their joint national war against the Japanese invaders.

Of course, none of these historical developments happened simply out of "objective necessity," devoid of "objective freedom." Rather, they were all embodiments of purposeful behavior by all concerned nations, governments, political parties, and individual politicians. In regard to the Communist Party after the Long March, I have elsewhere depicted Mao Zedong as "a political entrepreneur," astutely interested in the party's internal management and external competition in order to take over the state power. It was under such general circumstances that Deng found his own star rising.

In June 1937, Deng accompanied Zhou Enlai, Zhu De, and Ye Jianying to the Nanjing government's national defense conference, serving as a senior aide but not yet as a formal member of the CCP delegation. Of course, Deng would later argue that he had been the real decision maker behind the scenes. From Nanjing, Zhou and Zhu flew directly to Xi'an and then drove to Yan'an to take part in the Luochuan Conference. Deng and other staff members returned to Yan'an by train a few days later.

Deng did not participate in the Luochuan Conference of August 22–24, 1937, at which almost all the leading CCP figures formulated a new strategy for the new situation; nor was Deng elected, as were almost all the senior party and army leaders, to the newly reformed Central Military Council. Nevertheless, he was appointed deputy political director of the Eighth Route Army (ERA), formally established on August 25, 1937. This position was pretty high, although not quite substantial in view of communist history, but it would pave the way for Deng's further promotion to far more substantial power.[1]

In September 1937, Zhu De and Ren Bishi led the ERA headquarters across the Yellow River toward the Wutai Mountains, presumably in order to fight the Japanese troops. Deng followed them. During the next few months—from September 1937 to January 1938—Deng showed himself the key document handler and was therefore one of the few recipients of secret telegrams on behalf of the ERA headquarters from the Military Council and the Party Center, headed respectively by Mao and Zhang Wentian.

The Eighth Route Army consisted of three major units: the 115th, 120th, and 129th Divisions, formed respectively from the First, Second, and Fourth Front Armies of the Long March years. Of these three units, Mao was particularly concerned about the 129th Division, which had formerly belonged to his political archrival Zhang Guotao. He preferred to have more personal control of that division but feared that any abrupt and radical change in its leadership might arouse resentment, if not resistance, from its officers and rank and file. To mitigate Zhang's influence, Mao first dismissed Chen Changhao as the division's political commissar and Xu Xiangqian as its commander and substituted Zhang Hao and Liu Bocheng for them at the beginning of the Sino-Japanese War.

Liu Bocheng was originally from the First Front Army but had later worked with Zhang Guotao in the Fourth Front Army for more than a year in Sichuan. An army veteran, familiar with military affairs and with high seniority and a good reputation, Liu had no obvious biases in intraparty affairs. Xu Xiangqian, who now became the deputy commander, should also have been fine from Mao's perspective. Although he was formerly the general commander of the Fourth Front Army, Xu was also a professional soldier with no clear sense of intraparty factional allegiance.

The crucial role remained that of political commissar. Zhang Hao—an alias for Lin Yuying, actually Lin Biao's uncle—was a veteran leader who joined the CCP in 1922 and had worked in various senior positions ever since. He returned from Moscow to northern Shaanxi in late 1935 as a Comintern representative and functioned as the mediator between Mao and Zhang Guotao in 1936. Although his seniority and neutrality made him acceptable to the rank and file of the 129th Division, it also made him vulnerable to Mao's purpose of ever tighter control. In other words, Zhang Hao was too neutral to be personally loyal to Mao and too senior to be personally controlled by Mao. That being the case, Zhang Hao was a transitional figure. Mao would eventually want somebody loyal and junior to himself, but also persuasive enough to indoctrinate the troops and intelligent enough to play politics within and outside the party apparatus. Deng seemed Mao's ideal choice!

Mao was concerned not only with personal affiliation but also with military policy. After the first several combat engagements in the latter months of 1937, he had to stress repeatedly the basic change in military strategy from large-scale mobile warfare to small-scale guerrilla warfare.[2] The essential purpose of what he termed "guerrilla warfare in the mountains" was to avoid fighting with the Japanese troops in order to preserve and develop his own strength. Not all the communist generals seemed to fully understand Mao's strategy or strictly abide by his instructions. Therefore, after the Pingxingguan Battle of September 1937, Mao sent one telegram after another to the ERA general headquarters and sometimes directly to the headquarters of individual divisions, reminding them of the guerrilla policy and sternly admonishing them against any reckless combat engagements with the Japanese troops.

From both a personal and a political standpoint, Mao felt an urgent need to reform the army leadership, particularly that of the 129th Division. Thus, in December 1937, we find that Zhang Hao was called back to Yan'an for a new appointment as chairman of the All China Labor Union—seemingly a promotion with which Zhang should have been happy; and Fu Zhong, the deputy political director of the 129th Division, took over Deng's position as deputy political director of the ERA general headquarters—also seemingly a promotion with which

Fu should have been happy. In the meantime, Deng was reappointed political commissar of the 129th Division—seemingly a demotion from the general headquarters to a subordinate army unit. But the true effect of all this hustle and bustle, all these ups and downs, was that Mao managed to put Deng, loyal to himself or likely to be so, in direct control of the 129th Division without generating too much commotion or arousing too much suspicion.

It is surprizing that a recent (1993) biography by Richard Evans still has it that "Deng was appointed political commissar of the 129th division" to "succeed a man who had just died."[3] Evans is a former British ambassador to Beijing, and his book is among the serious and unbiased Deng biographies. It is clear, however, he did not know about Zhang Hao or Lin Yuying, let alone the complicated circumstances that had led to Deng's appointment to the 129th Division.

As for Deng, the new position represented a "great leap forward," from ordinary political cadre to de facto guardian of one-third of the CCP military forces. He had thus stepped up the political ladder, firmly planted on military ground, and he was to carry out Mao's political and military line and remain personally loyal to Mao. This proved a decisive move for their mutual benefit. Deng would not disappoint Mao, nor would Mao disappoint Deng, as the following years surely proved.

Deng's appointment as political commissar of the 129th Division was first announced by the Military Council to the ERA headquarters on January 5, 1938, and subsequently transmitted by the ERA headquarters to the 129th Division headquarters on January 8. Deng arrived to assume his new duties on February 8. Because Liu Bocheng was away in Taiyuan for a military meeting at the time, Deng assumed overall responsibilities in the division headquarters the moment he arrived. Deng was not one to be bashful about his power or authority.[4]

Following Mao's strategic instructions, the communist troops fought few combat engagements with the Japanese in 1938 but did manage to achieve a staggering growth in their military forces and territorial bases. Under the joint leadership of Liu and Deng, the 129th Division quickly grew from six thousand to thirteen thousand strong and successfully established three base areas, each with a dozen counties, along the adjoining border regions of Hebei, Henan, and Shandong Provinces.

In the autumn of 1938, Deng left southern Hebei to attend the CCP's Sixth Plenum in Yan'an, which marked the establishment of the

Mao leadership in the CCP Center. The plenum was also important for Deng, as it marked the first time he attended a Party Center conference as a full participant. Deng did not speak, nor was he yet regarded as an essential figure, but he was there as the legitimate representative of the 129th Division. In all likelihood, the plenum's criticism of the rightist line of Wang Ming and, to a lesser degree, of Zhou Enlai strengthened Deng's shift of confidence from Zhou to Mao.

On October 15, while the Sixth Plenum was still under way, Deng telegraphed from Yan'an to Liu Bocheng and Xu Xiangqian instructing them on military arrangements: "The eastern column should be divided into two brigades; so should the western column. I will bring back several brigade leaders with me when I return. All our new troops should go through intensive training, with the key purpose of increasing their combat capabilities."[5] The exact contents of Deng's message from Yan'an did not matter much, but the message seemed to convey the Party Center's stance. Therefore, Liu and Xu telegraphed back to express their total agreement and support. For Deng, it was the Party Center's authority that kept him in firm command of his own troops, but it was also his own troops who won him high respect from the central leadership.

Deng was regarded as a party man in the eyes of his troops, while simultaneously being regarded as a military man in the eyes of the Party Center leaders. His duty as political commissar was to keep the political orientation of the 129th Division in line with the Party Center or, more bluntly, to keep an eye on the military for Mao. Deng played this role skillfully, so as not to hinder the work or bruise the feelings of Liu and others. Deng thus maintained a relationship of mutual respect and dependence with Liu, who was entrusted with tactical command of the troops and conduct of the actual battles.

From Liu's perspective, he needed somebody to work with who was trusted by the Party Center and capable of dealing with political matters but would not interfere with his military operations. In the recent past, Liu had followed Bo Gu and Otto Braun in the Jiangxi Soviet in 1934 and Zhang Guotao during the Sichuan expedition in 1936. Their political mistakes had not only hindered Liu's military duties but caused him many political troubles as well. Professional soldier as he was, Liu also needed a stable political background on which he could depend. Deng and his connection with Mao provided this for him. In a sense, Liu needed Deng as much as Deng needed Liu.

In July 1939, Deng was summoned from the battlefront to Yan'an once again to participate in an enlarged Politburo conference. He stayed there for more than two months conferring with the Party Center leaders before returning to his troops. During his stay at Yan'an, apparently through the matchmaking efforts of party leaders, such as Deng Fa, he got married for the third and final time. Both Mao and Zhou personally attended Deng's wedding. The bride, Zhuo Lin, was a former college student recently arrived in Yan'an from Beijing.

After the outbreak of the war against the Japanese, one group of "progressive youth" after another came from northern and eastern cities to the "revolutionary mecca" of Yan'an, thus providing the communists with many young, urban, intellectual females. This offered a perfect opportunity for some veteran party and army leaders to get either married or remarried. Mao Zedong picked up Jiang Qing, Lin Biao found Ye Qun, Deng Xiaoping chose Zhuo Lin, and so forth.[6]

Zhuo Lin was born in 1916, twelve years after Deng. She was also from a landlord and capitalist family in Yunnan. After finishing high school in Kunming, she came to Beijing for college, majoring in physics at the Normal University for Women. She was among those "progressive youth" who had left big cities for Yan'an in the late 1930s and had then become one of those intellectual females married to communist veterans. The thematic nature of this volume prevents us from dwelling on Deng's private affairs, but it should be mentioned that, unlike many others in her category—such as the wives of Mao, Liu, and Lin—Zhuo Lin proved to be more interested in family life than in politics; she never caused Deng any political trouble during their marriage.

The newly married couple spent half their honeymoon in Yan'an, receiving gregarious congratulations from Mao and other party leaders, and the other half on their journey back to the Liu–Deng army, along with a group of bodyguards and news correspondents. Madame Deng would give birth to a girl, Deng Lin (combining her father's surname and her mother's given name), in 1941 and a boy, Deng Pufang (named by Liu Bocheng at his father's request), two years later, in 1943.[7]

In the southern Hebei Base Area in the fall of 1939, Deng met Evans Carlson, a U.S. Army officer who had come to observe the Sino-Japanese War in northern China. With great enthusiasm and sympathy, Carlson met Nie Rongzhen in the Jin-Cha-Ji Base Area, He Long in the Ji-Sui Base Area, and Deng in the Jin-Ji-Yu Base Area.

Carlson had extensive conversations with Deng and left deeply impressed by "Tun Shao-pin," as he called him at the time. He described Deng as an army officer, "short, chunky, and physically tough," with a mind "as keen as mustard."

Major Carlson was one of the few Westerners Deng saw during the war against the Japanese. Another was Hans Muller, a German who served as a doctor in the Chinese communist army. "In the spring of 1940," Muller recalls, "I lay in the infirmary of the headquarters of the Liu–Deng Army, semiconscious with abdominal typhus. Unexpectedly, Political Commissar Deng Xiaoping stepped to my bed and presented me with a whole carton of the fancy Shanghai brand cigarettes. As I smoked about 60 cigarettes a day at that time, I was naturally pleased with this gift." Unlike Carlson, who was just passing through, Muller worked with the communist army for many years to come. He had treated hundreds of Deng's sick or wounded soldiers, but not Deng himself. Why not? "Deng was simply never sick."[8]

Upon his return from Yan'an to the front in October 1939, Deng brought back directives from Mao and the Party Center, notably about the communists' "frictions" with local KMT troops. Since these were frictions within the "united front," involving competition for territorial control and administrative jurisdiction, they were regarded not merely as military matters but mainly as political issues. Deng made political decisions, and Liu took military actions.[9] After some careful preparations, the 129th Division fought a number of successful battles against nationalist generals such as Sun Chu, Shi Yousan, and Zhu Huaibing in the spring and summer of 1940. These successes enabled the 129th Division to grow to 110,000 strong and expand its territory to more than seventy counties with a total population of more than eight million. In addition to being the political commissar of the 129th Division, Deng assumed another important title as party secretary of the Taihang Mountain Base Area.

The 129th Division was directly under the command of the ERA headquarters, formally headed by Zhu De and actually run by Peng Dehuai, and less directly under the CCP North Bureau of Yang Shangkun and others. Deng had to deal carefully with them all, not just with Mao at the Military Council and Party Center. Peng pushed for engagement with the Japanese enemy—culminating in the "Hundred Regiments Campaign," in which all the communist troops in northern China were ordered to launch attacks on Japanese-occupied cities and railways from August to December 1940. Mao received the news of the Hundred Regiments Campaign with mixed feelings. Publicly, he sent a telegram congratulating Peng for this victorious campaign, but at the same time, he was deeply worried about the losses of his own personnel. Mao was even more unhappy that Peng had initiated such a large military operation without first requesting his personal approval.

In the 129th Division, Liu was in charge of combat operations at the front, and Deng was in charge of support work at the rear. Deng did not take an active part in the Hundred Regiments Campaign, but neither did he prevent Liu and the 129th Division from participating in the campaign at the time, nor did he complain about Peng or the Eighth Route Army headquarters for initiating it. He later observed that "both the enemy and our own troops suffered considerable losses in the campaign, with the former larger than the latter by a ratio of 9 : 7."[10] In such a subtle manner, Deng managed to share the glory of the division's military successes and yet avoid any possible blame for their negative political consequences.

In short, while formally joining and praising Peng's military operations, Deng also expressed subtle reservations about the Hundred Regiments Campaign—more or less the same way Mao himself did. Peng would later be criticized by purely political cadres such as Lu Dingyi, but not by Deng, who, as political commissar of an army division, was not just a political appointee. Personal disposition aside, because of the nature of Deng's duties, as well as the seniority of his position, he could afford not to express himself as openly as Lu Dingyi did.

Deng occasionally contributed articles to central and local party and army journals at the time. On April 28, 1941, in an article entitled "Fight against Inertia and Overcome the Grave Situation in the Taihang Region," Deng also expressed his own ambiguous opinion on the Hundred Regiments Campaign. "The Hundred Regiments Campaign was a grave test for the 129th Division, as well as for all aspects of our work in the Jin-Ji-Yu border area," Deng wrote. "It proved that a solid foundation has come into being in this border area in terms of military, political, party, and mass work alike. But it also exposed our weaknesses. The most urgent task is to consolidate our liberated area, in view of the fact that the enemy-occupied area is expanding and our liberated area is shrinking."[11]

In 1942, the Rectification Movement started in Yan'an and gradually spread to the entire party and army. While Mao's main target in the movement was Wang Ming and his leaders who had returned from Russia, historical investigations caused many other high party cadres to fall victim. Deng was spared, however, and suffered no serious criticism or challenge. Besides his special relationship with Mao, Deng's military position leading thousands of troops at the battlefront actually protected him.

Although the battlefield sounds like a dangerous place, it served as a safe haven for Deng in these years of fierce intraparty struggle. Some people, like Mo Wenhua of the former Seventh Army, brought up the matter of Deng's "desertion of his troops" in 1931. Chen Yi, who was in charge of the investigation, tried to treat it mildly: "It was inappropriate indeed for Deng Bin to have left the army at that critical juncture." When the matter eventually came to the Party Center for a formal resolution, Mao rendered it null and void. Even Deng's involvement with the Li Lisan line in 1930 was ignored, and only Deng's glory as a victim of the erroneous Bo Gu leadership in 1933 was recorded. The reason was simple: Deng was at the front with his troops. Thus, Deng alone avoided not only being attacked by others— unlike Zhang Wentian, Bo Gu, Zhou Enlai, and even Zhu De for his cooperation with Zhang Guotao—but also attacking others, such as Liu Shaoqi and Kang Sheng did in the Rectification Movement. Nonetheless, as incumbent leaders were toppled, Deng's seniority naturally improved.

Zhou Enlai, who had himself been a conspicuous target of criticism during the Rectification Movement, presumably for his involvement with the "leftist lines" of the 1930s and the "rightist line" during the early phase of the war against the Japanese, later recalled: "Comrade Deng Xiaoping was in sincere accord with the Rectification Movement and proved at the time relatively or entirely free from any mistakes."[12] What Zhou felt reluctant to admit was that Deng had by then become less a follower of Zhou than a follower of Mao.

Nonetheless, Deng seemed more than willing to carry out the Rectification Movement among his colleagues and subordinates. Just as Mao did at the Party Center by means of the Rectification Movement, Deng also attempted to enhance his own political authority within the 129th Division and among local communist organizations. It was always preferable to rectify others than to be rectified by others. By the end of 1942 when the Taihang Sub-bureau of the CCP Center was formed with Deng as its first secretary, he had become the undisputed number one leader in the army, government, and party of this vast communist base area.

From 1942 onward, as a result of the Hundred Regiments Campaign and the Rectification Movement, both of which reduced the authority of the ERA headquarters, and also because the Sino-Japanese War had entered a "phase of protracted stalemate" in which military affairs gave way to political issues, Deng came even more directly under Mao's auspices and enjoyed more independence from Zhu and Peng. His writings and speeches of that period dealt less with army operations than with party policies such as governmental administration, relations with the nationalists, land reform, mass organization, economic construction, political propaganda, and education.[13] Deng had both the responsibility and the privilege of making regular reports to the Party Center and the Military Council. He was called back to Yan'an more frequently than other leaders and would spend long nights in Mao's cave, chatting about political and personal matters. A special relationship of mutual trust and reliance was established between them.

The year 1943 was particularly difficult for the communists in the Taihang Mountain region, not only because of Japanese military assaults but mainly because of the aggravating economic circumstances created by natural calamities and the Japanese economic blockade. "Thrifty living and earnest producing" became the main slogan. Deng's July 2, 1943, article "Economic Reconstruction in the Taihang Area," and his speech on September 21 of that year—"Produce Food, Overcome Hardship, and Welcome Victory"—illustrated the Jin-Ji-Yu border area's economic predicament and the extensive efforts to overcome it.[14]

"He who has food has everything," Deng once said, summarizing a key problem in one simple and yet precise sentence as was his wont. "Hitler will drop dead next year, as will Japan go to hell the year after," he also noted. "But we also will have the most difficult time in the next year or two. Our economic and financial situation will be truly horrible." According to his slogan "Reward the diligent workers and punish the lazybones," model workers and labor heroes were rewarded with money and grain, while unproductive units were left to suffer as they deserved. As we shall see, Deng later adopted the same pragmatic policy under similar circumstances in the early 1960s.

Together with four other individuals—Zhang Jichun, Liu Xiwu, Li Dazhang, and Zhou Huan, all high-ranking army and party officials—Deng formed a "production team." They offered to rent a portion of a rice paddy, making a joint pledge to produce a certain amount of rice by the harvest season of the following year. It was mainly for propaganda and inspirational purposes, of course. By the end of the next year, the Sino-Japanese War was about to wind down, and Deng and his comrades would forget their rice production and commit themselves to fulfilling a more serious pledge.[15]

Sometime in October 1943, Peng Dehuai, Yang Shangkun, Liu Bocheng, and almost all the other senior leaders of the Eighth Route Army and the CCP North Bureau were summoned to Yan'an to attend "rectificational studies"—with the exception of Deng. He remained in the Taihang Base Area as the acting secretary of the North Bureau. Deng had gone to Yan'an before—actually, more frequently than others—but he did not go this time. While Peng was undergoing rectification in Yan'an, Deng took over his command of party, government, and army affairs in northern China. The decision was Mao's alone, and the effect, if not the purpose, was to enable Deng to avoid the harsh intraparty struggles in Yan'an and also to gain greater authority in the front base areas. Both in his having included Deng previously, and in his excluding Deng now, one can equally sense Mao's personal favor toward Deng.

From October 1943 to June 1945, Deng worked as the sole senior communist leader in northern China. With all the responsibilities heaped on his shoulders, he was certainly busy, but it was an exciting and rewarding business—one that Deng actually enjoyed. Several decades later, his daughter raised a question about that period: "Father, wasn't it very hard for you to be left alone in northern China?" Deng answered with a proud smile, "I did only one thing—to swallow bitterness."[16]

Perhaps as an expression of his true feelings of gratitude and perhaps as a means of raising his troops' morale, Deng began publicly praising Mao by name—something he had seldom done before. In a speech to his subordinates of the North Bureau in late 1943, we find the following comment: "Under the guidance of Mao Zedong thought or Sinicized Marxism–Leninism, our party's cause has been surging forward in the past nine years, without any serious mistakes. Recalling the bitter lessons of the previous opportunist leadership, every one of us should feel happy and thankful about these recent years."[17]

In early 1944, as its underdog status became ever more apparent in the Pacific War, Japan launched a desperate offensive campaign along the Beijing–Canton railway, especially in Henan. The KMT troops—

commanded by generals Jiang Dingwen, Tang Enbo, and Hu Zong-nan—suffered immensely in the Henan Campaign. More than half of the four hundred thousand troops were lost in a couple of months, and the rest started a southbound stampede. Meanwhile, the communist troops in northern China emerged rapidly from their rural byways to fill the vacuum, just as they had done in 1937 and 1938. They carried out several aggressive campaigns in 1944 and early 1945, less to challenge the Japanese army's hold on the railway line and the large cities than to expel the KMT and pro-Japanese puppet troops from hundreds of small cities and spread their own organizations in thousands of villages.

It should be noted that these communist operations were under Deng's leadership in his capacity as acting secretary of the CCP North Bureau; he should be given due credit in this regard. However, it should also be noted that Deng's leadership was more nominal than substantive, that it was more a matter of political influence than of military command. In fact, the communist troops in northern China could have accomplished more or less the same feats with or without Deng. After so many years of guerrilla experience, they already possessed the capacity—and the obsession—to expand their territorial holdings. They would naturally do so once the slightest opportunity presented itself.

As the Sino-Japanese War began winding down, the Seventh Congress of the CCP was convened in Yan'an from April 23 to June 11, 1945. It turned out to be a great triumph for Mao personally as well as for the Communist Party in general. The Seventh Congress brought two crucial developments: it firmly established Mao's supreme authority in the party constitution, and it clearly decided the party's postwar policy of competition with the KMT government for supreme state power.

Deng did not personally attend the Seventh Congress, nor did he need to do so. Deng spent the congress with his two hundred thousand troops at the front rather than among the audience in the congress hall, yet his promotion to the central leadership was a virtual certainty. He was elected, by a large affirmative vote, as a high-ranking member of the party's Central Committee, which represented an appropriate reward for his distinguished work as well as a particular favor from Mao.[18]

Liu Shaoqi, in his report on the new party constitution, obsequiously dropped Mao's name more than a hundred times and boldly declared,

"Our Comrade Mao Zedong is not only the greatest revolutionary and politician but also the greatest theoretician and scientist ever since Chinese history began." Liu needed to do this, because he had supported Mao in the Rectification Movement to squash the leaders who had returned from Russia, such as Wang Ming and Zhang Wentian, as well as the members of the old guard, such as Zhou Enlai and Zhu De, and thus helped promote Mao as number one and himself as number two. Deng also received a promotion from Mao, but in a less obvious way and less by means of internal power clashes than through his own military achievements. He was not inclined to chant as extravagantly as Liu did, although he also had to sing some sweet praises to Mao.

It was only after the ritual congress was over that Deng arrived in Yan'an in June 1945 to attend the First Plenum of the new Central Committee, at which substantive issues of practical policies and personnel assignments for the postwar circumstances were discussed. Deng remained in Yan'an for the next couple of months, until the Sino-Japanese War finally ended. It was a restful break after the hectic fights of the recent past and also a period of cheerful warm-up for the more hectic battles to come. Deng would soon be sent, with some other army leaders, to wrest national power from Chiang Kai-shek in the upcoming civil war or, in Mao's own words, to "remove the mountain" of the KMT regime.

9

Battlefield as "Gold Mine," 1945-1949

Deng stayed in Yan'an, hearing one piece of good news after another about the war. Finally on August 14, 1945, came the surrender of the Japanese government and emperor. Mao Zedong's immediate reaction was to vie with Chiang Kai-shek to accept Japan's surrender—that is, to acquire the Japanese munitions and territory. Thus, a large number of troops and cadres was quickly dispatched to take over Manchuria. Outraged telegrams were exchanged between Mao and Zhu at Yan'an and Chiang in Chongqing, from August 13 to August 26, and orders flew from Mao and Chiang to their own generals for emergency actions against each other's forces.

Yan'an was gripped by militant excitement. As Mao and Zhu did with the communist army as a whole, Deng and Liu Bocheng sent out one directive after another to their own troops, ordering "every party committee and every military district in the Jin-Ji-Lu-Yu Base Area to immediately seize big cities and vital communication lines and prepare to resist the advances by Chiang and Yan Xishan's forces in northern China."[1]

On August 20, 1945, the Jin-Ji-Lu-Yu Party Bureau was formed, with Deng as secretary, and also the Jin-Ji-Lu-Yu Military District, with Liu as commander and Deng as political commissar. The former title of the 129th Division, which reflected an inferior status vis-à-vis the Nationalist Army, was abolished, as was the former Jin-Ji-Yu Base Area, which was expanded to include Lu, or Shandong Province. On

August 25, two days before Mao and Zhou Enlai flew to Chongqing for peace negotiations with Chiang, Deng and Liu flew on an American airplane back to their military base area. No sooner had they arrived at their army headquarters in southeast Shanxi than they began preparing for the Shangdang Battle with the Kuomintang (KMT) troops under Yan Xishan's command.

Accompanied by U.S. Ambassador Patrick Hurley, Mao flew to Chongqing for peace talks with Chiang on August 27, 1945. The talks lasted forty days and resulted in the so-called Double Tenth Agreement on October 10. The communists agreed to acknowledge the legitimacy of the KMT central government, while the nationalists acknowledged the Chinese Communist Party (CCP) as a legitimate opposition party. A national congress would be held to select a new joint government. It seemed that the two parties had reached a solemn agreement on all questions, even on reshuffling their armed forces.

In retrospect, one might say that neither of the parties, especially their chiefs, Mao and Chiang, really believed in any peaceful solution in the first place. The Chongqing talks and the Double Tenth Agreement could be seen as largely a political plot and propaganda ploy. Hindsight is always right, nevertheless, because it is merely hindsight. The true political situation at the time might not have been so simple and clear, and understanding it would require deeper and broader analysis.[2] This is not the place to perform such an analysis, but we can at least surmise that the prowar military elements in both parties helped smother the slightest predilections of Mao and Chiang to avoid civil war and helped destroy the slim prospects for national peace. As a matter of fact, Deng was among the military leaders on the communist side who were vigorously pushing for a civil war at that historic juncture.

The Battle of Shangdang formally erupted on September 10, 1945, two weeks after Mao and Chiang's peace talks began, and ended on October 12, 1945, two days after the CCP–KMT peace agreement was signed. These events should be regarded not as coincidences but as deliberate efforts, particularly on the part of Deng. For his extraordinary conduct at the Battle of Shangdang, Deng won high accolades from Mao in the name of the Party Center and the Central Military Council.

The communists alleged that the Battle of Shangdang was caused solely by KMT troops' encroachment on CCP territory. But historical documents indicate that Deng was at least as aggressive as Yan Xishan, and probably even more so. In addition to their telegrams of August 10 and 14, Liu and Deng telegraphed Li Da and Xie Fuzhi from Yan'an again on August 22, instructing them to attack Yan's troops and capture the city of Changzhi, which turned out to be the trigger for the Battle of Shangdang. As Mao was still in Yan'an at the time, he must have been aware of this telegram and may even have approved it. It was true that Mao held the philosophy that "the battle-field decides the negotiating table," but that did not mean that Mao expected the battle to proceed in the manner and to the extent that it did. There were subtle discrepancies between Mao's and Deng's approaches. No matter how large military confrontation loomed in Mao's mind, there was still some room for political negotiation. But for Deng as an army leader, military struggle was everything, and peace talks were not his responsibility, nor even his serious concern.

On August 25, Liu and Deng arrived back in the Taihang Mountains, ironically, by American airplane. On September 1, the Battle of Shangdang was finally decided upon. On September 2, Deng drew up a tentative timetable for the battle, which was soon agreed to by Liu and others. On September 10, the battle formally began. During the first couple of weeks, the Liu–Deng army mopped up half a dozen small county seats and encircled the larger prefectural center of Changzhi. The second phase entailed the destruction of the rescue forces in early October, and the battle ended with the capture of Changzhi and the annihilation of its garrison troops on October 12. In the entire battle, as Deng reported, several KMT divisions totaling thirty-five thousand troops were wiped out, a dozen cities were taken, and a dozen KMT generals were captured and held as prisoners of war.[3]

Under the slogan of stopping the civil war, both the nationalists and the communists were busily preparing for the civil war. Deng was among the most active in so doing. Immediately following the Battle of Shangdang came the Battle of Handan along the Beijing–Wuhan railway, from October 17 to November 2, 1945; the Liu–Deng army wiped out seventeen thousand KMT troops and forced ten thousand more to surrender. Even several decades later, Deng still recalled these episodes with joy and pride: "During the War of Liberation, from its beginning to its end, our Second Field Army always stood in direct confrontation with the enemy. We stood in the very forefront against the enemy. Military struggles with the KMT could also be found in other parts of the country, but they were concentrated in our Jin-Ji-Lu-Yu region."[4]

After several months of uneasy armistice between the KMT and CCP troops under the supervision of U.S. General George Marshall, full-scale civil war broke out in June 1946. The first seven months of the civil war saw nationalist attacks on all the communist base areas. Chiang took over a number of large and medium-sized cities but failed to destroy a substantial number of communist troops. Mao, on the other hand, took annihilation of nationalist troops instead of occupation of big cities as his priority objective and succeeded in wiping out roughly fifty-six enemy brigades, for a total of about 450,000 troops. During this period, the Liu–Deng army fought eight battles, wiped out about fourteen enemy brigades totaling approximately 100,000 troops, and managed to increase its own forces to about 250,000.[5]

Beginning in February 1947, Chiang had to shift his strategy from general attack to regional attack on northern Shaanxi, where the CCP Center was located, and southern Shandong, which was closer to the capital of Nanjing. The nationalist general, Hu Zong-nan, captured Yan'an on March 19, 1947. While the CCP Center, including Mao and Zhou, remained in northern Shaanxi, Liu Shaoqi, Zhu De, and Ren Bishi moved to Hebei as the Central Working Committee. In northern Shandong, Chen Yi's troops, formerly the New Fourth Army during the Sino-Japanese War, continued steadfastly resisting the KMT assault.

To cooperate with Chen's troops, Liu and Deng, on Mao's orders, crossed the Yellow River in June 1947 and drove south deep into Shandong Province. Their forces, in four columns totaling 120,000 troops, conducted the Southwest Shandong Campaign with considerable success but also heavy sacrifice. After the campaign, Liu and Deng were highly praised by Mao in the name of the Party Center: "Our Liu–Deng army successfully fought the Battles of Huncheng, Juyie, and Dingtao. They wiped out nine and a half regular enemy brigades and four divisional headquarters, and killed or wounded or captured more than fifty thousand enemy troops. That represents a great success, and we therefore award you the highest honor."[6]

To divert the KMT attacks further as well as to start the CCP's own offensive—not merely in the Central Plain but throughout the whole country—Mao got the idea of dispatching the Liu–Deng army to strike farther south into the enemy's heartland of the Dabie Mountains in

July 1947. That would constitute a direct threat to the cosmopolitan city of Wuhan as well as the nationalist capital of Nanjing, thus compelling Chiang to recall his offensive forces from northern Shaanxi and southern Shandong.

It should be noted that the idea of moving the Liu–Deng army to the Dabie Mountains originated with Mao alone, not with Deng or Liu. But Deng—after some initial objection and hesitation, along with Liu and their troops—showed himself quick and clever enough to seize the initiative. On July 29, 1947, Liu and Deng telegraphed Mao, conceding to agree to move southward: "We are determined to annihilate three to five more brigades of Wang Chonglian in order to break through the route toward the south." But Mao would have preferred that Liu and Deng proceed straight to the Dabie Mountains rather than engaging Wang in southwest Shandong; Mao meanwhile allowed them a little flexibility: "Well, how about your taking a rest of ten or more days first of all?"[7]

On July 30, 1947, Liu and Deng responded to Mao in the Central Military Council: "We have decided to take a half month's respite and preparation before starting off according to the general strategy. . . . It is indeed better for us not to hang on at the Yu-Wan-Su border but to move ahead to the Dabie Mountains, in order to form a pincer position with the Chen–Xie corps and create broader mobilities."

The very same day, Deng received a positive reply from Mao: "Very good. We appreciate your decision to leave the rear base and fight into the Dabie Mountains. We'll make sure that Chen and Xie have the same determination as yours." It should be noticed that Mao had pretentiously suggested that Liu and Deng take "a rest of ten or more days" while they were arguing over the whole operation. But once Liu and Deng had agreed to such an operation, Mao wanted to push it as soon as possible. While the military officer Liu still stuck to "a half month's respite"—hadn't the chairman suggested as much?— the politician Deng was smart enough to sense Mao's true mind-set and change the agenda accordingly. That was what Mao needed Deng for! When Deng informed Mao about the troops' immediate departure on August 6, Mao was obviously pleased, and his response was simple and clear: "You are absolutely correct!"[8]

The Dabie Mountains are located at the adjoining border of three provinces—Henan, Anhui, and Hubei—and adjacent to the city of Wuhan, the hub of central China. They had formerly been the base area of the Fourth Front Army, from which the Liu–Deng army had been formed. The whole region was the homeland of many soldiers in the Liu–Deng army, thus making it much easier for them to operate there.

On August 7, 1947, the Liu–Deng army, 120,000 strong, left southwest Shandong, starting the Southern Expedition. The troops marched through the Yellow River's "flood zone" in a couple of days. It was a vast swamp created by river floods, extending more than forty kilometers, with knee-deep water. To avoid enemy airplanes, the army marched from late evening to early morning, soaked in the heavy rain. Deng's order to the troops was simple and precise: "No rest. Keep moving, unless we want to be stuck and drown here." Both Liu and Deng gave up their horses and walked with the troops through the muddy water. In the next month, the troops traversed three provinces, crossed five big rivers, broke through numerous enemy blockades, and finally reached the Dabie Mountains in late September 1947.[9]

The Liu–Deng operation in the Dabie Mountains eventually proved to have been a strategic turning point for the communist army in the civil war—marking its shift from a defensive posture to an offensive one. From September to December 1947, the Liu–Deng army established a Dabie Mountains Base Area, drawing in thirty-three brigades of three hundred thousand KMT troops around them, thus making it virtually impossible for the KMT to sustain its continuous attack on the north and making it feasible for other communist forces to mount a counterattack in the Central Plain.

To serve the interests of their own troops, Deng, but not Liu, occasionally had to contact Mao in the Military Council and ask him to coordinate the activities of other communist troops with those of the Liu–Deng army. On December 22, 1947, Deng wrote to Mao:

> We hope the Chen–Su and Chen–Xie troops will make some strategic arrangement for assisting us in the Dabie Mountains. That primarily means that they should try to annihilate two or three enemy divisions to make the enemy pull some troops out of here. Our situation would be far better if just two enemy divisions could be diverted. We also understand it would benefit the general situation if we could carry a heavier load on our backs in the Dabie Mountains, and other troops in the Central Plain would then be able to wipe out more enemy troops and make more progress.[10]

On January 30, 1948, it was also the politician Deng, not the military officer Liu, who had to write to Mao explaining why their troops had not won as many combat victories as some other communist forces: "Because we had just arrived in the Dabie Mountains, we could not conduct large battles from September to December. But we still wiped out five enemy brigades totaling fifty thousand. More important, we marched more than one thousand li [about five hundred kilometers] and created three large base areas with a total population of forty-five million, establishing military and administrative networks and settling down steadfastly here."[11]

The land reform program was promptly implemented in the Dabie Mountains, in a more radical manner than elsewhere, in order to win quicker and stronger peasant support for the newborn communist base. The previous policy of rent and tax control was replaced by a policy of land and property confiscation: the confiscated goods were distributed to the troops and the land to the peasants. The only correct agrarian policy was one that could promote military success and had practical utility; it had little to do with Marxist or Leninist doctrine—a principle Mao and Deng both understood well.

Mao was not concerned merely with military affairs. As a politician himself, he cared a great deal about land reform and mass work in the newly occupied areas. Deng, also a political type, was good at reporting on such matters. In fact, Mao distributed one of Deng's reports to the whole party and army with very favorable comments: "The Dabie Mountains experiences as Xiaoping describes them here are extremely valuable. I suggest that all places and all troops should implement them."[12]

After two years of fierce engagement on the battlefield, there was a fundamental change in the national military situation in the summer of 1948. The KMT forces had lost their offensive momentum and were fast collapsing on all fronts. Chiang had been shifting from an "all-round offensive" to a "focal offensive" strategy, then to a "focal defensive" strategy, and finally to an "all-round defensive" strategy—if the last approach could be still called a strategy at all.

In March 1948, Liu and Deng directed their mainline troops out of the Dabie Mountains and joined forces with Chen Yi and Su Yu in central China. In May 1948, Mao, together with Zhou, led the CCP Central Committee and the Central Military Council out of northern Shaanxi to Hebei to merge with the Central Work Committee, headed by Liu Shaoqi. Liu resumed his previous position as first secretary of the North China Bureau, while Deng became first secretary of the Central China Bureau, with Chen Yi and Liu Bocheng as his deputy secretaries.

Within their army, Liu and Deng conferred extensively on various military affairs. At least in the eyes of their subordinates, they respected each other, complemented each other, and took good care of each other. Since Liu was older and physically weaker, Deng would allow him more rest and remain on duty at night himself. Regarding the Military Council's combat orders, Deng would study them first, express his opinions for Liu's consideration, and then decide jointly with Liu on final responses. As for general reports to the Party Center, Deng would draft or dictate them personally, not delegating this task to anybody else. Deng took complete charge of political affairs as well, while Liu was mainly in charge of military operations.[13]

On June 6, 1948, Deng drafted another series of directives on land reform and party organization. Mao passed one of Deng's papers along to Zhou Enlai and Liu Shaoqi of the Central Work Committee with a few remarks of approbation: "We pass on this Central Plain Bureau document. The center therefore does not need to draft another one on this topic."[14] Here Mao's message was succinct yet clear: Deng's report could simply be regarded as the Party Center's policy—at least, on that particular subject.

By the summer of 1948, the civil war was entering its final stage. As the KMT forces were rapidly approaching the verge of total bankruptcy, the key problem for the CCP military leaders became less one of tactical operations than of strategic initiatives. In other words, the bolder they were and the bigger the battles they dared to mount, the more military victories and rewards they could garner for the good of the party's cause as well as for their own individual or factional interests.

Prior to the grand showdown with the KMT government, which Mao was determined to launch, the communist forces were reorganized into several "field armies" in order to conduct large-scale mobile battles and campaigns. Despite their constant changes in titles, leaders, and locations, four mainline field armies emerged in the summer of 1948: the First Field Army, under Peng Dehuai in the northwest; the Second, under Liu and Deng in the Central Plain; the Third, under Chen Yi in the east; and the Fourth, under Lin Biao and Luo Ronghuan in the northeast.[15]

Among the four field armies, Mao did not quite trust the First, which was basically He Long's troops mixed with local Shaanxi guerrillas presently under Peng Dehuai's general command. Regarding the Second Field Army, which had originally consisted of Zhang Guotao's troops, the only leader Mao deemed his own was Deng Xiaoping, the political commissar. Chen Yi's Third Field Army had been formed from the New Fourth Army, which also had little personal connection with Mao. As for the Fourth Field Army, both the troops and its leaders, Lin Biao and Luo Ronghuan, were Jinggang Mountain veterans, whom Mao deemed the most trustworthy of all.

Mao therefore felt inclined to use the First, Second, and Third Field Armies as supplementary forces to check or divert the nationalist troops and to employ Lin's Fourth Field Army as the primary offensive force in fighting the KMT Central Army. Mao fancied that the First Field Army would strike northwest toward Xi'an, the Second would strike southwest toward Chongqing, and the Third would cross the Yangtze River and advance farther south, thus splitting Chiang's attention in several directions, so that the Fourth Field Army could focus on a triumphant showdown with the nationalist troops in the Yangtze valley.

Consequently, Mao conferred with Chen Yi and suggested that the vice commander of the Third Field Army, Su Yu, should lead two army corps of two hundred thousand troops to force their way across the Yangtze River and drive deep into southern China, far behind the KMT front lines. Chen agreed with Mao's suggestion and, upon returning to the troops, duly informed Su of the operation.

Instead of accepting his assignment of marching to the distant south, however, Su went to see Mao in person to argue against the southern expedition and propose concentrating his troops to destroy the KMT Central Army north of the Yangtze. He even offered to sign a "military pledge." Not only was Mao persuaded to change his mind, but to facilitate Su's new plan, Mao also transferred Chen temporarily to the Second Field Army and appointed Su as acting commander and political commissar in full charge of the Third Field Army. Mao certainly possessed the domineering power as well as the overbearing ego to shuffle his army personnel somewhat like playing cards!

Su Yu indeed fulfilled his pledge. In the following couple of months, he directed the Third Field Army to victory in the Battles of

Yudong and Jin'an, each of which wiped out more than one hundred thousand KMT troops, thus sparking the enthusiasm of other military leaders to pursue large-scale mobile engagements and to compete with one another for war trophies and rewards.[16]

Eventually, Su's general strategy of concentrating major forces to engage the KMT troops north of the Yangtze River culminated in the monumental Huaihai Campaign, in which the joint forces of the Second and Third Field Armies wiped out 550,000 KMT troops, mostly from its Central Army, in two months, from November 1948 to January 1949. Chiang's troops consequently had to withdraw south of the Yangtze, and the KMT regime totally lost its vigor and vitality.

To execute this Huaihai Campaign, Mao, acting in the name of the Central Military Council, appointed a five-man "General Front Committee," consisting of Liu Bocheng, Chen Yi, Su Yu, Tan Zhenlin, and headed by Deng, who served as its secretary and had overall responsibility. The formation of the General Front Committee was no doubt based on complicated political, military, and personal considerations, yet one fact was clear: the appointment of the younger Deng as its secretary, over party and army veterans like Liu and Chen, reflected Deng's intimate relations with Mao more than anything else.[17]

The Huaihai Campaign was for the communists a monumental military victory, and Deng was the secretary of the General Front Committee, which had successfully conducted the campaign. This fact seems to have convinced many Deng biographers, Chinese and Western alike, of his outstanding capacity and capability in military affairs. David Bonavia actually covers Deng's experiences in the civil war under the chapter title "Strategist." I would instead suggest that Deng was a *zhengzhi ganbu,* or political cadre, rather than a *junshi ganbu,* or military cadre; and that Deng's true function throughout the war was one of political control rather than military command, either strategic or tactical.

In connection with Deng's role in the CCP–KMT civil war, a simple question may be raised: why did the communists lose in 1934–35 but win in 1946–49? In both stages of the civil war between the KMT and the CCP, the opposing military commanders were basically the same— such as He Yingqin, Chen Cheng, and Gu Zhutong on the KMT side and Peng Dehuai, Liu Bocheng, Chen Yi, and Lin Biao on the CCP side. But in the former stage of the war, all the communist troops, no matter who their commanders were, suffered grave defeats, while in the latter stage of the war, almost no communist troops failed to win great victories. Why? Although answering this question fully is beyond the scope of this biography, to put it simply, I would say that the outcome of the war was primarily decided by general historical and political conditions and that the performance, positive or negative, of any individual military commanders did not count too heavily.

It also seems interesting to offer a more profound insight into Mao's strategy in the civil war in general and Deng's military performance in particular. Mao's obsession with the idea of sending troops to fight in the enemy's rear can be traced back to the Jiangxi Soviet years of the early 1930s. More recently, from late 1944 to early 1945, Mao had dispatched one army corps of twenty thousand led by Wang Zhen to cross the Yangtze far down to the south. Hoping to drive a fateful wedge into the KMT enemy's heart for post–World War II development purposes, this "small long march" ended in sheer disaster. It started with twenty thousand troops and finished with barely two thousand struggling back north. In June 1948, Mao had tried to do the same with Su Yu, as mentioned above, without success. Had the Third Field Army fought single-handedly into southern China, it might have faced a destiny as precarious as Wang Zhen had experienced and Su Yu anticipated. At the very least, we can hardly imagine that the Third Field Army could have won any greater victories in the south than those of the Ji'nan and Huaihai Campaigns in the north.

The Liu–Deng army's long-distance drive into the Dabie Mountains happened to be a turning point in the civil war. It was a big deal in one sense and yet not in another. One may, along the latter line of argument, even raise a question about Mao's own ability as a military strategist. Mao was by no means the invincible military genius that many tend to believe. In this regard, Zhang Guotao might have made a telling point about Mao on the Long March: "Not always a practical politician or a successful military leader, Mao was oftentimes overwhelmed with fancy ideas and romantic dreams."[18]

The expedition to the Dabie Mountains was originally proposed by Mao and reluctantly accepted by Liu and Deng. As for the Huaihai Campaign, more strategic credit should be given to Su than to anybody else, Deng included. In the final analysis, the communists would probably have won with or without the Liu–Deng expedition to the Dabie Mountains, and the Huaihai Campaign would probably have succeeded with or without Deng as the Front Committee secretary. It should also be noted that, on both occasions, Deng assumed general leadership owing to Mao's political concerns rather than to Deng's own military expertise; and on neither occasion was Deng responsible for combat operations, which were mainly handled by Liu and the military staff.

To say that Deng's role was more political than military does not mean that he took no part whatsoever in combat activity. Where appropriate and necessary, as David Goodman correctly indicates, Deng was actively involved in military decisions on the battlefield. Deng was with Chen Yi at the front for two months during the Huaihai Campaign, for instance. At one point, they both led the troops on a speedy assault on the city of Yancheng, a communications hub between Xuzhou and Nanjing. They set off at dusk and covered thirty miles by dawn in order to seize Yancheng before the arrival of KMT reinforcements. They succeeded, and it proved a remarkable maneuver. Simply put, Deng did participate in real battles, and this was but one of them.

The communists' victory in the civil war was pretty much guaranteed after the Huaihai Campaign, coupled with the military triumphs in Manchuria and northern China. Deng was summoned to attend the Second Plenum in Xibopo, from March 5 to 13, 1949, to discuss the takeover of the whole country. During the plenum, he assumed a new position as first secretary of the East China Bureau, with Rao Shushi as second secretary and Chen Yi as third secretary. His seniority was further established among party and army veterans. This appointment also indicated Mao's determination to force across the Yangtze shortly to topple the KMT government, as the East China Bureau already included Nanjing and Shanghai under its territorial jurisdiction.

As usual, the military defeats caused factional disputes within the Nanjing regime. Chiang was forced to resign his presidency, and Li Zongren became the acting president. At Li's suggestion and with Mao's agreement, another round of peace negotiations took place in Beijing from April 1 to 22, 1949. The bottom line of Li's position, as the communist side well knew, was to maintain his own provincial troops and his home base of Guangdong and Guangxi intact. Yet Mao would permit nothing short of Li's complete surrender. The Beijing talks thus proved abortive. Had Mao not been so dizzy with his military success and so uncompromising in his political demands, the KMT, the CCP, and China might have had quite a different history.[19]

There is no need to speculate over Deng's frame of mind and

activity in the months following his meeting with Mao at Xibopo in March 1949. In his "Report to Chairman Mao Regarding Our Work after the River Crossing," dated May 10, 1949, Deng offered his own vivid description:

> The last three or four months were extremely hectic and busy. After the Second Plenum, we could not reach the front until March 18. Despite the rainy weather, muddy roads, and all kinds of difficulties, the troops reached the riverbank on schedule and speeded up preparations for the River-Crossing Campaign. By April 10, except for the Eighth and Tenth Army Corps of the eastern front, all the army corps were ready for the crossing and felt confident about it. Finally, on the night of April 20–21, all the troops succeeded in crossing the Yangtze as previously planned.[20]

On March 31 and April 8, Deng had already drafted two military papers, both regarding the details of the "River-Crossing Campaign"— one for Mao to approve and the other for his troops to implement. Obviously, Deng had totally ignored the peace talks still under way in Beijing, just as he had ignored those in Chongqing four years earlier.[21] Deng seemed once again to have read Mao Zedong's thoughts accurately—albeit the Machiavellian aspect of those thoughts rather than the Marxist aspect. Once again, as in 1945, Deng inspired the part of Mao's mind that favored military actions rather than peaceful negotiations to solve the national problem.

All of northern and central China had fallen to the communists' rule after the River-Crossing Campaign, but the overall domestic and foreign policies of these areas remained uncertain. Li Zongren still harbored a hope for further peace talks with the CCP; Joseph Stalin ordered the Russian Embassy to follow the KMT government to Canton, but U.S. Ambassador Leighton Stuart stayed on in Shanghai, ready to recognize the new communist regime. Deng was one of the few individuals with whom Mao could confer on general national and international matters. On July 19, 1949, Deng personally communicated Mao's directives to senior officials in the East China Bureau: "Our military policy is to occupy all China; our domestic policy is self-reliance and self-development; and our foreign policy is one-sided affiliation with the socialist camp and the Soviet Union."[22]

Liu and Deng entered Nanjing in the wake of their successful River-

Crossing Campaign in late April 1949. They both remained there with the Second Field Army headquarters while their troops were pursuing the KMT forces farther south. Sometime in September, Deng left for the north to join the preparations for a new communist state. He participated in the Political Consultative Conference in Beijing from September 21 to 30 and was elected a member of the central government. On October 1, Deng attended the grand ceremony in Tiananmen Square in which Mao formally proclaimed the founding of the People's Republic of China.

As the title of this chapter suggests, the battlefield, seemingly a dangerous place, actually served Deng as a "gold mine" in terms of military credentials and political capital, which he exploited to the limit. When comparing himself with his political archrival Lin Biao, in regard to their respective military achievements, Deng retorted sometime in the 1960s: "You had your Liaoshen, and I had my Huaihai. You fought from the northeast to the southeast, and I fought from the Central Plain to the southwest. So what?"[23]

Although Deng's victories during wartime proved his political acumen more than his military skills, they definitely had a great impact on his future career. In the course of twelve years, the troops under his command grew from the 129th Division of six thousand soldiers active in a few counties in 1937 to the Second Field Army of almost one million covering a dozen provinces in 1949. As Deng's military achievements mounted, his political influence in the party and army was firmly established, in the eyes of Mao and his senior colleagues as well as the rank and file. Thousands of his soldiers became officers and officials at all levels in the communist regime. They would respect Political Commissar Deng as their rightful superior, as they had in the past. The communist regime was established by military force, and therefore, one's military service would naturally turn into political capital. When the war ended, so did Liu Bocheng's career as a soldier, but not Deng Xiaoping's as a politician. Deng had been a politician even during wartime, and after the war came the real politics, so Deng's true career was just taking off![24]

Consistent military successes as well as his own steady promotions had created in Deng a firm belief in and direct reliance upon Mao. The close relations between them exhibited during wartime were to continue in the postliberation years. Such a relationship may be understood to consist of two aspects: personal opportunity and political strategy. Both aspects seemed fine to both individuals during the civil war—with their common objective of wresting state power from the ruling nationalists. Deng had proved capable both of implementing Mao's policy line and of maintaining his loyalty to Mao personally.

10

The Lord of the Southwest, 1949-1952

Shortly after the founding ceremony of the People's Republic of China (PRC) on October 1, 1949, Deng Xiaoping and Liu Bocheng returned to their military duties in the south—leaving others in Beijing to enjoy celebration banquets and receive central government posts. They took the train to Nanjing and then rode by jeep to the battlefront. Although the decision to create the Southwest Bureau had been made several months earlier, it was not until November 23, 1949, that the establishment of the bureau was formally announced in Changde, Hunan, with Deng as its first secretary.[1] The bureau's immediate mission was to take over southwest China. By the time Liu and Deng arrived at Changde, one of their army corps, led by Yang Yong, had already taken a deep detour through Guangxi and successfully seized Guiyang, the capital of Guizhou Province. A grand military expedition toward Sichuan, the center of the southwest region, from the south, north, and east was imminent under Liu and Deng's general leadership in late November 1949.

The central authority assigned Liu and Deng to direct the Second Field Army to conquer the entire southwest of China. They managed to fulfill this assignment quickly and smoothly—in retrospect, perhaps too quickly and smoothly. In the next month or two, their troops rolled swiftly over the vast southwestern highlands, picking up one metropolitan city after another: Guiyang on November 15, Chongqing on November 30, Kunming and Xikang on December 9, and Chengdu on December 27.

In the name of the Central Military Council, Mao Zedong had sent Liu and Deng a telegram on November 27, 1949, suggesting that they postpone taking Chongqing for a while in order to lure in and wipe out more Kuomintang (KMT) troops. Mao's suggestion, mild in itself, was not accepted by Deng. The communist troops were already on the move, and the nationalists inside Chongqing were rapidly destroying the city, Deng argued; there should be no change in the original offensive plan. Receiving Mao's approval on November 28, Deng immediately issued the order to attack on November 29, and Chongqing was taken the following day.[2]

After the losses of Nanjing in April and Canton in October, the KMT leaders had fallen into great confusion about what to do and where to go. Some had argued for withdrawal to the southwestern highlands, while others had preferred to retreat to the island of Taiwan. Reluctant to abandon the mainland, Chiang Kai-shek had for a while harbored the idea of making Chongqing his "temporary capital" and adopting the southwest as his final defensive line—as he had successfully done during the Sino-Japanese War. For that reason, Chiang had actually transferred his central government apparatus from Canton to Chongqing in late October 1949.

The seizure of Chongqing by the Liu–Deng army apparently left Chiang no choice but a final decision to move his government personnel and surviving troops to Taiwan. Ten days after Chongqing was lost, Chiang pronounced the establishment of his government in Taipei on December 10, 1949. Once the KMT government and army had withdrawn to Taiwan, it would prove far more difficult for the communists to engage them, militarily as well as politically.[3] In retrospect, therefore, Deng's quick capture of Chongqing was tactically correct but strategically questionable. This was one of the situations that give us the impression that Mao was not only rougher and tougher than Deng in terms of practical leadership but more farsighted and broadminded as well.

Escorted by the Second Field Army headquarters staff, Deng marched into Chongqing on December 8, 1949, and soon afterward assumed the post of mayor of the city. Thirty years ago, he had left as a shabby teenage student. Now he returned with pride and glory, power and prestige. He was seated in an army jeep with his bodyguards running ahead and shouting off the watching crowd. What an awesome sight! His entire family, including a brand-new baby girl, followed to settle in Chongqing. Deng was to remain there for the next three years as the most conspicuous and influential figure in the city.

By the end of 1949, the communists had occupied almost the whole country except Tibet, a marginal area in the southwestern highlands, and a few islands, notably Taiwan and Hainan, off the southeastern coast. Mao's foremost objective for the year 1950 was to "Liberate All China," as the New Year's celebration editorial of *People's Daily* indicated.[4] Lin Biao's Fourth Field Army was therefore assigned to take Hainan, Chen Yi's Third Field Army to take Taiwan, and Liu and Deng's Second Field Army to take Tibet.

Hainan Island was seized easily, as expected, by Lin Biao's Fourth Field Army in March 1950, with a loss of no more than a few thousand soldiers on the communist side. The Tibet issue could have been settled even more easily, except that it involved not merely military operations but also various political and international factors, which Mao preferred not to tackle too rapidly. As for "liberating" Taiwan, the last bastion of the nationalists, Mao entrusted Su Yu of the Third Field Army to conduct another massive campaign—this time, an "ocean-crossing campaign."

Taiwan was not like Hainan. It was much bigger, farther off the coastline, and far more heavily defended by the KMT army. Given the Third Field Army's disastrous defeat in the Golden Gate Islands earlier in October 1949, Su Yu did not want to rush into combat. Instead, he kept asking for more troops to participate in the "Taiwan campaign": first, two army corps; then, the whole Third Field Army; then, another field army—say, the Fourth Field Army; and finally, the navy and the air force as well. Eventually, the Korean War broke out, however, and Mao had to assemble forces for the "People's Volunteer Army" to be sent to North Korea; meanwhile, America's Seventh Fleet moved to block the Taiwan Strait. Both developments rendered Su Yu's "ocean-crossing campaign" practically impossible. Mao had to put the Taiwan issue on the back burner and finally give up on it, to Mao's deep regret in his later years and also to Deng's disappointment until the end of his days.[5]

Apart from the Tibet problem, there seemed little for Deng to do in the southwest region in the early 1950s other than routine work. The extermination of local bandits, the establishment of urban and rural governments, the land reform movement, the fiscal and financial administration, and the suppression of reactionary elements—all these were policies stipulated by Beijing and carried out throughout the country, including the southwest region. Besides, all these policies seemed quite reasonable and necessary to Deng, and he was more than willing to implement them.

For the first few years of the People's Republic, the Chinese mainland was divided into six administrative regions, each consisting of several provinces. With exceptions in the north and northwest, which had already been under communist control for several years, the regional governments or councils of military administration were formed on the basis of the four field armies, which possessed dominant influence in their respective occupied territories.

The Southwest Region consisted of five provinces—Sichuan; Guizhou; Yunnan; Xikang; and nominally, Tibet. In that time and place, the government, the party, and the army constituted the three major political institutions, and Liu Bocheng, Deng Xiaoping, and He Long were the three senior political figures. In the Southwest Council of Military Administration, Liu was appointed chairman, Deng second deputy chairman, and He third deputy chairman; in the Southwest Bureau of the Communist Party, Deng was made first secretary, and Liu and He, respectively, his second and third deputies; and in the Southwest Military District, He Long served as commander and Deng as political commissar.[6]

Liu and He were both military veterans, whereas Deng was a younger politician. It seemed to be a carefully calculated move on Mao's part to form the triumvirate of Liu, He, and Deng with seemingly equal shares of authority: each as head and the others as deputies in one of the three institutions. But in fact, it was only a way to give Liu and He some titular respect for their seniority. They were both figureheads, and the real power was held by Deng alone. The party leadership was, by all means, the most crucial matter, and there Deng had a firm hand. Liu and He were old soldiers, neither versed, nor much interested, in governmental politics. Liu, who had lost one eye in the civil war, was soon to leave the southwest for a new post in Nanjing. He Long, who could barely read and write, had to command the troops raised by others. Well, he did not really have to do even that—for General He showed himself to be the kind of person who would rather enjoy good meals and sports matches than command any troops!

Moreover, Deng held other official positions such as the mayoralty of Chongqing and the directorship of the Southwest Financial and

Economic Committee, both with practical responsibility and executive power. His energetic working style and firm-handed approach made his actions seem even more authoritative than his formal titles warranted. All in all, it seemed no exaggeration to call him the "Lord of the Southwest"—as the Red Guards did during the Cultural Revolution—with supreme leadership over the entire region.

During his official tenure in the southwest from 1950 to 1952, Deng did not make new policies on his own initiative, nor did he really need to do so. What distinguished Deng from other regional leaders inside or outside the southwest was the practical way in which he implemented general policies communicated from Beijing according to the particular conditions within his territorial jurisdiction—something he had done vigorously and effectively, and his organizational skills and administrative perspectives had proved very much in evidence.

Among Deng's immediate tasks were to eliminate remnants of KMT troops and local armed bandits and to take over governmental control at all levels and in all places in the vast Southwest Region. Assisted by one army corps transferred from the north, the Second Field Army fought numerous small battles in late 1949 and early 1950 in the southwestern highlands and mountains and successfully mopped up about five hundred thousand leftover KMT troops and local bandits. At the same time, some two hundred thousand soldiers of the Liu–Deng army were dispatched to thousands of cities and towns to establish governmental administration. Consequently, communist control was rapidly and firmly established throughout southwest China.[7]

For the country and for the southwest as well, 1950–52 was a period of postwar restoration and reconstruction. For that purpose, one movement after another was instituted under various names, such as agrarian or land reform, suppression of counter-revolutionaries, fiscal and financial adjustment, rectification of party styles, support of Korea against American imperialism, and so on. Mao in Beijing initiated these movements, and Deng in Chongqing implemented them. For the newly founded communist regime, all these were only commonsense tasks, which Deng would take for granted as being his appropriate responsibilities.

In March 1950, Deng, in his position as director of the Financial and Economic Committee of the Southwest, chaired a conference on financial and economic work in the region. In a highly professional manner and using highly professional language, he called for governmental

regulation of monetary circulation, for management of market conditions to control price inflation, and for restoration of agricultural production.

Deng was also concerned with news media and publications (as he
said on one occasion, "Writing is an important method of leadership,
and our leading comrades should snatch up the pen") and also with
proper policies on intellectuals and businesspeople (as he said on another occasion, "The united front is a temporary tactic, but it also has
the nature of a fundamental strategy—that is, to unite with as many
people as possible").[8] Reading between the lines, one finds Deng to
have been a resourceful communist politician, which could hardly have
been said of his military colleagues, either Liu Bocheng or He Long.

On June 6, 1950, in his report to a conference of Chongqing party
representatives, Deng gave a speech about rectification of party ideology and work attitudes. "It is very dangerous for some of our comrades
to think that the revolution is now completed and we can just take a
comfortable nap and be conceited and enjoy our personal life, and that
there are no more serious efforts to be made anymore." Deng went on,
lecturing the audience as well as admonishing himself: "As communists, we must regard our party's work, not just personal material
enjoyment, as the first priority of our life. It must be made crystal clear
that our own material conditions cannot surpass the level of the general
society's."[9]

When the Korean War broke out between China and the United
States in October 1950, the Second Field Army contributed one army
corps of one hundred thousand troops to participate in that interna-
tional conflict. The troops were commanded by Yang Yong, one of
Deng's most favored generals. After a truce was reached and Marshal
Peng Dehuai returned to China in 1953, Yang eventually took Peng's
place as the general commander of all the Chinese troops and stayed in
North Korea until their final withdrawal in 1958.

Deng himself took full charge of agrarian reform in the countryside.
By the spring of 1951, when this massive movement was completed in
the Southwest Region, turning approximately one hundred million
landless peasants into landowners, Deng made a summary report to the
Party Center in Beijing. This report, dated May 9, 1951, once again
won from Mao an intimate-sounding accolade: "Comrade Xiaoping
has just given us another excellent report!"

Tibet was one of the few issues, perhaps the only key issue, unique to the southwest that required Deng's particular attention. The problem was special enough in itself, and his boss's personal concern made it even more so. While still on a trip to Moscow in January 1950, Mao telegraphed Deng in person: "Since Britain, India, and Nepal have all recognized us, the Tibet problem now becomes much easier to solve." A few days later, Mao further instructed Deng: "In regard to the Tibet problem, the Southwest Bureau should take the major responsibility."[10]

According to instructions from Mao with which Deng complied, or according to suggestions from Deng that Mao accepted, the problem of Tibet should be solved by "peaceful persuasion plus military coercion." This was nothing new for either Mao or Deng. They had used such tactics with the KMT before. While specific army units were designated as an expeditionary force to the Tibetan highlands, a Tibet Working Committee was carefully formed. The committee was, needless to say, headed by a Han communist cadre, but it also carefully included a noncommunist Tibetan, Tian Bao, or Heavenly Treasure. Another communist cadre, doffing his army uniform and donning a long Tibetan gown, embarked on a mission as liaison between the communists and the Tibetan authorities. The man assumed a religious identity as a Buddhist layman and renamed himself Master Pure Mind.[11]

Deng personally received the Tibet Working Committee and the expeditionary troops before they left Sichuan for Tibet and carefully instructed them: "It is a military task to liberate Tibet, and for that, we need a certain amount of military force. Nevertheless, the primary problem is one of politics, not military force. Historically, the Tibet problem could not be solved despite numerous military expeditions. Some problems were solved, but mainly through political measures."[12]

After several rounds of contacts and negotiations between Beijing and Lhasa, the ice began melting, although it had not yet totally thawed; one more blow seemed needed. Therefore, from October 6 to 24, 1950, Deng's army conducted the Changtu Campaign and annihilated fifty-seven hundred Tibetan troops, to strengthen Beijing's negotiating position with Lhasa. Of the Dalai Lama's nine thousand troops, some six thousand had thus far been lost. The communists were, at the same time, pushing for a peaceful solution. They insisted on deploying their troops in Tibet but promised not to interfere with its social and political systems for the next twenty-five years.

The military victory proved persuasive enough: on May 23, 1951, a peaceful agreement was signed in Beijing. Deng sighed with relief in Chongqing. This agreement affirmed Beijing's titular authority over Tibet as part of China's sovereign territory while allowing the Tibetan government to maintain its substantial local rule intact. As we all know now, and as Mao and Deng had perhaps expected in the first place, the titular would turn into the substantial in just a few years.[13]

As the agrarian reform and suppression of counter-revolutionary movements surged ahead in 1950, they were almost beyond the personal control of any individual, even Deng. Deng's landlord family and his youngest brother, who had previously served as a department chief in the KMT county government, became the targets of local peasants in his hometown in Guang'an County. There arose a delicate contradiction between the party's policies and Deng's personal concerns.

Deng called his youngest brother, Deng Shuping, from Guang'an to Chongqing for a conference and instructed him to return home quickly and bring back to Chongqing several family members and relatives, just on the eve of the land reform campaign in early 1950. This group—which included Deng's elder sister, younger brother, and a few in-laws—stayed with Deng in the headquarters of the Southwest Council of Military Administration, thereby avoiding the violent action of local peasants against them as landlords. When five militiamen came from Guang'an to Chongqing to arrest Deng Shuping, they were told that Deng Xiaoping did not know his whereabouts.

The local peasants in Deng's home village recalled the episode as follows (of course, this recollection was expressed at the time when Deng was out of favor politically in the late 1960s): "If Deng Shuping had not fled in time, he would have been the first to be executed in Xiexing township. Even if the government didn't want to shoot him, the poor peasants would have beaten him to death for sure."[14]

By and large, nevertheless, 1950 and 1951 were for Deng two years of peaceful life—something he had rarely found before and would rarely find afterward. In the southwest, he also had the undiluted satisfaction of power, authority, and responsibility. His work duties were for the most part normal and understandable and proceeded smoothly to achieve the desired results. He and his family had comfortable, if not lavish, living conditions. They resided in the "Great Hall of the People," a magnificent building that had once been the KMT city hall, now renovated and renamed. His wife bore a baby girl in 1950 and a baby boy in 1952, who were cared for by Deng's stepmother and a government-assigned helper. Madame Deng worked as the principal of an elementary school for children of party and army cadres.[15] Everything, including Deng's busy official duties and noisy family life, seemed delightful. Unlike the earlier military struggle and unlike the subsequent political struggle, these years were for Deng a period of work. He had struggled all his life but had seldom simply worked! Although, ideally speaking, it would seem that Deng would probably have preferred work to struggle, the opposite might actually have been even more true.[16]

In the southwest, besides his old subordinates in the Second Field Army, Deng became acquainted with a number of party and government cadres who had recently been assigned to the region, such as Li Jingquan and Hu Yaobang, with whom a personal, if not factional, relationship was established for the coming years. The Southwest Region and the Second Field Army constituted Deng's political power base, although he did not need such local backup as much as some others did. Relying on his own political expertise more than anything else, Deng would look forward toward the future rather than back toward the past and keep his eyes on the central rather than the local leadership![17]

Deng seemed to be the only leader in the southwest who could maintain direct telephone and telegraph communications with Mao in Beijing. Mao called him to the capital on several occasions. Because of his personal communication and compliance with Mao and the Party Center, Deng could exert more authoritative influence in his own domain. In fact, it was a two-way street: because of his communication and compliance with Beijing regarding southwestern affairs, Deng could win more respect from Mao and the Party Center. Thus, we may say that centralism supplemented localism, and localism also complemented centralism. If such a dualism still seemed too abstract, its concrete realization would come soon, in the form of Deng's being summoned by Mao to serve in Beijing in the summer of 1952.

11

The Shoulders of Victims Form Rungs on the Ladder of Official Success, 1952-1956

In Chongqing, on July 1, 1952, Deng attended the ribbon-cutting in-auguration ceremony for the Chengdu–Chongqing Railway, and later, on August 1, Deng was seen with Zhu De and He Long at the Beijing stadium, watching an army sports match. Thus, it can be established that he was transferred from the southwest to the central government sometime in July 1952. He had visited Beijing several times pre-viously, but this time, he would work there permanently. His whole family—including wife, stepmother, three daughters, and two sons—followed. A family residence was arranged adjacent to, but not yet within, the Party Center compound of Zhongnanhai.

Roughly at the same time, four other regional party leaders were also summoned to work in Beijing, thus prompting a popular saying, "Five horses have run into the capital, one ahead of the others." Here, the "one ahead" meant Gao Gang, who had the highest position as a member of the party Politburo and vice president of the state. Having come from the Northeast Region to Beijing, Gao became the director of the State Planning Commission. The "others" meant Rao Shushi, who came from the Eastern Region to become the director of the Organizational Department of the Chinese Communist Party (CCP) Central Committee; Deng Xiaoping, who came from the Southwest

Region to become a deputy premier of the State Administrative Council; Deng Zihui, who came from the Central South Region to become the director of the Agricultural Office of the State Administrative Council; and finally, Xi Zhongxun, who came from the Northwest Region to become the chief secretary of the State Administrative Council.

It is commonly believed that Mao Zedong made these assignments to reduce "localist tendencies" and strengthen the central authority. Some observers even go so far as to suggest that these transfers were all part of Mao's political scheme, to substitute real regional power for titular central leadership, as the founding emperors of the Song and Ming dynasties had done once their victorious rebellion was over.[1] Valid as this argument may be, its converse is equally so: these "five horses" had been fighting for years for the establishment of the new regime and should therefore have been rewarded with central positions for their military services. Moreover, one might say that Mao, who had for years mainly been in charge of military affairs, would like to transfer his army leaders to Beijing in order to strengthen his control of the central party and state apparatus.

Whatever the precise rationale for these changes might have been, it did not look unusual or problematic for these communist leaders to leave their regional posts for new assignments in the capital. As for their respective future performance under the new circumstances, that was another question. A careful study of Deng's words and deeds in the years 1949–52 leads to the impression that he, in particular, did not seem to have limited his horizons to local affairs and always looked forward to moving up to Beijing.

Upon his arrival in the capital, Deng had no difficulty in discerning the configuration of the central leadership in the early years of the communist regime. Military work was still focusing on the Korean War, where Peng Dehuai was in full charge. Back home, Zhu De was the titular army commander in chief, as always. But with the civil war concluded and the new regime established, military affairs gave way to governmental administration. Liu Shaoqi was in charge of routine duties in the CCP Central Committee; Zhou Enlai handled governmental and foreign affairs as both premier and foreign minister; and Chen Yun shouldered financial and economic responsibilities as director of the Central Financial and Economic Group. Mao's general authority remained as strong as ever, but in practical terms, he grew less interested in any of those routine matters. Mao did not yet seem accustomed to the shift from "military destruction" to "economic construction" that governmental rule necessarily entailed.

Deng had assumed a number of official titles: besides being one of five deputy premiers of the State Council, he was simultaneously a member of the Central People's Government, the Central Military Council, the Central Committee of the Communist Party, the National Political Consultative Conference, the State Planning Commission, and the Association of Sino-Soviet Friendship. In November 1952, he was again appointed vice chairman of the Southwest Administrative Council, despite his physical absence from the Southwest Region.

Although all these official positions afforded Deng plenty of opportunities to attend conferences and make public appearances, none of them seemed to involve any substantial executive responsibilities, which is what he excelled in and aspired to. Deng was forty-eight years old, younger and more competent than most of his colleagues; he had accumulated high seniority through his wartime service and was patiently looking for real political power and waiting for opportunity to knock.

Deng's activities in his early months in Beijing, as can be seen from *People's Daily* news reports, included watching sports events, observing national holiday celebrations, receiving minority-race tourists, attending conferences on women and youth, reporting on election laws, speaking about supervisory regulations, and so on and so forth. In Deng's eyes as well as in reality, all these activities involved ritual formality more than political substance.[2]

Simply put, Deng had not yet found his real niche in the central leadership. His first year in Beijing, roughly from August 1952 to May 1953, was like a training or testing period rather than a period of regular employment. As far as Mao was concerned, in watching for a future trustworthy lieutenant, Deng was simply one of a few being considered and not yet the sole one selected. But that seemed just fine to Deng. Don't worry and don't hurry! Deng's opportunity would soon come, in the form of the Gao–Rao incident during 1953–55.

The year 1953 marked the Korean War armistice as well as the formal completion of postwar restoration. The transitional phase seemed over, and Chairman Mao began seeking a new orientation for the party and state. There arose between Mao and Liu a theoretical divergence over new democracy and socialism, as well as a practical difference over agrarian collectivization. Mao was inclined to make changes both in policy and in personnel, which would potentially contribute to the occurrence of the Gao–Rao incident.

In June 1953, a national conference on finance and the economy was convened in Beijing under the supervision of the State Council. Zhou Enlai, in his role as premier of the State Council, chaired the conference, and Chen Yun, head of the Central Financial and Economic Group, was the main speaker. Gao Gang, as director of the State Planning Commission, and Deng Xiaoping, as a deputy premier, also attended the conference, while the lower levels were represented by a few dozen senior officials in the financial and economic fields.

In examining the country's economic and financial status, a subject apparently brought up at the conference was the problem of the deficit. During the first half of 1953 alone, expenses reportedly exceeded revenue by three billion yuan on the national level, mainly because of the rapid increase in investment in basic infrastructure, compounded by the slow growth in revenue. Bo Yibo, as the minister of finance, should therefore be held directly responsible.[3]

How could revenue have shrunk? The conference discovered that it was because the Ministry of Finance had applied a "new policy" that levied proportionally less taxes on private businesses and commerce than on state enterprises. This turned into a political problem: Bo was blamed for implementing a "probourgeois rightist line." It was not merely a matter of taxes and revenue; all the banking, commercial, financial, fiscal, and economic policies also seemed wrong. Thus, Bo became the target of attack. Zhou ordered Bo to submit a formal self-criticism, which he did accordingly. But this failed to end the matter, and the conference grew even hotter and more divided.

Deng was quick to realize that the real debate was not just over the matter of finance and the economy per se, nor just over Bo as an individual. At the same time, a Politburo conference was under way in Zhongnanhai, at which Mao became furious with what he termed a "general rightist tendency" in the agricultural cooperative movement. Mao's argument went further—to address the issue of whether the country as a whole ought to maintain its new democratic status or carry out the socialist reform straightaway. Gao Gang, Zhou Enlai, and Chen Yun, all Politburo members who were also participants at that Politburo conference, were well aware that Mao's real target was none other than Liu Shaoqi.[4]

Coincidentally or not, Bo Yibo, who had for many years worked under Liu Shaoqi's leadership in the CCP Northern Bureau during the war, was regarded as Liu's follower, and his lenient taxation policy toward private businesses was thus regarded as part of Liu's rightist line. Mao did not want to name Liu openly yet, so Bo was singled out instead. At Mao's request, Zhou had to report to him personally each evening after the daily session of the financial and economic conference had concluded.

Among the most outspoken individuals at the financial and economic conference were Tan Zhenlin, Liao Luyan, and a few others whose ranks were virtually equal to Bo's. While the senior leaders in general seemed less emotional, Gao appeared the most active and outspoken, followed by Zhou, Chen, and Deng. Deng would let others jump on Bo while he himself remained restrained, despite his hidden determination. "Bo Yibo's mistakes are plentiful indeed," Deng would intone pedantically. "They should be measured by the ton, not by the pound." This proved to have been the smartest stance. The most notable change in personnel assignments at the conference was that Deng replaced Bo as minister of finance and subsequently assumed the deputy directorship of the Central Financial and Economic Group.[5]

This conference on finance and the economy in the summer of 1953 marked Deng's first successful performance in central power politics. Its end result turned out to be a clear and clean victory for him. He did the least but got the most; it was like killing without getting bloody. Soon afterward, there would come another opportunity for Deng to show the same political skill—at the national conference on party organizational work, held in Beijing from September to October of the same year.

Before Rao Shushi's arrival in Beijing, An Ziwen, another subordinate of Liu Shaoqi with a Northern Bureau background, had been in charge of the Organizational Department of the CCP Central Committee. After Rao came to take over the directorship, An lost his primary position but remained influential as deputy director of that department. As was often the case in CCP history and politics, friction would quickly arise between the newcomer and the old-timer.

Because the department was responsible for organizational preparation for the party's forthcoming Eighth National Congress, a draft list of candidates for the Central Committee and the Politburo had been prepared under An's auspices; the draft seemed to have included more former "underground urban cadres" than "liberation area cadres." Rao discovered the draft and reported it to Mao. An was chided. At the national conference on organizational work in the autumn of 1953, An and a few others became targets of Rao's further attack for their "factionalist maneuvers," ostensibly with Mao's approval. Rao was directly backed by Gao, who seemed more interested in accusing An as a means of getting at Liu.

In the wake of the organizational conference, November and December turned into a period of heated factional activities. Rao began making a new list of candidates for leadership positions for the Eighth National Congress, to replace An's draft list. In the interests of promoting the list among other party leaders, Gao ran around inside and outside Beijing. The cooperation went so far as to become an attempt to overhaul the party and government structure. Presumably, it was a safe and solid chain: behind Rao was Gao, and behind Gao was Mao.

A presumption was but a presumption! The Rao–Gao–Mao chain proved neither as solid nor as safe as had been presumed. Once a whole hornets' nest of commotion and confusion had been stirred up in the central and regional leadership, Rao as a department director had no authority to control the situation. An easy target, Rao instead faced a "boomerang effect," in which he became the object of various complaints himself. People like Chen Yi and Tan Zhenlin, who had been at odds with Rao in the Eastern Bureau for years, turned their old grudges into new spite. Because he had no direct link with Mao, Rao could only appeal to Gao for help.

Gao and Deng were two individuals who enjoyed sufficient intimacy with Mao to be able to discuss intraparty personnel matters with him easily. It must have been sometime in early December 1953 that they went to see Mao in person—separately, of course. Gao firmly backed Rao and earnestly requested Mao's support on Rao's behalf. Deng made a suggestion to Mao that sounded less affirmative and yet proved more effective: although Liu might not be above reproach, it seemed inadvisable to alter the entire leadership just for the sake of one or two individuals.[6]

An enlarged Politburo conference was convened on December 24, 1953. Mao decided to give Rao up for criticism. As for Gao, Mao still had an ambiguous attitude toward him, neither extremely positive nor extremely negative. "There are two headquarters in Beijing: mine is open, and the other of some folks is hidden," Mao announced at the conference. But what did this really mean? Did this refer to Liu or Gao? Nobody knew for sure—perhaps not even Mao himself at the time. Mao also allegedly murmured something like, "Dongjiaomin Lane is always so crowded with guests and friends, but nobody cared to visit Yinian Hall."[7] Dongjiaomin Lane was the location of Gao's residence, and Yinian Hall was where Mao lived. Mao sounded unhappy with Gao's social or factional activities. But did this signal a harsh attack or just a mild scold? Again, nobody knew for sure—perhaps not even Mao himself at that moment.

The next event that can be confirmed was that Mao left for a southern tour in early January 1954 and stayed away from Beijing for more than two months, obviously to avoid involving or embarrassing himself with what he would later call an "eighth-degree earthquake." While on tour in Hangzhou, he sent a few words to Liu, generously calling for the party's solidarity, but politely rejecting Gao's appeal for a personal meeting with him. By leaving Beijing, what Mao had really left were Gao and Rao to be slaughtered by Liu!

While Mao remained down south celebrating the Chinese New Year, Liu presided over the Fourth Plenum of the Seventh CCP Central Committee in Beijing from February 6 to 10, 1954. Some forty people—notably, Liu, Zhou, and Deng—rose to speak against Gao and Rao. For Gao, the situation turned into a vicious circle: the increasing pressure caused him to attempt suicide, and his suicide attempt further increased the pressure. The plenum ended up passing a resolution ironically entitled "Strengthen the Party's Solidarity!" In reality, the spectacle became a relentless power struggle!

There is little doubt that Deng played an extraordinary role during the Fourth Plenum. His formal speech calling on the party to guard against conceit and complacency does not tell the full story,[8] but just consider the ensuing personnel shuffle: Deng was appointed to head the Rao investigatory group at the plenum, and Zhou to head the Gao investigatory group. On March 1, soon after Mao's return to Beijing, Deng, together with Chen Yi and Tan Zhenlin, made a special report to Mao in person.[9] On April 27, Deng replaced Rao as director of the Organizational Department and, shortly afterward, assumed the even more crucial position of chief secretary of the CCP Central Committee.

This is what we outside observers know about Deng's involvement in the Gao–Rao incident now. What happened then behind the scenes might have been even more impressive! In a certain sense, Deng might even be regarded as the key figure. In all likelihood, it was through Deng that Liu and Zhou made sure of Mao's intention not to bother with the purge of Gao and Rao in the first place, and it was also through Deng that Mao accepted the final accusation against Gao and Rao as an antiparty alliance.

The Gao–Rao incident was a complicated matter. Few of the relevant documents—which were actually insignificant compared with the unrecorded private meetings and secret dealings—have been released even now. At the time of Deng's death, they still remained locked in the party archives. It is the only major political purge of Mao's era that has not yet been formally reviewed, obviously because of Deng's personal involvement. It is also the only major political incident that was never given a clear identification as to its line, either leftist or rightist. But in one sense, this incident was quite simple. It involved outright factional clashes and power struggles: Mao wanted to use Gao to check Liu at first and gave up Gao to bargain with Liu at last, while Deng smartly followed each step that Mao took.[10] The incident led Liu and Mao to reach a tacit compromise: Mao allowed Liu to maintain his position intact, while Liu learned to be more obedient to Mao, both personally and policywise; while Deng rose, Gao fell as the tragic scapegoat.

The Gao–Rao incident brought Deng many benefits at the time, but it also caused him a slight headache later on. Occasionally, he had to offer an explanation of this event and his role in it. Recalling the incident in 1980, he had this to say:

> Gao Gang wanted to win me over to pull down Liu Shaoqi. He told me Liu was politically immature. I replied that Liu's position within the party was a result of historical evolution. All in all, Liu seemed all right, and it would be inappropriate to alter his position. Gao also spoke to Chen Yun, saying that more vice chairmen should be named, and that Chen would be one and he himself another. By then, Comrade Chen Yun and I realized the seriousness of the situation. Therefore, we made direct reports to Comrade Mao, calling the matter to his attention.[11]

Here, we find Deng trying to portray Chen as having been in full accord with him regarding the Gao–Rao incident. A few simple questions arise, however: Why did Chen himself never second Deng's remarks in 1980? Why did Chen's official responsibilities remain unchanged while Deng was rapidly promoted in 1954? Why did Chen, unlike Deng, play no official role in the investigation? Logically and factually, there must have been some areas of disagreement between them!

In point of fact, Chen did join in the criticism of Bo at the financial and economic conference, but he did so from a practical economic perspective. Once the nature of the criticism shifted from a review of Bo's job performance to a power clash, Chen stepped back. Chen did express to Mao his concern about Gao and Rao's activities in late 1953, but he did so only to protect the incumbent leadership. Deng, on the other hand, was less interested in practical policies than in power assignments, and he wanted to change the status quo while pretending to maintain it. The leadership had finally changed, hadn't it? Gao was out, Liu was down, and Deng alone was up!

The Gao–Rao incident continued to offer Deng a superhighway to ride, or a straight ladder to climb, in his bid for supreme power. In late March 1955, a special national conference of party representatives was convened in Beijing. As the keynote speaker, Deng made a report on the Gao–Rao issue, relentlessly condemning the two as having formed a conspiratorial alliance to usurp party and government leadership. Both were stripped of their party membership. Gao had already committed suicide in prison in May 1954, and Rao would spend the rest of his life in custody.[12]

In the formal resolution on the Gao–Rao affair, drafted under Deng's direction, one finds Gao accused of such transgressions as having established an "independent kingdom" in the northeast, having allowed his subordinates to shout "Long live Chairman Gao," and having betrayed party and state secrets to Joseph Stalin and being rewarded with a fine automobile; Rao was accused of having been a communist traitor and nationalist agent, having attempted to pull down Premier Zhou, and so forth. This prompts another simple question: Why were they not purged at the time? Although these accusations actually represented the official communist propaganda *after* the incident, they have unfortunately become the consensus among many Western Sinologists. In some of their latest works, one can still find opinions that echo the official line, such as that Gao and Rao colluded to defy Mao's authority and that Deng firmly opposed them on Mao's behalf. Their authors seem defenseless in the face of official communist propaganda, and it appears that to the ignorant any small tidbits of information may sound credible.[13]

In the wake of the national conference was held the Party Center's Fifth Plenum, at which Deng was elected or selected to the Politburo as a full member. Afterward, Deng gave up his stepping-stone posts (that is, his positions as minister of finance and director of the Organizational Department) and focused instead on general executive duties in his powerful position as the chief secretary of the CCP Central Committee and, later on, as its general secretary. It should be noted, by the way, that Lin Biao was also promoted to the Politburo around that time. The decision was also Mao's alone, with the obvious purpose of checking the potent influence of Peng Dehuai in the Liberation Army—since the Korean War was over.

Besides producing a power realignment among the party's central leadership, the Gao–Rao incident also had a definite impact upon the state's practical work. It actually established the broad context for later radical policies. The communist leadership in general and Liu in particular would be more inclined to bow to Mao's autocratic rule and utopian line; the years 1954–56 would witness one powerful upsurge after another of "socialist revolution," especially the collectivization campaign in the vast countryside.

In February 1956, the Communist Party of the Soviet Union (CPSU) was scheduled to hold its Twentieth Congress in Moscow. That congress was to offer Deng another chance to show off his political ability. The CCP was invited to send a delegation to the congress as guests, which was the standard practice at the time. It was expected to be a routine event, just as Zhou and Liu had attended similar occasions in Moscow before. This time, Zhu De, whose seniority would represent a symbol of respect to the host party, was appointed to head the five-man CCP delegation, and Deng was made deputy head.

Deng had neither much knowledge of foreign affairs nor much experience in that area. Despite his five-year sojourn in France and his year in Russia, he did not speak French, much less Russian. He had been to North Korea in late November 1953 and met with Kim Il Sung in Pyongyang for the first time. His role was simply that of minister of finance offering North Korea financial aid after the war. But this mission to the Soviet Union would assume a more political nature.

Relations between China and the Soviet Union were in a state of flux after Stalin's death in 1953. Among others factors, Mao's attitude toward the new Soviet leader, Nikita Khrushchev, played a particularly important role. Mao had been to Moscow once, in 1950. It was not an entirely pleasant trip. He was never fond of Russia and the Russians. Nevertheless, Mao respected Stalin's seniority and authority in the communist world, and he respected Russia as a source of practical aid to China. In Moscow in 1950, he managed to show just enough stubbornness to make Stalin feel uneasy but not enough to make him flare up.[14]

Mao had little respect for Khrushchev in terms of either seniority or personality. But at least for the time being, the CPSU remained the leader of the international communist movement, and the Soviet Union's economic and military aid kept flowing to China. Exchanges of official visits by senior party and government leaders continued, including Zhou's to Moscow in 1953 and Khrushchev's to Beijing in 1954. The year 1956 proved by any standards to be a transitional period in an ambiguous relationship.

Although no expert in foreign affairs, Deng was an expert in domestic politics. To him at the time, domestic politics meant Mao's state of mind. Deng met with Mao before his departure from Beijing for Moscow to see whether the chairman had specific instructions. To the whole party, the Soviet Union was still the leader of the socialist camp and China's "elder brother," as it was called at the time. Zhu De, who had been touring abroad for the past few months, took this routine appointment to visit Moscow for granted and did not bother either to meet or to talk with Mao.

At the CPSU's Twentieth Congress, held from February 15 to 28, 1956, the CCP delegation was among the dozens of other communist delegations invited as guests and observers. Everything went well until the final days. In a closed session on the evening of February 26, Khrushchev delivered an emotional speech in which he fiercely denounced Stalin. The speech was filled with striking quotations. It reported that hundreds of thousands of good comrades had been brutally murdered by Stalin, and Khrushchev's conclusion went so far as to condemn Stalin as a cruel dictator.[15]

No foreign delegates were allowed to attend the closed session, and they did not get a transcript of Khrushchev's secret speech until the next morning. They were all flabbergasted but dutifully supported the speech anyway. Zhu was no exception. It would have been almost unimaginable for this dogged, loyal veteran soldier to have behaved otherwise. The Russian party was the leader and elder brother, and it couldn't be wrong. Besides, the Chinese delegates were only invited guests. Khrushchev had been talking about Stalin and the Soviet

Union's internal affairs. Anyhow, everybody else clapped their hands; why and how could the Chinese not do so as well?

Deng was also shocked but soon calmed down. He calculated that this was a watershed event and that he needed to consult his boss at home before expressing any opinion pro or con. He regarded himself as being responsible less to Khrushchev or Zhu than to Mao. Deng called Mao at home. The transcript of Khrushchev's speech was immediately cabled to Beijing. The Chinese delegation was consequently instructed to give neither a positive nor a negative response in Moscow. Zhu's clumsiness and Deng's shrewdness formed a sharp contrast during this dramatic episode.[16]

As it turned out, Mao did have deep reservations regarding the Stalin issue, which caused the first confrontation between the CCP and the CPSU. But from Deng's own perspective, at least, what really mattered was not the Stalin issue per se but the manner in which Deng had handled it. Once again, Deng had shown himself to be capable of dealing with emergencies while remaining faithful personally to Mao. Once again, Deng won Mao's accolades and more confidence—just what he wanted most.

Deng, rather than Zhu, gave a full report to the Politburo upon his return home. Mao chaired the conference and expressed his opinions, which were at variance with Khrushchev's. Mao complained that since Stalin had been regarded as the leader not only of the Soviet Union but of the communist world, Khrushchev should have informed other fraternal parties in advance of his speech. Although Mao had not highly respected Stalin before, neither would he totally deprecate Stalin now, both in contrast to Khrushchev. Mao preferred a divided evaluation of Stalin, something like six- or seven-tenths good and four- or three-tenths bad. If nothing else, that was at least a way to demonstrate his own individuality vis-à-vis Khrushchev.

Deng, together with Mao and a "theoretical squad," drafted two articles on the Stalin issue. They were published as *People's Daily* editorials in April and December 1956 to elaborate China's independent position. As China still had to depend upon the Soviet Union for many things, it was not yet time for Mao and his comrades to openly defy the CPSU and Khrushchev. The two articles therefore argued, subtly but clearly, over the issue of "historical experiences of the proletarian dictatorship," which in fact signaled the first independent move on the part of the CCP and Mao.[17]

Deng's extraordinary performances in the Gao–Rao incident and, to a lesser degree, at the CPSU's Twentieth Congress as well as his flawless image—in terms of both political capability and personal loyalty—so much impressed Mao that they would enable Deng to enter the supreme echelon of the CCP at its Eighth Congress in September 1956. That was what Deng had wanted, and that was exactly what he would receive.

Preparations for the Eighth Congress had started as early as 1952. After the Fifth Plenum in April 1955, which marked the formal conclusion of the Gao–Rao incident, the issue of the Eighth Congress became the top priority on the Party Center's agenda. It was the first national congress after the founding of the new regime. Its objectives were twofold: to lay out general programs for the party and the state, and to set up personnel assignments for the central leadership.

There should be no doubt that Deng played one of the most outstanding roles in the preparatory process. In October 1955, at the Sixth Plenum, Deng, as the spokesman of the Politburo, made the keynote speech regarding the Eighth Congress. Then, in late August to early September 1956, while Mao presided over the Seventh Plenum, Deng was entrusted with the responsibility for drafting and revising the key documents and selecting the participants for the forthcoming national congress.

On September 8, at a special conference held to decide on the makeup of the Eighth Congress's Central Committee, Mao stated, "As for the new Central Committee of the Eighth Congress, it will, as Comrade Xiaoping has just mentioned, consist of 150 to 170 members, in contrast to the 77 members of the Seventh Congress. That means a little more than double the previous membership, which I also think is appropriate."[18] Clearly, it was Deng who had worked out the new central leadership. Mao had the final say, of course, but the Eighth Congress's participant list was basically at Deng's discretion, not Liu's or Zhou's. Needless to say, that represented the most important function.

The Eighth Congress was convened in Beijing from September 15 to 27, 1956. Liu Shaoqi made the general or political report on behalf of the Party Center. Because the democratic revolution had purportedly been completed and the capitalist class annihilated, Liu logically asserted that China had become a socialist country in which the main conflict would no longer be between the exploiting and exploited classes but between backward productive forces and people's demands for better living conditions. In other words, economic reconstruction, not political revolution, would be regarded as the party's and the state's main task from now on.[19]

Deng's speech on the party constitution was in accordance with Liu's general assessment of the current situation and the party's objective. It particularly stressed party discipline and style—notably, the principle of democratic centralism in party organization. Just like Liu's speech, Deng's speech had originally been drafted by staff assistants, then revised by Deng himself, and finally approved by Mao. It was a collective product; nevertheless, there remained something genuine from Deng's personal inputs.

There was what might be termed a "double irony" in Deng's passage on the "personality cult" question. On the one hand, he called for overcoming the cult of personality within the Communist Party, but on the other hand, he cited Chairman Mao as the impeccable example of doing so! Moreover, Deng himself had ascended to higher power through Mao's sole authority, and yet he pretended to be opposed to autocracy![20]

There might have been some elements representing Deng's true, subtle feelings. In the original draft of the Deng speech, there were a couple of references to the guideline of "Mao Zedong thought." In the final version, that phrase was deleted. It was the blunt Marshal Peng who first suggested such a deletion; Liu immediately agreed; and Deng seemed more than willing to accept their opinions. This was just a small episode at the time, but it reflected a rift from which would flow the most serious consequences in the years to come.[21]

In the final vote for the new party Central Committee, Deng ranked fourth—behind Mao, Liu Shaoqi, and the elderly Lin Boqu, but surprisingly ahead of Zhu De and Zhou Enlai. He was subsequently elected a member of the Politburo Standing Committee. As Mao's special reward to Deng, the Secretariat was established as the central executive institution, and Deng was appointed as the general secretary.

For Deng, the Eighth Party Congress represented the completion of a sequence of ascending steps from a regional cadre to one of the supreme leaders. The Politburo Standing Committee represented the apex; there, Deng was formally ranked sixth, still junior to Mao, Liu, Zhou, Zhu, and Chen. However, Deng's actual power was second only to Mao's and equal to, if not greater than, that of Liu and Zhou, both of whom Mao had recently criticized, while neither Chen nor Zhu was a power-minded person. To put it more bluntly, one might say that Mao had entrusted Deng to assume responsibility for the party and government in general as well as to check Liu and Zhou in the central hierarchy in particular.

The Secretariat stood as an intermediate body between the Party Center's General Office and the Politburo Standing Committee. With its functions ranging from drafting and implementing party policies to appointing party personnel at all levels, the Secretariat became the most important executive institution, somewhat like a supercabinet, functioning on a day-to-day basis. In his post as general secretary, Deng showed himself to be the party's chief executive, responsible to almost nobody else besides Chairman Mao alone.

All the members of the Secretariat were relatively young and highly capable individuals. There were no titular figureheads: they all had executive duties, and all concurrently held other substantial positions: Peng Zhen, mayor and party secretary of Beijing; Huang Kecheng, chief of staff of the People's Liberation Army; Lu Dingyi, director of the Propaganda Department of the CCP Central Committee; Wang Jiaxiang, deputy foreign minister of the State Council; and Yang Shangkun, director of the General Office of the CCP Central Committee. One could surmise that the Secretariat functioned as a general supervisor over the party, the government, and the army. Yang was not responsible only to Liu Shaoqi, nor Wang only to Zhou Enlai, nor Huang only to Peng Dehuai; they all had to be responsible also to Deng Xiaoping as head of the Secretariat.[22]

Deng's steady rise from 1952 to 1956 was primarily due to one or two factors: Mao's authoritative influence and Deng's crafty application of this influence. It occurred more through internal power struggle than through constructive work as had been the case during the earlier wartime period. In reality, it reflected, if it did not create, a situation of mutual dependence: Mao's autocratic power made possible Deng's spectacular rise, and Deng's rapid ascension helped enhance Mao's imperial rule—together, unfortunately, with Mao's ever more arbitrary and fanatic utopian line!

— 12 —

Exuberance after Consecutive Promotions, 1956-1959

The 1956 national congress was supposed to have guided the party and the state for a long time to come. In reality, however, its carefully prepared and solemnly pronounced resolutions, including Liu Shaoqi's on the general line and Deng's on the party constitution, would almost immediately be invalidated. Chairman Mao Zedong, contrary to these resolutions, was quick to begin harping on the need for "two-class and two-road struggles" and calling for "socialist reform and revolution."

Quite a number of Mao biographers have pointed out his dualistic character. Although, in some respects, this may be a very complex matter, in other respects, it is simple and clear. I would suggest that the key lies in the basic shift in Mao's disposition before and after 1949, the year of the communists' takeover of state power. Before 1949, Mao's revolutionary idealism served his political realism; after 1949, his political realism served his revolutionary idealism. Some biographers have also alluded to the challenges Mao had faced from within the party leadership. In my own opinion, since 1938— and especially from 1949 until his death in 1976—nobody even came close to challenging Mao as the highest authority. Ross Terrill's comparison of Mao with an emperor in a newly founded dynasty is therefore appropriate. In other words, Mao remained in autocratic control of all his subordinates in all circumstances. He was always capable of stepping up to, or drawing back from, a radical policy with its adverse consequences, which he himself had created in the first place.[1]

With the Communist Party as an unchallengeable system and Mao as an unchallengeable authority, most if not all of the dramatic incidents or accidents that took place in the People's Republic of China (PRC) from 1949 until 1976 can be understood in terms of Mao's own mentality and behavior. The "Great Leap Forward" and the "people's communes" seemed to be socioeconomic movements, but in fact, they were nothing more than expressions of Mao's personal political enthusiasm. Because they were not social or economic events per se, there should be no surprise at their ultimate failure in socioeconomic terms.

Deng's political fortunes from 1952 to 1956 were directly connected with Mao, just as his thinking and behavior were primarily linked to those of Mao. As mentioned previously, Deng won his political power through astute speculation on Mao's state of mind rather than through his own practical achievements—not like Peng Dehuai in military command, or Chen Yun in economic management, or Zhou Enlai in diplomacy. Indeed, we may surmise that Deng had successfully followed "Mao Zedong thought" in the past and would most likely continue to do so in the future.

At the party's Second Plenum of the Eighth Congress on November 10, 1956, Zhou Enlai and Chen Yun were entrusted to make reports on the state of the government and the economy. They pointed out the severe inflation and the sharp imbalance between shrinking revenue and swelling expenditures caused by excessive investment in heavy industries and infrastructure projects in 1956. To balance the budget for 1957, they both suggested switching to a general policy of "appropriate concessions and protection of key projects."

In contrast to Zhou and Chen, Mao preferred to lecture on philosophical principles rather than dwell on statistics. Economic planning was and should always be a matter of balance plus imbalance, Mao pontificated abstractly. Any balance could only be temporary and conditional, whereas imbalance was permanent and unconditional; we need to break up balance, not just maintain it. We must either advance or retreat; we might need to do both, but primarily the former rather than the latter.

Liu Shaoqi did not speak at the conference, but Deng showed up in firm support of Mao. Zhou and Chen were criticized as representatives of a "rightist tendency," and their admonishments about economic disorders and financial deficits were totally ignored. Forced to choose between Zhou as the individual he loved or Mao as the authority he feared, Deng would opt for the latter rather than the former, at least during the period 1956–58.[2]

For several decades, since the late 1920s, the Chinese communists had attempted to define their revolutionary history in two stages: the democratic revolution and the socialist revolution. According to this rough division, the year 1949 seemed not as important as the year 1956, because the former marked only a superficial change in state power or political form, whereas the latter represented a substantial change in social and economic content. In other words, Mao could not claim China as a legitimately socialist country until after the "socialist reforms" were completed.

But that should be simple! The last couple of months of 1956 had witnessed the Chinese communist leaders' competing with one another to speed up the socialist reform campaign. By the end of the year, the socialist reforms were declared to be basically accomplished. In the countryside, 96 percent of peasant households gave up individual tilling for collective farming, with 88 percent of them having joined "higher-level production cooperatives." In the cities and towns, 85 percent of industrial and commercial enterprises were reformed under joint public and private ownership, and 91 percent of handicraft shops were replaced by handicraft cooperatives.[3]

During this socialist reform campaign, Deng once again showed himself the most active figure in the party's central leadership, which was entirely understandable. Having been promoted by Mao repeatedly in the recent past, Deng could not but follow Mao, even if it was somewhat at the expense of his own intelligence and conscience. Between left and right, Deng would choose to be left rather than right, mainly to please Mao. To put it a bit less bluntly, I would characterize Deng's mentality and public behavior at that time as "exuberance after consecutive promotions."

The grandiose accomplishment of the socialist reform movement, however, raised a few logically problematic questions. Since classes, defined by fundamental Marxism as an economic phenomenon, had already been abolished, there should no longer be any need to conduct "class struggle," should there? Since the socialist reforms had been completed and the capitalist road blocked, there should no longer be any "road struggle," should there? Although these points were exactly what the Eighth Congress had formally decided, they would soon be discarded by Mao, who would both boast of the abolition of classes as a previous achievement and call for class struggles as a future objective!

As the annual economic statistics came out, Chen Yun dutifully warned of the problem of the financial deficit again in January 1957. For that, Mao subjected him to further criticism. Thus, we see Liu both in 1953 and in 1955, Zhou and Chen in 1956, Chen again in 1957, and Zhou again in 1958 all being attacked for "rightist tendencies" by Mao. They constituted almost all the members of the Politburo Standing Committee except for Mao himself; Zhu De, who always remained a figurehead; and Deng, who served as Mao's constant follower and accomplice.

In response to the popular protests against the communist regimes in Hungary and Poland, Mao first expressed the "double hundred" slogan in April 1956, calling for "a hundred flowers to bloom" and "a hundred schools of thought to contend"—presumably, an invitation to the Chinese people to freely express their opinions and voice their grievances. At the same time, Mao also called for a "Rectification Movement" within the Communist Party to expose and correct party cadres' defects. At the Eighth Congress, Liu had not mentioned the movement at all, nor had Deng paid particular attention to it. Neither of them yet seemed to have taken these matters seriously at that juncture.

Presumably in order to prevent a repetition in China of what had happened in Eastern Europe, Mao made a well-known speech, "On the Correct Handling of Contradictions among the People," in February 1957, promising to allow common citizens greater freedom of speech, publication, social organization, and even political demonstration. Two months later, in April 1957, at Mao's personal instructions, the Rectification Movement was publicly launched, encouraging people to expose and correct "bureaucratism, factionalism, and subjective idealism" within the Communist Party itself.

In the Politburo Standing Committee, Zhou showed some support for the "double hundred" policy, because it sounded good for the people and also because it was what the chairman really wanted. Liu remained reluctant to follow Mao's lead, uncertain whether the policy was good for the party and whether it was what the chairman truly meant. Deng remained cautiously neutral for a few months in early 1957, awaiting further developments in the political situation and in the chairman's state of mind.[4]

Deng proved correct once again! As mass criticism of the party bureaucracy rose, so did worries and complaints from the party bureaucrats, and Mao suddenly reversed his stance. In the end, the "double hundred" of 1956 turned into the "antirightism" of 1957. Deng responded promptly, showing far more enthusiasm for squashing nonparty dissidents than he had for rectifying party bureaucrats. It was with the sponsorship of the Secretariat that *People's Daily* published the editorial "Why So?" on June 8, 1957, which marked the official commencement of the antirightist campaign.

In the following six months or so, nearly one million people were labeled as "antiparty and antisocialist rightists." Mostly intellectuals, they generally belonged to one of three categories: college students and professors; liberal scientists, entrepreneurs, and writers; and democratic party leaders and officials. The majority of the rightists were sent to labor camps in the distant countryside, and the very least punishment they could expect was a quick demotion from their present posts and a sharp reduction in their salaries.

The Communist Party leadership was indeed strengthened through this massive purge: the "united front" or "joint government" was totally abolished, and noncommunist ministers were generally eliminated from the State Council. All "poisonous weeds," or dissident voices, were gagged and muffled, and henceforth, one could find only "fragrant flowers," or obsequious voices, everywhere. Although the antirightist campaign of 1957 was in itself fanatic enough, it had also laid the foundation for the even more incredible "Great Leap Forward" of the following year.

At the Third Plenum, September–October 1957, Deng was entrusted to deliver a "Report on the Rectification Movement" on behalf of the Chinese Communist Party (CCP) Center. Despite its title, the report, bristling with combative rhetoric, was on the antirightist campaign. Deng alleged that "these rightists had their programs, their organizations, their plans and their objectives in order to overthrow the communist party leadership and the socialist state, and that their contradiction with the communist party was of an unconciliatory life-and-death nature," and therefore, it had to be regarded as "an absolute necessity to fight against them."[5]

Two decades later, under new political circumstances, Deng had to acknowledge his personal mistakes in the antirightist campaign, though in a rather delicate manner: "We should not allow an impression that only one individual is correct while all the others are wrong, or that only one is wrong while all the others are correct. I have the right to say this because I myself have committed some mistakes in the past. We were all activists in the antirightist campaign in 1957, weren't we? Wasn't I the general secretary at the time? I should therefore share some responsibility."[6]

Yes, Deng had indeed been the general secretary at the time. But he also headed the Antirightists Group in the CCP Central Committee—something he now pretended to forget. It was under Deng's own sponsorship that the antirightist campaign was initiated and extended. None of Deng's talks and speeches on this matter are included in his *Selected Works,* and official Deng biographers have avoided this topic. Although there are many details that we don't yet know and cannot find out, it should be sufficiently evident that Deng played a very decisive role in the antirightist campaign, far more so than others, perhaps even including Mao.[7]

Apart from, or partly because of, the antirightist campaign, the Party Center's Third Plenum in October 1957 passed the radical "twelve-year program of agricultural development." The program either was too bold or may simply have been unrealistic in its call for quickly surpassing Britain and catching up with the United States in terms of gross national product. Mao chided Zhou and a few others for their conservatism, while Deng once again stood by Mao and at some point even served as Mao's personal spokesman.

In November 1957, Mao personally led a Chinese Communist Party delegation to Moscow, choosing Deng as his deputy. That was Mao's second trip abroad and also his last. The delegation was to participate in formal celebrations marking the fortieth anniversary of the October Revolution and also attend a summit of sixty-four world communist leaders. In addition, Mao wanted to take the opportunity to negotiate renewed Soviet military and economic assistance and lecture the communist world on his own views of international communism.

During his two-week sojourn in Moscow, Mao met Nikita Khrushchev several times. He confided to Khrushchev his frank evaluation of his colleagues, or to put it more accurately, his subordinates. Mao indicated that he had nothing good to say about Liu, Zhou, or Zhu, while Deng seemed to be the only one worth a few complimentary words. At one of the informal gatherings, Mao pointed to Deng from afar and quipped to Khrushchev, "Look at that little guy over there. He is highly intelligent and has a great future ahead of him."[8]

After they both returned to Beijing, Mao asked Deng to report on his behalf to the Politburo about the visit to Moscow. Deng stressed the consolidated unity of the communist world as well as China's success in obtaining renewed economic support from the Soviet Union. Nevertheless, he knew better than anybody else that it had by no means been a perfect trip, and he understood Mao's deep resentment of the Russians. Although Deng might have shared the same patriotic sentiments as Mao, it was mainly Mao's feelings, not his own, that he really cared about.

Ever more radical policies were accompanied by ever more drastic changes in the central leadership in 1958, the year of the "Great Leap Forward." There was one party conference after another in the early months, constantly pushing Mao's radical line forward: January 5–9, the Hangzhou Conference, in which Mao criticized Zhou and Chen for their conservatism; January 11–23, the Nanning Conference, where the slogan "Great Leap Forward" was coined, while Mao chastised Zhou again and forbade anybody from even mentioning the term "antirashness"; March 9–26, the Chengdu Conference, which decided on the "general line" and brought renewed criticism of Zhou; the May 5–23 National Party Conference, which featured the slogans "One day is worth twenty years" and "Surpass Britain in seven years and catch up with America in fifteen years"; the May 23–25 enlarged Politburo conference, at which Lin Biao was promoted to the Politburo Standing Committee and three radical regional leaders were promoted to the Politburo; the May 27–July 22 conference of the Central Military Council, which singled out Liu Bocheng and Peng Dehuai as targets of criticism for exhibiting "foreign dogmatism"; and so on and so forth.[9]

It seems that each time Mao met with Khrushchev, he would attempt soon afterward to take some fancier, bolder, and more spectacular action within China. Thus, we find that Mao's general slogan "More, faster, better, and thriftier" was sounded in early 1958 in the wake of the late 1957 Mao–Khrushchev meeting in Moscow; and Mao's call for "people's communes" came on August 5, 1958, coupled with bellicose challenges to the United States over the Taiwan Strait, shortly after Mao's early August meeting with Khrushchev in Beijing.

Although few of the speeches Deng made in 1958 are officially published, the records that are available suffice to reflect his political performance, if not his personal thoughts, during the Great Leap Forward. Among the top party leaders, Deng was the most conspicuous in siding with Mao to push for radical policies in 1958.[10] The fact that Deng's talks and speeches during the Great Leap Forward were carefully omitted from his later official publications represents a kind of evidence in itself, perhaps more telling than anything that was published.

Actually, Deng's cooperation with Mao reached its very zenith in the heat of the Great Leap Forward in 1958. On several occasions, Deng acted as the chairman's representative and was referred to by Mao as "boss number two" and "deputy commander in chief at the party headquarters." Together with Mao, Deng, in the name of the Party Center, even assigned specific duties to Politburo members such as Chen Yi as deputy premier and minister of foreign affairs, Peng Zhen as mayor of Beijing, and Nie Rongzhen as minister of military industry.[11]

The Great Leap Forward touched off the massive campaign of establishing "people's communes" in the countryside. The people's communes were extravagantly touted as the "Eden of communism," among the greatest merits of which were their qualities of being "large and public"—large enough to include a whole township of a few hundred thousand peasant households in just one productive unit and public enough to deprive individual peasants of their own rice bowls and chopsticks. Accompanied by Deng, Mao toured several provinces, promoting the people's communes, in the autumn of 1958. The chairman was fanciful enough to suggest that commune members should take half a day to work in the fields and the other half just to play games. How would the land get farmed? The chairman further suggested that one-third of the land be used for raising crops, one-third for growing grass, and the final third simply left fallow, and that the land be rotated among these three uses every three years. What a wonderful idea!

Two decades later, under new political circumstances, Deng had to review the Great Leap Forward and his own role in it, also in a nuanced manner: "Talking about previous mistakes, we shouldn't just blame Comrade Mao Zedong alone. Other Party Center comrades also committed mistakes. We used to say that Comrade Mao Zedong's head was overheated during the Great Leap Forward. What about ours? Weren't they overheated, too? Comrades Liu Shaoqi and Zhou Enlai and I did not object to it, nor did Comrade Chen Yun speak out."[12]

The plain fact is that Liu, Zhou, and Chen were repeatedly criticized by Mao for their "conservatism" and "rightist tendencies" from 1953 up until early 1958; they did try to speak out, while Deng insistently stood by Mao. From the standpoint of sheer political power calculation, Deng would be happy to see others like Liu and Zhou stand out as Mao's targets of attack. Their demotion or loss of Mao's favor meant Deng's promotion or gain of Mao's favor in the party's central hierarchy! There might be some people whose heads were "overheated," but not Deng, whose head remained pretty cool, as far as politics was concerned—cool enough to do what Mao wanted done and to say what Mao liked to hear.

As late as April 1959, the Secretariat under Deng's leadership proposed pooling all resources to conduct an "iron and steel campaign." The campaign was supposed to consist of three battles in three consecutive months: in the first battle, in May, steel output must increase from thirty thousand tons per day to forty thousand tons per day; in the second, in June, to forty-five thousand tons per day; and in the third, in July, up to fifty thousand tons per day.[13] Despite the earnest efforts of Deng and his colleagues, the campaign failed miserably. Instead of rising, iron and steel production steadily declined in the latter months of 1959.

It did not take long for the Great Leap Forward and the people's communes to reveal their fatal flaws. From the latter months of 1958 onward, the Party Center had to call conferences at Wuhan, Shanghai, and Lushan to deal with the ever more apparent problems. Mao, this time as on many other occasions, would push the situation to the brink and then draw it back a bit himself. He did not seem too mindful of people like Chen Yun, who quietly worked on changes in his radical measures, without openly challenging his general authority. Deng followed Mao in denouncing the "five evil winds" in late 1958 and early 1959, but he did so not only through his own inclination but mainly because of Mao's change of mind at the time.

The Great Leap Forward of 1958 was just one of several periods of radical or leftist lines in CCP history. The difference between this period and previous ones, such as the Li Lisan line of 1930, lay not in their initiators—both Mao and Li might truly have believed in what they stood for—but in their followers: Li's followers were mostly his true believers, but Mao's were not quite so. The Great Leap Forward thus became a melodrama, in which Mao acted like an emperor running about naked and shouting wildly throughout the country, while his subjects clapped and cheered for his invisible new clothes!

With one veteran leader after another being either purged or muffled, Marshal Peng Dehuai was left as the only individual with high
enough seniority and great enough courage to dare occasionally to
cross words, if not swords, with Chairman Mao. Such a potential opposition would sooner or later turn into an actual confrontation, as it did
indeed in the form of a Party Center conference convened at Jiangxi,
the Lushan Mountains resort, from July to August 1959.

The Lushan Conference was originally scheduled as an ordinary
work conference of the Party Center to adopt some further moderate
policies. Although Peng raised exactly the same issues as Mao had
before, Mao took it as a personal offense. He grew enraged. The conference subsequently became the Eighth Plenum of the Eighth Congress and shifted from correcting "leftist errors" to fighting against
Peng's "rightist crimes." Liu and Zhou had to follow Mao's line, and
few dared to stand up for Peng. The conference ended with Peng and
three others being purged from the party leadership and with a resolution calling for a fight against rightist tendencies.

Deng did not personally participate in the Lushan Conference. He
remained in Beijing handling the Party Center's routine affairs while
nursing an injured foot. But he did take part in the enlarged conference
of the Central Military Council held in Beijing in September 1959, at
which he joined the harsh criticism of Peng and Huang Kecheng. As a
result, Peng was replaced by Lin Biao as minister of defense, and Luo
Ruiqing took over Huang's position as chief of staff of the army and a
member of the Secretariat. The conference also promoted Deng to the
Standing Committee of the Central Military Council—an extraordinary
privilege for him under the current circumstances. Mao and Deng were
the only two civilians in the committee, while all the other members
were formally ranked army officers.[14]

An article by Deng was published in both Russian and Chinese in
October 1's *Pravda* and October 2's *People's Daily* in commemora-
tion of the tenth anniversary of the PRC. After praising the CCP's
various achievements under the leadership of Mao, Deng turned to
recent intraparty relations: "The rightist elements in the party ignore or
refuse to recognize the great achievements of the Great Leap Forward.
They use some defects in our work to attack the party's line and the
people's communes. . . . This rightist opportunism reflects bourgeois
hatred and fear of the mass movement being conducted by the party."[15]

It should be noted that, in his article, Deng refrained from specifying just whom he was criticizing. Although he obviously meant Peng Dehuai, Deng for some reason seemed unwilling to mention him by name. That seemingly small detail actually represented a big issue. By the latter months of 1959, as far as I can judge, it became fairly apparent to Deng that a nationwide economic crisis was under way. Deng might not have been so concerned about Peng's personal ordeal, but deep in his own mind, Deng did not quite agree with Mao in criticizing the rightist line anymore.

All the events of late 1959 grew ever more insulting to Deng's intelligence and conscience. One might say that Deng was a communist politician of maximum intelligence and minimum conscience. But there had to be some marginal equilibrium between the two factors, and there had to be some bottom line or outer limit. Mao did not seem to allow Deng any! Deng knew better than anybody else that it was Mao who had promoted him step by step to the supreme leadership. However, unlike during the war years, when he had greatly respected both Mao's authority and his political line, now Deng still greatly respected Mao as an unshakable authority—perhaps even more than before—but he no longer respected him so much as an impeccable policy maker. The incredible Great Leap Forward and the resultant disastrous "three bitter years" would gradually transform Deng's overall attitude toward Mao.[16]

Deng during work-study program in France.

During a break at the September 1956 Eighth National Party Congress. From left: Lin Boqu, Zhu De, Deng, and Dong Biwu.

With Liu Shaoqi in June 1958.

With (from left) Deng Yingchao [Madame Zhou Enlai], Li Xiannian and Zhou Enlai at the airport in Beijing in March 1963.

Deng and Zhuo Lin in the Taihang Mountain Revolutionary Base Area after their marriage in Yan'an in August 1939.

Zhou Enlai, Chen Yun (back to camera), Liu Shaoqi, Mao Zedong, and Deng at an enlarged work conference of the Central Committee in early 1962.

實事求是

Deng's inscription, "Seeking truth from facts," which he believed to be the essence of Mao Zedong Thought.

With Mao Zedong (early 1960s).

Deng addressing his troops before a battle, in Licheng County, Shanxi, in the spring of 1938.

With President Jimmy Carter on the balcony of the White House, January 1979.

Deng, Zhao Ziyang, and Li Xiannian with Prime Minister Margaret Thatcher of the United Kingdom toasting the signing of the Sino-British Joint Declaration on the Question of Hong Kong (December 1984).

The families of Liu Bocheng and Deng Xiaoping in Wu'an County, Hebei Province, in 1945. From left: Liu Bocheng, Wang Ronghua, Zhuo Lin, and Deng Xiaoping with their children.

Seventy-five-year-old Deng on his way to the summit of Huangshan Mountain in Anhui Province (1979).

Deng greeting high-ranking military officers at expanded meeting of the Military Commission of the Central Committee.

Meeting with Soviet President Mikhail Gorbachev, May 16, 1989.

A favorite pastime.

— 13 —

Fatigue after Leaping Forward, 1960-1965

A momentary resurgence of the Great Leap Forward, spurred by the antirightist atmosphere, continued for a few months in 1960 before it came to an absolute impasse. The economic crisis became too evident and too severe. On June 6, 1960, the Party Center had to issue an emergency order for grain and other food to be brought to the capital. In the previous few months, barely half the required amount of wheat and rice for Beijing, Tianjin, and Shanghai had been sent in by the concerned provinces. As a result, the granaries in Beijing had stocks for no more than ten days' consumption; in Tianjin, seven days; and in Shanghai, effectively no stocks were available at all. The Shanghai granaries could hardly meet the city's basic needs on a day-to-day basis.[1]

Relatives and maids and security guards in Zhongnanhai, the Party Center compound, spread the news that a lot of peasants—there must have been quite a lot of them—were dying of starvation in the country-side. You had to believe them! These staff members had just returned from their homes yesterday or the day before. Some of them were teenage soldiers, crying while telling about their own uncles and aunts; others were old people vividly talking about their own neighbors, whom Mao Zedong and other party leaders had known when they were youngsters in their native villages.

As is now known, and as the communists themselves have admitted, 1959 marked the commencement of the "three bitter years" of 1959–61, in which more than thirty million people, mostly peasants died of outright starvation. Thirty million people! It virtually overshadows the total number of casualties China has sustained in all its domestic and international wars in the twentieth century.

In retrospect, it is no wonder that such a national catastrophe could have happened. In the previous year, 1959, China's grain production was falsely claimed to have been 300 million tons, or a 25 percent increase over that of 1958. In reality, it was only 170 million tons, but the state levied 18.6 million tons more in taxes than the year before. With a 15 percent decrease in production, coupled with a 14.7 percent increase in state collection, the aforementioned disaster and tragedy should have come as little surprise.[2]

After some desperate yet hopeless calls to "Defend the grain quota" and "Defend the steel quota," the party leadership gradually had to manage a "small leap backward" in the latter months of 1960. The Ninth Plenum of the Eighth Congress, held in Beijing in January 1961, formally adopted a so-called eight-characters policy—that is, "adjustment, consolidation, supplementation, and improvement." The whole country was once again divided into "six large regions," each encompassing half a dozen provinces. That measure represented both decentralization to permit more efficient economic management and Mao's attempt to appeal to local-level political support, as his central control was slipping away.

Chen Yun and his economic coterie were brought back to cope with the critical situation. They set to work immediately. Among the most effective measures they took was to dispatch approximately 8.7 million urban residents to the countryside in 1960–61 and another 6 million in 1961–62, thereby greatly easing the material burden of the cities and also substantially enhancing the agricultural labor force. In addition, the state investment budget for infrastructure construction was firmly and drastically reduced (by 67 percent), which sharply decreased not only heavy industrial output but the fiscal deficit as well.[3]

The year 1960 ended with agricultural production further reduced by 12.6 percent and the grain yield down by another 15.6 percent. The nationwide economic crisis reached its nadir in the winter of 1960–61. After two seasons of good harvests in the summer and fall of 1961, however, the nationwide famine and widespread deaths were by and large halted, and the national economy was brought back under control by the middle of 1962.

From March 10 to 13, 1961, in Canton, Mao presided over a conference of high party cadres of the three southern regions, to discuss the
people's commune problems, while Liu Shaoqi, Zhou Enlai, Chen
Yun, and Deng Xiaoping convened a similar conference of the three
northern regions in Beijing. Then, at Mao's order, a joint conference
continued in Canton from March 14 to 23. The conference adopted a
document called the "Sixty Points on Agriculture," which attempted, to
a certain extent, to correct the over-radical nature of the people's communes and restore agricultural production in the countryside. It should
be noted that this document was drafted not by Deng's Secretariat but
by Mao's own "intellectual squad"—notably, Tian Jiaying, Chen
Boda, and Hu Qiaomu.

Soon after the Canton Conference, at Mao's suggestion, the Party
Center leaders went on various tours of inspection and investigation.
They were to examine the effects of party policies on the people's
communes, especially the rural populace's response to public dining
halls. Liu went to Hunan; Zhou to Hebei; and Deng, together with
Peng Zhen, to the suburbs of Beijing. By early May, their reports
reached Mao. Their opinions were unanimously negative, despite vari-
ations in wording. Liu said boldly, "As they are no good, the dining
halls should be dissolved rather than dragging them on." Zhou said
mildly, "Commune members in general do not favor the dining halls;
even bachelors want to cook and eat at their own home." Deng said
meekly, "In order to raise peasants' incentives in agricultural production, some measures need to be further improved and some policies
rectified, such as those regarding provisional assignments, grain collection, spare grain distribution, labor quotas, dining halls, and so on."
In his response to Zhou's report, Mao finally approved the termination
of the unconditional policy of making commune members eat in public
dining halls.[4]

For most of the latter months of 1961, Mao remained in the south,
absent from Beijing, leaving other leaders to clean up the economic
mess. In August 1961, under Deng's direct supervision, the Secretariat
drafted the "Seventy Points on Industry," for the purpose of strength-
ening factory management and regulation to promote industrial production output, and the "Sixty Points on Culture and Education," for
the parallel purpose of rectifying radical policies and normalizing
schools and universities, scientific research, and liberal arts activities.

From late January to early February 1962, an enlarged conference

of the Party Center, later called the Seven Thousand Cadres Conference, was convened in Beijing to review the past three years' economic work in general. In his speech at the conference, Liu ascribed
the economic crisis not to natural calamities or the Soviet Union's
betrayal, as the party used to do, but mainly to the errors of the Party
Center's leadership. Mao took the blame generously and yet grudgingly: "With regard to the errors in the previous few years, I should be
held fully responsible, not only for those of the Party Center directly
committed by me, but also for those indirectly related to me."[5]

On the one hand, Deng tried to avoid any direct criticism of Mao;
yet on the other hand, he tried to concentrate on the problems: "Our
party has five good things: good thought—that is, Mao Zedong
thought; a good Party Center—that is, the center headed by Mao
Zedong; a group of good leaders; a good tradition and style; and a
good people loyal to the party."[6] As for the root of past errors and the
way to achieve future success, Deng emphasized the party's need for
the principle of "democratic centralism," with which Mao, Liu, Zhou,
and perhaps everybody else could not help but agree.

A few years later, during the Cultural Revolution in 1966, Mao
recalled a change in his relationship with Deng in the early 1960s:
"From 1959 up to the present time, Deng has never come to see me
about anything. Deng is a deaf mute, but whenever he was at a conference, he always chose to sit in a spot far from me. He respected me but
kept away from me, treating me like a dead ancestor."[7] Mao must have
been right in this regard. Deng still respected Mao for his awesome
authority but no longer for his correct leadership. Indeed, Mao was no
longer a correct leader. Deng had tried hard to follow Mao's policies in
the years 1956–59, only to find that the whole nation had fallen into an
inexcusably disastrous condition and that he himself had fallen into an
embarrassingly isolated position among his Party Center colleagues.

It is true that a basic change in Deng's attitude toward Mao had
taken place since 1959, but it was less a matter of personal relations
than of policy orientation. It should be noted that their relationship had
always involved a delicate balance of subjective and objective factors,
and the obvious failure of the Great Leap Forward caused a tilt in this
balance. From the Seven Thousand Cadres Conference of January
1962 to the Tenth Plenum of September 1962, Deng lined up with Liu
in carrying out what Mao later called a "right opportunist line." Only
his respect for Mao's authority and his disrespect for Liu's personality

kept Deng from allying himself irrevocably with Liu. In other words, Deng followed Liu in terms of social and economic restoration, but not in personal affiliation.

Soon after the Seven Thousand Cadres Conference, Mao left Beijing for Wuhan. He deliberately stepped out of the "first-front leadership" and left Liu and Deng in charge of the Party Center's daily affairs. In late February 1962, Liu chaired a Politburo Standing Committee meeting, known as the Western Hall Conference, attended by Zhou, Deng, and Chen. The conference accepted Liu's assessment of the current economic situation as being "on the brink of bankruptcy." A Central Financial and Economic Group was reinstated, with Chen Yun as its head and Li Fuchun as its deputy head, to start a nationwide rectification campaign.[8]

Following Liu's lead, Deng in the Secretariat drafted a resolution to restore the posts of all those who had suffered in the 1958–59 antirightist movement. Deng called for a one-shot solution: all the victims should be restored at once instead of looking into each individual case. But when a letter of appeal from Peng Dehuai was forwarded by Yang Shangkun of the Party Center's General Office to the Secretariat for resolution, Deng had to pass the letter on to Mao and meanwhile send a note on the matter to Liu and Zhou. They all agreed that this was a matter the chairman should handle personally. Even so, Mao still felt offended by Peng's letter as well as by Yang's and Deng's having passed it to him.

On July 7, 1962, Deng was invited to speak to a conference of the Communist Youth League, at which he delivered some well-known remarks. He told the audience, "Speaking about which is the best system of production, I would support whatever type can relatively easily and rapidly restore and increase agricultural output, and whatever type the masses are willing to implement should be adopted. If it is not yet legal, then it should be legalized. Yellow or white, a cat that catches mice is a good cat."[9]

The Great Leap Forward was an excessive action, for better or for worse. Once this excess had been removed, the national economy would return to normal functioning—that is, it would recover. Although Mao must bear the blame for the previous economic decline, neither Liu nor Deng can be fully credited with the later economic recovery. The economic rebound did not demonstrate Liu's or Deng's abilities in economic management. It mainly involved rectifying the radical policies or jettisoning the excessive measures in agriculture and industry, which was more a matter of political conscience than of economic expertise.

By the way, both the Indian government and the nationalists in Taiwan had misjudged the timing and extent of the "three bitter years." Despite the severity of the economic crisis, the communist regime in China was politically far from the point of breakdown or bankruptcy, even in its worst moments of 1959–61. As for the economic situation, furthermore, by the time Prime Minister Jawaharlal Nehru and Generalissimo Chiang Kai-shek finally decided to start their military adventures against China in 1962, China's crisis was pretty much over—which accounts for their decisive defeats by Chinese troops.

Mao remained politically astute and sensitive, as did Deng, both far more so than Liu. As soon as the economic crisis was brought under control, Mao would fight back. At the Tenth Plenum, held September 24–27, 1962, chaired by Mao in person, agriculture was declared to be the foundation and first priority of the national economy, followed by light and heavy industries. Mao seemed content in thus creating a Chinese way to build up a socialist economy, at variance with the Soviet model. Another unique discovery by Mao was the existence of classes and class struggle within a socialist state. "For a fairly long historical period after the proletariat seizes state power, there remain classes and class struggles as well as possibilities for the bourgeoisie to restore its lost regime," Mao stated. He therefore posited the need to "talk about class struggle every year, every month, and every day."[10]

The Tenth Plenum marked a turning point from Liu's economic rectification to Mao's continuous political revolution. Peng Dehuai's letter to the Party Center was repudiated as a rightist attempt to reverse previous verdicts. Deng Zihui's policy of "assigning grain quotas to peasant households" was labeled a rightist wind intended to squash the collective production of the people's communes. The Party Center's Department of Rural Work was thereupon abolished, together with Deng Zihui's directorship of said department.

During the "three bitter years" of 1959–61, the party leadership, central as well as local, was busily involved in economic production and policy adjustment; no special attention could be paid to problems involving individual cadres. The Tenth Plenum gave only a hint of a change in Mao's mind-set in the latter direction. It was not until May

1963 that Mao found a way to take his revenge in the form of the "socialist education campaign."

The socialist education campaign was nonetheless not an entirely artificial invention. With millions having died of starvation in the countryside, it seemed only natural that a great number of local cadres would be tainted by corruption, embezzlement, theft, bribery, licentiousness, and other illegal activities, as well as pessimism and cynicism in defiance of their communist allegiance. Such phenomena, indeed, did not have as much to do with class identity and class struggle as Mao claimed.

At a joint conference of Politburo members and major regional secretaries, convened in Hangzhou in February 1963, quite a few participants raised the problem of corruption among local cadres in the countryside. Consequently, a resolution was passed under Mao's auspices to launch an Education and Rectification Movement in the countryside. The document, later called the "Early Ten Points," quoted some of Mao's previous speeches as its introduction. "At the present time, there happens to be a serious situation of class struggle in Chinese society," it intoned, and called for "reorganization of revolutionary class forces to repel the combined assaults of capitalism and feudalism."[11]

Although Mao's remarks sounded quite radical and leftist, they were actually more theoretical rhetoric than concrete policy. After a few months' experimentation, the Secretariat, headed by Deng, was entrusted with producing a supplement to Mao's original draft. Deng's new version, or the "Later Ten Points," presented little substantive alternative to the earlier one concerning the "two-class and two-road struggle" but did supplement it with more concrete guidelines, especially in regard to the "four cleanups" of account books, granary stocks, fiscal files, and work records. Corrupt or "unclean" cadres were to be appropriately investigated and punished, while agricultural production was not to be impeded.

Because of various ambiguities in the previous literature, it should be noted that Mao did not seem unhappy with Deng's "Later Ten Points"—either at the time or afterward; nor did Deng himself ever confess, even during the Cultural Revolution, to any wrongdoing in 1963, as he did to other actions in earlier and later years. By all accounts, the major problem Mao had with the socialist education campaign was not with Deng in 1963 but with Liu in 1964.

In September 1964, under Liu's personal guidance was drafted the "Revised Later Ten Points," which, in a tone as bold and radical as the "Early Ten Points," proclaimed: "More than one-third of our rural administration is now lost to the five types of evil elements (i.e., landlords, rich peasants, reactionaries, criminals, and rightists)." The document required that "the work teams assigned to the rural locales should brush aside the incumbent cadres, get rooted with the peasant masses, expose and criticize the corrupt cadres, and establish a new leadership." In fact, Liu's draft was basically a product of his wife's five-month experiment as a socialist education campaign work-team leader in the village of Peach Orchid, Hebei.[12]

Despite the similarities between Mao and Liu in terms of their boldness, there were some fundamental differences between them. Mao's emphasis on classes and class struggle in a general ideological sense did not necessarily equate with Liu's judgment of party cadres from an economic perspective. If one were to be so serious and so strict about applying pure and clean standards to judge those peasant cadres, he or she might well conclude that not just one-third of the rural administration but all of the rural administration was lost to the evil elements! Liu certainly had a criterion problem there. Besides, Madame Mao's jealousy of Madame Liu seemed to have played an important role. But even without that additional irritant, Mao was already furious enough. He ordered Deng to arrange another central conference to review the socialist education campaign and Liu's document.

Deng did so and promised to chair the conference personally. As he recognized Mao's anger at Liu, Deng attempted to dissuade Mao from attending in person. Mao refused. At the Party Center conference on January 12, 1965, Mao declared that the socialist education campaign was a matter of socialism versus capitalism, not a matter of "four cleans" versus "four uncleans." As Liu tried to interrupt with some explanation, Mao flared up: "Here are two books in my hand: one is the state constitution and the other the party constitution. Both as a citizen of the state and as a member of the party, I have my right to speak. Now one of you does not want me to come to this conference, and another does not allow me to speak. Do you guys dare to deprive me of my constitutional right to come and speak?"[13]

Another socialist education campaign document, the "Twenty-three Points," was drafted under Mao's own supervision. The new document stressed reliance on 95 percent of the masses and 95 percent of the cadres and was therefore more moderate in practical terms. However, it expressed the main objective of the socialist education campaign as being to "expose and attack a small handful of capitalist roaders within the party leadership" and was therefore more radical in terms of high principle. Liu's 1964 document was harshly criticized as one of "apparent leftism but essential rightism."

As can be imagined, Mao's anger was directed primarily toward Liu, but it was directed partly toward Deng as well. Underlying Mao's argument regarding the nature of the socialist education campaign lay his resentment of Liu's encroachment on his political authority and of Deng's betrayal of his personal confidence. It was also at this juncture in early 1965 that Mao reached the final determination to remove Liu from the central leadership, according to his statement to Edgar Snow.[14]

During and after the Tenth Plenum, Deng began noticing the disagreement between Liu and Mao and attempted to step out of the "hot water" of domestic politics. He tried to avoid intraparty problems and devote his attention to international communist affairs, but he found it nearly impossible to do so. With Deng's high political position came great political responsibility. Members of his Secretariat, such as Peng Zhen, were in charge of various domestic duties. Peng was Deng's deputy in the Secretariat as well as the mayor and party secretary of Beijing; he was also a longtime subordinate of Liu since the late 1930s. Besides, given Deng's own personality and disposition, it was difficult for him to keep his hands off power politics, as Chen and Zhou did. Deng was a politician in the true sense, helplessly obsessed with personal connections and power relations.

Even if only the countryside needed "four cleanups," the whole country must need "socialist education." Thus, the matter of the socialist education campaign was raised in the cities in 1964. In the capital, Beijing University was chosen as a "test spot" for the urban socialist education campaign. A work team, formed from members of the Beijing Party Committee and the Central Propaganda Department, entered the university in January 1964. A deputy director of the Central Propaganda Department named Zhang Panshi became the team leader. The whole matter was under the direct supervision of Deng and Peng at the Secretariat.[15]

The socialist education campaign work team quickly ferreted out problems at Beida (short for Beijing University). The university president, Lu Ping, and the majority of the department heads were from either capitalist or landlord families, and most of them had received their educations in schools under the KMT government. (How could they possibly have done otherwise!) Veteran army cadres like Nie Yuanzi, who graduated from the Anti-Japanese University in Yan'an in the late 1930s, had allegedly been expelled from the leadership for lack of academic knowledge. The work team therefore attacked Lu as an executive of a "bourgeois line" and praised Nie as a "revolutionary leftist."

Yet unlike a production brigade leader in a village, who could easily be fired by the socialist education campaign work team, Lu Ping was a high-ranking official, who could not be lightly removed without approval by central authority. After a period of stalemate and confusion, Mayor Peng said, "I know Lu Ping. He is a good comrade"; and General Secretary Deng declared, "Lu Ping's attitude and opinions are both good, and Beida is still a socialist university." The work team leader, Zhang Panshi, was dismissed from his position instead. Lu Ping resumed his presidency of Beida, and Nie Yuanzi was pressed to apologize.[16]

In September 1964, when Liu's "Revised Later Ten Points" were disseminated, however, Nie Yuanzi and other leftists used this latest Party Center document to rechallenge the university leaders. But they were again pushed back by Mao's "Twenty-three Points"—which sounded more friendly to incumbent leaders than to resentful challengers—in January 1965, until the Cultural Revolution broke out in May 1966 to turn the entire issue upside down. Speaking of the socialist education campaign in Beijing University, Deng once referred to Nie and her kind as follows: "There are people who would make themselves a fortune by snapping at others. They are a bunch of jerks, just wanting to climb higher on other people's shoulders."[17]

Since the Tenth Plenum in 1962, more through personal inclination than through official assignment, Deng shifted a large portion of his attention to international communist affairs, mainly debates with the Communist Party of the Soviet Union (CPSU). He was the most prominent figure on the Chinese side during the grand polemics between the Chinese Communist Party (CCP) and the CPSU from 1963 until 1965—regarding this a safe way for him to please Mao yet not offend his own conscience.

On February 21, 1963, the CPSU delivered a letter through the Russian Embassy in Beijing to the CCP, proposing bilateral talks in

Moscow. On March 9, Deng called in the Russian ambassador and handed him the CCP Center's response, which agreed in principle that it was necessary for the two parties to hold talks on some important issues regarding the international communist movement. By April 2, when another letter from Moscow arrived in Beijing, the composition of the Chinese delegation had largely been decided.[18]

The CCP delegation, led by Deng, departed from Beijing on July 5, 1963, and arrived in Moscow the same day. Also included in the delegation were Peng Zhen, Kang Sheng, Yang Shangkun, and Liu Ningyi—all Secretariat members—and Ambassador Pan Zili, who was already in Moscow. This delegation was small but very strong. All its members were responsible leaders and capable orators, with no figurehead included at all.

Deng, who stood out as the Chinese side's chief spokesman throughout the talks, engaged in heated arguments with his Soviet counterpart, Mikhail Suslov, head of the Soviet delegation. Suslov was a senior member of the Secretariat of the CPSU Central Committee and a well-known Marxist ideologue. It did not take the Russians long to realize that Deng and company had come to Moscow to quarrel, not to talk; to protest, not to negotiate. At the conference, Deng just read off his statements in Chinese, drawn up for the most part in advance in Beijing, and responded to Suslov's interjections with stony silence. To questions such as whether any nonviolent approach could be adopted to establish socialism, Deng would reply with some simple, contemptuous remark, like "Idle chatter," "No need to repeat," and so on.[19]

The CCP–CPSU talks lasted nearly two weeks and yet could reach no agreement other than to publish a joint communiqué, which said, "[B]oth parties have agreed on further talks at some suitable place and time in the future." This sentence was just a diplomatic confirmation of the talks' total breakdown, and as it turned out, the two Communist Parties broke off formal contacts for the next twenty-odd years.

Before leaving for Moscow, the CCP Secretariat had gathered together a dozen Russian specialists and Marxist scholars and hammered out a sixty-four–page document, drafted chiefly by Kang Sheng, under Peng and Deng's direct supervision, and with Mao's final approval. The document, pompously entitled "The Polemic on the General Line of the International Communist Movement," overflowed with notes and quotes from Marx and Lenin and other famous communist leaders. But its premises and conclusions were both quite obvious: the document was simply an attempt to stuff a bouquet of sweet flowers into Mao's harsh dogmatic vase!

It should be noted that most, if not all, of the anti-Soviet activists such as Deng and Peng would become "revisionists" themselves a couple of years later. As for Deng, he neither knew much nor cared much about Marxist-Leninist theories. His staunch position during the Sino-Russian debate was taken for practical rather than theoretical reasons; for domestic rather than international reasons; finally, for personal rather than public reasons. To put the matter more bluntly: Mao liked it! By all means, a bit of yelling at Nikita Khrushchev in Moscow seemed to do no harm, certainly not as much harm to Deng's own conscience as his earlier support for the Great Leap Forward.

In the final analysis, one may justify Deng's position in the Sino-Soviet polemics as a kind of Chinese nationalism or patriotism or even chauvinism. Without getting too far-fetched, however, I would simply ascribe Deng's performance to his personal desire to please Mao under the current circumstances. The more radical his position and the harder he argued with the Russians, the happier the chairman and the safer Deng's own political position. As for those works of Marx or Lenin, Deng had never cared to read them before, nor did he ever care to do so afterward.[20]

Even a casual review of Deng's public schedule reveals that, from after the CCP–CPSU talks in 1963 until the start of the Cultural Revolution in 1966, Deng continued to be intensively involved in international communist affairs, which fell under the jurisdiction of the CCP Central Committee, as opposed to state-to-state diplomatic affairs, which were handled by Chen Yi's Foreign Ministry in the State Council.

The radical position taken by the CCP in general and Deng in particular with regard to international communist affairs in 1962–65 did cause practical consequences—not always as harmless as Deng might flippantly have presumed. The dispute was not just a matter of idle chatter and cheerful quibbling; nor was it simply a matter of making an entertaining show abroad for the chairman to watch and enjoy at home, as Deng might apologetically have thought.

One example of immediate consequences was the disastrous defeat of the Indonesian Communist Party in 1965, for which the CCP should be held heavily responsible. General Secretary Aidit of the PKI (the Indonesian Communist Party) visited China three times during 1965, the last time in August of that year, just one month before the PKI's

September revolution. Aidit was warmly received by Deng each time. In that year alone, the CCP provided the PKI with as much as four hundred million yuan, for the latter to experiment with the Chinese model of armed struggle for the capture of state power. Although their confidential deals have not yet been fully revealed, the public result was the destruction of the PKI and the humiliation of the CCP.[21]

Another adverse consequence of the Moscow–Beijing dispute was the rapid rise in China's foreign aid expenditures from 1964 onward. While sweetly pontificating about world revolution, the Chinese communists also had to make a tangible contribution to world revolution. Prior to the Moscow talks of 1963, China's expenditures for foreign aid were rather modest. But in 1964, China's foreign aid rapidly grew to 1,240 million yuan, or 3.1 percent of the national budget. In 1965, the figure rose to 2,080 million yuan, or 4.5 percent of the national budget.[22]

The various eloquent positions that Deng expressed during the Sino-Russian polemics were, for the most part, patently absurd: world war(s) is (are) allegedly inevitable as long as imperialism exists; the only way to achieve socialism is through armed struggles, not parliamentary elections; neither cooperation nor even coexistence with any capitalist country can be allowed; the Communist Party is a party of the proletarian class, not of the people; and so on and so forth. It is interesting that there has been no official correction or even discussion of these ingenious themes in modern China—obviously, because of Deng's personal involvement—even though the CCP has practically abandoned almost all these revolutionary fantasies.

It was in the wake of the Moscow talks that China began dispatching troops to North Vietnam, both to compete militarily with the United States and to carry out its doctrine of world revolution. From October 1964 onward, an average of 100,000 soldiers were secretly dispatched each year. By early 1968, the total number of Chinese troops in Vietnam had reached 320,000—mostly construction, railway, logistics, and antiaircraft forces—before a sudden withdrawal at Vietnam's earnest request. Although the full details of this story are also yet to be revealed, enough is known for us to conclude that China spent more than one hundred million U.S. dollars to expel the hostile Americans, only to create a more hostile Vietnam.[23]

It seemed in accordance with Deng's radical doctrines in international communism that Lin Biao, the defense minister and Deng's chief competitor for the role of Mao's successor since the mid-1950s, raised the even more radical notion of "the epoch of people's war" in 1965. Lin divided the contemporary world into the world of the cities and the world of the countryside—and the communist strategy was to incite the world's countryside to encircle the world's cities. Thus, what Deng thought a safe way to please Mao actually provided a foundation for his political archrival![24]

The "eighth commentary," composed by Deng's "writing squad" shortly after the Moscow talks, scaled another fresh theoretical height. It seemed that the CPSU's problem was not merely Khrushchev's revisionist policy in international affairs. The Soviet Union was domestically not a socialist country anymore! It had allegedly degenerated into a country of "socialist imperialism," boasting "a new capitalist class with special privileges," exploiting and suppressing the working people.

Mao could do nothing about the Soviet Union—Khrushchev's fall from power in 1964 did not have as much to do with the CCP's "nine commentaries" as Deng and his associates joyfully claimed—but Mao could do a great deal to fight revisionism in China under his own rule. Didn't the forthcoming "Great Proletarian Cultural Revolution" start with the slogan of fighting and preventing capitalist restoration? Didn't it attack as its main target "the newborn bourgeoisie with special privileges" and "the capitalist roaders in power"? For his happy and safe tour of Moscow, Deng would soon have to pay with humiliation and disgrace at home!

—— 14 ——

Bombardment from Within the General Headquarters, 1965-1972

On November 11, 1965, the *Literary Daily* in Shanghai published an article entitled "Commentary on the Newly Composed Historical Drama of Hai Rui's Dismissal," which did not catch the particular attention of ordinary readers at the time but eventually became the start of a huge political drama later called the "Great Proletarian Cultural Revolution." The author of the commentary, Yao Wenyuan, worked as a literary editor with the *Liberation Daily,* another influential Shanghai newspaper, so why was his article not published there? The title of the article made it sound as if it might be a piece of academic criticism on historical research and artistic performance, but it proved rather political, since it openly named Wu Han, the deputy mayor of Beijing, as the target of its harsh attack.

Understandably, once Mayor Peng Zhen of Beijing was informed of Yao's article, he suspected there might be more to the article than met the eye—perhaps some "weird background" behind the scenes. In view of party discipline, it would be abnormal for a Shanghai newspaper to publish an article attacking a senior Beijing official without the capital's Party Committee having been informed in advance. Peng's hunch proved quite right: Yao's article did indeed have a suspicious background. It was later revealed that Madame Mao and Chairman Mao Zedong himself had directly participated in drafting and revising

161

the article as many as eleven times over a period of nine months before it was finally published.[1]

On the same day in Beijing, coincidentally or not, Yang Shangkun was dismissed from his position as director of the General Office of the CCP Central Committee. The ostensible reason was that Yang was found to have installed a bugging device in Mao's guest room to record his private conversations. The real reason was that Chairman Mao wanted someone else, more obedient to himself personally than to the Party Center as an abstract whole, in charge of the General Office on the eve of an extraordinary political campaign he was determined to launch.

December 8, 1965, came as another special day. Luo Ruiqing, the army's chief of staff, was unexpectedly summoned to Shanghai from an inspection tour in Yunnan. A Military Council conference was already in session in Shanghai, at which Lin Biao, the minister of defense, was featured as the main speaker. Lin, his wife, and some high-ranking military leaders like Ye Jianying and Yang Chengwu competed with one another in attacking Luo Ruiqing. Luo was finally charged with various blunders and crimes such as organizing a military competition campaign to divert emphasis from politics and plotting to usurp Lin's superior command in the army.

In reality, Ye himself had sponsored the military competition campaign in 1964, which Mao had personally attended and enthusiastically approved. As far as Ye and Yang were concerned, Luo's dominant role in the army hierarchy in recent years, which had aroused resentment and jealousy among army leaders, might have been a more appropriate explanation, aside from following Mao's and Lin's orders. As a result of their anti-Luo performances, Ye moved ahead of several other marshals in the Military Council ranks, while Yang was appointed acting chief of staff in Luo's place, immediately after the conference.[2]

Although Mao chaired that Shanghai Conference in support of Lin's position, he himself had no ill feeling toward Luo. Because Marshal Lin also needed a more personally trustworthy lieutenant in the army, Mao was simply granting him the right to make that choice. Since Mao had by then chosen Lin Biao and the army as the basic foundation for his forthcoming showdown with Liu Shaoqi in the Party Center, Mao had little reluctance about granting Lin some minor concessions. Luo's ordeal was merely one such case in point.

Deng was anything but politically insensitive. He left for a tour of his old domain of the southwest in late November 1965, ostensibly to inspect war preparations there but actually to avoid involvement with the tangled political struggle in Beijing. Together with his family and staff, Deng took a specially appointed train and received a rousing welcome at Chongqing. Li Jingquan, the party secretary of the Southwest Region, held a banquet in Deng's honor. All possible delicacies, like swallows' nests and sharks' fins, were served; Deng drank only mao-tai and smoked only Panda-brand cigarettes. As the dinner ran late into the night, the general secretary stood up, smiling from ear to ear. "Shouldn't we also work a bit?" he asked, and then, to reassure the startled audience, quickly pulled a box of playing cards out of his pocket. "I mean work on this!" The cheerful group played bridge until dawn, without anybody uttering a word about Beijing politics, although it loomed large in everyone's mind, particularly Deng's.[3]

Deng returned to Beijing in late December 1965, only to find that, instead of having settled down, the chaotic situation had intensified and grown even more complicated. That was particularly true of the Peng Zhen issue, which could hardly be avoided by either Deng or Liu Shaoqi. Peng had worked with Liu ever since the 1930s in the North China Bureau; for many years, since 1956, Peng had also been Deng's chief deputy in the Secretariat, and they both shared so many things, public as well as private, in common. Wu Han was, in fact, one of Deng's bridge partners. Personal concerns aside, Deng did not like the contents of Yao's Shanghai article and, above all, the abnormal manner in which it had been published. Both Liu and Deng felt a great deal of sympathy toward Peng. Hence, there arose a subtle confrontation between the Party Center in Beijing and its chairman in Shanghai in late 1965 and early 1966.

Peng proved the hardest and nastiest nut for Mao to crack at the initial stage of the Cultural Revolution. Peng could not be fired as easily as Yang and Luo, for various reasons. Besides, given his strong base in Beijing, Peng did not flinch from openly crossing swords with the Shanghai people. Regardless of Yao's background behind the scenes, and regardless of his article's hint of a linkage between Wu Han and higher politics, in Peng's opinion, Yao should be held responsible for his public argument: whether there were some good government officials in older dynasties who had done some good things for the people and, more bluntly, whether an incorruptible official was even worse than a corrupt official in premodern history because his kindness to the people would simply mitigate their class struggle and thus prolong the feudalist regime, or vice versa. That was an academic subject, and Peng had no difficulty in gathering a group of the most famous historians in Beijing to debate it.[4]

The matter remained stalemated until March 1966. But as Mao in Shanghai increased his pressure, Peng was pushed further against the wall. Liu and Deng could not easily turn one way or the other. In routine fashion, they appointed a central group—including Peng Zhen, Lu Dingyi, Kang Sheng, Zhou Yang, and Wu Lengxi—to investigate these academic and cultural affairs. The five-man group produced a written report to the Party Center in February 1966. Peng's final position, as shown in the report, was that even though Wu Han and his like might be bourgeois intellectuals, the issue of whether they were anti-party elements politically should be decided by the party organization, not just by an individual writer.

Peng depended on party norms to defend himself. The later accusation against Peng, Luo, Lu, and Yang as a confidential antiparty clique had no factual validity; ironically, it somewhat resembled the way Deng had branded Gao Gang and Rao Shushi thirteen years before. Far from being a "political coup" engineered by Peng and company, what happened at the turn of 1965 and 1966 seemed more like a "cultural coup," so to speak, jointly engineered by Jiang Qing, Lin Biao, and Mao Zedong.

Mao and Lin kept working together. Some military units were moved about; hence, Lin's trusted Thirty-eighth Army was transferred to Baoding, close to Beijing. What did Peng do? In fact, what could he do? He consulted with Liu and Deng in Beijing and called on Mao in Hangzhou a couple of times. Neither tactic seemed to have worked in his favor. During Liu's absence from China on a state tour abroad, Mao won Zhou Enlai over on the Peng issue through Kang Sheng, who shrewdly rejected Peng and took Mao's side. Mao then won Deng over through Zhou, who had no special affection for Peng or Liu. Once Mao and Zhou showed a united front, Deng had little reluctance about abandoning Peng.[5]

Deng called an emergency conference of the Secretariat on April 9, 1966, and made the problem crystal clear to Peng—what can you say, as both Chairman Mao's and Premier Zhou's directives here are against you?—and subsequently flew, together with Zhou and Peng, to attend a Politburo conference ordered by Mao in Hangzhou on April

16, 1966. Mao was adamant, Zhou and Deng were supportive, and Peng's fate was sealed. Liu returned home only to chair another conference in Beijing the next month, just to settle an already settled issue.

The real issues nevertheless remained to be resolved—the issue of Liu Shaoqi himself and, complexly intertwined with Liu as an individual distasteful to Mao, the issue of the mass movement, or the Proletarian Cultural Revolution. On May 25, 1966, with the personal encouragement of Kang Sheng and his wife, Nie Yuanzi put up a big-character poster on the campus of Beijing University. The poster's contents—nothing more than chastising the university president, as she had done in the socialist education campaign two years earlier—were not as important as the very manner of its publication. It set a precedent of expressing opposition to local party leadership by publicly exposing and attacking individual leaders rather than by officially appealing to higher-level party committees.[6]

Nie's poster caused great commotion and confusion among teachers and students, and Beijing University was soon ablaze with unrest. Kang shrewdly reported on this "spontaneous mass movement" not to Liu or Deng at the Party Center in Beijing, but to Mao in his private villa in Hangzhou. Mao directly ordered Kang to have the *People's Daily* publish Nie's "first Marxist-Leninist poster" on June 1, followed by a supportive editorial drafted by Mao's secretary, Chen Boda, with the amazingly bold title "Sweep Away All Demons and Ghosts!"

Liu and Deng were caught off guard, and Beijing seethed with protests! Teachers and students at all universities and most high schools followed the Beijing University example and rose up to denounce their own party leaders. It looked like 1957 but proved unlike 1957. This time, the party chairman stood firmly behind the intellectual rebels. Liu and Deng rushed to Hangzhou again, urging Mao to return to handle the emergency situation himself. Mao refused and simply encouraged Liu to continue to lead.[7]

Mao had said he believed that "Rebellions have justified reasons" and that "Chaos is a good thing." Unless Liu shared those beliefs, however, he would have to do something about the student uprisings. Liu could imagine no other solution than the old socialist education campaign tactic of sending work teams to the universities and colleges. To play it safe, Liu consulted with Deng and Zhou in Beijing. Deng agreed, as did Zhou. Neither of them could regard it as normal for students to rise up against party officials and professors.

Still fresh in Liu's and Deng's minds was the Mao-instigated "Twenty-three Points," which forbade merely relying on the masses at the expense of party cadres. The work teams were therefore instructed to support the students but also to protect the school leaders. In reality, they found it nearly impossible to do either! The students wanted to "kick out the party committee to make revolution"—something with which the work teams could hardly agree. The students then wanted to "kick out the work teams to make revolution"—something with which Liu could hardy agree, nor could Deng.

Deng always paid more attention to high politics than to mass movements. It was not the students—or what he used to call the "young babies"—but the power players whom Deng cared most about. Without directly challenging the students, who were presumably backed by Mao, Deng tried to take as moderate a position as possible. At one time, during his tour of Beijing Normal University in June 1966, he told the students, "There is at least one thing I would like to clarify for you. There has been a rumor about what is called Peng Zhen's 'February mutiny.' Here I can assure you: Peng Zhen could not move any of our troops; neither could I myself. Only Chairman Mao can transfer our troops, and nobody else."[8]

On July 18, 1966, Mao finally returned to Beijing, after the work teams' predicament had grown quite apparent. Two weeks later, Mao personally attended a mass rally in the Great Hall of the People. Zhou Enlai was entrusted to announce the immediate recall and dismissal of all the work teams. Liu and Deng were pressed to admit their mistake in "dispatching the work teams to suppress the revolutionary masses."

In his forced self-criticism speech, Liu could not help complaining a little: "You ask me how to make the Cultural Revolution. Here I answer you frankly that I don't know, nor do I think other Party Center comrades know." By contrast, Deng confessed more profoundly, "During the past two months, the chairman was away from Beijing, and Comrade Shaoqi and I were in charge of the Standing Committee's routine affairs. Soon after we sent out the work teams, there occurred suppression of the leftists, struggles among the masses, and conflicts of the masses with the work teams. . . . I have committed various mistakes in general direction and line. Dispatching the work teams was one of my mistakes, among numerous others."[9]

It took a couple of more months for Liu to realize, "No matter what I had done then, sending or not sending the work teams, I would always have been wrong. My very position in the Party Center was wrong. Let me step down, and let them come up. Then everything should be all right." Well, that was right, but not yet all right. Liu should have said that his very existence was wrong. He would eventually be carried out of Zhongnanhai, the Party Center compound, on a stretcher, beaten and sick, and die in Kaifeng, Henan, in November 1969.

It should be noted that, throughout these years 1960–66, when the two men shared the same moderate stand against Mao's radical policy, Deng still kept a certain distance from Liu—quite apparent at certain times, more subtle at other times. Deng always maintained a high respect for Mao's authority. Perhaps he had not entirely forgotten his original mission to check the Party Center personnel on Mao's behalf, for which he had been promoted in the mid-1950s. Each of them— Mao, Liu, and Zhou—might think that Deng had somewhat betrayed them, but none of them would ever really hate Deng.

The Eleventh Plenum of the Eighth Congress, held in Beijing in August 1966, was perhaps the only occasion in post-1949 communist history on which two rival leaders, Liu Shaoqi and Mao Zedong, not only openly argued against each other but also privately lobbied the voters on their own behalf. Deng shifted his position toward Mao once again. Consequently, he was included in the Politburo Standing Committee, ranking behind the new stars, Tao Zhu and Chen Boda, but ahead of Liu Shaoqi, Zhu De, and Chen Yun for the first time. Who knew what Mao might really intend to do, within or outside the party? Who knew what might eventually happen to Deng, good or bad?[10]

The great Cultural Revolution was, if nothing else, "historically unprecedented" indeed. Chairman Mao seemed to have adopted an approach that could be characterized as "the messier, the merrier." He called fourteen million high school and college students, or Red Guards, from all over the country to Beijing for nine mass rallies blessed by his personal attendance and then sent them back to "make rebellions" against their governors, mayors, and party leaders. In the meantime, Deng suffered ever harsher criticism, politically and personally, from within and outside the party apparatus.[11] He felt increasingly at a loss over the entire situation; the one matter he remained clear on was the need to strive for his own survival, political as well as physical.

After reading yet another of Deng's exaggerated confessions at the party work conference in late October 1966, Mao wrote a few words of reply on Deng's paper: "Don't be so pessimistic. Add some things more encouraging for the future!" Deng must have felt slightly comforted by the fact that Mao's remarks sounded rather mild and amiable. It should be noted that even Mao's well-known criticisms of Deng, such as "He never came to see me" and "He treated me like a dead ancestor," did not sound really hateful; rather, they sounded more like an aging father's complaint about a heedless child.[12]

On August 5, 1967, at the mass trial of Liu and Deng in Zhongnanhai, Liu appeared more dignified and held his own ground throughout the trial. Questioned by the revolutionary rebels, he did not admit any serious crimes and thus got his back broken by the Red Guards. Deng, on the other hand was, or at least appeared, far more submissive and repentant and, as a result, suffered no physical torture. The following is an excerpt from the Zhongnanhai trial published at the time:

> RED GUARD: Aren't you a capitalist roader in power within the party?
> LIU: No, I am not, though I did make some mistakes while working for the party.
> DENG: Yes, I am.
> RED GUARD: Do you oppose our great leader Chairman Mao?
> LIU: No, I don't.
> DENG: No, I don't. But I opposed Mao Zedong thought.
> RED GUARD: Why did you trust and support Peng Zhen?
> LIU: Because he would never deceive me.
> DENG: Because he had deceived me.[13]

That was the only public trial of Deng during the Cultural Revolution—and it was not exactly public, as it took place inside the Zhongnanhai compound. It happened at the very crest of the radicals' push, just after the Wuhan revolt, in which local troops detained two Party Center envoys, and before the British Consulate was burned down in a mass riot. A few days after the latter incident, Mao had the radicals Wang Li and Guan Feng purged. The leftist momentum was subsequently reversed in the fall of 1967, as far as the central power struggle was concerned.

Then came 1968, a year of messy and muddy violence at the grassroots level throughout China. Ironically, Deng lived peacefully in an isolated house, though much smaller than his previous one, in Zhongnanhai, together with his wife and stepmother. One might call it house arrest or whatever. The Dengs were not free to go outside, but neither did they want to. Here, life was safer! Food and groceries were regularly delivered, and they managed the cooking and household chores by themselves. Their children, including the handicapped Pufang and the fifteen-year-old Zhifang, were all out of touch, but besides missing and thinking of them, what else could they do in those extraordinary days?[14]

The Twelfth Plenum of the Eighth Congress, in October 1968, formally decided that both Liu and Deng should be removed from all their party and government posts; that went without saying. Liu was expelled from the party and would undergo further investigation by a special committee, actually headed by Zhou. Deng, on the other hand, was allowed to keep his party membership, without the need for a special investigation— that was a big difference between Deng and Liu. Mao did not treat the two equally; he reserved the possibility of another chance for Deng.

In October 1969, as a result of nationwide preparations for war with the Russians, Deng was among a few dozen party veterans dispatched from Beijing to distant provinces. Almost all these veteran cadres had lost their posts in the Cultural Revolution, but they were nevertheless divided into two categories: those of "contradictions among the people," like Zhu De and Chen Yun; and those of "contradictions with the enemy," like Liu Shaoqi and Peng Zhen. The case of Deng seemed a bit unclear. He was the "number two capitalist roader" and yet still kept his Communist Party membership.

Along with Chen Yun and Wang Zhen, Deng Xiaoping was sent to Jiangxi Province. Before their departure, Zhou Enlai personally conferred with Jiangxi provincial officials about policy instructions and practical arrangements. He called Chen and Wang comrades, mentioned that Deng even remained a party member, and specified that they should all be well treated physically and never abused.[15]

Deng's three-year banishment—from October 20, 1969, to February 20, 1973—in Xinjian County, Jiangxi, was the least known at the time but has become the best known today because of the recent publications of his own daughter's reminiscences and several journalistic reports. It seemed to be an ideal period for the eventual production of hagiographic literature: one of few national secrets, few complicated power clashes, few embarrassing criticisms and self-criticisms, and yet a lot of family harmony and political glory when viewed in retrospect.

The Dengs lived in a two-story building, previously occupied by a junior general and the master of an infantry training school, then closed and vacant. It was half an hour's walk away from Xinjian County's tractor-repair factory, where Deng and his wife worked in the mornings, he as a machine operator and she as a workshop cleaner. The Dengs took one room and the stepmother another, both on the first floor, while two People's Liberation Army soldiers, as security guards and housekeepers, had the second floor. Later, when the political atmosphere improved for Deng, and one child after another came to join them, the Deng family took over the entire building.[16]

But during his stay in Jiangxi, for instance, did Deng really peruse the twenty-four classic histories, as his daughter Deng Rong reported and Harrison Salisbury believed? Hardly! Deng was no Mao, for better or for worse. He could barely read the classical language. It was not his habit to read through anything long, to say nothing of those formidable historical volumes. Like many a Sichuanese, Deng could talk, and sometimes talk rough, but he could not read tough.

Every day, Deng would walk back and forth in his little courtyard in front of the building, until his feet wore a narrow path in the brown soil. "Watching his sure and yet fast-moving steps," his youngest daughter, Deng Rong, recalled in her memoirs, "I thought to myself that his faith, his ideas, and his determination must have grown clearer and firmer, preparing himself for the struggles lying ahead."[17]

From its very outset, the alliance between Mao Zedong and Lin Biao bore the stamp of mutual expediency, which Mao was aware of far earlier than Lin. Reading through Lin's speech at the Politburo conference of May 1966, Mao grew worried, as he certainly should have. The chairman might indeed have disliked Peng and Yang, Liu and Deng, but what about now hearing Marshal Lin declare, "These SOBs want to kill us, and we must kill them. If we do not kill them, they will kill us," and listening to him lecture that "Chinese history is nothing but a history of coup d'état, of candle flashes and knife shadows"![18]

Despite his bluffing statements, such as that China had no fear of sacrificing one-third of its population in a nuclear war with the Russians, did Mao really expect to have a Sino-Soviet war in October 1969 and therefore require a "number one national emergency combat order," as Lin declared? Even if he did, Mao would have issued the order himself rather than having Lin do so. Mao particularly resented Lin's breaking the rule that he alone could issue war orders and transfer troops. Mao thus called Huang Yongsheng, the chief of the army's general staff, to have Lin's emergency order rescinded at once.

With Liu and Deng removed from the Party Center through the joint efforts of Lin Biao and Jiang Qing—each thought his or her contribution was the bigger one—and with Zhou Enlai of the State Council remaining instrumentally useful as ever, Lin of the Military Council and Jiang of the Cultural Revolution Group found themselves embroiled in another round of the intraparty power clash. The matter of succession was not as settled as the party constitution said and as people like Chen Boda thought. Chen, who truly regarded Lin as the future party leader and himself as Lin's literary deputy, became Mao's first and easiest target of punishment at the Lushan Conference in August 1970.

Lin did not seem to appreciate the problem fully until it was too late. Under Mao's devious pressure and incitement, he apparently grew desperate. He tried to flee to the Soviet Union but ended up dying when his airplane crashed in the Mongolian desert on September 13, 1971. From one extreme of antirevisionism to the other extreme of prorevisionism, Lin at least provided an illustration of Mao's philosophy on contradictions and also of his own philosophy on Chinese history, both in ironic ways![19] In handling the Lin Biao incident, Zhou Enlai proved useful indeed to Mao. More than that, Zhou took charge of overall party, government, and army affairs soon afterward, from late 1971 until late 1972.

Secluded in the distant south as a political exile, it was not until two months afterward, in November 1971, that Deng learned of the Lin Biao incident. The whole family was thrilled, as Deng's chief enemy was removed and the general political condition changed overnight. It was reported that, when informed of Lin's fate, Deng's first words were, "Heaven damned Lin to death!" He promptly wrote a letter to Mao on November 15, 1971. In the letter, Deng said that he felt infuriated at Lin's treachery and overjoyed at Mao's victory. He asked gingerly whether it would be possible for him also to take part in the mass criticism of Lin.

Although it seemed at first that Deng's letter neither received a formal response nor had an immediate effect, it was hardly in vain. Mao got the letter, read it, and put it aside—but kept it in his heart. A few months later, in January 1972, while attending Chen Yi's funeral, the chairman made a few seemingly casual remarks to the mourners:

"Chen Yi is a good comrade . . . and Deng Xiaoping's case is also one of contradictions among the people."[20]

Did Deng learn of Mao's remarks? Obviously he did, one way or another. Subsequently, Deng found that his living conditions were gradually improved, and a couple of provincial leaders even came to visit him. In the early months of 1972, Deng must have written quite a number of other letters to Beijing for various purposes. At least one or two were concerned with better treatment for his eldest son, Deng Pufang, who had suffered severe injuries at Beijing University during the Cultural Revolution several years before.

Deng Pufang was allowed to return to Beijing for treatment in May 1972. He was accompanied by his younger sister, Deng Rong, as he checked into the No. 301 Army Hospital, one of the best in China. To Deng Rong's surprise, Wang Zhen, already back in Beijing, sent word that he wanted to see her. During their meeting, Wang asked the girl to convey a message to her father that his problem would soon be solved and that Wang promised to try to talk with Mao personally about it. Did Wang really talk to Mao, or even if he did, did it have any effect? As corny a veteran soldier as he might be, Wang already sensed that Deng's return to power was imminent and felt it was high time to show Deng a little personal concern.

To strike while the iron was still hot, Deng addressed another letter directly to Mao on August 3, 1972. The letter began with, "As the chairman knows, Lin Biao and Chen Boda hated me and would rather have put me to death. I can hardly imagine what might have happened to me but for the chairman's protection." He went on to apologize for his past errors and to conclude sentimentally, "It has been almost six years since I have been out of work and out of society. I have always been looking forward to an opportunity to return to the chairman's revolutionary line. Being sixty-eight years old and still in decent health, I may still work seven or eight more years for the party and for the people, redeeming some small part of my previous blunders."[21]

This time, Mao was sufficiently moved. Deng was no Peng Dehuai, who had stubbornly refused to write to Mao in person in early 1962. But once Mao received Peng's apologetic letter in 1965, he responded positively, thus ending their mental tug-of-war. As regards Deng's letter, Mao issued a rather long response. "Despite his serious mistakes," Mao stated, "Deng Xiaoping differs from Liu Shaoqi." Mao then listed three of Deng's key merits: his having had no serious historical problem, his having been persecuted as Mao's follower in the Jiangxi Soviet, and his wartime performance and anti-Soviet activities. Mao's edict concluded with some emphasis, "I have said all this many times before, and I am now saying it once again."[22]

It should particularly be noted that the tone of this last sentence appeared quite heavy. It sounded as if Mao had grown impatient with some people who had been holding the Deng issue up, though it is hard to pinpoint exactly who they might be. Anyhow, Mao's directives decisively paved the royal road for Deng's rehabilitation. Yet it took Deng another half a year of anxious waiting, for one reason or another, before he would actually be called back to Beijing in February 1973.

— 15 —

The Capitalist Roader
Back on the Road, 1973-1975

Notified of a summons by the Party Center, Deng Xiaoping and his family left Jiangxi by train on February 20, 1973, and arrived in Beijing the next day. But it took a few more weeks for the top leaders to work out a formal resolution of his case. There were debates over Deng's work assignment. Some suggested appointing him to a technical or research job. (Hadn't Deng himself asked for that in his own letter to the chairman?) The final decision was Mao Zedong's, but it is not entirely unbelievable that, as she herself later claimed, Jiang Qing showed more favor to Deng than many others. A Party Center resolution was formally passed on March 20, 1973, restoring Deng's "party organizational life and deputy premier position."[1]

At an evening banquet hosted by Premier Zhou Enlai in honor of Prince Norodom Sihanouk of Cambodia in the Great Hall of the People on April 12, 1973, Deng made his first public appearance since his 1966 disgrace. It was a surprise to the audience, but a happy one—greeted by a sudden outburst of loud applause. After six years of exile, Deng seemed almost to have forgotten the entrance to the Great Hall. Wang Hairong, Mao's niece and a foreign affairs official, had to usher him in. Zhou then introduced Deng to Sihanouk as the "deputy premier."[2]

Three days later, Heishirou Ogawa, Japan's first ambassador to the People's Republic of China (PRC) after the normalization of diplomatic relations, encountered Deng at Beijing Airport. Together with Deputy Premier Li Xiannian, Deng was seeing a Chinese delegation off to visit Tokyo. He still appeared a bit uncomfortable and lacking in

174

confidence during his brief conversation with Ambassador Ogawa. When questioned by Ogawa, Deng would frequently turn to consult his Chinese colleagues before responding.

For quite a few years, the consensus of belief has been that it was Zhou Enlai's idea to bring Deng back to the central leadership. Supposedly, Premier Zhou was found to have incurable cancer in 1972 and had to look around for a faithful and capable assistant. He therefore twisted Mao's arm to request that Deng be restored to work as deputy premier. Mao eventually granted Zhou's request, despite the strong opposition of Jiang Qing and other radicals.[3]

This consensus, superficially sweet and smooth, was nevertheless not quite accurate, for communist politics seldom proves so sweet and smooth. In Deng's own words, it was Chairman Mao, not Premier Zhou, to whom he owed his 1973 restoration. "Under certain circumstances, Mao thought I could again be useful and therefore brought me back from the grave." Deng then added in conclusion, "That is the whole mystery."[4]

Deng offered no further explanation as to exactly what circumstances had made Mao think Deng could again be useful at that moment. It seems to me that Deng's statement quoted above presented another mixture of truth and falsehood—and definitely did not explain the "whole mystery." To say the very least, for instance, how about Deng's own considerable effort in having written one letter after another to the chairman admitting his previous errors and asking that his party work be restored?

Needless to say, Deng would not just have dropped his letters to Mao into a local mailbox on the nearest corner. Normally, letters of such an important nature would hardly have been held up at intermediate levels. Instead, they were most likely passed through the Jiangxi Provincial Committee to the General Office of the Party Center and eventually to Zhou and Mao themselves.

Zhou, who was in charge of the Party Center's daily affairs, must have known about Deng's letters, but he lacked the authority, as well as perhaps the inclination, to bring Deng back to Beijing. Had he showed such an inclination, it might have sidetracked the whole deal rather than expediting it. Zhou indeed asked Mao to allow Deng to work with him in the State Council, as Hu Yaobang later implied, but that was in all likelihood after Deng's return to Beijing. Already, at that point, the real question was not whether Deng should be restored, but how.

As a matter of fact, Zhou himself ran into great trouble at that time, not only physically but also politically. Most Western biographers have learned by now that Zhou was first diagnosed with incurable stomach cancer sometime in the spring of 1972, but few of them yet seem to have fully realized his political predicament during the years 1972–74.

The early months of 1972 seemed fine for Zhou, who was put in charge of the Politburo's routine affairs because of Lin Biao's sudden death and Mao's continuing refusal to play any frontline role. He worked hard on rebuilding the national economy and rehabilitating veteran cadres to central or provincial leadership posts, both under the general slogan of rectifying Lin's "leftist line."

Zhou's moderate policy did not last long; Jiang Qing and her radical colleagues soon found another ideological weapon with which to fight back. They argued, and Mao seemed to agree, that Lin's problem was not an "ultraleftist" one, as Zhou said, but rather an "ultrarightist" one. Hadn't Lin attempted to appeal to the revisionist Soviet Union? Zhou's criticism of Lin as a leftist and what Zhou did in general in 1972 therefore became a rightist tendency and a target of renewed intraparty struggle. It was only through great patience and political expertise that Zhou managed to maintain his position intact.[5]

In this biography of Deng, space constraints prevent me from delving into the complicated details of Chinese Communist Party (CCP) politics at that time. Rather than simply accepting the idea that Zhou persuaded Mao to call Deng back to the central leadership, however, we may surmise that Mao wanted Deng back precisely because of his disillusion with Zhou, both personal and political, coupled with his illusion that Deng might serve as a check against Zhou's overall influence, more or less as Mao had used Deng against Liu Shaoqi during the 1950s.

Anybody who cares to flip through the *People's Daily* news reports from 1973 should have little difficulty reconstructing Deng's schedule of governmental activities during that year. From mid-April onward, Deng appeared publicly on about one hundred occasions, mostly receiving foreign visitors and sometimes attending holiday ceremonies, offering a greeting at conferences, going to funerals, and so forth.

Normally, at that time, when foreign heads of state arrived, Premier Zhou, together with Deputy Premiers Li Xiannian and Deng Xiaoping, would welcome them at Beijing Airport; hold formal talks with them in the Great Hall; accompany them to meet Chairman Mao at his Zhongnanhai residence (without Li and Deng); arrange for Li and Deng to escort them on tours of places like the Palace Museum and the Great Wall in Beijing and of other cities such as Shanghai and Canton; and finally give them a sendoff at Beijing Airport with Zhou, Li, and Deng all present or at another airport more convenient for their travel plans with only Li and Deng present.

Here is a list of Deng's meetings with foreign dignitaries after his rehabilitation in April 1973. Although some of these visitors were not heads of state, they were highly respected by the Chinese communists at the time: April 12, Prince Norodom Sihanouk of Cambodia; April 19–22, the president of Mexico; April 25, the prime minister of Cambodia; May 8, Prince Sihanouk of Cambodia; June 4–8, a delegation from the North Vietnamese Communist Party and government; June 21–27, the president of Mali; July 27–31, the president of the Congo; August 11–14, the president of France; August 21–24, the deputy prime minister of Egypt; October 10–17, the prime minister of Canada; November 1–4, the prime minister of Australia; November 6–10, the president of Sierra Leone; November 18–23, the chairman of the South Vietnamese National Liberation Front; December 7–14, the king and queen of Nepal.[6]

Except for Mao's rare receptions—presumably the highest honor for both foreign visitors and their Chinese companions—Deng participated in the entire process of diplomatic etiquette. In the case of foreign guests holding official positions below the level of head of state, Li and/or Deng would normally take full charge of the visits from arrival to departure, without Zhou's personal involvement.

Day in and day out, Deng kept ushering in and sending off one group of foreign dignitaries after another. It seemed that he was serving as a diplomatic functionary with no high political ambition. It was like a repetition of his experience twenty years before, when he had just come from Chongqing to Beijing. Deng seemed to be merely one of several deputy premiers, having no substantial influence in either the party or the army.

In retrospect, the years 1973–74 indeed bore some similarity to 1952–53 as far as Deng's own political performance was concerned. Both were periods during which Mao retrained Deng and retested his suitability for higher leadership. Deng's patience would eventually pay off. Actually, Mao kept his eyes wide open to what Deng was currently doing but kept his mouth tightly shut about what he might want Deng to do later. Once that mouth opened, however, it would issue firm orders!

The CCP's Tenth National Congress in August 1973 was marked by a sharp division in the Party Center between Zhou's majority veteran leadership and Jiang's radical opposition. Surprisingly and yet understandably, Mao decided to have Wang Hongwen, a junior member of Jiang's group, promoted to become deputy chairman of the party and his candidate for the role of Mao's successor. As a freshly restored cadre, Deng didn't yet seem to belong to either side. Nevertheless, Deng resumed his membership on the CCP Central Committee—nothing more and nothing less.

Enough was enough! The testing period should be over. Thus, on December 12, 14, and 15, 1973, Mao mentioned Deng's name in a positive way on three formal occasions, saying, "Deng is pretty resolute in tackling problems," and, "Deng is a man of 'softness melded with toughness,' just like 'a needle wrapped in cotton.'" Finally, Mao proposed that Deng be included as a full member of both the Politburo and the Central Military Council.[7]

Coincidentally or not, it was also at this very juncture when he was rapidly promoting Deng that Chairman Mao once again harshly chastised Premier Zhou, who was responsible for the Politburo's routine duties, and Marshal Ye Jianying, who was in charge of the Central Military Council. "The Politburo does not care about matters of politics," Mao loudly complained, "nor does the Military Council care about military affairs."

Besides his concern with the central leadership, Mao ordered that the assignments of the eight military district commanders be rotated. Only a bodyguard and an assistant were allowed to accompany each commander to his new appointment in another military district. This measure stemmed less from any practical necessity than from Mao's quixotic mentality. Before the generals left for their new posts, Mao called them together in Zhongnanhai and personally led them in singing a chorus from the old Jinggang Mountains army song "Three Disciplines and Eight Attentions." What a sensational scene!

There is a widely circulated story that, sometime in the fall of 1973, Mao dispatched Deng Xiaoping and Wang Hongwen on a joint inspection tour throughout the country. Upon their return, Mao summoned them for a report and asked them what they thought would happen in

China after his death. Wang answered, "[T]he whole country will continue to follow the chairman's revolutionary line and unite to carry out the revolution to the end"; Deng responded, "Warlords will emerge, and a civil war will break out, and there will be national division." Mao, apparently more satisfied with the response from the elderly Deng than with the response from the young Wang, thus decided to rotate the military district commanders.[8]

This story, which originated with some source in Hong Kong and seemed ideal for adoption by certain Deng hagiographers, is not quite accurate. No factual evidence or logical ground can be found for Mao having sent Deng and Wang off on such a joint tour in late 1973. Nevertheless, it must be true that Mao's growing discontent with Wang's naïveté and immaturity, among other factors, had contributed to Deng's rapid promotion in 1973 and 1974. Mao once told Wang to his face, "Politically, you are no good, and Deng Xiaoping is far better."

From April 4 to 16, 1974, Deng led the Chinese delegation to a special session of the United Nations General Assembly in New York City. Previously, in March, at a Politburo meeting held to discuss the matter, Jiang Qing had objected to Deng's having been chosen to head the delegation. This prompted a letter from Mao in which he told her, "Deng's appointment abroad is my idea. It is better for you not to stand against it. You should be cautious not to oppose my opinions."

The central topic of the United Nations session was international cooperation and development, but Deng, in his forty-minute speech on April 10, dealt with far broader issues. Somewhat analogous to his argument with the Russians in Moscow in 1963 about the CCP's position on the general line of international communism, his speech sounded like a declaration of the PRC's general line of world politics. In 1963, it had been the doctrine of proletarian revolution and dictatorship; now, it was the "three worlds theory."

Deng alleged that the planet today was divided into three worlds. The first world consisted of the two superpowers—namely, the United States and the Soviet Union—which were the international exploiters, oppressors, seekers of hegemony, and instigators of war. Somewhat to the relief of American listeners, Deng stressed that "the superpower that flaunts the banner of socialism is particularly vicious and dangerous." The existence of the superpowers and their hegemonic ambitions would most probably result in the outbreak of world war. By the second world, Deng meant industrially developed countries such as those of Western Europe and Japan. These countries had a dual nature: sometimes, they shared the superpowers' benefits and interests, and at other times, they resented the superpowers' threats and control.

Deng's third world consisted of the undeveloped or developing countries of Asia, Africa, and Latin America. These countries constituted the revolutionary force fighting against superpower imperialism and hegemonism and advancing the course of world history. China belonged to the third world and would always stand by the third world countries. It would never become another superpower, according to Deng's speech, despite its potential to do so.[9]

Deng did not leave New York immediately after the UN conference. He decided to stay on for a few more days touring the city. This was his first visit to America and his first to the West in nearly fifty years. The Broadway skyscrapers and Times Square subway station seemed awesome to him. The sharp contrast between American progress and Chinese backwardness was too obvious to deny. He would never afterward talk lightly about catching up with America in a few years. Later, in 1980, he encouraged his youngest son, Deng Zhifang, to study in America, saying, "You will see what a modern world looks like."

Deng's UN speech had been carefully drafted at home by foreign affairs officials and international relations scholars. Once again, they crammed the pretty flowers of their world knowledge into the vase of the revolutionary dogmas that Mao was selling. Deng just had to recite the text to the General Assembly. He did this very well—calmly, firmly, and fluently—as he had done in Moscow in 1963. From a personal standpoint, it turned out to be a successful performance for him. Deng was no theoretician and did not even think too much about the contents of the speech. As time passed and his own position changed, Deng practically tossed out most of this dogma in later years.

Deng's UN speech drew a lot of attention and won him considerable publicity outside China. More important, back at home, Mao was pleased with Deng's performance. A large part of Mao's later life hinged on international activities. He received foreign visitors far more frequently in 1973–75 than during any previous period of his life. The three-world theory was regarded as one of his most creative contributions to the international communist canon. Mao was therefore happy that its first public presentation went well, thanks to Deng as his spokesman.

Upon his arrival at Beijing Airport on April 19, 1974, Deng was warmly greeted by Premier Zhou and almost all the senior party, government, and army leaders, including Jiang Qing and her radical colleagues. Here I say almost all, because Chairman Mao himself was not present, but that did not really matter. Mao would soon make up for that, and what Mao would offer Deng was far more than just a simple greeting!

After his return from abroad, some change, perhaps considerable change, could be seen in the nature of Deng's public appearances. When Mao received foreigners, Zhou Enlai and Wang Hongwen used to be present. Obviously, Mao had wanted to train Wang as a candidate to succeed him. After a few months' trial and error, however, Mao found that this former steelworker still could not learn to conduct himself appropriately and remained an embarrassment in the presence of foreign dignitaries. Mao had Deng take Wang's place from May 1974 onward, when the following dignitaries were received: May 11, Prime Minister Zulfikar Ali Bhutto of Pakistan; May 18, the president of Cypress; May 25, former Prime Minister Edward Heath of Great Britain; September 4, the president of Togo; September 17, the president of Mauritania; October 5, the president of Gabon; October 20, Prime Minister Poul Hartling of Denmark; November 12, the presidential chairman of South Yemen; December 17, the president of Zaire.[10]

Access to Mao had become an absolutely crucial determinant of one's standing in Beijing's power structure. Not only was it a symbol of one's existing political fortune, but it also represented an opportunity to further enhance one's political fortune. An individual's entire political fate might be sealed just by getting a quick signature, a simple word in writing or orally, a nod of assent or a shake of the head in dissent from this octogenarian lying flat on his sickbed!

In June 1974, Premier Zhou checked into Beijing Hospital permanently. He would remain there for the last eighteen months of his life, leaving rarely and briefly, only for a few special occasions. At roughly the same time, Chairman Mao left Beijing for Changsha, in the south, because of his own declining health. He remained there recuperating for more than half a year and did not return to Beijing until the spring of 1975.

In Beijing, the central leadership became more divided and mutually isolated. The Party Center was headed by Wang Hongwen; the State Council, by Deng; and the Military Council, by Ye Jianying. Only

Wang could officially contact Mao through Zhang Yufeng, his secretary and mistress. But in fact, Deng could see Mao more often than Wang by accompanying foreign visitors to Mao's receptions.

As his position grew higher and his responsibilities heavier, it became more difficult for Deng to avoid conflict with the radicals, especially the quick-tempered and self-willed Jiang Qing, or Madame Mao. At a Politburo meeting chaired by Wang Hongwen on October 17, 1974, Deng and Jiang crossed verbal swords for the first time. The argument started over a casual matter. It was reported that a Chinese-made cruiser, the *Fengqing,* had just successfully finished its maiden voyage abroad. It was a good thing, and everybody was happy. But Jiang claimed this event as a grand victory in the class struggle of the proletariat over the bourgeoisie and went on to condemn any purchase of foreign ships as constituting a capitalist line. Deng could not easily accept that kind of extravagance. Regardless of Jiang's pushing him to express his opinion, Deng sat there silent. Pushed again, Deng did express his opinion: "What's the big deal? It is just a ship, not even as large as the one that carried me to France fifty years ago!" Jiang flared up, and fierce altercations broke out. Eventually, Deng stood up and walked out of the conference hall.[11]

It was unusual for a Politburo conference to be this fractious. Shocked and angered, Jiang and the radicals decided to send Wang to see Mao in Changsha about this and other issues involving not only Deng but also Zhou, Ye, and other veterans. In the face of such common challenges, Deng and Zhou were drawn closer together. Zhou called Deng to the hospital for a talk and afterward called in Wang Hairong and Nancy Tang, two young female diplomats who were scheduled to accompany a group of foreigners to meet Mao in a few days. "They [Jiang Qing and her like] have been bullying Comrade Deng Xiaoping for quite a long time," Zhou told Wang and Tang, obviously intending not so much to complain to these young women as to use them to pass the same message along to Chairman Mao. "Comrade Deng Xiaoping can hardly put up with them anymore."[12]

On October 20, Deng accompanied Prime Minister Poul Hartling of Denmark to meet Mao in Changsha. Deng performed his duties as usual, not mentioning his recent quarrels with Mao's wife to the chairman. He would rather leave the two young women to do that on his behalf. As it turned out, Deng's low-key approach worked well. During his meeting with Wang Hongwen a few days later, Mao scolded

Jiang as an egoist and warned Wang against forming a "Gang of Four." As for Deng, Mao proposed assigning him greater responsibilities in party, government, and army affairs.

The problem of succession continued to loom large in the mind of the elderly Mao, but he had still found no solution. Two of his designated successors, Liu and Lin, had failed him, or he had failed them. Mao had ruled out Zhou as his successor as early as 1972 and did not even want to die leaving Zhou alive as such. At the Tenth Congress and shortly afterward, Mao had toyed with the idea of Wang Hongwen as a candidate for the role of his successor. The idea did not work out well. Now, in 1974, Mao began amusing himself with the possibility of choosing Deng as his successor. Mao did not like the radicals as individuals, nor did he like the moderates as a group. Perhaps Deng could be an exception, standing above the flaws of both camps.

On December 25, five days after Deng had accompanied President Seseseko Mobutu of Zaire to see Mao, Mao met with Wang Hongwen and Zhou Enlai; the pair had flown from Beijing to Changsha to confer with him regarding personnel arrangements for the upcoming Second Plenum of the Party Center and Fourth National People's Congress. "Deng is a man of rare talents. He has a strong sense of politics," Mao told Zhou and Wang. At the same time, he proposed that Deng be appointed concurrently to the posts of deputy chairman of the CCP Central Committee, first deputy premier of the State Council, deputy chairman of the Military Council, and chief of staff of the People's Liberation Army. The only thing Mao stopped short of saying was that he had made Deng his new successor. Actually he did, but actually he did not!

Mao had attempted to use Deng to check Liu in the 1950s, and eventually Deng shifted to side with Liu in the 1960s. This time, Mao tried to use Deng to check Zhou in 1973–74, but eventually, Deng shifted to side with Zhou in 1974–75. Deng cared a lot about power relations, but there had to be a limit beyond which he would not go. To check Liu Bocheng in the 1940s was fine, and Deng did so willingly and deliberately, not just because of his respect for Mao's authority but also because of practical imperatives. To check Liu Shaoqi in the 1950s seemed fine at first, but with the approach of the "three bitter years" from 1959 to 1961, Deng had to step back. To check Zhou now in the 1970s did not seem personally or politically palatable at all: in choosing between two opposing sides, as he had to, Deng could by no means opt for Jiang Qing and her Shanghai folk as individuals or for their fanatic policies, such as the joint criticism of Lin Biao and Confucius.

By the time the Second Party Plenum and the Fourth People's Congress concluded in Beijing in January 1975, Deng had received all the positions for which Mao had recommended him. With both Zhou and Mao basically bedridden, Deng assumed the overall leadership of party, government, and army. Before returning to the hospital, Zhou held a conference of senior State Council officials on January 8, at which he enthusiastically announced that Deng would be in full charge of that body on his behalf.

Deng lost no time and set to work promptly. The year 1975 turned out to be an extremely hectic one for the seventy-year-old Deng, who worked with a vengeance. He used to be a rather "lazy guy," not a workaholic type like Zhou. Never in his life, neither previously nor afterward, would Deng work as hard as he did in 1975. Under the general slogan "rectification of disorders," he energetically and resolutely tackled all kinds of problems: domestic and foreign affairs; party, government, and army issues; industrial and agricultural matters. In the following ten months, until he was again forced out of central power, Deng received dozens of groups of foreign dignitaries, spoke at dozens of conferences and meetings, and signed hundreds of documents and directives.

On January 25, 1975, Deng spoke at the General Staff headquarters on "cleaning up the mess of factionalism within the army." He spoke at the national conference of industrial leaders on February 25, calling it the greatest blunder to talk about socialist revolution alone without paying any attention to economic work. On March 5, at another conference of provincial industrial leaders, he gave specific instructions for solving the serious problems of railway transportation and suggested dismissing and even arresting factionalist ringleaders who had caused problems. At a May 29 meeting, he called for the leaders of the steel industry to overcome "softness," "laziness," and "looseness" in order to increase iron and steel production. He presided over a June–July conference of the Military Council and made a speech entitled "Tasks for Rectifying the Army," calling for solid and efficient "leading squads" in the army and for "preparation for war." He talked to the study classes of the Party Center on July 4 and stressed the need to strengthen the party's leadership and rectify the party's working style.[13]

Under Deng's personal guidance, the State Planning Commission drafted a document entitled "Several Questions on Speeding Up Industrial Development," or as it was commonly called, "Twenty Articles on Industry." In September, Hu Yaobang, the head of the Chinese Academy of Sciences and a close friend of Deng, produced another document entitled "Promote Scientific Research and Applications." In October, Deng personally endorsed the "General Working Program of the Party and the Country," drafted by Hu Qiaomu and Deng Liqun of the Party Center's Institute of Political Research, which clearly posited economic production, not political revolution, as the focal task of the entire party and the entire country, militantly denouncing anybody who claimed otherwise. These three documents, all produced under Deng's direct supervision, were later criticized by the radicals as "three poisonous weeds" aimed at the restoration of capitalism.[14]

The only endeavors Deng tried to ignore or tolerate were ideology and propaganda, which he preferred to leave to Madame Mao and her radical colleagues, conducting their anti–Lin Biao and anti-Confucius campaign and penning their articles about it. Deng derided the campaign's absurdity in private but condoned it in public—which he had to do, as long as Chairman Mao seemed to like it and as long as it did not interfere too much with Deng's own domain of state and government work.

Deng's position in the Party Center remained rather ambiguous. Although he was in charge of its general affairs on a de facto basis, Wang Hongwen outranked him in terms of formal seniority. Besides, Madame Mao's influence was everywhere, and all it lacked was a formal rank! Confrontations in the Politburo between the moderates and the radicals were inevitable, and only Mao's imposing authority kept the two sides in temporary balance, preventing an immediate explosion. Mao tried to control his wife for Deng's sake in the early months of 1975. On May 3, Mao personally held a Politburo conference and there labeled Jiang and her coterie as a "Gang of Four," admonishing them with the famous "three dos and three don'ts." Deng followed suit at a June 3 Politburo conference and forced Jiang to submit a paper of self-criticism. Of course, all this was more or less like the master of a house siding with his butler to chide his wife. Eventually, it would be easier for the master to dismiss the butler than to divorce the wife!

Hu Yaobang, who showed himself to be Deng's most resolute supporter during this period, once raised a worried question: "Aren't we pushing it too far?" He added, "There may be some people who do not like what we are doing and will find fault with us." To Hu's concerns, Deng replied playfully, "I tell that you shouldn't be too scared. I myself am a Moslem maiden, with many pigtails on my head for those people to grab at."[15]

On September 20, 1975, right outside the operating room where the final and ultimately ineffective operation on Zhou's stomach cancer was about to be performed, the premier noticed Deng bending over his stretcher. "You have done a good job this year," Zhou gasped in a low but firm voice, grasping Deng's hand in his own—"far better than I could have done myself."[16]

Indeed, Deng had done and said many things—things that Zhou himself might have wanted to do and say but could not or would not. Deng was not like Zhou. Deng was resolute in tackling problems, which was what Mao had liked about him before but also what Mao would come to dislike about him later! In retrospect, Deng had perhaps been too resolute in tackling too many problems. By October 1975, Mao seemed to have seen and heard enough!

Mao had returned to Beijing in the spring of 1975 and confined himself to his own study in Zhongnanhai even more than he had done previously. An old and sick man, he chose to shut himself up in his private residence and indulge just in the classics, ancient poetry and music, and young ladies—all physically attractive but politically ignorant. In August 1975, his nephew Mao Yuanxin came to Beijing, moved into Mao's residence, and began working as Mao's liaison and spokesman with other party and state leaders. That brought about a big change. Mao loved and trusted Mao Yuanxin. Unlike those naive girls around Mao, Mao Yuanxin was a former Red Guard who would later become a provincial leader in Manchuria on the radical side. After he took up residence with Mao, nobody, not even Jiang or Deng, could see the chairman without permission from both Mao Yuanxin and Zhang Yufeng—Mao's nurse, secretary, and mistress.[17]

On October 13, Liu Bing, vice president of Qinghua University, sent a report via the Ministry of Education to the State Council, complaining about the adverse impact of the "proletarian educational revolution" in the university. "The quality of education is falling to such a point," Liu said, "that a college graduate may still be an illiterate, unable to read and write." Deng sympathized with Liu's report and passed it along to Mao, in hopes that the chairman would share his views.

It must have been a misjudgment on Deng's part. He should have known that the worker–peasant–soldier propaganda team—through which the educational revolution was carried out in Qinghua—had two leaders, Chi Qun and Xie Jingyi, both of whom were well acquainted with Mao. Mao was particularly fond of Xie, a female radical he had known for years. Mao read Liu's report but, for personal and political reasons, did not accept it at all. He regarded it as an attempt by Liu to usurp Chi and Xie's leadership in Qinghua University and, moreover, to reverse the cultural and educational revolution. Because the report had been passed along through the Ministry of Education and the State Council, their leaders would be held responsible for it.[18]

Mao's repudiation of Liu Bing's report in order to side with Chi Qun and Xie Jingyi occurred in late October 1975. Jiang Qing and her radical peers were more than overjoyed to communicate the news to Qinghua University, where mass rallies and large-character posters immediately erupted throughout the campus, hailing the chairman's latest directive and denouncing Liu Bing and his sympathizers.

At Mao's suggestion, a Party Center "notification conference" was held in early November 1975. A draft paper approved by Mao and entitled "A Few Points of Notification" was communicated at the very beginning of the conference. Mao had evidently offered some directives: "What happened in Qinghua University is not a single casual incident but a reflection of a rightist tendency in general." The conference quickly passed a resolution repudiating the "rightist wind of reversing verdicts."[19]

An outburst of mass rallies soon spread from Qinghua to other universities and colleges in Beijing. Critical articles abounded in *Red Flag* and *People's Daily*. By December 1975, the movement of "repulsing the rightist wind of reversing verdicts" had spread throughout the country. Liu Bing and Zhou Rongxin, the minister of education, were publicly exposed as targets of attack. Deng was not singled out by name yet, but his Party Center leadership was almost automatically rescinded.

Deng Xiaoping indeed stood behind Liu Bing. When Liu told him of the radicals' call to repulse the "rightist wind," Deng retorted in contemptuous defiance, "Wind? We'll make it a typhoon."[20] Deng pretended, especially before his subordinates, to stick fearlessly to his political stance. But in reality, he was getting into big trouble, much bigger than he had probably anticipated.

On November 1, 1975, Deng accompanied a group of foreign guests to meet Mao in his Zhongnanhai residence. After Chancellor Helmut Schmidt of West Germany had left, Deng stayed behind and took advantage of the opportunity to pose a simple and clear question to Mao: "How does the chairman view my work this year?" What could the chairman possibly reply? Briefly and meekly, Mao mumbled, "Good."[21]

Chairman Mao said that Deng's work was good, as did Premier Zhou. Furthermore, the facts spoke for themselves regarding the quality of his work: under Deng's leadership of the party and government, 1975 had witnessed a phenomenal 11.9 percent growth in China's gross national product. That figure was in sharp contrast with the 1.4 percent increase that had been seen in 1974 and the 1.7 percent increase that would be seen in 1976. Unfortunately, as far as Deng's political fate was concerned, what Zhou and the economic statistics said mattered little or perhaps not at all. What Mao said did matter, but what he said would prove not entirely true!

─── 16 ───

The Year of the Dragon, 1976

According to the Chinese lunar calendar, 1976 was the year of the dragon. More often than not, the dragon symbolized a year of natural disasters and human calamities. Although the Chinese are a people without religion, they have a lot of superstitions instead. Only those who were in China at the time could feel the tension in the social and political atmosphere. I was then in northern Shandong, teaching in a high school. On December 31, 1975, the prefectural broadcast warned of an imminent earthquake. People were to stay awake on the street all night. Nothing happened. As the dawn broke, everybody headed home with a feeling that an extraordinary new year had arrived.

At the turn of 1975/1976, Julie and David Eisenhower, the daughter and son-in-law of former President Richard M. Nixon, were visiting China. On January 1, 1976, the couple met Mao in his private study. While discussing one of Mao's recently published poems, they heard the old man murmur, "There will be more struggles within the party." Deng attended the meeting as usual but sat there silently, occasionally toying with his wristwatch. Deng's mood was undeniably glum, perhaps owing to Zhou Enlai's physical condition as well as to his own political situation.[1]

Deng had gotten into even bigger trouble in the past two months because of Mao's directives regarding Liu Bing's letter. But that did not mean that Mao was determined to eliminate Deng. As an elderly patriarch, Mao pretended to treat his quarreling subordinates even-handedly when it came to punitive measures. He had sided with Deng once in October 1974 and again in May 1975. Both times, Jiang Qing and her radicals were pressured to admit their errors. This time, Mao

189

would prefer to side with the radicals against Deng. Mao might have wanted to play a balancing game between the leftist Jiang and the rightist Deng.

Soon after the start of the new year, on January 8, 1976, Zhou died in Beijing Hospital. He had mostly been unconscious and in a coma since early December 1975. Together with Madame Zhou, Deng had kept watch over him around the clock in the hospital during the last couple of days. With the exception of Mao, all the party and government leaders, including the sick ninety-year-old Zhu De, streamed to the hospital to pay their last respects to the premier.

Zhou left no will, other than an oral instruction not to have his ashes deposited at the Babaoshan Cemetery of Revolutionaries but instead scattered over "the rivers and soil of my motherland." Nor did Zhou insist that Deng handle his funeral arrangements. Probably because of the reluctance of radicals like Zhang Chunqiao and the unsuitability of other moderates like Li Xiannian and Ye Jianying, Deng was designated to deliver Zhou's funeral eulogy on January 15, 1976.

For physical as well as political reasons, Mao decided not to attend Zhou's funeral service at Babaoshan. All he did was send a pine wreath with one cool phrase, "In Memory of Comrade Zhou Enlai." While Deng spoke fulsomely to the five thousand assembled senior cadres, Wang Hongwen awkwardly presided over the funeral service. That would be Deng's final public appearance for the whole year.

Zhou became a symbol of virtue and justice for China, somewhat like Mother Teresa for the Western world. Even Mao's maid–mistress, Zhang Yufeng, resented Mao's apparent indifference to Zhou's death: "Shouldn't you also go attend the premier's funeral?" To this barb, even Mao had no easy answer; instead, he only muttered a feeble excuse, "Sick as I myself am now, how can I go there?"[2]

It may be true that, with Zhou's death, the buttress for Deng's attempt to maintain a post-Mao alignment of power was lost and a barrier that had prevented the radicals from wresting away Deng's official post was removed. But more pertinently, I would say that Zhou's death intensified the urgency for Mao to make up his mind about his successor. The political deadlock or stalemate, which might otherwise have continued, had to be broken promptly. It was necessary to choose and announce a new head of government right away, wasn't it? Could Mao allow the government to remain without a premier, as he had already allowed the country to remain without a president? The succession should have been no problem—hadn't Mao already decided on Deng two years ago?—but now it suddenly became a problem as a result of recent developments.

The decision about who would succeed Zhou as premier was Mao's alone and at bottom had nothing to do with any Politburo conference or discussion at all. Sometime and somewhere in this old man's changing heart, Deng might still have been considered, however briefly, as a candidate for that vacancy, but he would be dismissed equally quickly as being obviously unsuitable under the circumstances of late January 1976.

It was a time when all Beijing campuses had just begun a mass drive to fight against "the rightist wind of reversal of verdicts" and against "that unrepentant capitalist roader," while Deng himself remained stubborn and unrepentant indeed. Zhang Chunqiao, as the second deputy premier, seemed to be another possible choice. But Mao had never really trusted Zhang or Yao Wenyuan, his Marxist theoretician "twin" from Shanghai.

The elderly Mao felt pressure, mentally more than substantively, from both sides. Moreover, for Mao, this decision actually involved two choices in one: it was not merely a matter of picking a new premier but also of picking his own successor. Mao knew all too well that Jiang Qing could easily offend everybody and make a mess of everything, while Wang Hongwen had proved lacking in political capability and could hardly be expected to control the situation, either internal or external.

Surprisingly, and yet not unreasonably, when faced with a choice between the radical Zhang Chunqiao and the moderate Deng, Mao finally chose the nonpolitical Hua Guofeng as acting premier. At least Mao had no strong negative opinions about this tall, amiable, modest, and honest former party secretary from his native province. Although Hua might not be entirely right for the position, neither was he particularly wrong. Hua might not be as smart as Deng, but in Mao's own words, he was "not that stupid" either.

On February 3, 1976, the eve of the Chinese New Year, the CCP Central Committee issued its "No. 1 Document," formally announcing Hua's appointment as acting premier. For a while, it was still unclear what impact this appointment might have on the Party Center leadership, in which Wang remained a vice chairman while Hua was just an ordinary member of the Politburo.

It was reported that Marshal Ye, who was in poor health, felt disgusted by Hua's appointment, among other matters, and left Beijing for his hometown of Canton in the distant south, presumably to recuperate. Chen Xilian—obviously because of his recent acquaintance with Mao Yuanxin—then assumed temporary charge of the Military Council's routine affairs.

The radicals were equally unhappy with Hua's appointment. In his own diary, Zhang Chunqiao wrote grudgingly, "Another New Year! And another 'No. 1 Document'! Those who rise quickly will also fall quickly."[3] Here, Zhang referred to both the "No. 1 Document" of 1975, by which Deng had been appointed deputy chairman of the Party Center, and this latest "No. 1 Document" of 1976, by which Hua, instead of himself, was designated acting premier of the State Council.

There was still some ambiguity in the new configuration of power, which reflected the ambiguity in Mao's own mind at the time. Hua was only the acting premier, not yet the full premier, and only a member of the Politburo, not yet a member of its Standing Committee. Wang Hongwen, Ye Jianying, and even Deng Xiaoping remained vice chairmen of the Central Committee, formally outranking Hua in the party's hierarchy.

On February 25, 1976, Hua convened a Politburo conference, which passed a resolution criticizing Deng and his "rightist tendency of reversing the verdicts." The resolution was later communicated within the party apparatus. Deng's name was not yet exposed to the public, nor was he formally removed from his leadership positions. Some conversations about Deng's problem between Mao and his nephew Mao Yuanxin from October 1975 to January 1976 were quoted as the main support for the resolution.

In that resolution, it was recorded that, sometime in October 1975, Mao Yuanxin had said to Mao, "I have been paying much attention to Deng Xiaoping's speeches these last couple of months. There is a problem. He seldom mentions any achievements of the great Cultural Revolution or criticizes Liu Shaoqi's revisionist line." At another point, Mao Yuanxin said, "Of what Deng calls the three directives, actually only one was the key point—that is, to promote production."[4]

The elderly uncle must have been moved by the young nephew's remarks. In his later years, Mao used to say that he had done just two things in his entire life: one was to overthrow the Kuomintang regime and drive Chiang Kai-shek off to the island of Taiwan, and the other was to start the great Cultural Revolution. Mao thus regarded the Cultural Revolution as the last half of his political career, and he was hypersensitive to any possible reversal of its evaluation after his own demise. "Deng said that he would not reverse the verdicts," Mao lamented to his nephew. "How could these words be reliable?"[5]

As long as certain political undercurrents existed, no matter how unreasonable they might be, there would be smart or stupid people popping up as their public spokespersons. Thus, it was seen that, in Shanghai, big-character posters appeared on the streets demanding Zhang Chunqiao's appointment as premier. Also, as long as two or more conflicting political positions existed, there would be smart or stupid people pushing one position or the other to its very extreme, no matter how absurd that might be. Thus, an article appeared in the *Literary Daily* making such statements as "that capitalist roader in the party had helped this unrepentant capitalist roader to ascend to the leadership."[6] It was fine to attack "this unrepentant capitalist roader," which meant Deng, but it certainly went far beyond the norm to denounce "that capitalist roader in the party," which obviously referred to Zhou.

Mao was still undecided about Deng. He was reluctant to strike Deng down outright. At one point, he said, "Deng has a clever mind," and at another, he suggested that Deng be put in charge just of foreign affairs. Hua's attitude toward Deng was the same as Mao's: "Deng has committed some grave mistakes. But the Party Center still hopes that he can acknowledge his mistakes and accept the help of his comrades, in order to return to the chairman's correct line and rejoin our revolutionary ranks."[7]

Several more Politburo conferences were held to criticize Deng during March 1976, one being attended by some young college students in the name of "representatives of the revolutionary masses." As the motions, emotions, and commotions escalated in the conference hall, Deng stood up and walked out, muttering, "I am a deaf old man, and I could not hear what you folks were yelling about."[8]

Under the same adverse circumstances in the past, Deng had admitted his errors quite a few times. But not this time! Although he stopped short of open defiance, he did remain silent at the Politburo meetings. It would have been too much for him to have bowed down before Jiang and Zhang, whom he so greatly despised. He did submit a paper of self-criticism to Mao and the Politburo. Beyond that, he did not want to budge or dodge any further. Nor did he pitifully appeal to Mao, as he had done before. Since Mao was now physically incapacitated, it would be too insulting to Deng's seniority and dignity for him to beg for leniency in front of Mao's young nephew and mistress. What would be the use anyhow, other than to humiliate himself before a dying old man!

On March 8, 1976, believe it or not, an extremely rare natural phenomenon was observed in northeast China. A meteor shower occurred over an area of about five hundred square kilometers in the suburbs of Jilin in Manchuria. Presumably, a giant meteor had exploded into thousands of pieces, which then fell to earth with horrible flashes and whistles. Although astronomers had their scientific explanation, the common people had their own metaphysical rationale. It was regarded as an ominous sign for both the nation and the ruling regime.

April 5 was the Qingming Festival, or the festival of spirits, traditionally an occasion for the Chinese people to celebrate the memory of their deceased ancestors and display respect for them. In the abnormal year of 1976 and the abnormal place of Beijing, however, the festival's observance would become the April 5 incident, which would eventually turn Deng's political fortunes upside down.

It all started in late March with a small bouquet of pink roses placed on the marble pedestal of the People's Heroes Monument by a few schoolboys and schoolgirls. No message was left, nor was one needed; the flowers were in memory of the late Premier Zhou. More people and more flowers followed. By early April, the monument was buried beneath thousands of wreaths with all kinds of messages. One wreath was an iron and steel frame more than five meters tall, with a huge tag: "The People Miss the Premier." On April 4, Sunday, almost two million people visited the monument in Tiananmen Square. The inscriptions on the wreaths ran from simple, innocent sentences such as "Immortal Is Our Beloved Premier" to political pledges like "Defend the Premier with Our Life and Blood!" There were also poems with a strong political flavor, such as: "As we observe the premier's death in mourning, those demons and ghosts are laughing. Let us draw our swords and chop off their ugly claws!"[9]

The Beijing municipal government was shocked. After getting permission from the Politburo, Mayor Wu De ordered the metropolitan police to remove all the wreaths during the night. The next day, April 5, about one million people came back, shouting, "Return our wreaths!" Thus, a memorial for the dead turned into a demonstration against the living. Confrontations between the masses and the police led to a riotous situation that lasted throughout the afternoon and late into the night. Then, as most of the people left for home, some ten thousand militiamen and three thousand security police, brandishing clubs and sticks, swept through Tiananmen Square. They cornered the few hundred individuals who remained around the monument, struck many of them down, and threw a few dozen into police trucks, leaving bloodstains all over the monument's marble stairways. It was a terrible scene, which required the police to block the entrances to the square the next day in order to wash off the blood. Nevertheless, it should be pointed out that there were few casualties in this incident, certainly not as many as fifty thousand—a deliberately exaggerated figure published in the Taiwan press and naively believed by many Western writers.[10]

The Politburo called an emergency session. Hua was at a loss, and the radicals were highly excited. The meeting voted to condemn Deng as the sole instigator of this "mass riot." Mao Yuanxin reported the vote to Mao on April 6 and heard Mao blurt out the remarks, "Nature has changed," and "Throw him out." That was good enough for Mao Yuanxin to call Aunt Jiang and inform her of Uncle Mao's approval.

On April 7, two resolutions of the Politburo were announced in accordance with Mao's instructions. The first mandated the removal of Deng from all his leadership positions inside and outside the party. That was what the Politburo had decided, and that was what the radicals had wanted. The second appointed Hua as premier and first vice chairman of the Party Center, actually Mao's designated heir apparent. That was Mao's own addition. It was what the radicals should have expected but did not.[11]

As near death as Mao was, he clung to a minimum of sanity up until the last moment of his political life. Deng was out, but the radicals were not in. In the final analysis, the April 5 incident was less a success than a failure for the mindless radicals. They succeeded in pressuring Mao into removing Deng from the leadership, a situation that had already existed on a de facto basis since January. But they failed to get power realigned the way they wanted. The formal appointment of Hua as Mao's successor was something new—something that totally blocked them from legitimately competing for supreme power during Mao's life and after Mao's death.

Finally and significantly, Deng lost his party leadership but not his party membership, thanks once again to Mao's leniency. Deng's problem was still regarded as one of "contradictions among the people." Thus, he could keep his normal residence in Beijing and would not suffer any physical punishment. Given all this, Deng could afford to stay with his family and just wait—wait for the chairman's demise and the future's mandate.

Mao met with the prime minister of New Zealand in late April and with the prime minister of Singapore in early May. Now Hua was with Mao in both meetings. It was an embarrassing scene for the foreigners as well as for the Chinese. The elderly Mao behaved somewhat like a handicapped infant. Even the retouched photos published in *People's Daily* could scarcely hide the fact that the chairman did not have long to live.[12]

Zhu De died on July 6. People were already used to the funereal music from the Central Broadcasting Station. "Who this time?" one listener asked. "Just Zhu," another answered in a hushed tone. The death of Zhu, former commander in chief of the communist army and current chairman of the National People's Congress, seemed not yet enough! Historically, the names of Zhu and Mao had been linked as a symbol of the entire communist regime, ever since the Jinggang Mountains years.

Nobody respected Hua as an individual politician, but everybody had to respect him as a legitimate authority. The radicals did not realize that until it was too late. They did what they would normally have done. They wrote articles to push the anti-Confucius drive to a new height. Some clever scholars in the "two schools" discovered that Confucius had once served as minister of public security and then as acting prime minister; Hua had also held these positions![13] This allusion was indeed ingenious and resourceful. But what was its practical use, other than to plant in Hua's mind seeds of suspicion against the radicals, which would bear fruit in retaliation after Mao's death?

On July 28, an extremely severe earthquake struck Tangshan, a city of 5 million residents in the municipal district located eighty miles from Beijing and thirty miles from Tianjin. The Tangshan earthquake was officially recorded as having a magnitude of between 8 and 8.2 on the Richter scale and an intensity of 11 degrees on the Mercalli scale at its epicenter. Some 240,000 people were killed and 160,000 badly injured. The whole city was totally ruined, with not even a single building of two or more stories left standing. Unofficial estimates suggested that the casualties might have numbered as many as 600,000 or 700,000. If communist China held few world records for accomplishments, this event certainly ranked among the world's greatest disasters.[14]

The giant quake could be felt strongly in Beijing. Mao was nearly tossed off his sickbed and for a while was at a loss as to what had happened. Later, he insisted on receiving detailed reports on the situation. Mao was of peasant origins and retained a peasant mentality all his life. Chinese peasants had for centuries believed that severe natural disasters, especially earthquakes, foretold the demise of an emperor or a dynasty. Versed in Chinese classics, Mao must also have been familiar with the doctrines of the Han Dynasty scholar Dong Zhongshu about sympathetic interactions between heavenly disorders and human ordeals.

China was filled with confusion. Various rumors spread like wildfire throughout the country. Mao's reign was falling and fading. People speculated about another even larger earthquake still to come. In Sichuan, an earthquake having a magnitude of 7.2 on the Richter scale did indeed occur in August, with a number of aftershocks ranking between 6 and 7 on the scale. Most of the residents of Beijing had to live in camps and tents on the streets throughout the summer. Outside the capital, railway accidents, especially along the Beijing–Zhengzhou line, became routine affairs, numbering as many as eighty within the space of a couple of months. At one time, there was a pile-up involving twenty trains, which were jammed one into another, unable to move for a week. All in all, the whole nation was in a state of near panic.[15]

Amid all these extraordinary circumstances, Mao's death, on September 9, 1976, came more or less as many people had expected, albeit not as they wished. Death was not always a bad thing. In his last years, Mao had become too great a burden to almost everybody, perhaps even to the radical "Gang of Four," who would probably have liked to see Mao gone to heaven so that they themselves could have free political rein on earth.

Battles for supreme political power began immediately after Mao's death or, to use Jiang Qing's words, "while the chairman's body and bones were still warm." In this regard, the radicals, or the "Gang of Four," were vigorously swinging their two swords—the flamboyant Madame Mao and the omnipotent *People's Daily*—as they had thus far so successfully done!

Jiang Qing indeed lost no time in offending everybody and messing everything up. At one time, she kept pestering Zhang Yufeng for some of Mao's leftover letters and papers. After being rejected, she appealed to Wang Dongxing and finally to Hua Guofeng himself. On another occasion, for heaven knows what reason, she telephoned Hua at midnight to order him to call a Politburo Standing Committee meeting the very next morning. "What for?" Chairman Hua asked meekly. "You'll know by then," coolly replied Jiang, who was not even a member of that committee herself. She seemed to have forgotten a simple and yet crucial point: her husband, the "king," was dead. In the past, it had been a matter of family feud, and now it really became a matter of class struggle.[16]

Both Zhang Chunqiao and Yao Wenyuan wrote well and quite thoughtfully. They argued with Hua for days over the exact wording of Mao's testimonial. Despite Hua's rejection, Yao had the *People's Daily* publish an editorial on October 4, 1976, relentlessly attacking "whoever does not act according to the decided policy." Indeed, Hua was "not that stupid" as to ignore the fact that the article constituted the opening salvo in the radicals' planned fight with him for party and state power.

Restless and reckless, Zhang and Yao also seemed to have forgotten the simple and yet crucial point: the chairman was dead. No matter how ludicrous or adventurous their previous lurches of line had been, Mao's presence had been a constant—a final source of authority, a limit on end results. They should have realized that their seemingly omnipotent pens had always depended on Mao's living breath alone. Now that Mao was gone, so was the potency of their own writing.

While the radicals were bluffing loudly with their pens, the moderates were quietly taking up their guns. It proved quite simple and easy. On October 6, the "Gang of Four" was just brushed away: Zhang, Wang, and Yao were arrested at a Politburo conference and Jiang at her own residence. On the moderates' side, three men played the decisive roles: Hua Guofeng, Ye Jianying, and Wang Dongxing. In addition, Li Xiannian, a veteran member of the Politburo, and Chen Xilian, the commander of the Beijing garrison troops, also took part in this de facto military coup.[17]

Deng remained in Beijing during the entire period, from his downfall in April 1976 until his rehabilitation in July 1977, as he himself told Joseph Strauss. He and his family were not "thrown out of Zhongnanhai" because of his 1976 ordeal, as they had not resided there since October 1968. He did not flee, nor was he smuggled, to the distant south to "hide out" at some hot springs resort near Canton, nor did he actually participate in the October 1976 coup to arrest the "Gang of Four"—as some outside writers have claimed. All these claims, albeit arguably resulting from shortages of accurate information, defy the basic logic and mechanisms of CCP politics at the time.[18]

On October 20, 1976, a mass parade of one million people took place in Beijing to celebrate the Hua center's victory over the "Gang of Four." On the Tiananmen rostrum reviewing the giant demonstration were Hua, Ye, and other leaders. While marching through Tiananmen Square, the participants kept shouting slogans such as, "Carry out Chairman Mao's revolutionary line to the end!" and "Carry out the criticism of Deng Xiaoping to the end!"[19]

Please don't underestimate the Chinese sense of irony and mystery! When they cheered for Mao's line, they might really have been railing against Mao's line. When they hailed Hua's leadership, they might really have been ridiculing Hua's leadership. When they pledged to fight against Deng, they might really have meant to sympathize with Deng. What did seem clear and definite, nonetheless, was the expression of their discontent. What really mattered was that these Chinese could gather together by the thousands and even millions for one political cause or another. This apparent form was in itself profoundly substantive.

Oh, yes, as more than one million Beijing residents shouted in support of carrying out Mao's line and the criticism of Deng to the end, they might have been correct in a certain sense. For both Mao's line and the anti-Deng drive, the end game was indeed in sight! In other words, Mao's line would soon reach its final conclusion, as would the anti-Deng movement. An entirely new epoch, Deng's epoch, and an entirely new line, Deng's line, were in the process of being formed!

— 17 —

Back to Supreme Power, 1976-1980

As noted in the preceding chapter, Deng stayed in Beijing throughout 1976 and was never in Guangdong under the confidential protection of Xu Shiyou or Wei Guoqing. After the Tiananmen incident in April of that year, he was removed from all official positions and practically confined to his home. He lived privately with his family, avoiding, or being prevented from making, any public appearances. He had no direct involvement with the capture of the "Gang of Four," either in advance or soon afterward. Deng did learn of the political melodrama soon after it took place, but only because he was present in Beijing and this event was not kept as secret as the Lin Biao incident of September 1971.[1]

On October 10, 1976, shortly after being informed of the downfall of the "Gang of Four," Deng sent a letter to Hua Guofeng, the new boss of the Chinese Communist Party (CCP) Center, as he had done with Mao Zedong in 1971. The letter oozed with excessive flattery: "Comrade Hua Guofeng is the most appropriate successor to Chairman Mao. His youth guarantees that the proletarian leadership will remain stable for at least fifteen or twenty years."[2]

Given its exaggerated tone, such as "Hurrah! Hurrah! Hurrah!"— which was entirely inappropriate for Deng, who was older than Hua— the letter might have been drafted by someone else, like one of Deng's children, rather than by Deng himself. Its basic purpose, nevertheless, was clear and must have been Deng's own: Deng asked Hua to allow him to participate in the criticism of the "Gang of Four"—the same thing he had requested of Mao with respect to Lin Biao in 1971. On both occasions, what Deng was really asking for was the restoration of his own political role.

It seemed reasonable and logical that, once the "Gang of Four" had fallen, Deng as its chief foe and victim should be redeemed. Yet it was not such a simple matter. Hua, whom Mao had promoted to be his successor, would tend to stick to the wishes and will of Mao, who had personally sponsored the anti-Deng movement. Besides, Hua was once again "not that stupid." He and some other members of the new leadership—notably, Wang Dongxing and Wu De—were concerned that Deng's restoration could spur a challenge to their incumbent positions and lead to retaliation against them for their anti-Deng words and deeds in the recent past.

It was true that Hua proved to be a rather lame-minded person—not astute enough to realize the inevitability of Deng's reinstatement. But if Hua had been so smart, Deng might not have been able to re-emerge—at least, not as successfully and thoroughly as he actually did. Although Hua was reluctant to let Deng come up again, he was not determined enough to keep Deng down. That was his dilemma. Had Hua been a truly power-conscious individual, of course, Mao might not have chosen him as his successor in the first place!

Hua's response to Deng's letter sounded pretty cold and somewhat pretentiously arrogant: "You have committed errors and should be criticized, although the Tiananmen incident had nothing to do with you. You should be put to work on the front line, but on the combat front line." The last sentence is not very clear even in its original Chinese, nor perhaps was it very clear in Hua's own mind at the time. In November 1976, Hua said other things to the same effect: "At this moment, our primary task is to criticize the Gang of Four, but we should also criticize Deng as well. We should take care not to alter whatever Chairman Mao previously instructed and approved."[3]

It was not merely a matter of high-level power relations or elite-level politics. The people, the masses, the party cadres, and government officials in general—after so many years of suffocating suppression and revolutionary excesses during the Mao era—were looking forward to basic change in the status quo. At the very least, Deng's restoration would represent the negation of the disgusting past and the possibility of moving toward an improved future.

January 8, 1977, brought the first anniversary of Zhou Enlai's

death, and there were various commemorative activities, some officially organized and others spontaneous. On that date in Beijing, more
than one million people gathered in Tiananmen Square to pay tribute to
the late premier and denounce the "Gang of Four." Among the crowds
could be found quite a number of people holding posters and shouting
slogans requesting Deng's immediate restoration.

It was most likely under such circumstances that veteran party leaders such as Xu Shiyou and Wei Guoqing in the Politburo and Wang
Zhen in the State Council began actively pushing for Deng's rehabilitation. In the meantime, some newspapers also grew courageous
enough to carry news reports and articles to the same effect. All in all,
it gradually became a popular trend to call Deng back, a trend that was
hard for Hua and his followers to resist.

On February 7, 1977, *People's Daily,* directly controlled by Wang
Dongxing at the time, published a joint editorial in its own name and in
the names of the *Liberation Army Daily* and the party organ *Red
Flag*—the most authoritative way to express the Party Center's official
position. The editorial prominently set forth the principle of "double
whatevers," stating that "whatever decisions Chairman Mao had made,
we should firmly support, and whatever Chairman Mao had instructed,
we should always observe."

Needless to say, the matter of Deng Xiaoping was among the most
prominent issues that Mao had decided and on which he had instructed, and therefore, no reversal should be allowed. Under such
delicate circumstances, Deng wrote another letter, on April 10, 1977,
this time addressed to "Chairman Hua, Vice Chairman Ye [Jianying],
and the Party Center." He admitted in the letter that he had made some
mistakes before and would not attempt to reverse Mao's decisions on
them. But he seemed to take his eventual restoration for granted and
yet stated modestly, "When and in what position I should resume my
own work should depend entirely upon the Party Center's decision."
At the very end, he shrewdly proposed that his letter be circulated
internally within the party apparatus. The letter was indeed thus circulated on May 3, arousing a general sense within and outside the party
leadership that Deng's political restoration was quite imminent.[4]

May 14, 1977, happened to be Marshal Ye's eightieth birthday, and
several marshals and high-ranking generals such as Xu Xiangqian, Nie
Rongzhen, Wang Zhen, and Yang Chengwu were invited to a party at
Ye's mansion in the Western Hills. Hua was not invited, nor did he

seem interested enough to attend. Just before the dinner began, to the surprise of all present, Deng and his wife came to the door. They were ushered into the dining hall. Smiling from ear to ear, Deng exclaimed: "Ah ha! So many old soldiers are gathered together here!" "Aren't you also an old soldier?" Ye replied happily, "Nay, you are the chief!" The attendants hurriedly added a couple of chairs for the Dengs at the head table.[5]

Obviously, Deng was herein playing a calculated political game. He did not really respect Ye, nor even Hua—among other reasons, because both of them had been his subordinates for many years in the recent past. There seemed little doubt that, during the early months of 1977, Deng was trying his best to please Ye and also to allay the worries of Hua and other incumbent leaders merely in order to return to power.

There were still suggestions within the Party Center that Deng should be rehabilitated only as deputy premier, as in the precedent of 1973. Didn't Deng himself also admit that he had made some mistakes? Hua was hesitating again. But Ye Jianying and Li Xiannian were resourceful enough to realize that, since Deng's restoration was inevitable, they would rather have Deng resume all the positions he had lost after the Tiananmen incident of April 1976. They realized Deng's great potential. Instead of Deng trying to please them, it was their turn to please Deng. Why not do something now rather than later?!

The next important party conference, the Third Plenum of the Tenth Congress, was held in Beijing from July 16 to 21, 1977. The plenum decided on a full restoration of Deng's former positions as deputy chairman of the Party Center, first deputy premier of the State Council, deputy chairman of the Military Council, and chief of staff of the People's Liberation Army. By March 1978, furthermore, Deng became the chairman of the National Political Consultative Conference; Ye was appointed chairman of the National People's Congress. With Hua remaining as the topmost leader in the Party Center and on the State Council, there appeared a triumvirate of Hua, Ye, and Deng, sharing supreme power for the time being.

As deputy premier of the State Council and head of the Chinese government delegation, Deng paid a visit to Japan in the autumn of 1978, to preside officially over the signing ceremony for the Sino-Japanese peace and friendship agreement. He was received by the

Japanese emperor and empress with the honors due a head of state, although he had not formally assumed such a position. Deng comported himself like a head of state, so he was treated as such. The Japanese were an astute people indeed. They had already realized that Deng, not Hua, would soon be China's top leader. Four "quickie" Deng biographies were put out during his visit. Deng's trip abroad turned out to be both a diplomatic success and a personal triumph.[6]

Where there is a will, there is a way! It all started as a matter of academic discourse; on May 11, 1978, *Bright Daily* published an article entitled "Practice Is the Sole Criterion for Truth." Despite its academic tone, the article, sponsored by Hu Yaobang, was directed against Wang Dongxing, who was in charge of the party's ideology and propaganda work. It opposed the "double whatevers" principle, expressed by Wang and approved by Hua. Theoretically, there was a paradox. The article's title and main theme could not be faulted, because the title was a direct quote from Mao. But what if Mao or some of Mao's words were proved wrong in practice? The real issue, however, was not a purely theoretical one. The theme of the article eventually became for Deng an expedient device to sort out pros from cons, friends from foes, despite the possible sacrifice of some academic scholars.[7]

In this kind of academic debate, it was almost impossible to reach a conclusion agreeable to all concerned. If practice is the criterion for truth, isn't this proposition in itself a truth? Another paradox for sure! While Wang and Hua were repelled by the article, Deng showed up at the June 2 conference on the army's political work and openly argued in support of the article. An academic debate turned into a political one. Deng was supported by Luo Ruiqing, who had recently been restored as chief secretary of the Central Military Council; Luo sponsored an editorial in the *Liberation Army Daily* accusing those who had opposed the *Bright Daily* article of being ignorant of the most basic principles of Marxism and Mao Zedong thought.

On December 13, 1978, Deng gave a speech at the Party Center's work conference, entitled "Liberate Our Minds, Seek Truth from Facts, and Unite to Look Forward." Deng expressed the view that the party's first priority was to liberate people's minds. Only through a free mind could one reach a correct understanding of Marxism and Mao Zedong thought and solve both past and future problems. "Any party, any country, or any nation, if its mind is bound by doctrines and superstitions, cannot advance, and it will lose its vital life and eventually die away."[8] Deng further stressed the importance of democracy—institutionalized and legalized democracy. Such institutions and legalities would not change their substance just because of the opinions of any individual.

The Party Center's Third Plenum of the Eleventh Congress, held on December 18–22, 1978, marked the official commencement of the Deng epoch. The plenum turned into a repudiation of the Hua leadership and its Eleventh National Congress of the previous year, in terms of both its policy orientation and, more important, its personnel alignment. The Third Plenum was theoretically and practically guided by Deng's December 13 speech. Deng himself was formally and completely rehabilitated; the 1976 resolutions of the Party Center regarding the Tiananmen incident were reversed and the "double whatevers" repudiated. The Cultural Revolution was denounced, while economic development was designated as the focus of party and state. No slogans like "Carry on class struggle" or "Continue the revolution" could be found in any of the plenum's resolutions.

A whole contingent of party veterans and Deng's former colleagues and subordinates—notably, Peng Zhen, Bo Yibo, and Yang Shangkun—were brought back to the central leadership. Chen Yun was appointed vice chairman of the party and chairman of its Discipline Commission, and Hu Yaobang was made the party's chief secretary. Although Hua Guofeng and Wang Dongxing maintained their titular positions, their authority and practical functions were substantially reduced.

Coincidentally or not, the winter of 1978–79, around the time of the Third Plenum, also witnessed a turning point in Deng's attitude toward popular democracy and mass movements. It was a sharp turn from a supportive, liberal, or rightist approach to a restrictive, conservative, or leftist approach. Of course, we should keep in mind that the terms *leftist* and *rightist* here are loaded political jargon whose definitions might often bewilder even their contemporary users.

Starting in the fall of 1978, big-character posters appeared along the walls of Xidan Street off Chang'an Boulevard in downtown Beijing. As the posters became more numerous and attracted more public attention, people dubbed the place Democracy Wall, a reference to Hyde Park's democratic corner in London. Although most of the posters posed no direct challenge to the party and government, extreme views did show up. Some posters expressed concrete personal complaints about party officials, while others were bold enough to condemn Mao as a feudal dictator and demand greater democracy and political freedom.[9]

The pressure fell primarily on Hua and the conservatives. Deng did not object to the Democracy Wall; actually, he condoned and encouraged the movement in its early phases. By the end of 1978, however, because the Third Plenum had ended and Hua's supreme authority had become a thing of the past, and also because young extremists like Wei Jingsheng had begun to attack the Communist Party as a whole and Deng as an individual, Deng's attitude suddenly changed. Obviously with his personal approval, the Beijing security police blocked off access to Xidan Street and directed that all the posters be placed in Moon Park, far from the city center.

Deng visited the United States for the second time in early February 1979, this time at the official invitation of the U.S. government. Formal diplomatic relations between the People's Republic of China (PRC) and the United States had just been established, and it was a period of "China fever" in the United States. During the visit, Deng took the opportunity to rail against "socialist imperialism," obviously referring to the Soviet Union, in order to win America's sympathy and support. Although, for most of his trip, Deng was occupied by official business in Washington, the capital, he did manage to visit other cities, such as Atlanta, Houston, and Seattle.

It was not that Deng really believed in the Soviet military threat or its revisionist line but that, under the current circumstances, Deng and China were expecting financial and economic assistance from the Western world in general and the United States in particular. Calling the Soviets a few bad names therefore seemed like a sure way—a cheap one as well—of winning American sympathy.

The day before his delegation was scheduled to leave Washington, Deng requested a final private session with President Jimmy Carter. At the meeting, he came directly to the point—that is, the Vietnam issue. Deng told Carter that China was determined to teach Vietnam a lesson and thereby shake up the Soviet Union's world strategy a bit. He outlined several possible responses the Soviets might make. Even the worst possibility could be dealt with by China alone, Deng said gracefully, but China might need moral support from America. The next day, after consulting his aides, Carter mildly suggested to Deng that China should try to tolerate Vietnam a little more rather than resorting to military action.[10]

In fact, China had not yet made a final decision regarding military action against Vietnam, nor did Deng really need Carter's advice or moral support. He might have wanted to use America's condoning of his position to influence his colleagues Hua and Ye at home. America, for its part, was more than happy to see China bruise Vietnam a little— it would be indirect revenge for the Vietnam War—despite President Carter's show of indifference and neutrality. It was both a political and a diplomatic game that Deng was playing, and he played it pretty well.

Back home, Deng took action at once—first, to push Hua and pull Ye for a final decision regarding the military operation against Vietnam. For Deng, the operation was, among other things, a personal exercise of military and political power in his position as chief of the army's general staff. As for the southern battlefront, Deng appointed Yang Dezhi and Xu Shiyou as commanders, putting each in charge of an offensive route with a total of more than five hundred thousand troops.

The Sino-Vietnamese War broke out on February 17, 1979. Originally, Deng had planned to fight for a few days, win a symbolic victory, and then call it off. As it turned out, however, it took the troops more time and losses than expected to take Lang San, a significant Vietnamese provincial capital, before they announced a truce and withdrawal on March 16. Militarily, it could hardly be called a victory for China, which had met tenacious resistance from the Vietnamese army. The action exposed the weakness of the Chinese troops and the incompetence of the Chinese high command. Yet politically, it was a great victory for China, even more so for Deng as an individual politician.

Deng well knew that an international war could have a strong impact on domestic politics. As the war with Vietnam was proceeding, Wei Jingsheng and other political activists were arrested in Beijing at Deng's personal order, and the Democracy Wall was strictly banned. The formal charge against Wei was that he had attempted to sell military secrets to a British correspondent. In November 1979, Wei was sentenced to fifteen years' imprisonment, again through Deng's direct influence. The rough accusation and tough punishment surprised many people, both Chinese and foreigners alike.

On March 30, 1979, Deng gave a speech at the Party Center's theoretical conference entitled "Persist in the Four Cardinal Principles," in which he listed the four principles as the socialist road, the proletarian dictatorship, the Communist Party's leadership, and upholding Marxism–Leninism and Mao Zedong thought. The tone and content of this speech differed sharply from the one Deng had given to the party work conference just a few months before, on December 13, 1978.[11]

Was this shift in Deng's attitude meant to benefit Hua and the conservatives? Hardly! The actual situation was that, by early 1979, Deng's superior position had been established within the party apparatus, thanks in part to the outside popular movement; and he would not allow the party apparatus and his own interests within that apparatus to be damaged by that same popular movement. Thus, Deng could be seen to be shifting either to the left or to the right, careful not to slip over the edge in either direction, but striding straight ahead in his drive for supreme power.

Notably, 1979 was a year of "reversals of verdicts," under Deng's personal guidance. First came the reversal of the verdict on the 1976 Tiananmen incident, then on the 1966 Cultural Revolution, the 1959 anti–Peng Dehuai movement, the 1957 antirightist campaign, and so on. Consequently, one group after another of former victims of these political movements were vindicated and restored to various levels of party and state leadership.

These reversals reflected not only Deng's true sympathy with those innocent victims but also his calculated approach to the current power struggle. The rehabilitated party cadres would certainly constitute a force in Deng's personal and political favor. In other words, these veteran cadres were brought back to central and provincial leadership not only for their own good but also to strengthen Deng's hand in challenging Hua and his recently promoted lieutenants.

Of course, some nasty complications arose in reviewing the political struggles during the course of the Mao epoch, such as the Gao–Rao incident. Deng's personal involvement and responsibility in that case prevented its verdict being reversed or even reviewed. For the same reason, the antirightist campaign could be only partly reversed: the campaign was now held to have been necessary in the first place but excessive in terms of its final result.

Logically as well as practically, the restoration of old cadres meant the expulsion of new leaders. Hua was gradually stripped of his supreme power, while Deng stepped forward as his replacement. Here is a list of the major events in this process: September 25–28, 1979, at the Fourth Plenum, Deng's followers Peng Zhen and Zhao Ziyang

were brought into the Politburo; February 23–29, 1980, at the Fifth
Plenum, Hu Yaobang and Zhao Ziyang were brought into the Politburo
Standing Committee, and Hua's supporters Wang Dongxing, Ji
Dengkui, Wu De, and Chen Xilian were forced to resign; August 30–
September 10, 1980, at the National People's Congress, Zhao formally
became the premier of the State Council in place of Hua; November
10–December 5, 1980, at the Politburo conference, Hua surrendered
his chairmanship of the CCP Central Committee to Hu and his chairmanship of the Central Military Council to Deng; June 27–29, 1981, at
the Sixth Plenum, the above resolutions were formally approved.

There are good reasons to believe, and a great deal of factual evidence to indicate, that during the years 1976–80, Deng's first priority
was to return to supreme power and become the national leader; anything else was secondary. He first excessively praised Hua, then attacked him in all possible ways; he first encouraged and benefited from
the Democracy Wall, then abolished it; he first called for democracy
and freedom, then shifted to dwell on the four cardinal principles. In
my own judgment, all these apparent contradictions should be viewed
in the context of Deng's end and means mentioned above.

Interestingly—although it was hitherto either not known or under-
estimated—the political showdown between Deng and Hua took the
form of the former's attack on the latter's "leftist line" in national
economic affairs during 1979–80. In that struggle, Chen Yun was
drawn in as the main critic of Hua's economic policy, as Deng really
aimed at Hua's political power. There were subtle and yet important
differences between the two positions, which should be carefully
examined.

There had been a general desire and tendency, which Hua shared, to
develop the national economy after Mao's death. On April 18, 1977, at
the national conference called "Learn from Daqing," Hua intoned
lightly, "It is not enough just to have one Daqing in the petroleum
industry. We should have at least ten Daqings." The State Planning
Commission accordingly made two specific reports to Hua and the
Party Center. The reports set such bold goals as producing 60 million
tons of steel and 250 million tons of petroleum by 1985. Meanwhile,
infrastructure construction would be accelerated in 120 main projects,
including 30 electrical companies, 10 oil fields, 10 steel plants, 10
chemical factories, and 10 coastal harbors. By the year 2000, production levels would reach 200 million tons of steel and 1.5 billion tons of

grain, which would represent the effective accomplishment of China's economic modernization.[12]

The State Planning Commission's reports were basically the same as its "Ten-Year Project of Economic Development," drafted under Deng's supervision in 1975. Therefore, it was not Deng but Chen who, in January 1979, first offered some criticism: "There are a lot of gaps in the economic plan, and some of its quotas and projects should be reduced." Since Chen's criticism was directed at the Hua leadership, Deng was more than willing to follow his lead. "We need to have a general adjustment of our economic policy," Deng seconded; "we should handle our economy in the way that can achieve quick results and easy money. Large projects like iron and steel plants should be reduced."[13]

On March 14, 1979, Chen Yun as director and Li Xiannian as deputy director of the Central Financial and Economic Group signed a joint warning to Hua and the Party Center regarding a few fundamental principles of national economic development. The tone of these two veteran leaders sounded quite heavy, almost disrespectful to the Hua center: "Advance steadily; don't hurry up; avoid twists and turns! For the long haul, the national economy needs proportional growth, and the government needs a balanced budget."[14]

At the Politburo conference chaired by Hua on March 21, 1979, Chen admonished again, "There is a serious budget deficit, even more serious than in the years 1961 and 1962. We are trying just to set up 'bones' but not to put on any 'flesh.' " Deng echoed Chen's tone in declaring, "The central task is to adjust the economic plan as a whole. We should be determined to proceed in such a manner. Otherwise, you try to grab 'west,' you try to grab 'east,' and you will finally grasp nothing!"[15]

Hua seemed to have been cornered by Chen and Deng in combination. Actually, Chen, unlike Deng, was not greatly concerned with power relations. And Chen, unlike Deng, seemed truly worried about the ineffective investment in heavy industry, the large expenditure of foreign currency reserves, and the excessive dependence on foreign loans.[16] Hua could not control the practical work in the State Council, either professionally or in terms of personnel, while Ye Jianying, because of his advanced age and army background, also had little to do with economic and financial affairs.

The general situation in 1978–80 was not really as bad as Chen had suggested, despite Hua's blind rashness in economic reconstruction. Later on, Chen's economic criticism abated a bit, but Deng's political criticism did not. On March 14, 1980, Deng appointed Zhao Ziyang to replace Chen as head of the Central Financial and Economic Group, and the slogan of "economic adjustment" continued with renewed enthusiasm. Zhao's appointment was largely for political purposes, and he would soon replace Hua as premier in August 1980.

Finally, from November 10 to December 5, 1980, the Politburo held nine sessions of an enlarged conference. Deng played the key role, and Hua became the principal target. Aside from Hua's political problems—such as his performance during the 1976 Tiananmen incident, his push for the "double whatevers," and his propagation of a personality cult—he was particularly blamed for the "leftist economic line" of the past two years. Interestingly enough, a conference of governors and mayors took place at almost the same time as the Politburo sessions, from November 15 to 30, 1980. This conference was convened by the State Council and chaired by Zhao Ziyang, the new premier.

Zhao Ziyang addressed both the Politburo and State Council conferences, talking about the budget deficit, the excessive investment, the overheating of inflation, and so forth. He went so far as to declare that if these problems continued, the national economy would soon collapse! Of course, Zhao did not forget to attribute all these problems to the "leftist tendencies" of Hua's leadership in the past few years.[17]

Yet for the years 1977–80, no grave damages from such a "leftist line" can be verified. The economic situation had been fairly good, with a growth rate of about 8 percent annually in the gross national product. In 1978, agriculture showed 7.8 percent growth, while industry reported 13.5 percent growth. In 1979, agriculture increased by 8.6 percent and industry by 8.5 percent. In 1980, agriculture again grew by 3.9 percent and industry by 8.7 percent. Those figures were not bad! Besides, ever since late 1978, Chen and then Zhao had been in overall charge of economic affairs, not Hua. The budget for 1978 showed a surplus of 1 billion yuan; the budget for 1979 showed a deficit of 5 billion yuan; and the budget for 1980 again showed a surplus, this time of 4.3 billion yuan. Those figures were pretty normal, despite the deficit for 1979. There should have been no big deal and no big fuss—unless Deng wanted to drive Hua out.

Hua himself argued at the December 1980 conference that the economic situation was not at all critical and that, even if there had been some problems, he could not be held solely or mainly responsible. Hua might have been quite right in this regard. But alas, if you could not be held responsible, then you should be relieved of your responsibility! And that's exactly what was decided: Hua was ousted from the central leadership.

The basic truth was that Hua lacked Deng's political capacity and capability. Even without Deng's dexterous challenge, Hua had little chance of remaining in the central leadership for much longer. Among the common residents of Beijing at the time, various jokes and barbs already circulated about Hua's licking a thumb to help him turn each page of his speeches while reading them at public meetings, his counting on his fingers in order to tick off ten economic projects, and so on.

Nevertheless, one result of the economic and political debate was that Deng did indeed take a more cautious approach to financial and economic affairs. Because Hua's problems had presumably involved industrial matters, Deng preferred to shift the focus to agricultural reform. It might be dangerous to spend too much money buying foreign machines and building plants and factories, and consequently producing budget deficits. Agrarian reform, on the other hand, seemed to Deng much better and safer, much simpler and easier. It would just be a matter of drafting a few papers to eliminate Mao's people's communes and liberate the peasants to make money for themselves—as well as for the party and state.

To promote agricultural output, the Party Center first increased the price of the grain sold compulsorily by the people's communes to the state by 20 percent and the price of grain sold voluntarily by 50 percent. Meanwhile, the state cut the prices of its agricultural machines, fertilizers, pesticides, and other goods sold to the people's communes by 10 to 15 percent. The results were as positive as had been expected, and agricultural production showed obvious growth in 1978 and 1979.

Nobody in the late 1970s yet dared to broach the subject of the total dissolution of the people's communes. In Anhui in 1978, Wan Li had begun to expand the "fringe land" from 5 percent to 15 or 20 percent of the total, to be privately farmed by individual peasants, and to encourage peasant households to develop their own sideline businesses. Zhao Ziyang followed the same line in Sichuan in 1979. There were political factors involved; Wan already had, and Zhao soon would have, a close personal relationship with Deng. But their experiments did indeed mark the initial phase of Deng's agrarian reform, which would prove to be by far the most fundamental of Deng's accomplishments. In Anhui and Sichuan, agricultural production increased almost proportionally to the expansion of the fringe land and household farming.[18]

Deng's foremost objective was to become the national leader, both to satisfy his own ambition and as a means to push his social and national programs. He picked Hua as the prime target because, among other factors, Hua held the supreme power. Hua's complaints about Deng's unfair treatment of him and untrue accusations against him therefore have some validity. Nevertheless, Hua should not have complained too loudly, for he himself had been promoted to the central leadership in the first place through casual chance, scarcely because of his high seniority, great ability, or outstanding achievement. When you get it easily and come up fast, you lose it easily and go down fast!

To wrap up the official justification of Deng's ascension to the supreme leadership, a document entitled "Resolution on Certain Questions in the History of Our Party since the Founding of the State" was drafted by a special group supervised by Hu. Deng treated this document as a big issue and talked about it five or six times from 1979 to 1981. As regards Mao's historical role, Deng proposed a division into "three-tenths negative and seven-tenths positive" as the basic evaluation. Deng also instructed, "Whenever and wherever there had been mistakes in the past, we have to rectify them right now." Nevertheless, the Gao–Rao issue was not reviewed, and the debate between China and the Soviet Union was ignored, while the descriptions of the anti-rightist campaign and the Great Leap Forward were carefully couched so as to avoid staining Deng's own reputation.[19]

This document on party history could not—and would not—ignore the issue of Hua Guofeng in dealing with recent years. Hua and company were criticized in many subtle ways, though not yet by name. In fact, this historical resolution of Deng's was an imitation of Mao's similar resolution passed some forty years earlier in the wake of the Yan'an Rectification Movement. Although both Mao's and Deng's documents seemed to deal with party history, neither Mao nor Deng was concerned as much with past history as with current politics.

18

The Pinnacle of
Name and Fame, 1981-1984

It seemed a little puzzling that Deng had worked so hard to knock Hua Guofeng out of the leadership and yet refused to don the mantle of leadership himself. Despite persuasion and appeals from his colleagues, Deng thrice refused to formally assume the highest position as chairman of the CCP Central Committee. In July 1981, asked by an editor of a Hong Kong magazine to explain this puzzle, Deng replied with a sagacious smile, "Talking about name and fame, I already have a little of both, haven't I? No need for any more! One should be farsighted, not shortsighted. My health is still fine, no serious illness. But I am old and can only work for eight hours—more than that makes me tired. Hu Yaobang is sixty-six years old, not so young either. But he is very healthy, full of energy, and capable of working longer and harder. Let him do the job."[1]

Deng was indeed a farsighted and complex-minded politician. He did not care merely about his own "name and fame," either in a simple titular sense or in a purely personal sense. More precisely, he cared more about substantial power than about his formal title, and he also cared about impersonal policy issues, or what he thought would be good for the Communist Party and the Chinese nation.

Political power and political slogans could serve Deng—as they had many a contemporary politician—as either a means or an end, depending on particular and often delicate circumstances. At least in the years 1976–80, as I have stressed before, his primary concern was how to regain supreme power at Hua's expense. Once that goal had been

214

accomplished, he would begin to pursue economic and political reforms more seriously. The early 1980s marked a shift in the balance between these two kinds of concerns.

As a means of reversing the Cultural Revolution—in which millions of people, Deng included, had suffered arbitrary persecutions—Deng and the Communist Party began to emphasize the rule of law. The trial of the "Gang of Four" in January 1981 was publicly pronounced a purely legal matter. The trial was a good thing—by all means better than no trial at all. But as it turned out, the trial was neither so public nor so legal. Actually, it turned into an intraparty political deal and Deng's personal revenge on Jiang Qing and company. Behind the trial court, a special group headed by Peng Zhen was handling the matter, and behind Peng was Deng himself. Both the prosecutor and the defendant were well aware of the situation. Jiang yelled at the court, "Deng Xiaoping is a quisling and a fascist!" and Deng retorted accordingly, "Jiang Qing is a very vicious woman, too vicious to be described in words!"[2]

Nie Yuanzi, of Beijing University, whom the reader may remember from the Cultural Revolution, was sentenced to ten years in prison on Deng's personal order—certainly too harsh a punishment. Deng did not forgive and forget Nie, who had been the first to put up a large-character poster attacking Deng by name in November 1966. Besides, Deng assumed her to have been responsible for Deng Pufang's broken back in August 1968, just as Mao Zedong had assumed Peng Dehuai to have been responsible for Mao Anqing's death in the Korean War in 1950—although neither assumption is factually correct. Mao loved Mao Anqing as his eldest son and a possible successor, whereas his younger son and daughters all seemed politically hopeless; Deng loved Deng Pufang in precisely the same way, whereas his younger son and daughters also seemed politically hopeless.

Deng held that the party leadership should be diversified—seemingly a good thing. Thus, at the Fifth Plenum in early 1980, the Secretariat was restored, with Hu Yaobang as general secretary, while Hua remained as the party chairman. Deng also held that party and government functions should be separated—also not a bad idea. Thus, at the People's Congress in August–September 1980, Hua was forced to hand over his post as premier to Zhao Ziyang. But these kinds of policy excuses were somehow ignored at the Sixth Plenum in June 1981, when Hu replaced Hua as chairman and

Deng, Ye Jianying, Chen Yun, and Hua were expediently appointed deputy chairmen of the CCP Central Committee.

On January 13, 1982, the Politburo passed a resolution on rejuvenation of party and state leadership, establishing certain age limits for certain official ranks. Deng played the most active role in the rejuvenation effort, which again proved to be a case of public policy intertwined with power struggle. One side of the reality was that a majority of the party and state leaders were seventy or eighty years old, which definitely hindered the efficiency of leadership and had to be changed. Another side of the reality, however, was that Hua, who was younger than Deng, had pretty much lost all his power by that juncture, whereas Ye, who was much older than Deng, would be a new target for Deng to aim at through the rejuvenation effort.

The Twelfth National Party Congress, convened in Beijing on September 12–13, 1982, marked the final establishment of Deng's supreme authority, in terms of personnel alignment as well as policy orientation. The party's general line, expressed in the congress's political resolution, was "build up socialism with Chinese characteristics." Reunion with Taiwan, opposition to superpower hegemonism, and economic reconstruction were the three main objectives that Deng emphasized at the congress to be pursued during the 1980s. As for the longer term, Deng called for achieving a per capita annual income of one thousand dollars by the year 2000 and thus for the Chinese to reach what he called a "decent level" or a level of "small comfort." Simply put, while the political foundation would be kept intact, economic reconstruction would become the main goal of the Communist Party and the Chinese nation.[3]

Doubtless at Deng's order, the traditional posts of chairman and deputy chairmen of the party were all abolished. Hu was therefore reappointed general secretary, while Deng continued to chair the Central Military Council. Two new party institutions were created: the Central Advisory Commission, with Deng as its director, and the Central Disciplinary Commission, with Chen Yun as its director. Simply put, while Deng remained in primary control, Hu and others would assume secondary positions and handle routine operations.

If the Seventh Congress of 1945 was Mao's congress, the Twelfth Congress of 1982 could be regarded as Deng's congress. As a matter of fact, Deng himself made such a comparison between the two historic occasions. Meeting with Kim Il Sung at the Fishing Terrace

Guest Hall shortly after the congress on September 14, 1982, he proudly told the Korean leader, "The Twelfth Congress of our party bears some similarity to our Seventh Congress in 1945. The Seventh Congress had led to the victory of our revolution, and this Twelfth Congress will lead to the victory of our economic construction."[4]

As time passed, however, some differences became apparent. The Seventh Congress in 1945 had indeed paved a smooth road for the communist victory a few years later, but the Twelfth Congress in 1982 could hardly be said to have achieved a comparable feat. What about the later Thirteenth and Fourteenth Congresses—in which Hu and Zhao failed successively as Deng's successors—and the Fifteenth and Sixteenth Congresses, if the CCP continues to rule? Could the "victory of . . . economic construction" be so easily accomplished? There were further differences. The Seventh Congress had been marked by Mao's control over every aspect of party and army leadership, in name as well as in practice. At the Twelfth Congress, Deng held no formal or legitimate position as the party leader and could only operate behind the scenes. Mao had been fifty-two years old then, and Deng was seventy-eight years old in 1982—another significant difference.

The bewildering shifts in CCP personnel and institutions around the Twelfth Congress can best be understood in terms of Deng's psychology of name and fame: oftentimes, name and fame can be achieved by refusing name and fame! Deng wanted to expel Hua from higher power and demote Ye, who remained Deng's virtual equal in authority during the early 1980s. But Deng preferred to have Hu and Zhao pick up the official titles on his behalf.

Let's look at Deng's thinking in regard to party politics from another angle. At first, Hua was the party chairman, and the Secretariat was restored with Hu as general secretary, to check Hua's practical influence. That was no problem, as the 1956 precedent demonstrated. Then Hu replaced Hua as chairman but remained general secretary. That was unprecedented in party history—institutionally, a bit strange. Later still, Hu kept his chairmanship, whereas the Secretariat was abolished. Finally, the post of chairman was abolished, and Hu was shifted back to the post of general secretary. A puzzling maze indeed!

Deng's own thought processes provide the clue! He pushed Hua down but felt reluctant to take over Hua's post. He pulled Hu up but felt reluctant either to line up with Hu as deputy chairman or to grant Hu the title of chairman. After having worked with Chairman Mao for so many eventful years, the title of chairman had left Deng with a great many awesome and awful impressions. It would be too much to have another chairman—this time, Chairman Hu! Does this sound too banal as an explanation for the solemn reform of party leadership? Perhaps it is, but it happens to be the truth! This kind of intuitive analysis of Deng's thought processes, I would say, may be more fruitful than many "definitive quotes" and "hard facts."

In terms of seniority and authority, Ye Jianying alone remained in a position nearly equal to Deng's in the early 1980s. Chen Yun was not yet an issue. To check Ye in the Central Military Council, Deng put him alongside Xu Xiangqian, Nie Rongzhen, and Yang Shangkun, all as deputy chairmen. Ye was thus no longer as important as before in terms of his titular position, while in terms of practical work, Yang, as executive deputy chairman and chief secretary, ran the Military Council's daily affairs. Yang, a Sichuanese veteran with great capability and keen political instincts, began his intimate affiliation with Deng from this moment. At the age of eighty-five, Ye Jianying was sick and weak, inert professionally even in his own field of army affairs—albeit, unlike Hua, he did not lack seniority or capability.

Deng's apparently arbitrary reshuffle of party and army personnel displeased Marshal Ye, who left Beijing for his hometown of Canton in January 1981, as he had done in the spring of 1976—but with a very different result. He stayed in the south for some six months, until a personal envoy from Deng was dispatched to appeal for his return to Beijing in June 1981. Actually, Deng was just as glad that Ye had gone away for a while. By the time the old marshal came back to the capital, the Hua matter had finally been resolved, as had the matter of army leadership.[5]

What had been left for Ye was (1) one of the four deputy chairmanships of the Central Military Council, which Deng chaired, with Xu Xianqian as minister of defense and Yang Shangkun as chief executive with day-to-day responsibilities; and (2) the chairmanship of the National People's Congress, which was a rubber-stamp body in any event. Even in the People's Congress, Peng Zhen, in the post of executive deputy chairman, played a far more active and substantial role than Ye did.

It was under these circumstances that, from late December 1982 to early January 1983, a national conference of the army chiefs of staff was held, at which Deng, Xu, Nie, and Yang were all present, but Ye was noticeably absent. Presumably, Ye's advanced age, poor health, and frustrated state of mind prevented him from attending to army and/or party activities any longer. In helping to engineer the removal of the "Gang of Four," this old soldier had inadvertently paved the way, not only for Deng's rise, but also for his own fall.

By the early 1980s, Deng's position as China's paramount leader had been firmly established. It became a fact known to almost everybody, Chinese or foreign, party member or common citizen. Deng was chairman of the Military Council and held exclusive authority over the People's Liberation Army. Hu, as general secretary of the party, and Zhao, as premier of the government, were both his junior protégés, not even remotely comparable to Deng in terms of seniority or authority.

The two newly founded central institutions—that is, the Central Advisory Commission and the Central Disciplinary Commission, headed by Deng and Chen Yun, respectively—were fraught with delicate personal and political relations. Literally, Deng was supposed to offer advice on the party's overall policy initiatives, while Chen was just supposed to deal with the behavior or misbehavior of individual party members. Hence, Deng's function was more substantive than Chen's. Besides, despite his high seniority—as high as Deng's if not higher—Chen had always been more of a technical person than a political one, ever since the Long March years of the 1930s and particularly since the 1950s.

Chen differed from Deng and Ye in that he was detail-oriented and hardworking and held fast to moral dignity and political principles. He could work with Deng as he had with Mao, as long as their policy directives did not stray too far from points he deemed essential. Anyhow, Chen did not yet constitute a challenge or a threat to Deng—nor would he until the late 1980s, when he began to have serious doubts about Deng's reform and openness policy and its consequences.[6]

It should be re-emphasized that, for Deng political power was a crucial issue, but not the only issue. He also cared about policy. While both power and policy concerned him very much in a general sense, either this or that matter might capture his primary attention at a particular time and under particular circumstances. Following his firmer consolidation of central power in the early 1980s, Deng would push more vigorously for grass-roots social and economic reforms, particularly agrarian reforms in the vast countryside.

The earlier rural reform policy of the "household responsibility system" had evolved from experiments by Wan Li in Anhui and Zhao Ziyang in Sichuan in 1978–79 and culminated in an upsurge in the country's agricultural output in 1981–82. Deng encouraged Wan and Zhao. Their performance was an economic matter as well as a political one. One might say that Wan and Zhao entered the Politburo because of their pioneering work in the rural reforms. One might also say, equally correctly, that they both were bound for the Politburo from the moment Deng supported their experiments with rural reforms. One might also say, of course, that the cause and the result were intertwined.[7]

Although Hua's "leftist line" had caused problems in the financial and industrial fields, Deng's agricultural policy seemed to have had just the opposite effect: Hua worked hard and ended up being blamed, whereas Deng took it easy and ended up being praised. Why? It was because Deng's agrarian reforms involved no hardship on the part of the party or government but rather a sort of "hands-off" policy toward the peasants. There seemed neither harm nor cost in leaving the peasants free to get rich by and for themselves—and eventually for the benefit of the party and state as well!

In reality, there was no basic difference between the "household responsibility system" and *baochan daohu,* or the "household assignment of production quotas," implemented by Deng Zihui, condoned by Liu Shaoqi, and later prohibited by Mao in the early 1960s. It was largely a matter of common sense and political courage rather than economic expertise. It was nothing new. Before 1954–56, and historically for thousands of years, Chinese peasants had tilled and farmed their own private land!

From 1980 onward, the rural reforms spread rapidly throughout the country. Instead of the old policy of enlarging the fringe land, the new policy allowed distribution of all the land of the communes and their production brigades to individual peasant households. Although the land remained nominally under collective ownership, the peasants could farm their own share almost any way they preferred. In return, they were to pay a fixed amount of tax or rent in grain to the government and some fees to the village administration.

In January 1982, the entire system of people's communes, production brigades, and production teams was abolished; instead, the age-old divisions of village, township, and district were restored. More concrete regulations were also enacted: land allocation was stipulated as being unchangeable for fifteen years. On their plots, the peasants might grow "cash crops" other than just grain; they might even use their land for other purposes, such as raising animals and fish, as long as they paid their rents and fees in cash. It would also be acceptable for them to sublet their land to others and undertake other work in the village or outside it. A peasant who makes money is a good peasant—just as a cat that catches mice is a good cat!

The impact of Deng's agrarian reforms on agricultural production and the Chinese countryside in general proved simply breathtaking. From 1978 to 1984, the per capita output of grain for the total population grew by an average of 3.8 percent each year, compared to an annual average of 0.2 percent from 1957 to 1977. During the same period, the output of cotton rose by 17.5 percent, compared to a drop of 0.6 percent for 1957–77; and the output of meat rose by 9.0 percent, compared to a rise of 1.7 percent for 1957–77. The peasants' eating and living standards were greatly improved. For centuries in northern China, where I was raised, peasants had eaten "rough grains" such as corn, sorghum, and sweet potatoes as their basic diet and "fine grains" such as wheat and rice only as rare treats on holidays and other special occasions. Since 1984, wheat flour has become their staple food, and they eat sweet potatoes—no longer sweet potato flour—only rarely. It is a huge change, and a big deal indeed!

For many years during the Mao era, China maintained an independent or closed-door economy, shunning "foreign loans and debts" and refusing to import foreign machinery and equipment. That attitude changed immediately after Mao's death and the downfall of the "Gang of Four." Under Hua, China seemed to have had just the opposite problem: it attempted to spend too much money to buy too many foreign things. Both in response to this problem and as an excuse to undermine Hua, Zhao exaggerated the economic situation in 1980. Under the circumstances, Deng's open-door policy was temporarily downplayed and its focus shifted a bit. Instead of borrowing foreign money and purchasing foreign goods, Deng found that his interests were best served by opening more special economic zones (SEZs).

The first group of four special economic zones had been established in 1979, in Shenzhen, Zhuhai, Shantou, and Xiamen—all coastal cities adjacent to Hong Kong and Taiwan. Government and economic enterprises in those cities were allowed extra administrative independence and legal freedom to conduct business and trade with foreigners. From late January to early February 1984, Deng made an inspection tour of the special economic zones. He left an inscription in Shenzhen, "The progress and experience in Shenzhen bore witness to the correctness of our special economic zone policy," and another in Xiamen, "The SEZ matter should be done faster and better." Upon returning to Beijing, on February 24, 1984, Deng met with Hu and Zhao and called for more openness and more SEZs: "The special economic zone is a boon for technology, management, knowledge, and also diplomacy. It brings in all sorts of benefits. It will serve as the basis for our openness and benefit us not only in terms of economics but also in terms of the education of personnel and diplomatic influence. Besides the present special zones, we should open more locales and harbor cities in the same way."[8]

On orders from Deng, the Secretariat and the State Council held a joint conference from March 26 to April 6, 1984. As a result, fourteen more cities along the eastern coast and all of Hainan Island were designated special economic zones. The purpose was not only to conduct international trade as before but also to attract foreign investment. By combining foreign capital and Chinese labor, it was hoped that the special economic zones would enable China to build up its own factories and workshops to produce goods that would be exported in exchange for foreign currency.

Implementation of the SEZ policy passed through three stages, with varying results and consequences: a positive stage in the mid-1980s, a negative stage in the late 1980s, and another positive stage in the early 1990s. At this initial stage, the SEZs provided immediate stimulation for China's economic development with very little monetary input and managerial effort from the central leadership. Once again, it was a matter of political courage rather than economic expertise on Deng's part. He simply opened China's territory to the business world and permitted Chinese labor to work for foreign investors, leaving them together to get rich for their own benefit and also eventually for the benefit of the party and the state. It seemed like a good bargain and an easy bargain as well!

In 1983, a nationwide campaign was initiated to, in Deng's own words, fight against "capitalist spiritual pollution" and promote "socialist spiritual civilization."[9] The campaign eventually boiled down to a few popular slogans, which can be literally translated as "Five Talks on Four Beauties with Three Loves." This anti–spiritual pollution campaign started off vigorously enough by targeting girls' slit skirts and boys' oily hair, Beethoven's "rotten" music, and Sartre's "decadent" philosophy, but it soon ran out of steam. Its only lasting result was that Deng Liqun, its chief proponent, lost his official position. But from Deng Xiaoping's own perspective, the starting and the stopping of the campaign were OK, as long as both actions displayed his personal authority.

The anti–spiritual pollution campaign among the masses was matched by a parallel anticorruption campaign among the higher officialdom, which also failed to achieve no more than half-baked results. Many high officials and their children were indeed found liable for various types of corruption. Zhu De's grandson was executed, but Peng Zhen's daughter was exonerated. Hu Qiaomu's son was arrested, but Yu Qiuli's son was protected. Although the explanations were complicated, the underlying rationale was pretty obvious: Zhu was already dead, but Peng was still alive; Hu was a tender-minded scholar, but Yu was a tough soldier. This campaign also seemed fine to Deng as an expression of his authority and attitude, for Deng, unlike Mao, never wanted to carry any political drive to its extreme.[10]

It was also in 1983 that the *Selected Works of Deng Xiaoping* was published—with a total of as many as twelve million copies printed. This was another way for Deng to show his supreme authority, like Mao before him. In sharp contrast with Mao's writings, however, Deng's works consist merely of bureaucratic reports and conference speeches. They contain neither references to ancient history and classics nor quotations from Marx and Lenin. Even the few casual mentions of their names sound more negative than positive. "Marx and Engels lived and died in the last century," Deng said in one of his articles; "they were great, but we shouldn't expect them to come alive and help solve all our problems today."[11]

In regard to a world outlook, one might say that Deng seemed to substitute an optimistic for a pessimistic view about the possibility of a peaceful world; he stopped dwelling on the inevitability of world war(s). Nonetheless, one might also say that Deng seemed to exchange revolutionary optimism for political pessimism; he no longer ranted about international communism and world revolution. Both of the above changes just "seemed" to have occurred, however, without Deng himself having openly declared or clearly articulated them. Deng still regarded the major foreign threat to China as coming from the Soviet Union, but that reflected less the military reality than Deng's economic and diplomatic cooperation with the West, particularly the United States.

National reunification—a problem that fell somewhere between domestic policy and international policy—loomed large on Deng's agenda. That meant, of course, the Taiwan and Hong Kong issues. Deng received Winston Yang, a Taiwanese professor teaching at Seton Hall University in New Jersey, on June 26, 1983, and took the opportunity to express a new attitude on the part of the CCP toward the Kuomintang (KMT) in Taiwan: the key to the problem was national reunification, and anything else was only secondary, Deng told Yang; after reunification, Taiwan would be allowed to retain its existing social and economic systems and even its government and armed forces. All the communist mainland seemed to require was that the nationalist Taiwan change its name from the Republic of China (ROC) to the People's Republic of China (PRC).[12]

Out of this casual conversation eventually emerged an official policy called "two systems in one nation," which could supposedly be applied not only to Taiwan but to Hong Kong as well. Deng was fond of summarizing a complicated issue in a simple phrase. In the next couple of years, he would proudly dwell on his newly invented "two systems in one nation" concept with almost every foreign visitor he encountered, including U.S. President Ronald Reagan and British Prime Minister Margaret Thatcher.

The nationalists in Taiwan, still regarding Deng's remarks as nothing but the old united-front policy dressed in a new overcoat, offered no official response; it would take a few more years before there was any positive response. The British, who had leased Hong Kong from China, responded immediately and vigorously, however; London's lease on this colonial island would expire in 1997, and understandings had to be reached in advance regarding its future status.[13]

Official negotiations between London and Beijing over Hong Kong started in September 1982 with Thatcher's first visit to China and concluded in December 1984 with Thatcher's second visit and the signing of a joint statement with Premier Zhao. Deng met and talked with Thatcher on both visits. He did not take part in the formal negotiations, but his strong interest and decisive role in the entire process were obvious to both sides.

As renewing the lease—a faint hope harbored by some business-minded British politicians prior to the negotiations—appeared out of the question, the British side tried to apply Deng's "two systems in one nation" idea to Hong Kong. How about returning Hong Kong's titular sovereignty to China while maintaining British administration there? That was unacceptable to the Chinese, who wanted to take over Hong Kong's sovereignty as well as its administration. Beijing promised only to maintain Hong Kong's political stability and economic prosperity; after its return to China in 1997, Hong Kong could keep its capitalist system under an autonomous government for fifty years; and that government would be formed by the residents of Hong Kong themselves, not by the British.

After several preliminary rounds, the negotiations delved into more detail in the summer of 1984. Could China perhaps promise not to send its troops to Hong Kong after 1997? That was a serious matter, as few Hong Kong businesspeople would like to see bayonet-toting Liberation Army soldiers patrolling their office buildings. Such a promise had seemed like a good possibility because two senior Chinese officials, Huang Hua and Geng Biao, had already suggested it.

On May 25, 1984, Deng publicly received a group of Hong Kong representatives who were attending a session of the People's Congress in Beijing. The reception took place in the Great Hall of the People. To the surprise of all present, Deng said that he would make a special personal statement. Then everybody heard him declare loudly and clearly:

> Let me take this opportunity to clarify two issues. First, in regard to our policy toward Hong Kong, what I say counts, what Premier Zhao says counts, and the same with Foreign Minister Wu. Whatever others say does not officially count and is null and void! Second, let me clarify a rumor. What Huang Hua and Geng Biao said the other day is bullshit! It does not represent the central government's policy. There will be troops deployed in Hong Kong after 1997. As it is Chinese territory, why can't we deploy our troops there? You folks may go back and print as public news what I have just said.[14]

Nothing like that had ever happened before. The Hong Kong news reporters were startled, though perhaps happy and excited from a purely professional standpoint. It became the following day's biggest news story. The Hong Kong stock market reacted badly to Deng's remarks: its Hang Seng index dropped sharply, by 200 points. Of the two Chinese officials referred to by Deng, Huang was the former foreign minister and currently a member of the State Council, and Geng was a deputy premier and the minister of defense. They were not just ordinary citizens. Deng's despotic outrage was overwhelming, as bad as Mao's or even worse. Mao had rudely sworn at his subordinates on a few "closed-door" occasions, but Deng did so with an "open door" to the entire Hong Kong press!

In April 1984, Deng met with the leaders of Japan's Komeito Party in his Zhongnanhai guest hall. Obviously satisfied with his Japanese junior visitors bowing their heads and listening to him attentively, Deng lectured them in a monologue: "China will develop its own economy. China cannot close its doors and just defend its borders. It should be open to the outside world. This policy of China's will not change in this century. As for the next century, during the first fifty years, it will also not change. How about during the second fifty years?" Deng paused, seemed a bit indecisive, but finally declared resolutely, "No. No, it will not change then either."[15]

In May 1984, Deng met with U.S. President Ronald Reagan, also in Zhongnanhai—the first visit of an American president to China after the two countries' normalization of diplomatic relations. Beaming and in a confident mood, Deng declared, "We are firmly determined to achieve a peaceful reunification with Taiwan. We need your sympathetic understanding, but please don't interfere with China's internal affairs." Before that meeting, China had successfully negotiated with the United States certain restrictions on Taiwan's purchases of weapons. Like Mao, Deng seemed to prefer Republicans to Democrats. Reagan and Deng appeared to share a common ground in their opposition to the military threat posed by the Soviet Union.[16]

August 22, 1984, was Deng's eightieth birthday, a special occasion for an elderly person, which was celebrated privately at his own home. He turned away all high officials and had only his family members and some service staff attend the party. The birthday cake, three feet high, two feet across, and shaped like an ice cream cone, was a bit of the West with Chinese characteristics. Exactly eighty peaches and eighty candles were placed in several layers around the cream cone, fenced in with rolls of tissue paper on every layer. To the paper were glued eighty golden pairs of characters reading "Long Life!" As Deng's wife smiled, his daughters laughed, his grandchildren yelled joyfully, and the servants watched carefully, Deng puffed to blow out the candles. The old man was really happy and gratified![17]

October 1, 1984, was the thirty-fifth anniversary of the founding of the People's Republic—a special national holiday, celebrated with extraordinary fanfare. During Mao's years, the pattern (with a few exceptions, such as in 1961, 1962, 1971, and 1976) had been that Mao and his colleagues would watch the massive parade from the rostrum of the Gate of Heavenly Peace. But this time, it turned out to be Deng's one-man show!

The weather was perfect. Beijing basked in fresh autumn air and golden sunshine. Deng and his comrades watched a parade lasting more than three hours: columns of soldiers from all branches of the armed forces; followed by columns of men and women from all professions—students, workers, peasants; with lorries carrying ballistic missiles as the finale. A military band of some two hundred played the national anthem and then the army anthem. So far, the events were virtually a rerun of the Mao years.

Imitating Mao on the PRC's founding day in 1949, Deng also made a brief speech. Thirty-five years ago, Mao had stated, "The Chinese people have now stood up!" On this anniversary, Deng echoed, "The Chinese people are now stronger and wealthier!" Deng then broke with Mao's precedent by suddenly riding out of the Gate of Heavenly Peace in an open car to review the troops who were awaiting their turn to march by. Dressed in a green military uniform with a red star–studded army cap, Deng saluted each contingent as his vehicle passed. Thunderous cheers and applause burst out, "Terrific, Chief!" Deng yelled back, "Terrific, Comrades!"[18]

In the People's Republic, it was a national holiday, the most important one of the year. Nobody had to go to work. One billion people were watching Deng on TV at home. They observed, among other less apparent matters, that this old man was really happy and satisfied! Indeed, the year 1984 marked the zenith of Deng's personal and political triumph!

As 1984 ebbed away, Deng seemed quite content and confident. He had attained full control of the central power. Nobody could challenge his ultimate authority. Both Hu and Zhao were his junior disciples, devoted to him personally and to his reform and openness line. Ye was gone, and Chen was down. The national economy was growing at the fastest pace in China's history. The results of the agricultural reform were remarkable, and the urban industrial reform showed great promise. Relations with the United States were at their best. Deng had just subdued Great Britain over the Hong Kong matter. Even if he kept calling the Soviet Union names, Deng knew it was no real threat.

Everything looked good for Deng and could be expected to get even better. Although he held just a few nominal titles, he enjoyed a lot of substantial power. He was doing little but getting much. He was happy and at ease. Hence, I term 1984 the "pinnacle of name and fame" for Deng. He had reached the age of eighty, and the communist regime had reached the age of thirty-five—both special occasions. Five years earlier, October 1, 1979, it had not been Deng's national day but Hua's, and five years later, in 1989, as we shall see, the student protests would spoil both Deng's eighty-fifth birthday and the People's Republic's fortieth anniversary.

— 19 —

Unsuccessful Successors, 1985-1988

Deng received Prime Minister Lee Kuan Yew of Singapore at his Beijing residence in September 1985, with particular warmth and intimacy. For various reasons, Lee was one of the very few noncommunist foreigners with whom Deng would occasionally confer on private matters. Deng held Lee in high regard, for under his leadership Singapore had become one of the economic miracles, or "four small dragons," in East Asia, and Deng also liked his authoritative control of the Singapore government. All in all, Deng respected Lee as a successful Chinese statesman. Deng told Lee, "Everything in China is going smoothly. I am very glad. I have neither worries nor concerns at all."[1]

Production output had increased rapidly and continued to do so in China throughout the 1980s. The gross national product grew by 11 percent in 1985 and by 10 percent in 1986. Deng's policy of reform and openness seemed to be faring quite well. Nonetheless, all kinds of problems—social, economic, and political as well as ideological—that had remained somewhat hidden until 1984 became ever more apparent in 1985 and 1986. Deng seemed too content to notice these problems. Even the rural reforms about which he used to boast were not proceeding as smoothly as he had thought; the urban reforms would prove even tougher.

What the rural reforms had given the peasants in the countryside was primarily the private tenancy of land and the freedom of individual tillage. They were released from the previous shackles of the people's communes. In other words, Deng's policy removed the negative but did not build up the positive. Because China's arable land was very limited and its rural population enormous, what to do with the surplus labor force became an urgent problem, especially after the dissolution of the people's communes. First, much of the surplus labor force went into the category of the special households, or the rural industrial and commercial sectors, either individual or cooperative. By 1985, about one-tenth of the rural population, or 80 million peasants, belonged to that category. Still, about 60 million more had temporarily or permanently given up their rural residences and moved to the cities, especially those in the eastern coastal regions, to work or look for jobs. That large-scale emigration from rural areas partly accounted for the fact that, in 1985, grain output fell by more than fifty-three million tons.[2]

The dissolution of the people's communes, which had previously been not only a form of productive organization but also a local administrative system, coupled with the upsurge in specialized household activities, caused a variety of disorders and corruption in the countryside. In the central government, Deng had made no careful arrangements to deal with the new situation, while local governments and administrations were paralyzed for years; it was only natural that various problems cropped up and went unsolved.

This book is not intended as a comprehensive survey of the rural reforms and their consequences, either positive or negative. I will therefore just note that there existed three inter-related problems: the problem of China as a whole; that of the communist system in general; and that of Deng as the supreme leader, who was rather old and lacked the necessary hands-on control. In the mid-1980s, for instance, there was a very popular saying: "Out of the eight hundred million peasants, there are now eight hundred million businessmen." Although such a situation was, in a positive sense, at least inevitable and might have had certain advantages, it was definitely bad from the standpoint of rural governmental and administrative rule.

In January 1985, the Yangtze and Pearl River Valleys were hurriedly designated as special economic zones (SEZs) and declared open to foreign investment. That seemed too much for Chen Yun and other conservatives. In June 1985, Chen complained, "The special economic zones have strayed well off the socialist line." Chen further argued, "As every province wants to open one or more SEZs, foreign influences will rush in, and along with them, domestic corruption will rise up." At the same time, Hu Qiaomu stated even more boldly that the SEZs were tantamount to "foreign colonies."[3]

The special economic zones were supposed to absorb foreign capital and provide Chinese labor and raw materials in order to produce goods that could be sold abroad for foreign cash. They thus enjoyed various tax and tariff concessions, with each zone operating almost totally free from taxes and tariffs during its first three years. But the end results seemed just the opposite of what had been intended: officials and businessmen abused their favored tariff status to buy valuable consumer goods on the foreign market, like TV sets and automobiles, and then sold them to the inland market, deducting huge commissions. Bribery and embezzlement became unavoidable, and the 1985 Hainan automobile scandal, in which local party cadres grabbed millions of dollars by smuggling foreign cars and selling them at inland black markets, was but one example of such notorious abuses.

In his speech to an October 1984 symposium on China's economic and trading relations with foreign countries, Deng acknowledged: "I am just a layman in the field of economics. Sometimes I make a few remarks on this field, but all from a general political vantage. I have proposed China's economic policy of openness to the outside world, but as for the details or specifics of how to implement it, I have to say that I myself know very little indeed."[4]

That was a good confession and, I must say, truly a very honest one. Nevertheless, despite Deng's own acknowledgment of the problem, the problem itself remained. Deng's relevance to economic affairs and modernization in the 1980s was not comparable to Mao Zedong's relevance to military affairs and state power in the 1940s; nor was the problem Deng faced comparable to the problem Mao had faced. Mao knew his primary business well; Deng didn't. The economy was supposed to be the centerpiece of Deng's later career. A layman's knowledge and performance therefore seemed insufficient. Policy or politics, good as it might be in the first place, was not quite enough. Removing the political barriers to economic growth was a good starting point, but then what? How could the country progress beyond that point? Deng was forced to answer some questions that he was neither qualified nor even prepared to answer. Regarding the problem with inflation in 1987, for example, he could say no more than, "Break the impasse of price reform!" Although Deng was a pragmatic politician, his pragmatic insights would often be limited by the fact that he was a communist as well as an old-timer.

Despite the existing problems, Deng preferred to push even further forward. In fact, he regarded the year 1985 as a basic point of demarcation for China's, or his own, economic reform program: "Since the Third Plenum of the Eleventh Congress, we have had three years of economic reforms in the countryside, and the achievements are obvious. From now onward, after the Third Plenum of the Twelfth Congress, we will shift the focus of our economic reforms from the countryside to the cities. That represents an all-round development of the economic reforms, and we are expecting to make the same achievements in the next three years."[5]

Although they had never been clearly defined by Deng or anybody else, the urban economic reforms were gradually downgraded—or upgraded, if one likes—to "economic system reform" and finally "political system reform." Either way, the reforms went too far astray to be practically achievable. For 1986, Deng raised what he called "two hands," one to grab economic reconstruction and another to grab political system reforms. Of the two hands, he attempted to emphasize the latter in particular: "Economic reforms cannot go well without political reforms—that is, division of party and government functions, decentralization of political power, and reduction of administrative apparatus."[6]

Indeed, urban industrial and financial reforms could not succeed without political system reforms. But this problem was far easier to see than to solve. As part of the reform of the political system, for instance, Deng publicly pledged to reduce the People's Liberation Army by one million troops. But who was supposed to carry out this reduction? Not Deng himself but Hu Yaobang, who was in charge of the Party Center's routine affairs. Some of the troops to be demobilized were army veterans, who had served forty or fifty years and had deep personal and factional connections to the central authority. They would make numerous complaints and requests regarding their residences, pensions, medical treatment, and so forth, just as Vietnam veterans had done here in the United States.

Deng wanted to dismiss one-third, or two hundred thousand, of the six hundred thousand party and government bureaucrats. This downsizing also seemed like a pretty good idea, but again, who was going to carry it out and take the blame for it? Hu! Appropriate arrangements had to be made for the former bureaucrats' new positions, new salaries, new houses, spouses' jobs, children's schools, and a hundred other problems. The satisfied ones would be forgotten immediately, and only the unhappy ones would be remembered permanently.

Deng also wanted all corrupt officials, as well as their children and relatives who had benefited from their corruption, no matter how high their positions, to be legally punished. That sounded very good, too. But who was to carry out this reform and take the responsibility? Hu, again! Then came Peng Zhen's daughter and Wang Zhen's and Bo Yibo's sons, who had reportedly committed various economic misdemeanors; even Deng's own children, Deng Pufang and Deng Nan, were said not to be so "clear and clean." The complications and confrontations seemed endless!

As time passed, some of the political reforms barely succeeded, and others failed at an embryonic stage, but the tensions between Hu and veteran leaders such as Wang Zhen and Bo Yibo could only worsen; in the meantime, Hu's image as an ideal successor became more blurred in Deng's eyes. The gun had already been loaded, so to speak, and its trigger would be pulled by the 1986–87 student demonstrations.

Hu Yaobang had joined the revolution at the age of fifteen and took part in the Long March at the age of eighteen. He got to know Deng in the Jiangxi Soviet in the early 1930s and got along well with him in the early 1950s in Sichuan. When Deng was the "lord of the southwest," Hu worked there as a political director in an army corps and later as party secretary of a prefecture. They were both summoned to Beijing in 1952. Hu became the general secretary of the Communist Youth League and Deng the general secretary of the Communist Party.[7]

Hu's political affiliation with Deng in an intraparty factional sense, however, began only in 1975 during their common struggle against the "Gang of Four" and grew closer in 1978 against Hua Guofeng. Hu showed himself as the most outspoken in confronting Hua and Ye Jianying in favor of Deng's reformist line and would continue to confront Wang Zhen and Bo Yibo in the same manner. For various personal and political reasons, however, Deng did not want to offend Wang and Bo beyond a certain point. While Deng, already the national leader, attempted to maintain a power balance between Hu and Wang and Bo, his confidence in Hu necessarily eroded.

Although Hu had neither much formal education nor a subtle disposition, he was a candid and straightforward person. That was what Deng had liked about him in their alliance against Jiang Qing and Hua in the first place. Once he became the general secretary and was subjected to public scrutiny, however, Hu could not help making errors, especially during receptions for foreign visitors. Once, in a meeting with Lu Keng, a devious Hong Kong news reporter, Hu was reminded that he and Wang Zhen were born in the same locality. He fell into the trap. "It is true that we both were originally brought up in the same spot," Hu laughed, "but we are now traveling on different roads."[8] After the news report was published, Wang protested to Deng and accused Hu of exposing intraparty matters to a foreigner. On another occasion, when he received a group of Japanese visitors, Hu, obviously on impulse, invited a Japanese youth delegation, two thousand in all, on a free tour of China. Party veterans later scolded him for the huge expense.

Satirical stories and slanderous rumors about Hu began to pop up one after another. But that was not the problem. The real problem was his relationship with Deng. In a certain sense, relations between Deng and Hu were bound to be like a Catch-22—perhaps somewhat akin to the dilemma of the animal tamer and the wild animal in a circus act: on the one hand, the tamer wants the animal to move freely; on the other hand, the tamer does not want the animal to move freely!

In the fields of ideology and education, the salaries of intellectuals and teachers were raised, but they could hardly keep pace with the salary levels in society at large. It might not be so difficult for a professor of physics to earn some extra money by repairing electrical equipment in his neighborhood or for a professor of English to earn some extra money by teaching a night class at home to youngsters who wanted so desperately to go abroad. But what about those majoring in "pure theory" or "fine arts," like philosophy, history, literature, and political science? What could they do? They had helped Jiang Qing criticize Lin Biao and Confucius in 1975, and they had also helped Deng advocate the doctrine "Practice is the sole criterion for truth" in 1978. These people were Marxists by profession and political critics by nature, and now they were hopelessly unemployed.

Only a couple of years earlier, Deng had encouraged Hu to work with outspoken intellectuals such as Liu Binyan, Fang Lizhi, Wang Ruowang, Su Shaozhi, Guo Luoji, and Ruan Ming to "liberate people's minds." Now, Deng was asking Hu to fight against them as "bourgeois liberals." Hu tried his best but still found it difficult to please Deng on the one hand and these intellectual friends on the other. The end result was that both sides were displeased.

College students were even more unpredictable. Although they sometimes protested for good reasons—such as because their dormitories were too crowded (eight in a room) and their expenses for food were still too high (the food that had cost them twenty yuan per month before now cost them fifty yuan per month)—they might also protest for hardly any reason. They were a new generation of angry young men and women! They made as much noise when the Chinese women's volleyball team won as when the Chinese men's football team lost. They raised their voices in protest as patriots when the Japanese emperor visited Beijing, though all of them wanted to leave China for abroad—ideally, for Japan or America.

Deng had once listed "legalization" as one of the major objectives of the political system reforms, and the local elections of 1980 were part of that legalization endeavor. Party leaders called on college students to participate in elections of district representatives to local People's Congresses. In some cases, the students succeeded in getting their own candidates elected, grew excited, and wanted to push forward. In other cases, they failed, were unhappy, and would find opportunities to complain. Either way, the elections became for them a quasi mobilization for political participation.

An incipient student movement broke out at the University of Science and Technology in Anhui on December 9, 1986, and rapidly spread to Shanghai's Jiaotong University. There was an open debate between the students and the newly appointed Shanghai mayor, Jiang Zemin. Jiang was humiliated. Only one center could or would normally exist at any one time in a student movement, and the center, like the eye of a hurricane, soon moved northward to Beijing. What happened in Shanghai was quickly repeated in Beijing, particularly at Beijing University and the Chinese People's University. The students in Beijing had the advantage of access to Tiananmen Square in the middle of the capital city. They went there in late December 1986, shouting slogans like "Improve intellectuals' living conditions!" and "Down with corrupt officials!" It should be noted that most of their slogans were in compliance with the official line at the time, just as they would later be during the Democratic Movement in 1989.[9]

On December 30, 1986, Deng talked to a group of veteran leaders about the student demonstrations: "This student uproar is not in itself a big deal, but its very nature suggests a big deal. Firm measures should be taken against those who charged the Square of Heavenly Peace.

Since the Beijing government has announced regulations regarding parades and strikes, they have the status of law and must be implemented. We should not compromise in this regard." Deng continued, declaring, "This is not just an issue in only one or two places, nor just an issue of only one or two years. It is a result of these several years' ambiguity and hesitation in fighting against bourgeois liberalization."[10]

The student protest was indeed, as Deng had put it, "no big deal": it lasted only a couple of days and involved a couple of thousand youngsters from a couple of universities. It was soon peacefully ended. Beijing University's president rented a dozen trucks to drive his young people back to the campus and meanwhile negotiated with the metropolitan police to free the few who had been arrested. As so often happens in modern history, the university authorities, once caught between their own students' demonstrations and the government's suppressions, would come to act as moderate mediators between the two sides.

In retrospect, the 1986 incident may be seen as merely a prelude to the 1989 Democratic Movement. Already tired of Hu, however, Deng readily acceded to the demands of Wang Zhen and other veterans— none of whom any longer constituted a personal challenge to Deng. After a few days of a so-called party life conference in early January 1987, Hu was pressed to submit a self-criticism and also resign his position as general secretary of the Chinese Communist Party (CCP) Central Committee.

In order both to please Deng and to take advantage of Hu's predicament for his own benefit—this should particularly be mentioned, because many outside observers claim just the opposite—Zhao Ziyang lined up with the party veterans against Hu. Thereafter, at Deng's recommendation, Zhao became the acting general secretary immediately after Hu's dismissal. Needless to say, this new appointment meant that Deng had selected a fresh successor apparent.[11]

Zhao's personal relationship with Deng had started in the 1940s, well after Hu's. But once again, recent intraparty affiliation was more important than wartime cooperation. Zhao won Deng's confidence through his effective anti-Hua performance during the years 1980–82. Deng disliked Hu's rough manner and indelicate style; in that respect, Zhao seemed far better. Zhao was smart and prudent in official work and loyal to Deng's reform policy. Zhao's age and seniority were also suitable: he was born in 1919 and had joined the party in 1938—

neither so young that he might worry his Party Center colleagues nor so old that he would soon be a candidate for "rejuvenation."[12]

After Hu's dismissal and the expulsion of liberal intellectuals like Fang Lizhi, Liu Binyan, and Wang Ruowang from the party, Deng would nonetheless not allow his reform policy to be challenged; nor would Zhao, who was more than happy to follow Deng's line in this regard. Because of their respective positions, Deng could afford to play a "double-face" game, but Zhao could only play a "single-face" one. Therefore, the "announcement" of the CCP Central Committee, on January 28, 1987, drafted by Zhao and approved by Deng, sternly warned against any excessive measures in the antiliberalization campaign. The campaign would be strictly confined to the party leadership, to the field of political ideology, to the matter of high party principle, and so forth.[13] One group of restrictions after another led eventually to the campaign's de facto abolition, and it was, in reality, stillborn.

Deng instructed Zhao in May 1987, "We should not allow what happened last year to influence our reform and openness. We should not only continue sticking to the reforms but hasten our steps in carrying them out."[14] As a result, except during the first couple of months of the year, there was little talk and even less action with respect to the problem of bourgeois liberalization or spiritual pollution. Instead, even louder and bolder calls for reform and openness were heard from both Zhao and especially Deng throughout the rest of 1987.

But Deng, not Zhao, had the responsibility of explaining to the outside world why Hu had been dismissed. He did so by stressing to his foreign guests the necessity of unity and stability as a precondition for China's deeper economic reforms and faster modernization. Such were the main points of his conversations on March 3, 1987, with U.S. Secretary of State George Shultz and on June 29 with former U.S. President Jimmy Carter, among a dozen other foreign dignitaries who visited Beijing at about that time.

On October 25, 1987, at the party's Thirteenth National Congress, Deng made the opening speech, and Zhao gave the general political report, entitled "March Forward along the Road of Socialism with Chinese Characteristics." The Politburo Standing Committee, newly reformed during the Thirteenth Congress, consisted of Zhao Ziyang, Li Peng, Qiao Shi, Hu Qili, and Yao Yilin—all new members with the exception of Zhao, who formally assumed the title of party general secretary.

Before and during the Thirteenth Congress, Deng clearly stated that he did not want to be re-elected to the party's Central Committee, and his name was therefore not included in the list of candidates. Following Deng's lead, as they had to, Chen Yun, Li Xiannian, Peng Zhen, Bo Yibo, Wang Zhen, and almost all the other party veterans declared their retirement. Thus, none of their names could be found in the new Central Committee, let alone in the Politburo.[15]

Chen Yun took over the chairmanship of the Central Advisory Commission, and Deng, despite his having asked to resign, continued to chair the Central Military Council. At Deng's recommendation, Zhao Ziyang was appointed first deputy chairman of the Military Council, while Yang Shangkun remained executive deputy chairman in charge of the council's routine affairs. Li Peng assumed the post of acting premier upon Chen's recommendation; he was soon formally appointed premier at the National People's Congress.

Hence, while Deng got things mostly his way, he had to compromise with the other veterans—notably, Chen Yun. The promotion of Li Peng as a member of the Politburo Standing Committee and premier of the State Council was a big issue at the time, yet not as big as it would later prove to be. Li, the son of a party veteran killed by the Kuomintang in the 1930s, had been adopted by Zhou Enlai and his wife at Yan'an in the 1940s. It was through Madame Zhou's recommendation that Li had entered the Politburo in the first place. Everything about Li looked fine to Deng, except perhaps one matter: Li seemed too arrogant and stubborn to be Deng's own man, either personally or politically.

Despite his official retirement from the party leadership, Deng remained the paramount leader, who alone had the final say on all the party's key matters. In fact, the Thirteenth Party Congress passed a special resolution to make sure that "Comrade Deng Xiaoping would still hold the helm and have the final say." After the Thirteenth Congress, the new party leaders—General Secretary Zhao Ziyang, in particular—frequently reported to Deng and asked for his instructions on sensitive and important matters.

Deng's position as the paramount leader, or "decision maker behind the scenes," was an openly acknowledged fact, not a state or party secret, as some have claimed. Speaking at a public news conference shortly after the Thirteenth Congress, Zhao in fact admitted, "I respect Comrade Xiaoping very much. In my own opinion, nobody among our current leaders, whether those still on duty or those already retired, can compare with him in terms of political experience and wisdom. It is a privilege for me, on any crucial matter, to appeal to him for advice in order to handle it better, isn't it?"[16]

In terms of seniority and authority, Chen Yun remained the only person who could claim a status equal to Deng's. Chen became a Politburo member in the 1930s, when Deng had not yet even entered the Central Committee. In the 1950s, Chen was the party's vice chairman, while Deng was its general secretary. Chen's disagreements with Deng were less personal than truly political. While Deng focused on political power and personal relations, Chen focused on economic affairs and national, if not socialist, interests. Chen would not, and perhaps could not, challenge Deng's supreme authority.

For better or for worse, Chen was a man of principle and dignity, more so than Deng. Deng was more liberal or flexible. Careful development and implementation of economic and financial programs was not Deng's specialty, nor his primary concern, but it was definitely Chen's. Chen scarcely challenged Deng over sheer political power— for Deng, that was a plus—but he did occasionally challenge Deng over practical policies. Chen was not a generalist politician like Deng. He had little to do with the army, ideology, or foreign affairs; he did not like going abroad or seeing foreigners. Chen's main interest lay in the national economy, especially fiscal and financial policies.

The Thirteenth Party Congress of 1987 had decided on a new central leadership—which Deng did not expect to change soon, if ever— and 1988 was supposed to be a year of regular, collective party work. Ostensibly, that was true. The year brought no dramatic political movement or drastic personnel changes, but it did feature two prominent economic issues: price reform, which Deng wanted to tackle, and inflation, which Deng hated to see.

The inflation and price-reform issues in 1988 were important for various reasons, but they did not have as much bearing on the 1989 Tiananmen incident as some outside observers have tended to think. They would suggest that price liberalization, pushed forward by the liberal Zhao Ziyang and opposed by the conservative Li Peng, caused inflation and social resentment and eventually led to the following year's mass demonstrations.[17] Here, a simple counterargument can be made: if this scenario is accurate, why did the Tiananmen protest of 1989 target Li, not Zhao?

I would say that it was not simply the inflation and price reform that caused the Tiananmen incident; rather, the debate over how to handle the inflation and price reform exacerbated the political tensions between Zhao and Li; and behind them, between Deng and Chen; and more profoundly, between two basic "lines" or two basic "roads"—which would eventually lead to the spectacular drama of 1989.

Therefore, one might say that the intraparty contention for political power was one factor, and the general social disenchantments such as students' demands for freedom and democracy were an entirely different factor. These two factors could be intertwined with each other and could interact with each other, but they were not identical, nor did they operate simultaneously. Such delicate distinctions should not be lightly ignored or neglected, either in theory or in practice.

The Party Congress made the decisions, and the People's Congress announced them; that had been the norm of communist China's politics. At the Seventh National People's Congress, from March 25 to April 13, 1988, Yang Shangkun became president of the People's Republic of China (PRC), Wan Li chairman of the People's Congress, Li Xiannian chairman of the Political Consultative Conference, and Li Peng premier of the State Council. Because the Military Council was regarded as a party as well as a governmental institution—one of Mao's odd political legacies—Deng was appointed chairman of the PRC's Central Military Council.

Since Deng claimed to have retired, he did not want to bother attending the People's Congress. Instead, he stayed home watching the TV news reports while the congress was in session. But he did receive a number of foreign visitors at his private residence. He would tell them he was quite happy with the results of the Thirteenth Party Congress and the Seventh National People's Congress, in which two key questions had been settled: the continuation of reform and openness, and the succession of party and state leadership.

Throughout the summer of 1988, inflation and price reform became common topics in Deng's meetings and conversations with foreign guests. He met with U.S. Secretary of State Shultz on July 15, for example, and stressed that China was deepening the reforms and opening the "open door" wider and also attempting to break the impasse on price liberalization. It was risky and difficult, Deng told Shultz, but it had to be done, and breaking this impasse would create the conditions necessary for China's economic development in the next century.[18]

However, at the party's Second Plenum of the Thirteenth Congress, convened in Beijing and chaired by Zhao in September 1988, "arrangements for the economic environment and rectification of the economic order"—instead of reaffirmation of previous bold slogans on price liberalization—were designated the party's primary tasks for 1989 and 1990. This Second Plenum also called for combating official corruption, which was not so notable at the time but assumed great significance soon thereafter.

Ever since then, Deng himself stopped boasting to his foreign visitors about "breaking the impasse." Instead, he began to talk about "bold guts plus steady legs" as well as the unity in intraparty relations. On September 16, he told a delegation from Japan's Liberal Democratic Party, "Some Hong Kongers like to spread rumors that there are splits in our higher leadership and that there are liberals and conservatives in our party. These are groundless rumors. We have neither, only one group of reformers. Those who look forward to splits and confusions inside China will be disappointed."[19]

One explanation commonly accepted by Western observers for the policy shift involved in the 1988 price reform is that Zhao persisted in carrying out the reform program until Deng stopped backing him. As a matter of fact, Zhao himself had been well aware of the sensitive nature of price reform or price liberalization or price inflation—which were actually all one and the same. "The people may want a premier who raises their salaries and yet does not increase, or perhaps even decreases, the price of consumer goods," Zhao had said early in 1987. "I myself have not been able to accomplish that. Hopefully, the next premier can manage the matter better than I did."[20]

But Deng seemed to stand squarely behind his urban economic reform program. Unless Zhao did not want to pursue the program at all, price reform seemed to be the easiest and least politically risky issue to tackle. Herein, Zhao was just dealing with the common citizens, whereas other reforms, like reducing personnel in leadership positions and dissolving state enterprises, would impact directly on party and government officials. Thus, Zhao and his followers were the first to resume the price-reform effort in the spring of 1988. Li Peng, as newly appointed premier of the State Council, had to follow Zhao's lead at that point, however reluctant he might have been to do so.

It did not take long for price reform to produce social consequences as serious as both Li and Zhao had feared. Consumer prices soared, rising more than 20 percent in a couple of months. By the end of the summer of 1988, panic purchasing had spread from Shanghai to other cities. In September, the Politburo, including both Li and Zhao, decided to hold off on further price liberalization and instead called for rectification of the economic order.[21] As long as the slogans of reform and openness were still recited and no serious policy setbacks occurred, Deng did not mind acquiescing to Li and Zhao's decision. Thereafter, Deng quietly quit preaching about "breaking the impasse"!

Zhao's personal influence in the State Council—as represented by his protégés, such as Tian Jiyun—remained rather strong, and Li as incumbent premier could hardly have been happy about the situation. There were differences between Zhao and Li in basic political stance as well. Their disagreement over how to handle price reform resulted in a de facto power split between them, which would have a great deal to do with the outbreak, the course, and the conclusion of the subsequent 1989 Tiananmen incident.

In short, Deng remained positive about price reform or price liberalization, and verbally supportive of the effort, throughout the spring and summer of 1988, while both Li and Zhao gradually stepped back from that position for fear of further inflation and economic disorder. As always, the "retired" paramount leader Deng functioned mainly as a booster of reform and openness, who preached slogans but exerted little influence on the practical implementation of policy. The price-reform drive lasted a few months in early 1988 and came to a stop before 1989. It had few lasting effects, positive or negative, in the economic field but caused a wide and deep political rift in the central leadership.

20

Bloodshed at the Gate of Heavenly Peace, 1989

Nothing seemed really abnormal as 1989 arrived in China. It was a year of the tiger, anyhow, better than a year of the dragon. If there was anything special, the year would bring Deng's eighty-fifth birthday and the People's Republic's fortieth anniversary. The preceding year, 1988, had ended up as one of continuous growth in the gross national product, which rose at a rate of about 14 percent. The market was under control, and the panic over inflation was six-month-old history. The army, with its newly entitled seventeen full generals and newly appointed eight district commanders, seemed content. A busy schedule of state and government leaders' visiting abroad and receiving foreign guests at home was well under way.

Deng kept receiving foreign dignitaries as usual. He spent the Chinese New Year in Shanghai, where he called in the Soviet minister of foreign affairs and talked to him in early February, in preparation for his summit conference with President Mikhail Gorbachev in a few months. Between the lines of their conversation, one could get the sense that Deng regarded the upcoming summit as a very serious and personal matter.

Later that month, Deng returned to Beijing to meet George Bush, whom he had seen off as a U.S. diplomat based in Beijing years ago and who now came back as president of the United States. Bush's aides attempted ingeniously but without success to usher Fang Lizhi into the barbecue prepared for Deng by the American Embassy. Deng felt obliged to lecture Bush at length on why he could not accept

Fang's recent letter requesting the release of political prisoners: "China needs stability. You know China has a lot of people, each with his or her own opinion. You protest today, and I protest tomorrow, and one year has 365 days, and we will have protests every day. How can we continue our economic development?"[1]

In March, while the National People's Congress was still in session, Deng received the presidents of Thailand and Uganda, smiling and chatting and evidently feeling no premonition whatsoever of any imminent problem. "I did not take part in this People's Congress. I asked for leave, in order to preserve my own health," Deng stated at one time. "More important, I want to step down totally from the leadership myself and let the others take over the job."[2]

Fang Lizhi's letter caused something of a political stir. Fang had just finished a three-month visit to Australia and returned home via Hong Kong to Beijing; then he sent a public letter to Deng asking amnesty for political prisoners like Wei Jingsheng. When Fang's letter received no response from Deng, a group of thirty-three popular intellectuals—sponsored by Chen Jun, who had lived in New York for years before his recent return to Beijing—signed an open letter of appeal to the People's Congress to second Fang's request. Then another letter of appeal from forty-two scholars and scientists was circulated in late March.

Students from several universities and colleges in Beijing—notably, Beida (Beijing University) and People's University—grew excited. A variety of independent students' associations had already arisen in the wake of the 1987 student movement. Most of them took nonpolitical names such as Romantic Poetry Club or Foreign Philosophy Salon, for reasons of political safety or in many cases because of the youngsters' arrogant fantasies, but these groups were generally political in nature, as would soon become evident.[3]

The sudden death of Hu Yaobang became the trigger. Hu was said to have died of a heart attack after a heated argument with conservative veterans during a Politburo conference. Between Hu's death on April 15 and his funeral on April 22, a sizable student movement came into being in Beijing. The students, a few thousand at that stage, went to Tiananmen Square to demand that Hu's reputation be fully rehabilitated. Their request was pretty reasonable. They felt guilty because Hu had apparently lost his position as a result of their demonstration some two years before. Word spread that Deng himself, in retrospect, felt some regret about Hu's humiliating dismissal as well. That might be true because Deng chose to attend Hu's funeral in person.

As the funeral ceremony proceeded inside the Great Hall of the People on April 22, approximately one hundred thousand students from scores of colleges and universities gathered outside in adjacent Tiananmen Square, chanting slogans and singing songs. Deng must have noticed the amazing scene. Most of them dispersed late that day, but some decided to remain in the square until the government met their demands, which now included not just Hu's rehabilitation but broader matters as well, such as freedom of speech, democratic elections, release of political prisoners, punishment of corrupt officials, and the dismissal of Li Peng and other conservatives.

While Zhao Ziyang was on a previously scheduled visit to North Korea, Li Peng held a Politburo Standing Committee conference, with Yang Shangkun in attendance, to discuss the emergency situation. A decision was made to denounce the student movement. Li and Yang then went to consult Deng at home. Deng expressed his support for their decision and called the student action "a riot of young trouble-makers," although he himself did not yet go so far as to define it as, in the words of an April 26 *People's Daily* editorial, "an antiparty and antisocialist rebellion instigated and manipulated by a group of criminal elements."[4]

The *People's Daily* editorial was a mixture of Deng's and Li's directives, though it did not precisely attribute the original sources. Its title ("We Must Unequivocally Oppose the Riot!") and its main theme ("This is not an ordinary student movement but a political riot, and it aims at subverting the Communist Party leadership and overthrowing the socialist system"), as is known by now, were paraphrased from Deng's own remarks two days before.[5] Instead of pacifying the situation, however, the editorial made it even worse. The next day, thirty thousand students from thirty-eight colleges and universities poured into the streets and forced their way to Tiananmen Square at the center of the city. The reason, or at least one of the reasons, was that the student leaders had received information that Li had prepared the *People's Daily* editorial without Zhao Ziyang's knowledge and approval.

Zhao returned to Beijing on April 30, and there indeed appeared to be conflict between him and Li. It was true that Zhao had cabled his agreement with Deng's decision from Pyongyang. Nevertheless, it was one thing for Zhao to express his agreement with Deng from abroad but quite another for him to read the *People's Daily* editorial and listen to his followers' complaints at home now. Zhao talked to Deng, who seemed stuck with a tough decision. Zhao did not directly object to Deng but suggested that the April 26 editorial be disavowed. Deng was, for a while, persuaded to believe that he had been somewhat deceived into supporting the editorial, whose wording was not exactly his own. But it would have been too much of a loss of face for him to take it back. Anyhow, Zhao, as general secretary, continued to take charge of the Party Center's affairs. Another *People's Daily* editorial was thus published on May 4 in a tone that was clearly more moderate than the previous one.[6]

Had the student movement ended then and there, Zhao would have been in fine shape, Deng would have been quite glad, and Li would have been scolded for his rashness. But instead, from May 13 on, two thousand students started a hunger strike in Tiananmen Square. The students read the May 4 editorial as one sign that the communist leadership was ready to compromise. In fact, there was no unity among the communist leadership. Had there been, the student movement would not have continued, at least not on such a large scale and for so long. Li and his ilk were happy to see the student strike continue as a mockery of Zhao's liberal leadership, while Zhao's followers, if not Zhao himself, were also happy to see the strike continue as an indictment of Li's conservative stand.

Moral standards aside, I would say that Zhao fatally misjudged the political circumstances in general and Deng in particular. Deng did not like Li, nor did Deng want to replace his successor (in this case, Zhao) once again, so soon after Hu's dismissal. Deng held, nevertheless, that the student movement had to be stopped, one way or another. Zhao was careful and prudent in handling ordinary duties but less capable of dealing with political crises—quite the opposite of Deng himself.[7]

The Deng–Gorbachev summit was supposed to have been a victorious show for Deng because the "three obstacles to Sino-Soviet relations" had been removed in response to Deng's persistent demands. As it turned out, unfortunately for Deng, the meeting became an unqualified embarrassment. The welcoming ceremony, originally planned for Tiananmen Square, had to be canceled. On his way to meet Deng in the Great Hall of the People on May 16, Gorbachev had to drive slowly under heavy military escort through the thick crowds, which seemed friendly but were obviously out of official control. Passing Tiananmen Square, he observed a vast sea of riotous students yelling and shouting.

As soon as he saw Gorbachev, Deng proposed a toast: "Let me take this opportunity to declare that the relations between our two nations are now normalized. I would like to use eight Chinese characters to describe this meeting: Close the past and open the future!" In return, Gorbachev flattered Deng by calling him comrade: "The Chinese comrades, especially Comrade Deng Xiaoping, have made great contributions to the normalization of relations between our two great countries."[8]

While the Deng–Gorbachev conference went on inside the hall, outside, in Tiananmen Square, half a million students and citizens brandished posters, shouted slogans, and broadcast the "International" as well as rock and roll. News reporters and photographers, both Chinese and foreign, seemed far more interested in the angry crowd of protesters than in the summit.

As if all this were not yet provocative enough, Yan Jiaqi, presumably one of Zhao's political consultants, published a "May 17 Declaration" in Tiananmen Square, which openly condemned Deng as the biggest and stupidest tyrant in Chinese history and called upon the people to overthrow the Deng dictatorship.[9] At the same time, large-character posters, obviously in line with the position taken by Zhao and his followers, appeared on the streets to expose Deng and accuse him by name of all possible errors, political and personal.

The five members of the Politburo Standing Committee—Zhao, Li, Hu Qili, Qiao Shi, and Yao Yilin—were summoned to meet in Deng's residence on the evening of May 17. Deng did not yet seem outspoken about his own stand. "The current situation cannot drag on anymore," he said. "What should we do? How can we concede and how far?" He asked the five for a vote on whether martial law should be declared in Beijing. Zhao alone voted against martial law; Li and Yao both voted for it; while Hu and Qiao abstained. The matter was thus decided. After the meeting, Zhao did not return home but went directly to the square. The students there saw tears in his eyes and heard him apologetically mumbling something about his having come too late.[10] Because of his illness, political as well as physical, Zhao asked Deng to allow him to resign the next morning, but Deng refused even to see him anymore. By evening—at a conference of party, government, and army cadres—Li had formally declared martial law throughout Beijing in the name of the State Council.

Even at this juncture, there still appeared to be some lack of unanimity within the communist leadership. On May 21, it was announced on national television that Marshals Nie Rongzhen and Xu Xiangqian had promised that the students would not be repressed. The next day, eight senior People's Liberation Army (PLA) generals—including Zhang Aiping, former minister of defense, and Yang Dezhi, former chief of staff—circulated a joint message to the martial law headquarters, requesting that "the People's Army should never fire on the people."[11]

Rumors swept through the capital city, the country, and the world in the following days. Deng was said to have died of a heart attack at one point and to have left Beijing for Wuhan to summon rescue troops at another point. Li Peng was said to have been assassinated. The Twenty-seventh Army had supposedly revolted against the Thirty-eighth Army. Yang Shangkun was allegedly busy transferring billions (or trillions) of yuan (or dollars) to Switzerland in preparation for a possible flight abroad by the top communist leaders and their families!

But strangely, no sign whatsoever could be seen of Deng, nor could any word be heard from him. All the incumbent leaders in the party's Politburo and the army's Military Council remained silent. It should be clear that Deng stayed in Beijing the entire time, and at no time did he lose control. The delay in resolute action from May 20 to May 30 was less because of any loss of military command on Deng's part than because of his political concerns. It was not that the troops were incapable of forcing their way into the city but that Deng was reluctant to order them in hastily. Also, it took a few days to make sure that the whole operation was carried out under the unified command of the Military Council, not under the auspices of the State Council or the Defense Ministry or the Beijing Military District. The martial law headquarters was directly responsible to Yang in the Military Council; Yang, in turn, was to report personally to Deng.[12]

Several preliminary attempts by regular troops and armed police to move into Beijing failed late in the month, from May 25 to 30. This created an impression—a false one, as would soon be proved—that the communist leadership as a whole had lost control of the military forces. The entire capital city was overjoyed, and Beijing residents, reportedly two or three million of them, rushed to help the students erect barricades on the main streets.

The students at Tiananmen Square were in ecstasy as well as in pandemonium. These youngsters, whose leadership was divided from the very beginning, fell into tens of quarreling groups. Some elder intellectuals and officials—notably, "the four gentlemen"—plunged into a hunger strike for, as some of them later admitted, "reputational purposes." A so-called University of Democracy was founded in Tiananmen Square on the night of June 3, with a few young students appointed as its professors, amid the sound of bursting firecrackers—and approaching army tanks as well!

For better or for worse, foreign interests and influences, or what Deng later called the "general international climate," had indeed been acting upon this student movement. Hong Kong people provided three thousand tents for the hunger strikers. *China Spring* people hurried in from New York with monetary support. The Taiwan government held meetings to discuss possible emergency reactions. Furthermore, reporters from CNN, ABC, and BBC were hectically interviewing and broadcasting.

When the final assault was decided upon, on May 31, Deng spoke to Li Peng and Yao Yilin. His words were an interesting mix of resolute anger and deep sorrow: "After this riot, we should really do something for the people, primarily two things: first, we should change the leadership, and the new leadership should bring to the people a fresh look and a feeling that it is hopeful; second, we should take some measures, sound and solid, to show that we are against corruption, truly and not falsely, in order to win back the people's trust."[13]

Finally, the troops were coming! The army entered Beijing on the night of June 3. The military action lasted a few hours, until dawn on June 4. The soldiers approached from several directions, mainly from the western suburbs, to meet in Tiananmen Square. They forced their way in columns of tanks, crushing all blockades—human as well as inanimate—followed by armored vehicles with soldiers shooting at all sides along their routes of advancement.

In front of the Gate of Heavenly Peace is Eternal Peace Boulevard, Beijing's main artery, running from east to west through the capital city. The half-mile section of the boulevard from Muxidi to Xidan, a couple of miles west of Tiananmen Square, was turned into a bloody stream. Among those killed were not only students but local residents who had thus far been building and defending their street barricades against the troops so successfully. The tanks forced their way forward, crushing everything and everybody in their path. By dawn, the troops had all reached their destination and encircled the square, where the five thousand or so remaining students negotiated their way out without further bloodshed.[14]

Fierce battle? No! Massacre? Yes! At one point, foreign broadcasts reported that as many as thirty thousand civilians had been killed in the army's pointless shooting. Later on, official Chinese accounts gave the number of dead as between three hundred and five hundred. It is difficult for us to believe the reports or learn the exact figures, but in connection with this very question, I would suggest that the objective of the troops can and must be appropriately clarified.

The troops' objective, or the military order given to the troops, should be quite clear. It was to reach and take Tiananmen Square; that was the final end. Crushing with their tanks and shooting their rifles were what they considered the necessary means. As the troops covered the first mile, from Muxidi to Xidan, in the first couple of hours, they met the fiercest resistance, and hence, this portion of their advance had the bloodiest consequences. From Muxidi to the Gate of Heavenly Peace was about three miles, and it took the troops about four or five hours to cover this distance. The first couple of hours of the first mile were the bloodiest, with the heaviest casualties. Afterward, as the people realized that these were real bullets and real killings, they mostly fled. The last couple of hours, during which the troops covered the two miles from Xidan to the Gate of Heavenly Peace, went more smoothly and were less tragic.

Li Peng, who functioned as public spokesman while Yang Shangkun acted as chief military commander, appeared on national television on June 3 before the bloodshed began and again on June 5 shortly after the bloodshed ended. After having been out of sight for almost a month, Deng finally showed up on June 9, at a reception for senior commanders of martial law troops in Zhongnanhai's Benevolence Hall. He first of all asked everybody present to stand for one minute of silence in honor of those who had died martyred. In his opening speech, he sounded more philosophical than practical. He attributed the recent turmoil to the "general climate" of the world and the "particular climate" of China at the time, which were beyond the realm of all human desire and control. He went to considerable lengths to emphasize and re-emphasize the correctness of his general political line of "one center and two basic points."[15] Deng took it for granted that the turmoil was over, and the real effect of his speech was to alleviate doubts about the continuation of his reform and openness policy in the wake of the Tiananmen bloodshed. On June 16, 1989, Deng's position grew tougher and his spirit higher:

> The imperialist Western world attempts to make all socialist countries give up their socialist road and go under the monopoly rule of international capitalism. We should hold tight to resist the trend, holding the flag clear and high. If we do not persist in socialism, eventually we will only become a dependent nation, and it will not be so easy to become economically developed. Only socialism can save China, and only socialism can develop China. There is no hope for China other than the socialist road, not even mentioning the triangle of China, America, and Russia.[16]

An enlarged Politburo conference was held from June 19 to 21. It was called enlarged because Deng was no longer a Politburo member and the conference therefore had to be enlarged to legitimize his participation. Actually, he was the keynote speaker. The Fourth Plenum of the Thirteenth Congress immediately followed, on June 23–24, at which Li Peng spoke on behalf of the Politburo about Zhao Ziyang's mistakes. Deng chose not to speak. Zhao was stripped of all leadership positions and subjected to further investigation. That was something that had to be done. Deng could not have prevented it even if he had wanted to. The speech Deng had given on June 9 was unanimously applauded as the guiding line in reviewing the past, planning for the future, and uniting the whole party. The plenum delineated the party's key tasks as persisting in the reform and openness policy and stabilizing the domestic situation.

Surprisingly, Jiang Zemin was elected or selected the party's general secretary instead of either Li Peng or Qiao Shi. Meanwhile, Li Ruihuan and Song Ping were ushered into the Politburo Standing Committee after the ouster of Zhao and Hu Qili. The new leadership was certainly not collectively elected by the plenum. It was Deng's personal decision, made after some consultation with other veteran leaders like Chen Yun and Peng Zhen during the previous two weeks.

Why Jiang Zemin? Deng did not know Jiang well, nor did he particularly like him. In Deng's own words, he "selected and selected and eventually selected Jiang Zemin." Deng was more determined not to choose Li Peng than he was to choose Jiang or anybody else. An apparent reason for choosing Jiang was that he was the party secretary of Shanghai, where he seemed to have managed the student movement well. He had not given in, nor had the students risen up. More important, by comparison with the other candidates, Jiang seemed more favorable to Deng's reform and openness policy. He was not highly intelligent, nor was he stupid—remember Mao's comments on Hua? That seemed just fine; he would thus be more controllable.

Li Ruihuan, the party secretary of Tianjin, was known as an outspoken reformer, which Deng truly appreciated. Li was also fortunate that little student turmoil had taken place in Tianjin on his watch. In those days, having nothing happen was a good thing. In fact, being geographically so close to Beijing, the potentially rebellious students there were largely drawn to the Tiananmen drama, thus leaving Tianjin in relative peace. The problem this former carpenter faced among his colleagues lay in his lack of higher education—and political capacity.

Song Ping had obviously been sponsored by Chen Yun. Deng's attitude toward Yao Yilin was more or less the same as his attitude toward Li Peng. As Yao had to go at Deng's insistence, Deng would not object to Chen's bringing in Song as a temporary replacement. In any event, it already seemed rather paradoxical that the whole trouble presumably began because of Zhao's, and also Deng's, liberal approach and yet ended up with several conservatives tossed out of the party's supreme hierarchy.

Why not Li Peng as the new general secretary, as was commonly expected at the time? In fact, it was Deng's first priority not to have Li take Zhao's place. Li had come to the Politburo and its Standing Committee upon the recommendation of Deng Yingchao and Chen Yun. No reformer, Li was strong-minded and high-handed. Above all, Deng had felt pushed by Li throughout the Tiananmen incident, almost the same way Mao had felt about Zhang Chunqiao in early 1976. The results were also more or less the same. Mao dropped Deng but did not pick up Zhang then, and Deng dropped Zhao but did not pick up Li now. The last thing an old man liked was being pushed.

Why not Qiao Shi as another choice? Qiao had indeed been under consideration, until Deng finally rejected him. Among other reasons, Deng regarded his own reform and openness policy just as highly as Mao had regarded his Cultural Revolution. No reversal of, or even ambiguity toward, that policy could be allowed. In Deng's eyes, Qiao seemed like an instrumental, politically neutral bureaucrat; also, he seemed more resourceful and less controllable than Deng wanted his successor to be.

Western observers also speculated that Deng might allow Zhao to remain in the Politburo, provided he made a formal confession of his errors, just as Deng had done with Hu before. Zhao apparently refused to confess and therefore lost all his leadership positions.[17] That speculation was another rumor—and a rather implausible one as well. Actually, Zhao did admit his mistakes, but the 1989 incident was incomparably more severe than the 1986 incident. There was no way that Deng could allow Zhao to retain any leadership post and avoid being harshly attacked.

Two months after the Fourth Plenum, Deng handed the Chinese Communist Party Central Committee a letter, in which he formally asked to resign from his last post as chairman of the Military Council. Before that, he apparently told those colleagues who attempted to dissuade him, "I have made up my mind, period. If I have done nothing else for the party, at least I will set this precedent of voluntary retirement." In the meantime, Deng recommended that Jiang Zemin assume his position.

There were various speculations regarding Deng's motives. Deng did indeed want to enhance Jiang's authority, in title as well as in substance. But that reason was only secondary. The primary reason, which seemed improbable but true, was none other than Deng's personal temperament. He simply wanted to give up all his official responsibilities after the frustrating Tiananmen incident, after changing successors for the third time, and after passing his own eighty-fifth birthday.[18]

Deng thought first about his own departure from the post; only then did he consider the issue of to whom the post should be passed. Actually, once Deng had chosen Jiang as his new successor, there could be little choice—unless he wanted to call off the entire deal. When he chose Zhao in 1987, he appointed him deputy chairman of the Military Council. Now that he had chosen Jiang, he gave him his last and most powerful position—namely, the chairmanship of the Military Council, or the power to move China's troops.

As the year 1989 concluded, the communist regime was shaken but not routed, and Deng's authority and policy orientation were challenged but not defeated. Many residual strains from the Tiananmen bloodshed remained. International protests and sanctions were still overwhelmingly strong. Some of the student leaders were arrested; some were smuggled out through Hong Kong to France and America; Fang Lizhi fled to the American Embassy for asylum; and others remained at large. But basically, Deng knew that the past was gone and finished. It seemed really amazing that, only a few months before, millions of Beijing residents had gathered on the streets to condemn Deng as a feudalist dictator, but now, the same millions were gathering on the same streets to hail him as a socialist savior. The Chinese are an incredible people, and China is an incredible country. The Chinese and China must surely have some special mystique![19]

— 21 —

The Influential Retiree, 1990-1993

After his formal retirement, Deng Xiaoping mostly stayed at home, outside and yet close to Zhongnanhai, with his immediate family and other relatives. He was physically assisted by his daughters, and his elder son Deng Pufang offered him political advice, just as Mao Yuanxin had done with Mao Zedong before. There were also half a dozen officially appointed secretaries and assistants to form what was called the Deng office. Top secret documents and reports were delivered for his review on a routine basis, and some veteran leaders like Bo Yibo, Yang Shangkun, or later Wan Li would act as "go-betweens" to keep up Deng's occasional contacts with the Politburo executives—more or less the same as Mao had done in his later days, although with quite different consequences.[1]

Deng no longer talked about separation of party and government functions, or decentralization of industrial enterprises, or wage and price liberalization, or reform of the political system. When he had talked about those matters in the late 1980s, none of them seemed to fare well; but now, in the early 1990s, when he stopped talking about them, everything seemed to be working fine.

History is indeed mysterious. Its message is often hard to read! One might ask China hands or review their speeches and publications to see who among them had ever predicted that, in the wake of the political turmoil and mass bloodshed in Beijing in 1989, followed by the rapid collapse of Eastern European communism in 1989, communist China would experience a five-year period of rapid economic growth and smooth diplomatic expansion.

Even if one could not care less about the McDonald's and Burger King and Kentucky Fried Chicken restaurants that have opened in Beijing and Shanghai, it is impossible not to notice all those inexpensive shirts and shoes in Woolworth's and Ann & Hope marked "Made in China." Before 1989, when one went to China and chatted with the Chinese on the street, they would usually talk about politics. In the early 1990s, however, they would most likely talk about money and business.

There seems to exist among the Chinese an enormous energy, somewhat like nuclear energy: either for politics, as before, or for the economy, as now! Leaving aside his racist overtones, we might still find something enlightening in Georg Hegel, the classic German philosopher, when he compared China to a solid ONE and India to a vacant ZERO.[2] There had been a quiet but apparent shift in the nation's general direction and the party's general line. It must have been Deng's philosophy: let Chinese labor and foreign money run, by themselves and for themselves!

Weren't there some invisible connections or interactions in the communist world? Was it just pure coincidence that one communist regime after another fell in Eastern Europe from 1989–90? It seemed that what had happened in China in 1989 had something to do with what soon happened in Poland, Romania, Czechoslovakia, and East Germany. Despite the fact that the central television station and *People's Daily* downplayed these events, the Chinese people, inside and outside the party, watched and read about them with special interest. The case of Nicolae Ceausescu of Romania was the most shocking to Deng and all the Chinese communist leaders.

In the past three decades or so, Deng had met Ceausescu a dozen times. These fairly regular meetings had been interrupted only during the early years of the Cultural Revolution. Their most recent meeting had taken place in Beijing in October 1988, when Deng expressed sincere thanks to Ceausescu for having acted as a mediator between China and the Soviet Union and affectionately called his personal relationship with this Romanian leader one of "three olds"—"old friends, old comrades, and old cofighters."[3]

At Deng's suggestion, some Politburo members and veteran cadres gathered to watch videotapes of the recent Romanian rebellion, collected by the Ministry of Foreign Affairs mainly from Western news broadcasts. The uprising of the Bucharest people in the face of the security police seemed like a microcosm of the Tiananmen incident. What the VCR viewers were not familiar with was the subsequent part of the story—the arrest and execution of the Ceausescu couple. This old comrade and his wife looked pale and depressed. They were questioned and obviously had been physically tortured. The couple heroically refused to sign the judgment paper of the military court. They were dragged to the execution ground, forced against the wall, and finally shot. The bodies fell like heavy rocks, jerked on the ground, and eventually lay still in puddles of blood. The Chinese viewers gave a few soft sighs, followed by a few minutes of stunned silence.[4]

"We'll be like this," said a voice from among the viewers, "if we don't strengthen our proletarian dictatorship and repress the reactionaries."

"Yes, we'll be like this," said Deng, expressing his own opinion, "if we don't carry out reforms and bring about benefits to the people." It would have been hard to tell which opinion was right and which was wrong; but there was at least one thing on which everybody present seemed to agree: none of them wanted this horrible scene ever to happen to China and to himself.

China and the Eastern European countries shared something in common: they were all communist regimes with the same political system of one-party dictatorship. This was a big problem, which Deng did not seem to fully recognize or appreciate. But China and the Eastern European countries also differed in a variety of important respects. China was historically and geographically a pretty independent country, and the People's Republic of China had been founded through decades of armed struggle. The Eastern European countries were largely dependent on the Soviet Union in various ways. As a consequence of Mikhail Gorbachev's reform line, their connections—political, economic, and ideological—with the Soviet Union became ever looser; they could hardly resist the international and domestic pressures for fundamental change. Deep in Deng's mind, there was the belief that Gorbachev should be held somewhat responsible for the collapse of Eastern European communism.

In August 1991, Russian conservatives staged a coup d'état and detained President Gorbachev for several days. Conservative leaders like Wang Zhen were momentarily excited by the news. For many years, Gorbachev had been regarded as the leading reformer in the communist world, and Deng had always felt somewhat jealous; he might have been happy to see Gorbachev in trouble then. It might also be that Deng preferred the conservative communists, who had instigated the coup, to the liberal communist Gorbachev and that, in turn, he preferred Gorbachev to the noncommunist Boris Yeltsin.

The conservative-controlled news media in Beijing were overjoyed, and those of Wang Zhen's ilk even wanted to issue an official message to greet the leaders of the Russian coup. This jubilant mood lasted for only a day or two, before it was quickly quashed by Deng, who preferred to adopt a more cautious and restrained approach, at least publicly.[5] A few days later, when the Russian coup ended in failure, Deng was admired by his colleagues, liberal as well as conservative, for his coolheaded diplomacy.

After the dissolution of the Soviet Union, China became the largest purchaser of Russian weaponry and ammunition. In the years 1991–92 alone, China spent U.S.$ 6.8 billion and bought from Russia 246 advanced combat planes, including 72 Su-27s, 24 MiG-31s, and 150 MiG-29s. China was also reportedly negotiating with the Ukraine over the purchase of a couple of nuclear-powered aircraft carriers and oceangoing submarines. The results of these and probably other secret military acquisitions enabled the Chinese navy and air force to achieve a combat capability covering both Northeast and Southeast Asia.

The international diplomatic and economic sanctions sponsored by the United States were one of Deng's major concerns in the years 1990–92. On January 9, 1990, referring to the Western countries' sanctions after the Tiananmen incident, Deng said publicly, "Only if we can manage our own affairs well will they sooner or later come back to us."[6] At one point, he bluntly compared China's market and labor resources to a large chunk of fat meat, whose appeal the Western capitalists could hardly resist. On quite a few occasions, Deng instructed his colleagues on China's appropriate role and activities in world politics, especially the "golden triangle," which had referred to the United States, the Soviet Union, and China before and vaguely applied to the United States, China, and other countries now. During the Gulf War in 1991, China properly chose to abstain during the UN vote against Iraq, avoiding either excessive dependence on, or excessive defiance of, the American dominance in world politics.

Deng proved right, at least in a practical sense. Western diplomatic sanctions did gradually fade away. First came the prime minister of

Japan and then the prime ministers of Canada, Singapore, and Iran. U.S. Secretary of State James Baker arrived in 1991 and then Russian President Yeltsin in 1992. International trade and commerce and investment were even quicker to recover. Businesspeople from Taiwan, Hong Kong, and Japan did not seem to care about anything but making quick money. They kept rushing in, "munching this huge chunk of fat meat," in Deng's own words. Henry Kissinger regarded his meetings with Deng—whom he had called a "nasty little man" before and might call a "lovely little man" now—in Beijing in 1989 and afterward as not only a personal honor but a business contact for his firm, Kissinger Associates.

Later on in 1992, Deng expressed China's general diplomatic line in a set of aphorisms that came to be known as the "twenty-four-character policy." Literally translated into English, the policy—which consists of six phrases, each with four characters—reads: "Observe all situations soberly; confront all challenges coolheadedly; stick to our own foothold; confine and preserve our own strength; excel at tough defense; make no rush to show off leadership."[7] Without the slightest trace of any ethical or ideological concerns, Marxist or otherwise, the policy sounded more like a bunch of argots and cants in ancient, honored folklore!

Jiang Zemin, the general secretary and Deng's new successor, seemed like an affable and amiable individual. He had an uncle who died a revolutionary martyr, and Jiang himself had studied science and technology in Moscow in the early 1950s. He had worked as a technocrat for years in the 1950s and 1960s before being promoted to the posts of mayor and party secretary of Shanghai during the 1980s rejuvenation movement. Jiang appeared to fit the criteria for Deng's successor perfectly: young, knowledgeable, experienced, and reform-minded.

Deng tried to help boost Jiang's image and authority in 1990. It was something for which Deng felt a responsibility. He publicly suggested that the current leadership should be firmly supported and defended against any doubts in this regard. He bluntly admonished a group of party officials and army officers, "Don't crab about the Jiang center, don't be snobbish, don't be unconvinced, and don't attempt to defy the Jiang center. The current leadership headed by Jiang will not be altered for at least ten more years."[8]

However, the successor was not really like the predecessor. Jiang soon became the butt of jokes and mockery, as Hua Guofeng had in the late 1970s. Even the fact that Jiang knew several foreign languages seemed to be a problem, rather than a help, to his interpreters. During Jiang's meetings with foreign dignitaries, the interpreters found it difficult to work with him. Jiang would try to speak Russian to the Russians and English to the Americans, but nobody seemed to understand him. The foreigners thought he was speaking Chinese, and the Chinese thought he was speaking a foreign language. The interpreters felt reluctant to interpret his Russian into Russian or his English into English, not wanting to embarrass their boss, but they had to. Eventually, the Ministry of Foreign Affairs was obliged to call this matter to the Party Center's attention.

To Japanese or Taiwanese visitors, Jiang would boast of his knowledge of classical Chinese literature by reciting "Poetry on the Pavilion of Duke Teng," by Wang Bo, an ancient writer, and with American visitors, he would labor for minutes to recite President Abraham Lincoln's Gettysburg Address. Eventually, the minister of foreign affairs also had to bring all these embarrassing episodes to the Party Center's attention.

What began to worry Deng was not only Jiang's lame personality but his feeble political attitude. After the collapse of the Soviet Union, the slogan "Guard against capitalist restoration" appeared in official CCP documents. Then a literary war broke out between southern liberal Shanghai and northern conservative Beijing. The *Liberation Daily* in Shanghai called for reform and openness, while the *People's Daily* in Beijing stood for the four cardinal principles. As the former mayor of Shanghai and the current general secretary in Beijing, Jiang was miserably squeezed in the middle, not knowing which side to support.

At the CCP's seventieth anniversary celebration, on July 1, 1991, Jiang as the party chief gave a speech, published in *People's Daily.* Deng was happy to read Jiang's remarks in support of reform and openness, but he knitted his brow when he came across the remarks that socialist reform should be differentiated from capitalist reform, and proletarian openness from bourgeois openness. Certainly, Jiang was trying here both to please Deng and to bow down to the conservatives.[9]

The evening of September 1, 1991, viewers of the ten o'clock news on state television heard an announcement that an important editorial would be broadcast immediately and then published in *People's Daily* the next morning. The editorial, entitled "All for Reform and Openness," lasted about twenty minutes, before regular programming was resumed. At eleven o'clock, however, there was another announcement, saying that the same editorial needed to be rebroadcast and cautioning local newspaper editors to listen carefully and copy the new version exactly, with no mistakes.

People found the two broadcasts almost identical except for one minor change. The ten o'clock version had contained the sentence, "In carrying out the party's policy of reform and openness, we should also persist in the four cardinal principles, and we should not forget to distinguish Mr. Socialism from Mr. Capitalism." In the eleven o'clock version, the phrase about "Mr. Socialism" and "Mr. Capitalism" was omitted.[10]

Deng had been watching the ten o'clock news at home that very night. The editorial's title seemed OK to him, and its "all for reform and openness" theme sounded fine. But he grew furious at the end. He called in his secretary at once. Telephones made quick action possible. In the next few minutes, a message went from the Deng office to the Politburo, and from the Politburo to the *People's Daily* editorial board. It was like a combat order: Delete those words and rebroadcast the whole piece! "Why?" General Editor Gao wondered. "The general secretary didn't say there was anything wrong." He was firmly cautioned, "Don't ask why. Just do it. This is from the top of the top."[11]

The Beijing winter was cold, and Deng as an elderly retiree liked to spend some days in the warmer south, just as a New Yorker or a Bostonian might take a winter vacation in Florida. Escorted by his wife, children, and grandchildren, Deng left Beijing aboard a southbound train on January 18, 1992. The first overnight stop was in the city of Wuhan. The Hubei governor came to welcome him. "It is better to reform than not," Deng said, as the governor kept nodding his head. "Our policy of reform and openness will not change for one hundred years."

Arriving the next day at Changsha, the provincial capital of Hunan, Deng met the Hunan governor and asked him how his province had been faring lately. The answer—"We are carrying on socialist education among the people"—did not seem to be received as favorably as expected. "Socialist education?" Deng retorted. "You must first feed your folk well, not let them starve, while they attend your educational meetings."

In his subsequent visits to the special economic zones of Shenzhen and Zhuhai from January 20 to February 1, Deng was joined by President Yang Shangkun. During these visits, Deng made a number of speeches to the local party and government leaders. His message was clear: more reform and more openness. He did not hide his unhappiness with the status quo: "In carrying out our policy of reform and openness, what we should be worried about is not hastening but hesitating." More than once, Deng stressed, "Reform and openness are a historical trend. The country needs this policy, and the people like it. Whoever opposes the reform and open-door policy should just step down!"[12]

The last stop on Deng's southern trip was Shanghai, where he stayed on for more than a week, including New Year's Day in the traditional Chinese lunar calendar. There, his call for more reform and openness was repeated yet again. "I made a mistake previously," Deng told the Shanghai officials accompanying him. "I should have allowed Shanghai to be a special economic zone some years earlier."

There was no big reaction to Deng's trip, nor even much reflection on it. Business in Beijing seemed to proceed as usual. Somebody did ask Li Peng whether there appeared to be a "new spirit" in Deng's southern talks and received only a stern admonition from the premier: "You folks shouldn't just hear a breeze and then say it is a pouring rain. As regards party matters, you should just listen to Comrade Jiang Zemin, and as far as government matters are concerned, I am the person in charge here."[13]

Fine! Deng made another visit to the Capital Steel and Iron Plant on May 22, 1992. There, he made no attempt to hide his dissatisfaction: "As regards my talks in the south, some people do not take them seriously and just play games with me; other people remain silent but actually oppose them; and only a small minority make some active response." Turning to the mayor and the party secretary of Beijing, who were accompanying him on the trip, Deng uttered a few words in a deliberate tone: "You people may pass on what I have just said to the Party Center."

On that same visit, Deng also mentioned that Zhu Rongji, the former mayor of Shanghai, was a resolute reformer and an economic expert, who "is not used appropriately enough yet."[14] At the time, Zhu was already a Politburo member and deputy premier in the State Council. What did Deng mean by saying that Zhu was not used enough yet? Wasn't it obvious that Deng wanted, or was threatening to want, another reshuffle of the Politburo and the State Council's top leadership at the upcoming Party Congress?

This time, the Party Center folk got Deng's message loud and clear. Jiang Zemin took active measures immediately. He rushed to the Central Party School on June 9, 1992, and offered to make a speech. There, Jiang hailed Deng's southern trip, paraphrased Deng's words, and dwelled on all the merits of reform and openness, without the slightest reference to that capitalism versus socialism business.

For the next several days, *People's Daily* carried news reports of provinces and large cities throughout the country warmly welcoming Deng's call for bolder and faster reforms. The Party Center compiled Deng's southern talks into a formal document for the entire party to implement. These actions were facilitated by the fact that a number of hard-liners, including General Editor Gao of *People's Daily,* had been removed from their leadership posts.

"Hurricane Deng," as people called it, kept blowing in the summer and fall of 1992. It swept away many rocks standing in its path. Li Peng had to rewrite his report to the People's Congress, deleting 150 or so "anticapitalist" words and phrases from his original draft. Even Chen Yun had to make up for his May 1 speech, in which few references to reform and openness could be found, by publicly expressing his wholehearted support for Deng's southern talks.[15] To dramatize the situation a bit, military leader Yang Baibing called on the Liberation Army to "escort the warship of reform and openness."

It was just the wind, but the rain would soon follow—although it turned out not to be as heavy as had been expected. The Communist Party's Fourteenth National Congress was held in Beijing from October 15 to 25, 1992; the focus of its agenda was to review the party's general line in the previous years and also to reorganize its central leadership.

Deng himself did not show up. In his keynote speech at the Fourteenth Congress, Jiang called for "building up the socialist market economy"—which went one step further than the Thirteenth Congress's "planned economy as primary and market economy as supplementary." Jiang praised Deng as the general architect of China's reform and openness and pledged to apply both Mao Zedong thought and Deng Xiaoping theory in hastening the pace of reform and openness.

The Yang brothers' dismissal from the Central Military Council at the Fourteenth Congress was a major surprise, and Zhu Rongji's failure to replace Li Peng as premier of the State Council was a minor one. Yang Shangkun, a resourceful politician, was accused of trying to duplicate tape recordings on the Tiananmen bloodshed—in which Deng had presumably given the final order to shoot—to disavow his own responsibility. True or false? Nobody knows for sure. His younger brother, Yang Baibing, was blamed for saying that "the army should escort the party in carrying out reforms." Was anything wrong with that remark? Yes! Why did the party have to be escorted by the army?

The simple and yet complex reason for the Yangs' downfall lay in the fact that they seemed to have grown too powerful in the past few years. Neither army veterans like Liu Huaqing nor the party chief, Jiang Zemin, felt comfortable with them. At the very last moment, Deng therefore decided to pull both of them out of the military leadership. This event had nothing to do with the debate between liberals and conservatives.[16] The final result was, of course, that the Yang brothers lost both their control over the army and their political stronghold in the party. At least for the time being, Jiang's leadership in the Military Council was further consolidated.

There had been strong signs that Zhu Rongji would become the premier instead of Li Peng, who would, in turn, take over Yang Shangkun's post as president of the People's Republic. As it turned out, Jiang Zemin concurrently assumed the post of state president instead of Yang. Zhu became a member of the Politburo Standing Committee and the first deputy premier, while Li remained premier in charge of the State Council.

There was evidence suggesting that, in return for his public support of Deng's call for more reform and openness, Chen Yun won a compromise from Deng so that the current Jiang–Li joint leadership would be maintained intact. Besides, Li Peng evidently wrote a letter to "Uncle Deng," earnestly asking to be allowed to continue his job in the State Council. Apparently for all these reasons, Deng caved in a little.[17]

Anyhow, the membership of the Politburo Standing Committee had been enlarged a bit at the Fourteenth Congress. While Jiang, Li, Qiao Shi, and Li Ruihuan remained on it, the elderly conservative Song Ping was dropped, and Zhu Rongji, Liu Huaqing, Zhang Zhen, and Hu Jintao were added. Of the four newcomers, Hu and particularly Zhu might be called liberals or reformers; Liu and Zhang were both veteran soldiers, who would most likely remain neutral in matters of intraparty politics.

By the time the Eighth National People's Congress concluded in Beijing in March 1993, a fresh lineup of state and government leaders had also been completed: Jiang Zemin as president of the state; Li Peng as premier and Zhu Rongji as senior deputy premier of the State Council; Qiao Shi as chairman of the People's Congress; and Li Ruihuan as chairman of the Political Consultative Conference.

Almost all the veteran leaders were formally removed from the party and state leadership, except Liu Huaqing and Zhang Zhen in the army. Liu was in his seventies and Zhang in his late sixties. But the potential influence of veteran leaders like Deng, Chen, Peng, and Bo remained strong, as long as they were alive and mentally alert. Thus, it might be said that there were two rows of passengers in one vehicle: Jiang, Li, Qiao, and Zhu were the front seat drivers, while Deng and Chen were the backseat guides.

There was little doubt that Deng had the final say in choosing the party and government personnel, while Chen and others had played only a supplementary role.[18] Therefore, in view of Deng's personal psychology, how could Jiang have been appointed concurrently as chief of the party and also head of state, and why couldn't Zhu have been "used appropriately" to take Li's place as premier?

The Fourteenth Congress would presumably be Deng's last Party Congress, and Jiang would presumably be his final successor—at least, Deng must have felt that way at the time. Although he was not fully satisfied with Jiang, Deng did not think he would have the chance to make another choice. Despite his own concerns about Jiang, and per-haps precisely because of such concerns, Deng would rather bolster Jiang by putting him in full charge of party, state, and army together—more or less as Mao had done with Hua in 1976. Was this for Jiang's sake or for Deng's own sake? Both.

It was not just Chen who saw the Jiang–Li joint leadership as a symbol of political unity and stability: at least in part, Deng shared the same feeling. Admonishing Li Peng a bit would have to suffice; going beyond that seemed inappropriate. Zhu Rongji did not come from a "revolutionary family"—as Li Peng did—and had suffered a lot as a "rightist element" in 1957. Deng might have been somewhat worried about that. Zhu was also a man who pushed everything hard, which Deng liked at certain times but disliked at other times—again, more or less as Mao had viewed and treated Deng in 1975.

After Deng's southern trips and talks, China's national economy recorded another round of rapid growth in the years 1992–93. Its gross national product, which had grown by 8.4 percent in 1989 and by about 10.5 percent in 1990 and 1991, grew by 12.5 percent in 1992 and by almost 13.8 percent in 1993. That was simply staggering! In his original report to the Eighth People's Congress, Li Peng had attempted to keep the growth rate to about 8 percent for fear of overheating the economy and causing inflation. Although Li had some good reasons, to be sure, he proved a little too conservative. The annual industrial growth rates during those years were between 15 and 20 percent, and the agricultural growth rates were between 3 and 5 percent; meanwhile, the rate of inflation fluctuated between 8 and 12 percent.[19]

Although I am no economist, and this book is just a biography of an individual leader, it is certainly safe to say that the above statistics do not suggest an unhealthy situation. Other East Asian countries and regions like Singapore, Taiwan, and South Korea had comparable rates of economic growth and inflation in their economic "takeoff" stage during the 1960s and 1970s. By all means, China's economic growth was for real and a big deal! Although there may be various other explanations, one must agree that Deng, more than anyone else, should be given the credit, if not for China's great achievements then at least for China's not having experienced great setbacks, either economic or political, in the wake of the 1989 Tiananmen incident.

22

Supreme Maturity, 1994-1996

This author has known Deng Pufang since we were schoolmates at Beijing University in the late 1960s: The young Deng is a man with a good mind and a keen political sense, but his disabled body keeps him from much public activity. During his latest visit to Canada, Deng Pufang was reported as making some remarks about his father, whom he perhaps knew better than anybody else: "My father's thinking on politics seems to have recently reached a status of *luhuo chunqing,* or supreme maturity. When he said those who did not want reforms had to go, he did not exactly mean those who defied reforms had to go. You shouldn't take his words too literally. There may be something beyond words, that you cannot hear but you can just feel."[1]

Are these remarks of Deng Pufang metaphysical myth or profound truth? I would say a little of both! They may mean that Deng *needed not* personally do anything anymore—he had already decided the policy line to be achieved and the personnel to achieve it, and all he needed to do was to rest on his laurels with just occasional supervision. But it may also mean that Deng himself *could not* do anything anymore, because of his ever weakening physique and other reasons. Hence, supreme maturity seems as good and as bad a term to depict such an elderly person, as to depict a ripe fruit or a fattened fowl.

The year 1994 arrived presumably as a special year for Deng—of course, to somebody of his old age, any new year could be regarded as special—for he would celebrate his ninetieth birthday on August 22, and the People's Republic would celebrate its forty-fifth anniversary on October 1. The Chinese people care more about the decannual than the pentannual. The year seemed therefore more important for Deng than for his communist regime. How could Deng realistically expect to live another ten years to 2004 for his hundredth birthday?

On February 9, 1994, Deng publicly appeared on China Central Television or CCTV for the first time in more than eleven months. Tightly held on either side by the hands of his two daughters, Deng Nan and Deng Rong, Deng was shown meeting and talking with Mayor Huang and other Shanghai senior officials on the eve of traditional Chinese New Year.

The eighty-nine-year old, diminutive Deng looked frail and haggard, far more so than the previous year on the same occasion. His hearing ability was obviously further impaired. One of the daughters could be seen constantly bending close to his ear, carefully repeating the words of the people who spoke to him. Deng's actual voice was not broadcast, obviously to avoid any worse impression upon the viewers. Only the TV announcer transmitted his brief yet clear message, "I think Shanghai's economy has all the good conditions to grow even faster."[2]

The awesome pictures, instead of reassuring TV viewers of Deng's good health and high spirits, could only remind them of Mao's final years in the 1970s. Fortunately Deng had more helpful daughters than did Mao, who at that time had to depend upon his secretary/mistress. That was all we as outsiders knew for sure, and that was all we as outsiders could know for sure: Deng remained alive, albeit old and sick, and Deng still adhered to his policy of reform and openness.

In terms of party and state affairs, everything seemed fine, except for those nasty Americans. China failed in its bid to host the 2000 Olympics, despite energetic efforts including the release from prison of Wei Jingsheng, the country's most famous political dissident. But it was over, when it was over. By all means, the selection of Sydney over Beijing appeared to be a fair vote, which the Chinese leaders could hardly protest. They might privately blame Britain, whose final round of votes cast Beijing out. It must have been the "British devils'" retaliation for China's stand on the Hong Kong issue, in Deng's opinion.

America threatened to cancel China's Most Favored Nation or low tariff privileges in the American market unless it could make "overall significant progress" in human rights, including the release of political prisoners and permission for Red Cross inspection of labor camps and detention centers, acceptance of the independence movement in Tibet headed by the Dalai Lama, and so on.[3] In fact, the White House's staunch position could be taken as the continuation of the previous year's presidential election, in which Democrat Clinton challenged Republican Bush's diplomatic policy as "kowtowing to Communist China."

During the November 1993 conference of heads of state of the Asian and Pacific region in Seattle, President Jiang Zemin stated that China would make some positive efforts to respond to President Clinton's requirements. In February 1994 in Paris, the Chinese foreign minister, Qian Qichen, gave U.S. Secretary of State Warren Christopher the same impression, if not any concrete promises. Behind the public screen sat Deng as the paramount leader, seemingly ready to concede and compromise.

President Clinton's stringent requests forced Deng and the Chinese leaders into a truly resentful dilemma. This was one of the rare matters they had to take seriously: Cancellation of China's MFN status could result in a loss of billions of dollars due to higher tariff payments, and thus would be a substantial setback for China's economic growth. One of the keys to China's economic progress lay in the United States, where China sold as much as $40 billion worth of goods in 1993, a great leap forward from the $2.5 billion level just ten years before in 1983.[4]

If China accepted all the American conditions, on the other hand, its communist leadership might set itself on a path to another political crisis. Relaxation of political restrictions, especially under foreign pressure, could well reinvigorate another opposition upsurge. More intangible were the concerns regarding America's encroachment on China's national sovereignty and interference in China's internal affairs. For Deng himself, furthermore, it amounted to a challenge by the forty-eight-year-old Clinton to his seniority and dignity.

Secretary of State Christopher's visit to Beijing in March 1994 was a failure, at least in terms of U.S. diplomacy. He looked strong in appearance but proved weak in substance. All business, he turned down the sightseeing tour at the Great Wall. After two days of rancorous arguments with the Chinese leaders, in which he stuck strictly to Clinton's demands, Christopher had to leave empty-handed. "You cannot become a fat man, with just one big meal," President Jiang told him at one point during a long monologue peppered with popular aphorisms and historical references, meaning that America should not expect China to accept all its demands overnight.

Coincidental with the Sino-American confrontation appeared the

North Korean problem in the spring of 1994. Pyongyang seemed to be experimenting with nuclear weaponry, which greatly concerned Washington. The United States wanted, through the United Nations, to have this matter thoroughly inspected, and threatened North Korea with stringent economic sanctions—as it had done previously with Yugoslavia and Iraq. To do so, however, America wanted China's vote, at least not its veto, in the UN Security Council.

One doesn't need to be a CIA agent or a Pentagon expert, but just read carefully the *New York Times'* international news reports, to see that China's involvement with the North Korean problem was more than a matter of a simple UN vote. From January to February 1994, while China was offering the United States human rights improvements for MFN prospects, North Korea agreed to the UN inspection. In March, when Beijing played tough with Washington after Secretary Christopher's fruitless visit, Pyongyang turned down the UN proposal. In April, while Beijing and Washington were fumbling for some face-saving solutions, Pyongyang raised the possibility of further cooperation.

The relations between China's MFN issue and North Korea's nuclear weapon issue were as close as the relations between Deng Xiaoping and Kim Il Sung as paramount leaders of their two countries. Until his death in August 1994, Kim remained the longest-lasting communist dictator. He became North Korea's Communist Party chief in the 1930s and head of state in the 1940s, when Cuba's Fidel Castro was still a law student in Venezuela. He had ruled the country ever since. Born in 1912, Kim was eight years junior to Deng, and thus called him "elder brother," and told his son to call Deng "elder uncle." After Ceausescu's death in Romania, Kim was Deng's last remaining old guard foreign friend. Kim visited China publicly many times, and secretly even more—it was only a ten-hour ride by train from Pyongyang to Beijing.[5] Each time Kim came to Beijing, a meeting with Deng was *de riguer*. With Kim versed in Chinese, they could readily converse on the phone any time either of them deemed it necessary.

The U.S. ambassador to the United Nations, Madeleine Albright, said at the time, "It is very evident that the Chinese are as interested as any of us in a denuclearized Korean peninsula."[6] Ambassador Albright seemed to have little knowledge of the history and politics of Northeast Asia. Apart from other national and international concerns, Deng and the Chinese leaders were more interested in a de-Americanized Korean peninsula than in a denuclearized Korean peninsula! For the time being, they were mostly interested in utilizing North Korea as a bargaining chip to deal with the United States over the MFN problem.

Formally a retiree, Deng held no more domestic duties and seemed to have little to do at home. Engaging in a bit of foreign policy, like quarreling with the Americans, was for him a kind of entertainment. He was careful about money but, in the final analysis, old Deng did not seem to care much about losing a few billion dollars, just as old Mao did not care about losing a few million Chinese people, in defending the Central Kingdom's integrity or his own imperial authority!

The economic embargo of Kim's North Korea by Clinton's America could not go well without cooperation from Deng's China; China to North Korea was not what Hussein's Jordan was to Saddam's Iraq in 1991. There is a three-hundred-mile–long border between China and North Korea, and it remains totally out of UN or U.S. control. It is worth noting retrospectively that during the Korean War in the early 1950s, 180,000 Chinese troops moved into North Korea and it was several weeks before General MacArthur even realized they were there![7]

Eventually, both China's MFN problem and North Korea's nuclear weaponry problem were resolved according to Deng's expectations, if not his full satisfaction. China persuaded North Korea to soften its position a bit, and for its own part released a few political prisoners, notably Chen Ziming and Wang Juntao, and meanwhile lobbied American officials such as Commerce Secretary Ron Brown and American corporations such as General Motors and AT&T. As a final result, in June 1994 President Clinton not only renewed China's MFN status but also delinked it from human rights conditions once and for all. Deng had been prepared to give up more, but finally found it did not even need to!

Deng had, sternly and a bit proudly, stated that after the Soviet Union's decline, China would inevitably take its place as the chief competitor with the United States. During Christopher's Beijing visit, Deng again taught his junior colleagues the same world outlook. Once agitated, Deng as an old man could hardly wait for long to retaliate. MFN or no MFN, America's decision would equally provide a boost for his birthday celebration in August. It was only a mental boost, of course. But, for goodness sake, what else could one imagine a ninety-year-old needed most!

Nonetheless, people who had expected a grand celebration of Deng's ninetieth birthday were disappointed. August 22, 1994, came and went without much public fanfare, only a brief news report in *People's Daily*. The official explanation was that Deng preferred to protect his privacy. Why not in 1984? Finally, October 1 brought the People's Republic's forty-fifth birthday, presumably another ostentatious occasion. A mass parade was prepared but eventually canceled. Only some fireworks were set off at a few designated spots in Beijing. *People's Daily* reported briefly that Deng watched the fireworks at home, but did not carry any live photos of him.[8] The undeniable fact was that Deng's health was fast declining. It was better not to observe the birthday, or the holiday, in order not to reveal his weakened state of health.

Gradually, by late 1993 and early 1994, Deng had become a symbolic figure, somewhat like the Japanese emperor and the British queen. His national prestige had come way up, while his political function had gone way down. He might still be consulted with on personnel assignments and international policies, but his practical leadership was over. That was primarily because of his old age and poor health, but also because many of the new problems, especially in the economics field, went further beyond his professional capacity. The slogan of reform and openness, which once stood for a fresh policy, had now become dry doctrine. It was good that everybody shouted it, but not so good that nobody seemed to care about it.

For various economic and political reasons after the Tiananmen incident, inflation, as measured by increases in retail prices, fell under 10 percent in 1990 and 1991. Economic growth in 1992 and 1993 pushed the inflation rate over 10 percent, and in 1994 it reached 25.6 percent, even higher than the 1988 record of 18.5 percent. Deng did not like that figure. But 1994 also saw another year of rapid GNP increase with no apparent adverse impact upon the people's livelihood. No popular panic occurred as it did in 1988 either. Inflation could cause grief and protest, as Deng was told; but inflation could also accompany economic growth either as a necessary cause or as an unavoidable result—as Deng was also told. There were plenty of foreign models to support either perspective, but Deng was not quite familiar with them. He felt at a loss looking at those interest rate curves, banking account charts, mathematical equations, and computer calculations. All this stuff seemed far beyond his comprehension, let alone his practical management.[9]

Agricultural productivity and output had been dropping for several years, and 1993 and 1994 were worse than previous years. China had to import more staple agricultural products such as wheat, soybeans, and cotton to meet domestic demand. It was seen as a bad thing, as both Chen Yun and Deng took for granted the ancient political dictum that "the state will not be secure without sufficient grain." But it was not so bad a thing, according to some people. Industrialized Asian countries such as Japan and South Korea had been importing proportionally more agricultural goods than China. Despite its large amount of purchases from America in 1994, China still maintained a $30 billion trade surplus. It sounded like a profitable deal to import cotton as raw material from abroad and then export ready-made textile goods to abroad. Deng was concerned at first then relaxed a bit later on, and then became worried once again when America threatened to place sanctions on China's exports in January 1995.

Another practical problem brought up by the reforms and economic growth lay in the area of governmental finance. Partially because of the expansion of special economic zones (SEZ), which had been granted low tax privileges, the average tax share of the central government decreased from more than 50 percent in the 1970s to less than 15 percent in the early 1990s. The national revenue thus fell proportionally. The SEZ policy might be reasonable for stimulating rapid economic growth but, as time went on, it seemed to have contributed to creating the unpalatable situation in which the richest locales paid the lowest taxes, while poorer locales paid the highest taxes. To mitigate such a situation, Zhu Rongji had to spend days and nights negotiating with each province and municipality. How was the tax share between the central and local governments and among the local governments to be apportioned? Furthermore, how were the conflicting interests between the central and provincial governments as well among various local governments and industries to be properly dealt with? Deng had to acknowledge that he himself did not know the correct answers to these problems.[10]

State-owned enterprises were seen as the foundation not only of the socialist system but also of Communist Party rule. However, they fared less well than the private sectors and annually lost between U.S. $50 billion and U.S. $60 billion (RMB 400 billion and RMB 500 billion). The government had to subsidize them. Any drastic measures, such as letting them go bankrupt and selling them to private owners, Chinese or foreign, would immediately affect the about 50 million employees and one million executives in these enterprises and certainly cause great social upheaval. Sichuan, Deng's home province, attempted some experimental reforms but ended up with thousands of people on strike; the reform program had to be canceled immediately. It appeared to Deng Xiaoping that many problems went beyond his practical control, and so many people used things that he had said to argue their own positions.[11]

The succession problem or the Jiang-centered leadership had presumably been settled years before, but it remained quite worrisome. Sometimes Deng felt glad to see Jiang's authority strengthened, other times he didn't, especially when Jiang crammed his Shanghai cronies, notably Wu Bangguo, into the central leadership. Deng attempted to have his personal secretary, Wang Ruilin, operate the Central Military Council—with or without Jiang's acquiescence?—but failed halfway through. He used to not like Li Peng for his arrogance and stubbornness, but began to appreciate his apparent confidence in treating foreign visitors and his own subordinates. He sometimes harbored nostalgic feelings about Zhao Ziyang as a true reformer and allowed him more freedom of movement and activity; but he also continued to confer with Yang Shangkun, whom he relied on to suppress the 1989 democratic movement. All these conflicting concerns were partly due to China's tilting political scales, but also to old Deng's equivocal mentality. To a certain degree, old Deng was falling into the position of a King Lear, being flattered as well as humbugged by his courtiers!

The health or illness of Deng once again became a hot topic of domestic and international attention at the turn of 1994/1995. In January 1995, one of Deng's daughters made a public statement to the media regarding her father's condition. Because it was highly unusual for a relative of a Chinese leader to reveal his physical state, there was speculation that Deng Rong's statement might have been condoned by the incumbent communist leaders, even by Deng himself, and not just out of an attempt by Deng Rong to promote her biography of her father.

Deng Rong told the *New York Times* correspondent, "My father's health declines day by day. People have to understand that my father is 90 years old and the day will come when he passes away." She further said that Deng used to walk 30 minutes twice a day, but now he could not walk anymore, and needed to have two people supporting him to stand on his feet. But Deng refused to use a wheelchair, fearing that once he did, he would never be able to get up again.[12]

It was later reported that Deng had checked into Beijing Hospital for a few weeks after the Chinese New Year because of a high fever caused by a common cold. There seemed no sign of a fatal crisis in his health; yet the party leadership had reportedly completed its preparations for Deng's death. Another more dramatic but less credible allegation said all party, government, and army senior officials in Beijing, as well as most provincial and municipal leaders, were summoned to Beijing for an emergency conference to make post-Deng arrangements.

At least, what Deng's own daughter revealed must have been true. His health was declining, almost day by day. That Deng did not show up for the New Year celebration, as he had normally done, was convincing evidence. Deng Rong's statement seemed quite valid for various reasons, the least one being to boost the sales of her own book. Yet, just a few days later, she had to recant her story by meekly blaming the *New York Times* for exaggerating. Meanwhile the Chinese Ministry of Foreign Affairs formally stated that there had been no problem with Deng's health at all. Leaving aside what contradictions—"contradictions among the people" for sure—there might have been between party authorities and the Deng family, we can surmise that Deng had somewhat stabilized after a brief period of hospitalization.[13]

Deng became keenly interested in international affairs in 1989–91 in the wake of the Tiananmen bloodshed and the collapse of European communism. With some interruption in 1992–93, while he dealt with the Fourteenth Party Congress, he resumed his interest in foreign affairs from 1994 onward. By the time he died in February 1997, Deng Xiaoping had evolved from being a politician to being a statesman.

The Hong Kong and Taiwan issues do not exactly fall into the category of foreign affairs, but they are not exactly domestic matters either. China's recovery of Hong Kong, and its uncomfortable relationship with Great Britain are basically unsettled. July 1, 1997, came and went: Beijing took over the island colony, and despite Governor Chris Patten's quibblings and BBC's rumblings, a de facto new government has been established and the event was commemorated with a massive celebration ceremony. This may ultimately be Deng's greatest diplomatic trophy. Now that it is over, it is over. Hong Kong is a clearly defined matter, and Britain is not regarded as a big player in world politics—unlike Taiwan and its special relationship with the United States.

Another round in the U.S.-China-Taiwan diplomatic contest was triggered by Lee Teng-hui's five-day visit to America in June 1995. President Lee of the KMT government in Taiwan was allowed a temporary visa to attend an alumnae ceremony at his alma mater, Cornell University, in New York State. It was no big deal in the first place. Beijing didn't pay much attention to it until Taipei loudly boasted of it as a diplomatic breakthrough. Then it blew up into a much bigger matter. Despite Washington's downplaying of this "unofficial visit," China regarded it as American encouragement of Taiwan's independence movement. Apart from lodging strong protests, China recalled its ambassador, canceled all high-level diplomatic activities, expelled two American diplomats, and arrested Harry Wu, an American human rights activist. U.S.–China relations fell to their lowest point in the five years since the 1989 Tiananmen incident.

But each time diplomatic tensions between China and the United States persisted for a few months, something seemingly fortuitous and extraneous would pop up as a remedy. This time it was first lady Hillary Clinton's strong desire to attend the world women's conference in Beijing in September 1995—did she have to go?—and for that she felt she needed from China a symbolic invitation—did she really need that? She got it anyhow, in the form of China's sentencing Harry Wu to fifteen years in prison but setting him free to go back to California the same day! Isn't it an irony? More ironic is that Mrs. Clinton would go to China to protest its abuse of human rights. Another aspect of the irony upon irony was that Harry Wu, once released, began criticizing the Clinton administration's compromise with Beijing. Is Wu more of an American by his formal citizenship, or more of a Chinese by his natural birth, or more of a Taiwanese by his political affiliation?

Out of all this mist and dust appeared one salient event. While Washington became quiet and silent from August to October 1995, Beijing leapt into unprecedented action toward Taiwan. *People's Daily* published a series of articles labeling Lee Teng-hui everything from a former communist turncoat to a present national traitor; two giant military exercises, one a missile attack and the other an offshore bombardment, were conducted in the Taiwan Strait; the Taiwan stock market plunged 10 percent immediately, and Taiwan politics fell into a three-party division shortly afterward.

In regard to China's policy-making process in this latest Taiwan Strait crisis, there were various speculations, mostly in Hong Kong magazines and newspapers. One of the most broadly accepted was that a heated argument had taken place at a series of Politburo meetings between party and army leaders in late 1995 or early 1996. Worried about American reactions, Jiang Zemin was reluctant to take any unusual actions, while several high-ranking generals vigorously pressed for a military assault on Taiwan. A compromise solution was finally reached: Do not invade Taiwan itself but create a military commotion in the Taiwan Strait.[14] The underlying point of the story was that the incumbent Jiang, not the retired Deng, seemed to have played a decisive role.

Sincerely or otherwise, Deng also played down his own influence. He was reported as saying: "People outside China keep reporting that I am already dead or fatally ill. There are so many rumors that nobody will pay any attention to them anymore. Actually, my personal role is not so crucial. The crucial matter is that we are on the right track and our national affairs are making progress. Heaven did not fall because of Chairman Mao's demise, nor will it fall because of mine."[15]

None of the rumors about the Chinese leader's decision on the crisis, almost all claiming to come from reliable sources, can be verified. These rumors were in the vested interest of various people. It will probably take years or even decades for reliable documents of this secret military nature to become available. Now fifty years after the Korean War, the minutes of the few Politburo conferences revolving around China's participation, as referred to in several personal memoirs, remain unreleased. Such being the case, ingenious analyses based on general knowledge of communist political mechanisms, and careful studies of all available information would most probably lead closer to the truth than any one particular source.

I tend to believe that any final say on such an extraordinary event as military action against Taiwan would have to have come from Deng's mouth alone. Otherwise, it would have been a collective discussion in which half a dozen Politburo members plus half a dozen retired veterans would play an equally important or unimportant role. Rather than a result of compromise between two groups of conflicting people, I would opt for understanding what China recently did toward America and Taiwan as a compromise between two of Deng's own conflicting ideas![16]

We will hear Deng's words no more, but his ideas will persist. Actually, this author would say that in a sense Deng's ideas have become Communist China's collective wisdom. As far as U.S.-China relations are concerned, these ideas, or Dengism, may be defined in a simple way: confront America firmly and utilize America intelligently. With America constantly regarded as China's chief competitor in world politics as well as one of China's chief benefactors in the world economy, Beijing's foreign policy has gone through subtle but tangible changes during the 1990s, changes from, so to speak, the commercial defensive to the political offensive.

The Taiwan issue, seemingly an issue of national defense, serves as a focal point of China's diplomatic offense. The *New York Times* report that China would launch an immediate attack after Taiwan's presidential election in March 1996 proved to be another rumor spread by people with special interests.[17] In all likelihood, nevertheless, China will more vigorously pursue the Taiwan issue in the years to come, causing more confusion in Taiwan politics and further testing the extent of American tolerance. Even if they do not blow up now or soon, relations between the United States and China will, particularly over the Taiwan issue, blow up at some moment, on some excuse, and to some extent. Following in Deng Xiaoping's footsteps, Chinese leaders have become more determined, though less vocal, in such situations now more than ever before, far more so than their American counterparts. It is for them a matter of balance between anxiousness and cautiousness. Generally speaking, the incumbent party and state leaders will compete with one another in adopting more affirmative approaches in order to show their patriotism or nationalism as well as their personal loyalty to Deng's memory, just as Deng did in the Sino-Soviet polemics of the 1960s. Indeed, this author tends to believe that the post-Deng strongman will probably be created less through domestic routines than through diplomatic dramas.

—— 23 ——

Epilogue: Communist China
With or Without Him

It is not unusual for an elder politician, having attained influence in current politics, to begin pondering long-term history a little. Just like Mao Zedong in his later years, Deng Xiaoping in his later years became ever more sensitive about his own posthumous image. He actually raised the issue with Mao in a private conversation in the early 1970s, and appeared satisfied with Mao's response: "I think you are a person seventy percent right and thirty percent wrong." "This assessment sounds quite okay, better than I myself expected. Isn't this what we ascribe to Stalin?"[1]

Apparently giving himself the same mixed verdict, Deng did not want to write an autobiography; nor did he encourage others to write a biography on his behalf: "A good biography should include not just the good but also the bad one has done over his whole life. So it is better to have no biography at all." Deng therefore showed no interest in having Harrison Salisbury, a renowned American journalist, praise him in the first place; nor did he care about Harrison Salisbury's harsh criticism of him later, as long as he himself had not cooperated. The problem, as I understand it, lay less in Deng as a Chinese politician than in Salisbury as an American writer.[2]

In this epilogue three subjects are discussed, all closely linked with a general assessment of Deng and all presented more provocatively than conclusively. First, a few remarks on Deng's life and career are given in order to wrap up this biographic study. Second, a brief summary of Deng's philosophy (or Dengism) is discussed, particularly his basic strategies regarding Chinese politics—domestic and international, current and long term. Last but surely not least, the prospects for Communist China as a country and for Chinese communism as a political system in the foreseeable future are considered. This final topic interests this author very much, as presumably it does the reader as well.

The Deng Personality

During his more than ninety years, Deng followed a career path that was both ordinary and extraordinary—each step seeming common-place but ending up outstanding. He came from a rural landlord family and was greatly influenced by his father who himself was something of a pragmatist. With a vague idea of searching for "sagehood"—an old metaphor for great accomplishment in personal cultivation and also in public acclaim—Deng Xiaoping left for Chongqing and then for Paris to pursue his higher education and ended up becoming a professional revolutionary in Moscow. As a trend chaser rather than a path breaker, as Lucian Pye points out, Deng participated in the Chinese communist movement. For better or for worse, from the start he was not slavishly devoted to communist doctrines or dogmas, thus making it much easier for him ultimately to shake them off.

His intimate relations with Mao from the early 1930s to the mid-1970s constituted the first half of Deng's political career. He followed Mao from 1935 to 1952, in practice and in his heart, while the communist revolution was winning great successes in China and Deng himself was winning rapid promotions through the party ranks. The period 1953–59 was for Deng one of a rapid rise into the central leadership, owing to his careful study of Mao's thought and skill at playing political games. After the "Great Leap Forward," which turned into "Three Bitter Years," Deng combined a strong awareness of Mao's imperial authority with a modicum of practical reality and personal conscience. From 1959 to 1976 Deng constantly struggled between two polarized mentalities: an ever-higher respect for Mao as an unshakable power and an ever-deeper contempt for Mao as a source of benighted policy.

Deng was by no means the sole creator of the post-Mao "revolution of the revolution." He just swam with the tide of reformist upsurge in the 1980s, which was bursting forth after being held back for thirty years. Nonetheless, he proved to be the most clear-minded and firm-footed, the one who oversaw the shifting of the party's general line from political destruction to economic construction. At the same time, he believed either as a means or an end that the Communist Party had to maintain its rule, and he himself had to maintain his supremacy in the party apparatus. Although the end and the means may have sometimes been confused, these are the two ingredients always evident in Deng's performance from 1976 until his death.

Deng did not know much about military affairs in a professional sense, despite having been with so many troops on the battlefront for so many years in the 1930s and 1940s. He did not know much about world communism, much less Marxist or Leninist theories, even though he eloquently argued these matters with the Russians in the 1960s. He did not know much about modern economy or economics; but throughout the 1980s he engaged extensively in economic reconstruction. He was far from an expert in international affairs either—despite his six-year stay in France and Russia, he never learned to speak either language—yet he confidently lectured the United Nations and various foreign dignitaries.

The fact of the matter is that Deng knew a little about everything, but was an expert on nothing—except politics! He showed himself to be a politician first and foremost, and what he did know well was personal relationships and organizational power. But come to think of it, isn't that enough? Isn't that the core, if not the whole, of politics?[3]

One way to get a fix on Deng is to remember that he was a bridge player. He liked the game, not just as pastime but also, in his own words, as a general exercise of his brain: with a few rules, strict or loose, kept in mind; with a few cards, good or bad, received by chance; with a few quick ideas on how to deliver these cards; with a little cooperation from one's partner; with an occasional finesse of one's foes. Win or lose, it's a game and let's get on to a new round. Peng Dehuai and Zhu De, by the way, liked the straight fight in *xiangqi* or war chess. Chen Yi played the delicate intellectual *go*. Zhou Enlai and Chen Yun were workaholics, not playful at all. Mao did not play either, not after the founding of the communist regime, being reluctant to show any form of equality with others or perhaps to obey any set of rules.

For those who prefer to relate Deng to China's cultural tradition and historical heritage, I would suggest that Deng was a practitioner of Taoism, with its famous doctrines: the greatest way is the unspoken way, nonaction is the best action, governing a large state is like cooking a little fish, soft tongues outlive hard teeth, and so forth. Indeed, we may say Deng Xiaoping's great achievement, especially in his later years, lies not in his doing everything but in his undoing something! Among all the contemporary Marxists or communists, by contrast, Mao Zedong was more the traditional Legalist who would stress decisive action and strict discipline, while Zhou Enlai was a Confucian type who could abide by original rituals and routines.

Will Deng be eventually judged as the "butcher of Tiananmen" or the "architect of reform and openness"? As Mao's nemesis or China's savior? As communist old-timer or pragmatic modernizer? As narrow-minded nationalist or visionary internationalist? Some of these judgments are more of a political than a historical nature, while others may be too academic for Deng to deserve. An outright condemnation of Deng would have been a probability had he died when the Communist Party nearly collapsed in 1989, but not now. Deng Pufang once advised his father that the conclusion of his career should not be June 4, 1989. Indeed, despite Deng's earlier crises and his recent death, time has been on his side and will continue to be as long as China's economic growth continues and the Communist Party maintains its political leadership.

Despite all his historical faults and political flaws—many of which are detailed in these pages—I believe Deng will be remembered as a great politician and in purely historical terms as the dominant ruler of China in the last quarter of the twentieth century. In that epoch which bears Deng's name, furthermore, China has accomplished its initial and most decisive stage of economic modernization, the importance of which can hardly be exaggerated. To borrow from David Goodman, if any one person can be held responsible for China's economic growth after the 1970s, that person must be Deng. We need not, therefore, argue too much over whether Deng was a black cat, or a white cat, or a black and white spotted cat. What we need to recognize first and last is that Deng was a cat who could catch mice and who, indeed, caught a couple of monsters!

The Deng Philosophy

It has been conventional for Western observers to label Deng's political philosophy as "pragmatism." To a large extent this is a just and fair description, and Deng was indeed a pragmatist politician. Yet, the problem, of course, is that as much as pragmatism can be called a theory without theory, Dengism can be called a philosophy without philosophy!

There is no doubt that Deng, like other successful politicians, cared a great deal about his own political fortune and fate. At a certain time and under certain conditions, he indeed had the personal objective of power for power's sake, which dictated his approaches to his superiors, colleagues and subordinates, and how he dealt with both ordinary affairs and dramatic crises. While all this constituted an important part of Deng's political motivation and behavior, he never formally expressed it, and it cannot be easily summarized here. Fortunately, this is not our major concern.

What does interest us is that Deng cared not just about personal power, but also about public policy, which constituted another important part of his political philosophy. Deng cared a great deal, especially in his later years, about what was the most urgent agenda for China as a country and the Chinese as a nation, and how best to accomplish it.

When reading Deng's *Selected Works* and reviewing his record, especially in the 1980s and 1990s, one can discover Deng's two fundamental concerns: national integrity and, particularly, economic development, which he regarded as China's focal task during his lifetime and a little beyond.

China's need for a modern economy seemed to be quite simple and clear—almost all Chinese political leaders in this century, including both Chiang Kai-shek and Mao Zedong, had called for it.[4] But few previous leaders took it as seriously and none implemented it as effectively as Deng. For Deng, to focus on economic growth meant to apply some and to remove other social, political and cultural conditions at home, and also to withhold some and develop other international activities abroad. Hence the prodigious aid to poor Africa was reduced, while profitable trade and commerce with rich Europe and America increased, both at the expense of the fanciful Maoist claim of "leadership of the third world."

While stressing economic growth as China's focal target, Deng insisted on the four cardinal principles and the policies of reform and openness as the two supporting bases or, as Deng vividly put it, "one focus plus two basic points." How do we make sense of this Deng aphorism?

When he was talking about the four cardinal principles, Deng was actually referring to China's political unity and stability as either a defensive shield or an offensive spear in its battle for economic growth. Other than that, Deng had no clear interpretation of any of the cardinal principles. How does one define the Communist Party and its leadership? And, indeed, how did Deng define socialism? Should it be proletarian dictatorship or people's dictatorship? Did Deng really abide by Marxism–Leninism–Mao Zedong Thought?

Similarly, Deng's pursuit of domestic reforms and openness to the outside world should also be seen within the context and in the service of economic results. They too were a supporting base, a necessary means, or a "cat," while economic growth was the edifice, the end, or the "mouse."

It is not Chinese political identity, but Chinese national integrity, that will compete with economic modernity for priority in the Dengist political strategy for China's agenda, especially as time passes and circumstances change. Here, national integrity means China's prestige in international diplomacy, or China's increasing involvement in global politics.

One of Deng's ideas for China's agenda can be represented by the following estimated per capita income figures: 1980: $250/capita; 1990, $500/capita; 2000, $1,000/capita; 2025, $5,000/capita; 2050, $20,000/capita. This means that China must concentrate on it own economic development.

Another Deng idea for China's agenda is expanding regional and global influence: 1997, Hong Kong; 1999, Macao; early 2000s, Taiwan; middle 2000s, East Asia; late 2000s, the Asian continent. This represents China's nationalist progress into world politics.

Dengist China in the 1980s "focused on economic growth," and worried about "rushing into world affairs." But in the 1990s there appears to be a subtle shift in the two directions in the wake of an upsurge of nationalism and patriotism. In this regard, it should be mentioned that nationalist or patriotic sentiments can be either a consequence of or a precondition for economic growth. Furthermore, economy and commerce, especially for China, has a lot to do with international affairs. As for Deng and his successors, we should not forget that they are, after all, politicians more than economists, and that whenever they talk about nationalism, they are actually referring to China's position in world politics.

Western observers point out the disparity between Deng's economic liberalism and political conservatism, and therefore blame him for the limitations that entails. This is a fair criticism, but it should also be noted that application means limitation—anything applicable must also be historically limited. These are not just dry words, because it was precisely in Deng's position in the Communist Party—already a limit in itself—that Deng's authority lay.

As a matter of fact, Deng himself realized the problem of the Communist Party dictatorship. In his talks with George Shultz and George Bush in 1987 and 1989, respectively, Deng indicated his appreciation of American democracy, with its presidential election and bipartisan competition. China could not adopt this kind of system right now, he argued meekly: had it not taken America two hundred years to do so?[5]

Historically Deng may be wrong; it is not just that America has taken so many years to make democracy work, but also that the democratic political system has enabled America to endure for so many years. But politically Deng must be right, in holding that in order to build up its economy, China needed domestic stability as a basic condition. It seems practically and logically evident, to this author at least, that before a significant improvement in China's economy and before the appearance of some decently organized opposition, an abrupt collapse of the incumbent communist rule would lead China into national divisions and military conflicts, rather than political democracy and freedom.

Communist China With or Without Him

Has Deng's death caused any changes in China's political leadership? Of course, it has! Indeed, Deng's demise is in itself a substantial change. There has already been commotion and confusion inside and outside the party hierarchy. This is only natural. To expect otherwise would imply that whether he lived or died would not matter much.

Struggles for power alignment will continue within the CCP leadership, although it is hard for us, or anybody else, to foretell exactly how. With no supreme authority to appeal to, the political leaders have to compete for factional alliances and/or electoral legitimacy. Will there be another coup d'etat or mass strike like post-Mao 1976? Unlikely. The reason is simple: Deng in 1997 did not leave such an unreasonable policy orientation, nor such an incredibly malfunctioning power machine as Mao did in 1976. As far as we can tell at this moment, all possible problems such as inflation, corruption, intellectual opposition, regional divergence, and diplomatic inadvertence may fuel intraparty competition, but they can hardly destroy communist rule all at once. In all likelihood, leadership reshuffling will take place to the extent that it did in 1979–1980, but not in the manner that it did after Mao's death in 1976.

Even less likely is any drastic reversal of Deng's policy, as there was in Mao's policy after his death. Yes, there may be mild shifts closer to or further from one "standpoint" of the four cardinal principles, on the one hand, or the "standpoint" of reform and openness, on the other. Arguments over control of GNP growth rates may range from as low as 6 percent or 8 percent or as high as 10 percent or 12 percent; and opinions over troop deployment in Hong Kong may vary from sending as many as three armies to as few as a single division. Here again, these issues are more tactical than strategic in nature.

In the field of modern economics the term "bottleneck" is used to describe the uneasy preliminary stage of growth of an undeveloped or developing economy. Once the bottleneck is broken, there comes the phase of rapid growth or "quantum leap." The economy will subsequently slow down, after it has grown to be fully developed or modernized.[6] So the question for China's economic situation is simply: Is the bottleneck broken yet?

In his later years Deng Xiaoping served as a political buffer or safety valve—Deng himself understood this—while China maintained its pace and manner of economic growth. It is to be hoped that this residual influence will continue for a few more years. By that time, the bottleneck will surely be broken, and China will be poised to take off.

As for Deng's or China's communism in longer and, for now at least, broader perspective, wasn't Deng a communist and isn't China communist? Strictly speaking, we have to say, Yes, but there are many nuances. In terms of socioeconomic structure, for now at least, some 65 percent of China's businesses are now privately owned and 35 percent publicly owned—mostly large enterprises such as iron and steel works, ammunition factories, oil fields, railroads, and so forth. In the Western capitalist countries, private businesses consist of 75–85 percent of their national economy, while central and local government businesses amount for some 15–25 percent. Thanks to Deng, the difference between Communist China and Western countries has ended up more quantitative than qualitative.

The political system, the one-party monopoly of government power, is left as the quintessential characteristic of Chinese communism which Deng stubbornly refused to change; but it will change, sooner or later.

That it will change is as inevitable as was the disappearance of pigtails on Chinese men and bound feet on Chinese women. It entails not a particular geographic value, or a matter of *space*, but rather a general developmental phase or a matter of *time*.

Some predictions about China in the perspective of the world economy and world politics might be interesting and, in this regard, one should remember again the fundamental fact that China—its five thousand years of history and culture aside—has by far the largest land mass in the Eastern Hemisphere and still has the largest population in the world. It presently has almost 1.3 billion people and will have more, probably 2 or even 3 billion, before the end of the next century.

In the two decades of Deng's reign, China's GNP grew at an average annual rate of 10 percent, slightly more than the rates of between 5 percent and 7 percent achieved by the four "little dragons" in East Asia, and far ahead of that of the Western countries with less than 2 percent or 3 percent. The "big dragon" is quickly approaching a position as the third-largest economy in the world. If this comparative trend continues, China's gross output will soon surpass Japan's and catch up with the United States a couple of decades after 2000.[7] And it should be remembered that this does not include Hong Kong and Taiwan in the equation.

This will bring about great changes not only in the world economy but also in world politics. How will this affect America's overall leadership in the world, East Asia included, as it is now so widely perceived? Indeed, China has the potential to be an enormous challenge to the West in general and the United States in particular.

If, on the other hand, China does not fare well, and military conflict or regional disintegration—something like what happened in the Soviet Union and Yugoslavia—takes place there, it will be the last gasp of the Cold War, as well as the end of communism. But how about 1 billion refugees? We must ignore them! Otherwise we would have to provide U.S. dollars in billions or trillions more than we did with Russia, and probably to less avail. In other words, China also has the potential to be a huge burden to the world, too huge, by any stretch of the imagination, to be borne by anyone.

The potential for this is less now than before, thanks to Deng Xiaoping. If governmental authority had broken down in 1966–1976—remember, one of Marshal Lin Biao's plans in 1971 was to occupy Guangzhou in the south and confront Mao in Beijing in the north—there might have happened tens of Pol Pot's Cambodia in China. The current social and economic system is, by contrast, far more capable of absorbing any possible political crisis. In case of civil war or regional breakdown, newly emerged private traders might provide local citizens with grain and vegetables, while northerners and westerners might flee to the southeastern provinces, where fast growing private businesses might accept them as inexpensive labor force.

To avoid the worst or to cope with the best, either as passive observer or as an active participant—what is good for China is not necessarily good for America in this Olympics of world politics—we need to realize there is basically just one way out: let the Dengist line of reform and openness continue to push economic growth as far as it can, and let communist China or Chinese communism meanwhile go along its own evolutionary course, with all its contradictions and reconstructions. History is usually more patient than politics. Possibly and probably, we will see an affluent and democratic China—even better than Deng's "decent level" or "small comfort"—sometime in the new millenium.[8]

Notes

Notes to Chapter 1

1. See Deng's talk with American visitors, March 25, 1985, in Li Hongfeng, *Deng Xiaoping zhongyao huodong*, pp. 291–92.

2. For Deng's observations about the necessary confrontation with the United States, see Deng Xiaoping, *Deng Xiaoping wenxuan*, pp. 3:313, 325, 332, 348. To my own knowledge, some of Deng's remarks are more blunt in original than officially published.

3. The following are the most notable English-language Deng biographies published in the last decade or so: Lee, *Deng Xiaoping*; Franz, *Deng Xiaoping*; Bonavia, *Deng*; Evans, *Deng Xiaoping and the Making of Modern China*; Deng Maomao, *My Father Deng Xiaoping*; Goodman, *Deng Xiaoping and the Chinese Revolution*.

4. Lee, *Deng Xiaoping*, p. 40; Bonavia, *Deng*, p. 18; Goodman, *Deng Xiaoping and the Chinese Revolution*, p. 43; Evans, *Deng Xiaoping and the Making of Modern China*, p. 83.

5. Deng Rong offers uniquely valuable information on Deng's personal and family affairs. In terms of historical research and political judgment, however, her work is no better or worse than one would expect from a daughter of Deng.

6. See *Time*, January 1, 1979, and January 1, 1986. For a similar criticism of the magazine, see also Lucian Pye, "An Introductory Profile: Deng Xiaoping and China's Political Culture," in *Deng Xiaoping*, ed. Shambaugh, p. 25.

7. See Deng's talk with Japanese visitors, September 19, 1989, in Li Hongfeng, *Deng Xiaoping zhongyao huodong*, pp. 457–58.

8. Schwartz, *Chinese Communism and the Rise of Mao*, p. 21.

Notes to Chapter 2

1. Among the dozen or so Deng biographies produced outside China, I would say Lee's and Goodman's are the most serious ones, whereas Han Shanbi's and Franz's are the least so, with both oftentimes tending to make up sensational stories.

The information in this chapter on Deng's clanship and childhood is primarily based on my own surveys in Paifang village in June–July 1984 and in Guang'an County in July–August 1986, as well as on Deng Rong, *Wode fuqin Deng Xiaoping,* chs. 4–10.

2. Li Huang, *Xuedun shi huiyilu,* pp. 105–6. Since Li Huang—whose memoirs are full of factual errors—casually mentions that Deng was from a Hakka family, many Deng biographers have taken this for granted and stress its bearing on Deng's personal character and revolutionary performance. During my visits to Deng's native village, none of the villagers even seemed to have heard of his supposed Hakka background.

3. See *Genealogy of the Dengs,* quoted in Deng Rong, *Wode fuqin Deng Xiaoping,* pp. 24–26.

4. See *Gazette of Guang'an County,* quoted in Deng Rong, *Wode fuqin Deng Xiaoping,* pp. 29–30.

5. See "Deng Xiaoping's reactionary background exposed," Red Guard pamphlet reprinted in *Deng Xiaoping* (in Chinese) (Taipei: East Asian Institute of the National Political University, 1978), pp. 1–2; also, my June 1984 survey in Paifang village.

6. See "Investigation of the criminal life of Deng Xiaoping," Red Guard pamphlet reproduced in Makoto Yuasa, *Deng Xiaoping,* pp. 23–24.

7. Ibid.

8. My June 1984 survey in Paifang village.

9. Deng Rong, *Wode fuqin Deng Xiaoping,* pp. 46–50. Given her unique position, Deng Rong offers very valuable information on Deng's early life and activities, especially regarding his family relations.

10. My surveys in Paifang and Guang'an.

11. It should be noted that Deng attended and graduated from a secondary school (*gaoxiao*), not yet a high school (*zhongxue*), in Guang'an.

12. Franz, *Deng Xiaoping,* p. 23; Deng Rong, *Wode fuqin Deng Xiaoping,* p. 50. Did Deng Wenming have one wife after another or more than one wife and concubine simultaneously? Deng Rong attempts to argue for the former, but others, myself included, believe the latter.

13. Deng Rong, *Wode fuqin Deng Xiaoping,* pp. 64–65; Goodman, *Deng Xiaoping and the Chinese Revolution,* pp. 24, 316.

14. Snow, *Red Star over China,* pp. 140–49; Terrill, *Mao,* pp. 4–7.

15. See "Deng Xiaoping's reactionary background exposed."

16. See Franz, *Deng Xiaoping,* p. 25. My own survey in Paifang also confirmed this folklore.

Notes to Chapter 3

1. My surveys in Paifang village in June–July 1984 and in Guang'an in July–August 1986.

2. See *Sichuan shengqing* (Gazette of Sichuan Province) (Chengdu: Sichuan People's Press, 1986), pp. 55–56.

3. My surveys in Paifang and Guang'an; Deng Rong, *Wode fuqin Deng Xiaoping,* p. 64; Goodman, *Deng Xiaoping and the Chinese Revolution,* p. 166.

Goodman is right. As people from Guang'an told me, Deng and his uncle went to Chongqing together and attended a high school there before entering the preparatory school for France, which did not open until January 1919 and not, as Deng Rong mistakenly says, September 1918.

4. See Party History Research Group, *Pufa qingong jianxue yundong*, p. 1:135.

5. Ibid.; also Wang Yongxiang et al., *Lu'ou zhibu shihua*, p. 23.

6. Chen Yi, "My experience of work and study in France," Party History Research Group, *Pufa qingong jianxue yundong*, p. 2:157.

7. For Deng's remarks on his motives for going abroad, see Deng Xiaoping, *Deng Xiaoping wenxuan*, p. 2:124.

8. Jiang Zemin, "Reminiscences of diligent work and thrifty study in France and Belgium," Party History Research Group, *Pufa qingong jianxue yundong*, pp. 3:148–50. Note that the author of this article is another Jiang Zemin, *not* the individual chosen as Deng's successor.

9. Ibid.

10. Wang Yongxiang et al., *Lu'ou zhibu shihua*, p. 29.

11. My surveys in Paifang and Guang'an; Deng Rong, *Wode fuqin Deng Xiaoping*, p. 68; Bonavia, *Deng*, p. 7; Goodman, *Deng Xiaoping and the Chinese Revolution*, p. 25. Bonavia's speculation that Deng's leaving home for France might have resulted from some friction with his family is unfounded. Deng's father fully supported his going abroad.

12. Nie Rongzhen, *Huiyilu*, p. 1:25.

13. Jiang Zemin, "Reminiscences of diligent work and thrifty study."

14. Zhou Enlai's poem "Farewell Words," in Wang Yongxiang et al., *Lu'ou zhibu shihua*, p. 35.

15. See Feng Xuezong's letter from France to his family in Sichuan at that time, quoted in Deng Rong, *Wode fuqin Deng Xiaoping*, pp. 73–76.

16. For more on the "three beautifuls," see Jiang Zemin, "Reminiscences of diligent work and thrifty study."

17. See *Xinwen bao* (Newspaper), September 11, 1920; and *Lu'ou xinwen* (News in Europe), October 31, 1920.

18. For Deng's discussion of his purpose for going abroad, see Deng Xiaoping, *Deng Xiaoping wenxuan*, p. 2:124.

19. Terrill, *Mao,* p. 40.

Notes to Chapter 4

1. News report in *Shen bao* (Shanghai Daily), March 30, 1921.

2. He Changgong, "Work and study in France," in Wang Yongxiang et al., *Lu'ou zhibu shihua*, pp. 66–77.

3. Chen Yi, "My experience of work and study in France."

4. Li Huang, *Xuedun shi huiyilu*, pp. 105–6.

5. See Party History Research Group, *Pufa qingong jianxue yundong*, pp. 1:23–25.

6. Ibid.

7. Lee, *Deng Xiaoping*, pp. 27–28.

8. See Wang, "Deng Xiaoping: The Years in France," p. 698; and Good-

man, *Deng Xiaoping and the Chinese Revolution,* pp. 25, 166. Goodman too apparently didn't realize that Deng's trip from Shanghai to Marseilles could not have taken more than three months.

9. See official Deng biographies, and Deng Rong, *Wode fuqin Deng Xiaoping,* p. 110; and Ban Yang, "Verifications of the timings of Deng Xiaoping's joining the Communist Youth League and the Communist Party," *Tansuo,* March 1993.

Although Deng Rong admits that Fu Zhong had quite a different recollection, she still insists that Deng became one of the top leaders of the Youth League in Europe in 1924, thereby being naturally accepted as a Communist Party member. As a matter of historical fact, neither her premise nor her inference is beyond question.

10. Franz, *Deng Xiaoping,* pp. 43–44; Wang Yongxiang et al., *Lu'ou zhibu shihua,* pp. 62–73, 80–102.

11. See "Comrade Chen Duxiu's Report to the Third Party Congress on Behalf of the CCP CEC," in Saich, ed., *The Rise to Power of the Chinese Communist Party,* pp. 60–63.

12. Deng Rong, *Wode fuqin Deng Xiaoping,* p. 112. It would be interesting for someone with adequate financial resources and a knowledge of Russian to pursue further research in the Moscow archives, just as Nora Wang did in Paris, to make certain of Deng's activities, not only in 1926 but even before and afterward.

13. See Takagi Keizo, *Biography of Deng Xiaoping,* p. 23. Also see Wu Hao, "No. 1 Report of the Chinese Communist Youth League in Europe," Party History Research Group, *Pufa qingong jianxue yundong,* pp. 2:843–48. "Wu Hao" was Zhou Enlai's pen name. This valuable document shows, among other things, that it was against the Youth League's policy for its members to join the Communist Party without specific permission. In fact, Zhang Shenfu was expelled from the Youth League partly for his having concurrently held a Communist Party membership. For a fuller treatment of this subject, see Ban Yang, "Verifications of the timings of Deng Xiaoping's joining the Communist Youth League and the Communist Party."

14. For Deng's three "Look at" articles in *Red Light,* see Party History Research Group, *Pufa qingong jianxue yundong,* pp. 3:271–74.

15. Deng Xiaoping, "Look at the second slandering of the *Herald Weekly,*" in Party History Research Group, *Pufa qingong jianxue yundong,* pp. 3:271–74.

16. Wang Yongxiang et al., *Lu'ou zhibu shihua,* p. 55.

17. Wang, "Deng Xiaoping: The Years in France."

18. Numerous letters and announcements at that time indicate that Deng and his group's departure for Moscow had been prepared in advance, not attributable solely to the Paris police raid.

Notes to Chapter 5

1. Joseph Stalin, "On the political tasks of the Eastern University," in *Sidalin quanji* (in Chinese) (Comprehensive Works of Stalin), p. 23:355.

2. Takagi Keizo, *Biography of Deng Xiaoping,* p. 23; also Nie Rongzhen, *Huiyilu,* p. 1:29.

3. See Feng Hongda and Yu Hua,"Kind greeting and encouragement," in Ban Yang and Zhuo Xiaowei, "Black cat or white cat: review of Han Shanbi's biography of Deng Xiaoping," in *Tansuo*, no. 55, January 1986.

4. Deng Xiaoping's autobiography, quoted in Deng Rong, *Wode fuqin Deng Xiaoping*, p. 151.

5. Lee, *Deng Xiaoping*, pp. 38–40.

6. Ibid.; also Sheng Yue, *Sun Yat-sen University*, pp. 69–70.

7. See the assessment of Deng by the CCP branch of Sun Yat-sen University, June 16, 1926, quoted in Deng Rong, *Wode fuqin Deng Xiaoping*, pp. 149–50.

8. Sheridan, *Chinese Warlord*, pp. 110–12.

9. Lee, *Deng Xiaoping*, p. 40; Goodman, *Deng Xiaoping and the Chinese Revolution*, pp. 28, 166. Accompanying Feng on the trip from Russia back to China on September 16, 1926, was a small, confidential group, including just one Soviet adviser, one CCP agent, and a few assistants.

10. See Feng Hongda and Yu Hua,"Kind greeting and encouragement." Here what Deng called "Kulun" is the old Chinese name for Ulan Bator.

11. Deng himself once claimed that he had been the secretary of the secret party branch in Feng's army, but there seems no documentary evidence to support that claim either.

12. See Feng Yuxiang, *Feng Yuxiang riji*, pp. 7:58–77, 8:1–60. During the period from September 1926 to July 1927, there is no mention of either Deng Xiaoping or the Zhongshan Military Academy in Feng's diary. Even the very existence of the Zhongshan Military Academy is questionable, although the diary mentions the names of Liu Bojian as deputy director of the Political Department and a few other communists, as well as the operations of the "Cadres School," "Political School," and "Zhongshan Club."

13. See Feng Hongda and Yu Hua,"Kind greeting and encouragement."

14. Saich, *The Rise to Power of the Chinese Communist Party*, pp. 277–78, 296–308, 497–98. It should be noted that the conference minutes listed Deng among the service personnel, not among the twenty-one participants.

15. Ibid. Saich's work, especially for the period 1921–39, is excellent. Qu's confession of a "mistake of history" is based on my own knowledge.

16. Wang Jianying, ed., *Zhongguo gongchandang zuzhishi ziliao huibian*, p. 101; Li Weihan, *Huiyi yu yanjiu*, p. 243. Even Li Weihan sounds too reluctant to confirm that Deng was the chief secretary of the Party Center.

17. See Deng's talks with Chen Xingshen, November 3, 1986; Li Hongfeng, *Deng Xiaoping zhongyao huodong*, p. 372. It became almost a casual habit for Deng to brag excessively about his official seniority in the early 1980s. Despite my respect for Deng as a great politician, such a habit strikes me as odd and unnecessary. Deng should have known better than anybody else that, in Shanghai in 1928–29, the post of the CCP Center's chief secretary, or *mishuzhang*, had been held by Zhou Enlai and then Li Lisan, both of whom were full Politburo members, and could not possibly have been held by a non–Party Center member like himself.

18. Since he was still an insignificant figure, we have few records or memoirs directly regarding Deng at the time. For a general understanding of the underground Party Center activities in the late 1920s, which might have great bearing upon Deng's mentality, see Warren Kuo, *Analytical History of*

the Chinese Communist Party, vol. 2, ch. 17; and Benjamin Yang, "Complexity and Reasonability."

Notes to Chapter 6

1. See Liu Shaotang, *Minguo dashi rizhi,* pp. 2:450–75; also Benjamin Yang, *From Revolution to Politics,* pp. 12–15.

2. Zhang Yunyi, "The Baise uprising and a brief history of the Seventh Red Army," pp. 2:585–99; and Yuan Renyuan, "From Baise to Xiang-Gan," pp. 2:621–35, both in Party History Research Committee, *Zuo you jiang geming genjudi.*

3. Franz, *Deng Xiaoping,* p. 78. Franz does not give his source, which must be Harrison Salisbury's interview with Hu Hua. Unfortunately, both men are dead and can no longer shed light on the matter. Based on my own acquaintance with them, I gather that Salisbury might have misunderstood Hu. Even if Deng had ever taken a trip via Vietnam to Guangxi around that time, it could only have been on his return from Hong Kong to Longzhou in early February 1930.

4. Deng Rong, *Wode fuqin Deng Xiaoping,* pp. 204–5; Ban Yang, "Verifications of Deng Xiaoping's relations with the Seventh Red Army," *Tansuo,* no. 104, August 1992. Deng Rong's claim that Deng arrived in Guangxi and chaired the provincial congress of Guangxi Chinese Communist Party representatives in September 1929 is particularly at variance with historical records.

5. See "Letter of the CCP Guangdong Provincial Committee to the CCP Guangxi Special Committee," October 30, 1929, Party History Research Committee, *Zuo you jiang geming genjudi,* pp. 1:98–100.

6. See "Discussions and arrangements of the Red Army work in Guangxi," January 1930, Party History Research Committee, *Zuo you jiang geming genjudi,* pp. 1:174–200.

7. Deng Xiaoping, "Report of the Seventh Army," Party History Research Committee, *Zuo you jiang geming genjudi,* pp. 1:392–411. This twenty-thousand-character-long article—perhaps the longest ever to come from Deng's own hands—is an extremely valuable historical record.

8. Tu Zhennong, "Report of the Seventh Army," Party History Research Committee, *Zuo you jiang geming genjudi,* p. 1:385.

9. Deng Xiaoping, "Report of the Seventh Army."

10. Yuan Renyuan, "The red storm in Youjiang, Guangxi," *Renmin ribao,* December 9, 1978.

11. See "Comrade Yan Heng's report of the Seventh Army," April 4, 1931, Party History Research Committee, *Zuo you jiang geming genjudi,* p. 1:383.

12. Deng Xiaoping, "Report of the Seventh Army."

13. See "Deng Xiaoping, the deserter," a Red Guard pamphlet reprinted in Takagi Keizo, *Biography of Deng Xiaoping,* pp. 41–42.

14. Deng Xiaoping, "Report of the Seventh Army"; also Deng's letter to Mao Zedong, August 3, 1972, referred to in Lucian Pye, "An Introductory Profile: Deng Xiaoping and China's Political Culture," in *Deng Xiaoping,* ed. Shambaugh, p. 32. On the one hand, it should be clear enough, particularly from his own contemporary report to the Party Center, that Deng had no Front Com-

mittee resolution authorizing him to leave the Seventh Army. But on the other hand, as the supreme political leader in the Seventh Army, Deng had, according to the party and army's disciplinary rules at the time, the sole authority to make final decisions on any and all army activities. In this sense, Deng's leaving the troops was indeed "procedurally justifiable," even in the absence of a collective resolution. For a fuller discussion, see Ban Yang, "Verifications of Deng Xiaoping's relations with the Seventh Red Army."

15. Bonavia, *Deng*, p. 22; Evans, *Deng Xiaoping and the Making of Modern China*, p. 57.

16. Deng Rong, *Wode fuqin Deng Xiaoping*, pp. 287–89.

17. Deng Xiaoping, "Report of the Seventh Army."

18. See "Letter of the CCP Central Committee to the Front Committee of the Seventh Army, May 14, 1931," in Party History Research Committee, *Zuo you jiang geming genjudi*, pp. 1:412–14.

19. Han Shanbi, *Deng Xiaoping pingzhuan*, p. 1:212.

20. See Ban Yang, "Verification of Deng Xiaoping's relations with the Seventh Red Army." There are numerous historical documents that indicate that Deng might have been more actively involved in the Seventh Army purge. If proved true, that would have serious implications for Deng's reputation and would also be of considerable interest to us.

Notes to Chapter 7

1. There are different versions of Deng's early appointment in the Jiangxi Soviet even among Chinese official historians. Some believe he had worked in the General Political Department for a while upon his arrival. In any case, we must rule out the possibility of Deng being appointed party secretary of Ruijin as a reward for his role in the Changsha seizure in July 1930. See Sheng Ping et al., *Zhonggong renming dacidian* (Dictionary of Chinese Communists) (Beijing: International Broadcast Press, 1991), p. 98, and Donald Klein and Anne Clark, *Biographic Dictionary of Chinese Communism* (Cambridge, MA: Harvard University Press, 1970), p. 2:821.

2. None of their marriages—Zhou Enlai to Deng Yingchao in 1925, Mao Zedong to He Zizhen in 1928, and Zhu De to Kang Keqing in 1929—had involved any more ritual than just "moving in together."

3. Luo Ming, "A few opinions about our work," in *Zhonggong dangshi ziliao* (Materials on Party History), Beijing, February 1982, p. 275.

4. Li Weihan, *Huiyi yu yanjiu*, p. 125.

5. Luo Fu, "The Luo Ming line in Jiangxi," in Secretariat of CCP Central Committee, *Liuda yilai*, pp. 1:351–55. "Luo Fu" is Zhang Wentian's pen name.

6. See Luo Mai, "Struggle for our party's line," in Secretariat of CCP Central Committee, *Liuda yilai*, pp. 1:362–68. "Luo Mai" is Li Weihan.

7. Li Xinzhi and Wang Yuezong, eds., *Weida de shijian, guanghui de sixiang*, p. 96.

8. Deng was in trouble but not in prison. Also, I cannot understand why some authors think that Deng should owe his rehabilitation to Wang Jiaxiang. Because they both had studied in Moscow before? See Evans, *Deng Xiaoping and the Making of Modern China*, p. 65.

9. Yang, *From Revolution to Politics,* pp. 68–99; Salisbury, *The Long March,* p. 22.

10. See Benjamin Yang, "The Zunyi Conference as One Step in Mao's Rise to Power"; also see Thomas Kampen, "The Zunyi Conference and Further Steps in Mao's Rise to Power."

11. Of course, this is largely my own guesswork and cannot be conclusively verified. I remember giving a fuller discussion on this and some other issues at the Fairbank Center for East Asian Research, Harvard University in Feburary 1988.

12. Deng Rong, *Wode fuqin Deng Xiaoping,* pp. 357–58.

13. Deng's own excuse was that he left his position as chief secretary to Liu Ying in early 1935 because there was nothing to do in the CCP Center. How come? There were quite a lot of important things to do there, as it was the time of Mao's fierce struggle with Zhang Guotao!

14. Zhang Guotao, *Wode huiyi,* p. 3:137.

15. Deng Rong, *Wode fuqin Deng Xiaoping,* p. 353.

16. Yang, *From Revolution to Politics,* pp. 250–75.

17. Almost all of Deng's official biographies hold these positions. See Deng Rong, *Wode fuqin Deng Xiaoping,* pp. 374–85. But how much can these interviews of Deng's former subordinates by his own daughter really be trusted from a historical point of view?

18. My own knowledge based on an unofficial source; Peng Dehuai, *Peng Dehuai zishu,* p. 182; Snow, *Random Notes,* p. 137.

19. For a discussion of Deng's illness, see Evans, *Deng Xiaoping and the Making of the Chinese Revolution,* p. 155.

Notes to Chapter 8

1. See Central Revolutionary Military Council, "An order for reorganizing the Red Army into the Eighth Route Army of the Nationalist Army, August 25, 1937," in *Mao Zedong ji* (Works of Mao Zedong) (Tokyo: Soso Press, 1984), Supplementary Volume 5, pp. 101–2. This order—officially signed by Mao but actually not drafted by Mao—appointed Deng as deputy director of the Political Department of the Eighth Route Army. Since the political commissar system was temporarily abolished, directorship of the political department represented the highest political position in the communist army.

2. Yang, *From Revolution to Politics,* p. 313.

3. Evans, *Deng Xiaoping and the Making of the Chinese Revolution,* p. 83. In fact, Zhang Hao worked as chairman of the All China Labor Union for several years, until his death in 1943. All the communist leaders at Yan'an attended his funeral, and more notably, Mao served as one of the pallbearers.

4. Yang Guoyu, *Liu Deng huixia,* pp. 36–37.

5. See Deng's telegram to Liu from Yan'an, quoted in Li Xinzhi and Wang Yuezong, eds., *Weida de shijian, guanghui de sixiang,* pp. 55–56.

6. Terrill, *Madame Mao,* pp. 123–31.

7. Deng Rong, *Wode fuqin Deng Xiaoping,* pp. 417, 444, 449. There is no

doubt that Deng Rong's description of Deng's marriage with Zhuo Lin must be the most reliable and informative.

8. Carlson, *Twin Star of China*, p. 252, quoted in Lee, *Deng Xiaoping*, p. 78; Hans Muller's interview by Uli Franz, quoted in Franz, *Deng Xiaoping*, p. 116.

9. See "Liu and Deng's directive to the South Hebei Military District on frictions with the Kuomintang troops," *Jijiluyu genjudi shiliao xuanbian* (Collection of Historical Documents of the Ji-Ji-Lu-Yu Base Area) (Beijing: People's Press, 1989), p. 1:300.

10. Deng Xiaoping, "A brief account of our struggle against the enemy," January 26, 1943, *Deng Xiaoping wenxuan*, p. 1:35.

11. Deng Xiaoping, "Fight againt inertia and overcome the grave situation in the Taihang region," April 28, 1941, in *Deng Xiaoping wenxuan*, p. 1:45.

12. See Harrison, *The Long March*, p. 344.

13. For a fuller treatment of Deng and communist developments in the Taihang region, see Goodman, *Deng Xiaoping and the Chinese Revolution*, pp. 41–45.

14. Deng Xiaoping, "On economic reconstructions in the Taihang region," July 2, 1943, *Deng Xiaoping wenxuan*, pp. 1:78–86.

15. For a discussion of the production team, see Li Xinzhi and Wang Yuezong, eds., *Weida de shijian, guanghui de sixiang*, pp. 66–68.

16. Deng Rong, *Wode fuqin Deng Xiaoping*, p. 450. It should be noted that Mao showed his favor for Deng both when he called Deng to Yan'an and when he left Deng at the front.

17. Deng Xiaoping, "Speech at the mobilization conference for rectification in the party school of the Northern Bureau," November 10, 1943, *Deng Xiaoping wenxuan*, pp. 1:87–94.

18. Wang Jianying, ed., *Zhongguo Gongchandang zuzhi shi ziliao huibian*, p. 234.

Notes to Chapter 9

1. For Liu Bocheng and Deng Xiaoping's inspiring telegrams from Yan'an to all party and army units under their jurisdiction, see *Jijiluyu genjudi shiliao xuanbian*, pp. 4:1–2.

2. Mao Zedong, "Situations after the victory of the Anti-Japanese War and our tasks," *Mao Zedong xuanji*, p. 4:1045.

3. Mao Zedong, "Remarks on the Chongqing talks," *Mao Zedong xuanji*, p. 4:1055; also see Liu and Deng's directives and reports on the Battle of Shangdang, in *Jijiluyu genjudi shiliao xuanbian*, pp. 1:20–27.

4. Quoted in Deng Rong, *Wode fuqin Deng Xiaoping*, pp. 513–15.

5. For the Battle of Pinghan, see Deng Xiaoping, *Deng Xiaoping wenxuan*, p. 1:177; see also Academy of Military Science, ed., *Zhongguo renmin jiefangjun dashiji*, pp. 228–29.

6. Li Xinzhi and Wang Yuezong, eds., *Weida de shijian, guanghui de sixiang*, p. 61.

7. We should notice the subtle differences among Mao, Liu, and Deng regarding decisions on the precarious expedition to the Dabie Mountains: Mao was insistent, Liu reluctant, and Deng cooperative.

8. See Li Xinzhi and Wang Yuezong, eds., *Weida de shijian, guanghui de sixiang*, pp. 61–62.

9. For a description of the Liu–Deng army's expedition to the Dabie Mountains, see Academy of Military Science, ed., *Jiefangjun dashiji*, pp. 260–62.

10. See Deng's telegram to the Military Council on December 22, 1947, in *Zhongguo renmin jiefangjun dier yezhanjun shiliao* (Historical Materials of the Second Field Army of the Chinese People's Liberation Army) (Beijing: People's Press, 1989), pp. 71–72. Asking Mao to arrange for the strategic assistance of other army units was a political more than a military task, and thus, it was more appropriate for Deng rather than Liu alone to make the request.

11. See Deng's report directly to Mao on January 30, 1948, *Zhongguo renmin jiefangjun dier yezhanjun shiliao*, pp. 9–10. Winning over Mao's sympathy toward his own troops was a political task and thus one that would more appropriately be performed by the political Deng, not by the military Liu.

12. Li Xinzhi and Wang Yuezong, eds., *Weida de shijian, guanghui de sixiang*, pp. 71–72.

13. Generally speaking, telegrams on military affairs to the Central Military Council were drafted by Deng and jointly signed by Liu, but telegrams on political issues to Mao were written and signed by Deng alone. I also remember an interesting comment Bo Yibo made about Deng's complementary relations with Liu: "Comrade Bocheng treated small things as big ones, while Comrade Xiaoping handled big matters as small ones."

14. Li Xinzhi and Wang Yuezong, eds., *Weida de shijian, guanghui de sixiang*, p. 75.

15. See Academy of Military Science, ed., *Jiefangjun dashiji*, pp. 282–88. It should be mentioned that the four field armies were given their formal numerical designations a few months later.

16. For the strategic decision on the Huaihai Campaign, see Ban Yang and Zhuo Xiaowei, "Black cat or white cat," *Tansuo*, no. 57, March 1986, pp. 70–74.

17. To my own knowledge, Mao joked with Deng at Xibopo in March 1948, regarding the formation of the General Front Committee: "Here and now, I have put all the troops in your palms."

18. See *Mao Zedong junshi wenji* (Military Writings of Mao Zedong) (Beijing: Military Science Press, 1993), pp. 2:795–97, 2:817–18; see also Zhang Guotao, *Wode huiyi*, p. 3:1130.

19. Had Mao been as prudent in the Beijing talks as he was in the previous Chongqing talks, there might have been no Taiwan problem by now!

20. Deng Xiaoping, "From the river crossing to the seizure of Shanghai," August 4, 1949, *Deng Xiaoping wenxuan*, pp. 1:136–41.

21. Deng Xiaoping, "Operational plan for the Jing-Hu-Hang campaign, March 31, 1949," *Deng Xiaoping wenxuan*, pp. 1:131–34. Here "Jing" means Nanjing, "Hu" means Shanghai, and "Hang" means Hangzhou.

22. Deng Xiaoping, "Break the blockade imposed by the imperialists, July 19, 1949," *Deng Xiaoping wenxuan*, p. 1:135. Deng's communication of Mao's directives on the CCP's domestic and foreign policies on July 19, 1949, might have been the first indication that their cooperation had begun to shift from specific army matters to more general party affairs. Could we imagine Mao conferring with Liu Bocheng about such affairs?

23. Han Shanbi, *Deng Xiaoping pingzhuan,* p. 1:321.

24. See Academy of Military Science, ed., *Jiefangjun dashiji,* pp. 301–2, 308–9.

Notes to Chapter 10

1. Deng had been the first secretary of the East Bureau, with Rao Shushi and Chen Yi as the second and third in command, after the River-Crossing Campaign and before his new appointment as secretary of the Southwest Bureau, indicating changes in Mao's strategic concerns in the summer of 1949. In any case, Mao would promote the smart Deng to the most crucial post while demoting the blunt Chen to a role that was inferior even to that of the strange Rao.

2. See "Telegram to Liu and Deng regarding seizure of Chongqing," November 28, 1949, in Mao Zedong, *Jianguo yilai Mao Zedong wengao,* pp. 1:170–71.

3. Liu Shaotang, *Minguo dashi rizhi,* pp. 2:840–43. In retrospect, Mao's "chasing the retreating bandits" mentality as evidenced during the peace negotiations between the Chinese Communist Party and the Kuomintang was, if not ethically wrong, at least politically questionable. In this very regard, Deng Xiaoping, unlike Zhou Enlai, had exerted no positive influence upon Mao at all.

4. *Renmin ribao* editorial, "Liberate All China," January 1, 1950.

5. See Mao Zedong, *Jianguo yilai Mao Zedong wengao,* p. 1:195.

6. See Solinger, *Regional Government and Political Integration in Southwest China, 1949–1953.*

7. Academy of Military Science, ed., *Jiefangjun dashiji,* p. 311. Other sources even suggest that 850,000 bandits had been eliminated from the southwest region in 1950.

8. Deng Xiaoping, "Report at the conference on the media and press in the Southwest Region," May 16, 1950, *Deng Xiaoping wenxuan,* pp. 1:145–50; and "The entire pary should pay attention to the united front work," March 26, 1951, *Deng Xiaoping wenxuan,* pp. 1:172–76.

9. Deng Xiaoping, "Overcome the unhealthy tendencies within the party in the Southwest," June 6, 1950, *Deng Xiaoping wenxuan,* pp. 1:152–61.

10. For Mao's telegram to Deng from Moscow, see *Jianguo yilai Mao Zedong wengao,* p. 1:295.

11. Li Xinzhi and Wang Yuezong, eds., *Weida de shijian, guanghui de sixiang,* pp. 94–96.

12. For Deng's instructions regarding the Tibet problem, see Li Xinzhi and Wang Yuezong, eds., *Weida de shijian, guanghui de sixiang,* p. 94.

13. Party History Research Institute, comp., *Zhonggong dashi nianbiao,* p. 113; see also Harrison, *The Long March,* p. 450.

14. See "Investigation of the criminal life of Deng Xiaoping," Red Guard pamphlet reproduced in Makoto Yuasa, *Deng Xiaoping,* pp. 23–24.

15. Deng Rong, *Wode fuqin Deng Xiaoping,* pp. 640–45. Deng Rong's description of Deng's private iife in Chongqing must be considered the most informative and interesting.

16. The Chengdu–Chongqing railway and the Chengdu–Lhasa highway are among the most notable economic achievements under Deng's leadership in southwest China in the early 1950s.

17. See David Shambaugh, "Deng Xiaoping: The Politician," in Shambaugh, ed., *Deng Xiaoping;* see also Swaine, *Military and Political Succession in China.* Shambaugh and Swaine correctly specify the Second Field Army and the Southwest Region as Deng's power bases. It should be pointed out, nevertheless, that, partly because of his general supervisory role in the military as well as regional units, Deng would not depend, and did not need to depend, as much on the factional support of his former subordinates as did some others such as He Long and Lin Biao. Here lay Deng's strength, not his weakness. I know of Deng once making a statement: I never highly respected that petty factionalism *(xiao zongpai).* Each time I was moved to a new position, I went there alone, without even bringing my bodyguard.

Notes to Chapter 11

1. Han Shanbi, *Deng Xiaoping pingzhuan,* p. 1:245; Lee, *Deng Xiaoping,* p. 96; Bonavia, *Deng,* p. 257; and Goodman, *Deng Xiaoping and the Chinese Revolution,* p. 50.

2. See Party History Research Institute, comp., *Zhonggong dashi nianbiao,* pp. 131–32.

3. Bo Yibo, *Ruogan zhongda juece yu shijian de huigu,* pp. 25–35.

4. Ibid.

5. For Mao's criticism of Liu at the Politburo conference, June 15, 1953, see Mao Zedong, *Jianguo yilai Mao Zedong wengao,* p. 4:251. In terms of elite politics, we may say that the key to the Gao–Rao incident lay in the relations among Mao, Liu, and Gao, coupled with Deng's smart interplay with them.

6. Deng recalls his role in the Gao–Rao incident, in "Remarks on successive drafts of the Resolution on Certain Questions in the History of our Party since the founding of the People's Republic," March 1980–June 1981, *Deng Xiaoping wenxuan,* pp. 2:255–74.

7. For Mao's talks at the Politburo conference, see Mao Zedong, *Mao Zedong xuanji,* pp. 5:145–55; and for Mao's having allowed Gao to be subjected to criticism, see Mao Zedong, *Jianguo yilai Mao Zedong wengao,* pp. 4:432–40.

8. Deng Xiaoping, "Conceit and complacency are the arch-enemy of unity," February 6, 1954, *Deng Xiaoping wenxuan,* pp. 1:189–96.

9. See "Report of Deng Xiaoping, Chen Yi, and Tan Zhenlin Concerning the Discussion Meeting on the Rao Shushi Question," in Teiwes, *Politics at Mao's Court,* pp. 245–52.

10. Teiwes, *Politics at Mao's Court,* pp. 87–145. Teiwes's studies of this and other political purges under Mao are indeed the best in the Western literature.

11. For Deng's recollection of the Gao–Rao incident, see *Deng Xiaoping wenxuan,* pp. 2:255–74.

12. Deng Xiaoping, "Report on the Gao Gang and Rao Shushi Anti-Party Alliance," in Teiwes, *Politics at Mao's Court,* pp. 254–76.

13. The official statement, as well as perhaps the attention of ordinary or general participants and ordinary outside observers, was focused on Gao's establishment of an independent kingdom in northeastern China, his receipt of a luxurious automobile from Stalin, and so on.

14. Terrill, *Mao,* pp. 201–29. It is interesting to note that, just because he held less personal respect for the funny Khrushchev than for the awesome Stalin, Mao was fond of Khrushchev during 1953–57 (Sino-Soviet relations seemed better than before) and then he quarreled with Khrushchev during 1958–64 (Sino-Soviet relations became worse than ever).

15. For Khrushchev's secret speech on Stalin at the CPSU's Twentieth Congress, see *Khrushchev Remembers,* p. 234.

16. For Zhu's and Deng's performances at the CPSU Twentieth Congress, see Terrill, *Mao,* p. 245; and Shi Zhe, *Zai lishi juren shenbian,* pp. 576–98.

17. See Mao's instructions to Deng, April 2 and 4, 1956, in Mao Zedong, *Jianguo yilai Mao Zedong wengao,* pp. 6:59–67; see also Wu Lengxi, *Yi Mao zhuxi,* pp. 1–30.

18. See Li Xinzhi and Wang Yuezong, eds., *Weida de shijian, guanghui de sixiang,* p. 107.

19. For Liu's political report at the Eighth Congress, September 15, 1956, see *Liu Shaoqi xuanji* (Selected Works of Liu Shaoqi) (Beijing: People's Press, 1988), pp. 2:202–76.

20. Deng Xiaoping, "Report on the revision of the party constitution," September 16, 1956, *Deng Xiaoping wenxuan,* pp. 1:200–244.

21. The fact that Deng followed Liu and Peng's lead in denouncing the cult of personality and deleting the term *Mao Zedong thought* from his report might represent a mixture of true feelings and formal gesture.

22. Lee, *Deng Xiaoping,* p. 112; Shambaugh, ed., *Deng Xiaoping,* p. 68; and Goodman, *Deng Xiaoping and the Chinese Revolution,* p. 54. Careful as Goodman is elsewhere, his list of members of the Secretariat is uncharacteristically incomplete and inaccurate.

Although the nature of this biography does not permit a detailed analysis of the composition of the Secretariat and changes in its membership over time, what follows is a brief overview. Besides Deng, other Secretariat members in 1956 were: Peng Zhen, Wang Jiaxiang, Tan Zhenlin, Tan Zheng, Huang Kecheng, and Li Xuefeng. Alternate members were: Liu Lantao, Yang Shangkun, and Hu Qiaomu.

Li Xiannian and Li Fuchun were added as members in May 1958; Lu Dingyi, Kang Sheng, and Luo Ruiqing, in September 1962; Tao Zhu and Ye Jianying, in May 1966; and Xie Fuzhi and Liu Ningyi, in August 1966; and Huang Kecheng and Tan Zheng were removed in practice in October 1959 and formally in September 1962; Yang Shangkun, Luo Ruiqing, Lu Dingyi, and Peng Zhen were removed in practice from December 1965 to May 1966 and formally in August 1966.

The Secretariat as a whole was dismissed in practice in August 1966 and formally in April 1969. Although a Deng biography may not need a detailed analysis of the ins and outs of the above changes, they should be kept in the biographer's mind.

Notes to Chapter 12

1. For a discussion of Mao's dualistic character, see Pye, *Mao Tse-Tung: The Man in the Leader,* pp. 188–89; Wakeman, *History and Will,* preface; and Terrill, *Mao,* pp. 430–31.

2. Deng's siding with Mao against Zhou in 1956–58 marked Deng's more formal, albeit temporary, shift in allegiance and affiliation between his two mentors.

3. See Party History Research Institute, comp., *Zhonggong dashi nianbiao*, p. 143; and MacFarquhar, *The Origins of the Cultural Revolution*, vol. 1, pt. 1.

4. MacFarquhar, *The Origins of the Cultural Revolution*, vol. 1, pts. 3, 4.

5. Deng Xiaoping, "Report on the Rectification Campaign," in Bowie and Fairbank, *Communist China, 1955–1959*, pp. 341–63. It should be noted that, when Mao sponsored the "double hundred" and "rectification" campaigns, he might have indeed have meant it. Mao's grudge against the party bureaucracy in general and with Liu in particular was temporarily checked in 1953, 1957, and 1962, partly due to Deng's influence, but would find its full expression in 1966. The funny part of the communist political game at the time was that, while Mao was using Deng to check Liu, Mao also had to be checked by Deng for Liu.

6. For Deng's recollection of the antirightist campaign in 1980, see *Deng Xiaoping wenxuan*, pp. 2:255–74.

7. See Mao Zedong, *Jianguo yilai Mao Zedong wengao*, pp. 6:537–38. In June 1957, Mao estimated that there were approximately four thousand "rightists" in the entire country. The next month, the figure had jumped to eight thousand. By the end of 1957, when this campaign was completed under Deng's leadership, as many as eight hundred thousand were labeled rightists.

8. For Deng's 1957 visit to Moscow with Mao and Mao's referring to him as "the little man," see *Khrushchev Remembers*, pp. 252–53.

9. Bachman, *Bureaucracy, Economy and Leadership in China*, chap. 8; Tong Xiaopeng, *Fengyun sishi nian*, pp. 2:357–59. Mao derided and humiliated Zhou in 1958 on several formal occasions, during which Deng's supportive role for Mao's actions seemed quite apparent. It was through Deng that Zhou revised his self-criticisms and submitted them to Mao.

10. See Salisbury, *The Long March*, pp. 136–37; Evans, *Deng Xiaoping and the Making of Modern China*, pp. 148–49; and Makoto Yuasa, *Deng Xiaoping*, pp. 74, 83.

11. In my own knowledge based on unattributable sources, Mao made some striking remarks at a Party Center conference in late 1958 or early 1959: My name is Mao Zedong, and I am the general commander. Here is Deng Xiaoping, and he is the deputy general commander. One of us is No. 1, and the other No. 2. Then Mao turned to address Deng: You are not only the general secretary of the Secretariat, but also the general secretary of the Politburo Standing Committee as well as the Central Committee. You have the right, and you have the power. Don't you dare to exert them?

12. For Deng's recollections of the Great Leap Forward and his own role in it, see *Deng Xiaoping wenxuan*, pp. 2:255–74.

13. Fang Weizhong, ed., *Zhonghua renmin gongheguo jingji dashiji*, pp. 245–46.

14. Academy of Military Science, ed., *Jiefangjun dashiji*, pp. 366–71.

15. Deng Xiaoping, "The Great Unity of the Chinese People and the Great Unity of the Peoples All over the World," published respectively in *Pravda*, October 1, 1959, and *Renmin ribao*, October 2, 1959.

16. See MacFarquhar, *Origins of the Cultural Revolution*, vol. 2, pt. 2. Deng did denounce the "five radical winds" after late 1958—but that was also done in accordance with Mao's own "turn to the right" at that time—until the Lushan Conference.

Nonetheless, Deng did not show himself as active in 1959 as he had been before, and he would prove quicker to resort to a "small leap backward" than those true believers in the Great Leap Forward in 1960. The reason was simple: Deng had never quite believed in those fantasies in the first place and had supported the Great Leap Forward mainly for political, rather than economic, considerations.

Notes to Chapter 13

1. For a discussion of the food crisis in 1960, including the grain shortages, see Fang Weizhong, ed., *Zhonghua renmin gongheguo jingji dashiji*, pp. 272–73.

2. Ibid.

3. See Bachman, *Chen Yun and the Chinese Political System*, pp. 45–60.

4. Fang Weizhong, ed., *Zhonghua renmin gongheguo jingji dashiji*, pp. 300–302; Li Xinzhi and Wang Yuezong, eds., *Weida de shijian, guanghui de sixiang*, pp. 120–21.

5. For Mao's self-criticism at the Seven Thousand Cadres Conference, see Mao, *Mao Zedong sixiang wansui*, pp. 2:525–50.

6. Deng Xiaoping, "Speech at the enlarged work conference of the CCP Central Committee," *Deng Xiaoping wenxuan*, pp. 1:279–99.

7. Mao's remarks on Deng on October 24, 1966, in *Mao Zedong sixiang wansui*, pp. 2:655–61.

8. Party History Research Institute, comp., *Zhonggong dashi nianbiao*, p. 164.

9. Deng Xiaoping, "How to recover agricultural production," July 7, 1962, *Deng Xiaoping wenxuan*, pp. 1:304–9.

What Deng originally referred to was a "yellow cat or a white cat." Later on, this popular aphorism became "black cat or white cat." During the Cultural Revolution in the late 1960s, Deng carefully admitted that he had played a full role in the "1962 rightist tendency" and just a partial role in the "1964 formally leftist but substantially rightist tendency."

10. See Party History Research Institute, comp., *Zhonggong dashi nianbiao*, pp. 166–67.

11. It is generally accepted that the "Early Ten Points" and the "Later Ten Points" in 1963 were drafted under Mao and Deng, respectively.

12. The "Revised Later Ten Points" in 1964 was drafted under Liu's auspices. Together with this Party Center document, a report by Madame Liu on her "Peach Orchid experience" was communicated among high-ranking party officials. Madame Mao, who had joined the party ten years earlier than Madame Liu, was furious because she herself could not even qualify to attend such communication meetings.

13. Zhao Wei, *Zhao Ziyang zhuan*, p. 151.

14. Snow, *The Long Revolution*, pp. 17, 136; Bo Yibo also recalled Mao's abnormal behavior and remarks at his seventy-second birthday party on December 26, 1965.

15. Based on my personal knowledge at that time; see also "Ten cardinal crimes of Deng Xiaoping," *Shoudu hongweibing* (Beijing Red Guards), April 10, 1967.

16. Ibid.

17. Ibid.

18. Griffith, *The Sino-Soviet Rift,* pp. 104–19.

19. Franz, *Deng Xiaoping,* pp. 168–72; Evans, *Deng Xiaoping and the Making of Modern China,* pp. 159–61.

20. Griffith, *The Sino-Soviet Rift,* pp. 177–206, 372–88.

21. There were no doubts about China's direct involvement in the Indonesian coup, although even during the Cultural Revolution, such state secrets were not yet exposed.

22. For a discussion of China's foreign aid hikes, see Fang Weizhong, ed., *Zhonghua renmin gongheguo jingji dashiji,* pp. 403, 422, 438.

23. Regarding China's secret dispatch of troops to North Vietnam, see Academy of Military Science, ed., *Jiefangjun dashiji,* p. 376.

24. Lin Biao, "Long Live the People's War!" *Renmin ribao,* September 3, 1965. In a certain sense, Madame Mao's reforms in the performing arts in 1964 were also in line with Deng's radical stance expressed in the CCP–CPSU polemics in Moscow.

Notes to Chapter 14

1. Gao Gao and Yan Jiaqi, *Wenge shinian shi,* vol. 1, chapter 1; and also Tan Zongji, "Analysis of the May 16 Communique," in *Shinianhou de pingshuo,* pp. 1–38. It should be noted that besides Yao Wenyuan, Jiang Qing, and Mao himself, only the Shanghai party leaders Ke Qingshi and Zhang Chunqiao knew about the preparation of the article; even Kang Sheng and Chen Boda did not know at that time.

2. Ibid.

3. For a discussion of Deng's southern trip in November 1965, see "Investigation of Deng Xiaoping's crimes," in Makoto Yuasa, *Deng Xiaoping,* pp. 23–24. Deng took another trip to the northwest in March 1966, with the same hopeful motive and yet the same fruitless result.

4. Based on my personal knowledge at that time. For Mao's talks with Kang Sheng on March 28, 1966, in Shanghai and at the Politburo conference on April 28, 1966, in Hangzhou, see Mao, *Mao Zedong sixiang wansui,* pp. 2:640–41, 2:653–61.

5. See Tan Zongji, "Analysis of the May 16 Communique."

6. Based on my personal knowledge at that time.

7. Liu and Deng flew to Hangzhou to seek Mao's approval before sending off the work teams; see Gao Gao and Yan Jiaqi, *Wenge shinian shi,* vol. 1, chapter 2.

8. Deng's remarks on the "February Mutiny" are based on my personal knowledge at that time.

9. See Gao Gao and Yan Jiaqi, *Wenge shinian shi,* vol. 1, chapter 2. There were subtle differences among Liu, Deng, and Zhou in their speeches at the Great Hall of People on July 30, 1966. Liu shared more blame than Deng. Although Zhou had an interest in abiding by the party's rules and protecting himself, he might also have had some justifiable personal reasons for caring little about Liu's and Deng's ordeals. Liu's backstabbing in 1942–43 and Deng's feeder biting in 1956–58 merited Zhou's indifference at best.

10. See Party History Research Institute, comp., *Zhonggong dashi nianbiao,* pp. 182–83.

11. See "Deng Xiaoping's self-criticism at the central work conference on

October 23, 1966," *Zhonggong yanjiu* (Research on Chinese Communism), Taipei, November 1969, pp. 91–94.

12. Generally speaking, Deng was a family man who lived a family life. But I both remember and believe a story told in 1966 about Deng's romantic affair with a nurse while his broken leg was being treated in the Beijing Hospital in 1960. Madame Deng appealed to Yang Shangkun, who, as director of the General Office of the CCP Center, knew how to handle this matter properly: first, calm the wife down; then, move the young woman out of Beijing—without dropping even a hint to the troubling and also troubled husband.

13. For a contrast between the performances of Liu and Deng at the Zhongnanhai trial on August 5, 1967, see Zhao Cong, *Wenge yundong licheng,* pp. 3:147–53; and Shibata, *Deng Xiaoping,* pp. 213–14.

14. According to my own knowledge at the time, Deng Pufang attempted suicide in 1968 by jumping from his Beijing University dormitory building and ended up breaking his spine and was not, as commonly believed, pushed from the building by the Red Guards, let alone by Nie Yuanzi herself.

15. Deng Rong, "Days in Jiangxi," *Renmin ribao,* August 22, 1984.

16. Ibid.

17. Deng Rong, *My Father Deng Xiaoping.*

18. See Lin Biao's speech at the Politburo conference, May 19, 1966, in Zhao Cong, ed., *Wenge yundong licheng,* pp. 1:204–209.

19. An Jianshe, ed., *Zhou Enlai de zuihou suiyue,* pp. 154–68; Wang Nianyi, *Dadongluan de niandai,* pp. 382–433.

By the way, Yao Ming-le's *The Conspiracy and Death of Lin Biao* (New York: Knopf, 1983), once a popular book among Western Sinologists in the early 1980s, is fiction at best and its author definitely a fake.

The same can also be said of Jiang Zhifeng on the Tiananmen bloodshed in 1989 and Ai Pei on Zhou Enlai in 1993. Yao had nothing to do with the Lin Biao investigation, nor Jiang with Zhongnanhai secrets, and Ai is not Zhou's illegitimate daughter.

All this stuff is a shame for some and a mockery for others! The real question regarding the Lin Biao affair is whether Lin's plane crashed for lack of fuel or was shot down on orders from Zhou. Despite all the popular remarks and recollections, there remains the latter possibility, which is, in my own judgment, rather strong.

20. See Zhang Yufeng's reminiscences, *Wenhui bao* (Literary Daily), Hong Kong, July 23–25, 1988.

21. See "CCP Central Document No. 14, 1973," quoted in Zhao Wei, *Zhao Ziyang zhuan,* pp. 194–95.

22. Zhao Wei, *Zhao Ziyang zhuan,* pp. 194–95.

Notes to Chapter 15

1. See Party History Research Institute, comp., *Zhonggong dashi nianbiao,* pp. 199–200.

2. For a discussion of Deng's reappearance, see Lee, *Deng Xiaoping,* pp. 157–60; and Terrill, *Mao,* pp. 373–75.

3. See Terrill, *Mao,* pp. 373–75.

4. Deng Xiaoping, "Answer to the Italian journalist Oriana Fallaci," Au-

gust 21, 23, 1980, *Deng Xiaoping wenxuan,* pp. 2:303–12.

5. Tong Xiaopeng, *Fengyun sishi nian,* pp. 2:519–32; An Jianshe, ed., *Zhou Enlai de zuihou suiyue,* pp. 299, 302–5. Mao's renewed grudge against Zhou started roughly in June 1972 and became quite obvious by December of that year, ostensibly over the *pi-Lin pi-Kong* movement. Here "pi-Lin pi-Kong" means "joint criticism of Lin Biao and Confucius."

6. Regarding Deng's activities soon after his restoration, see *Renmin ribao* news reports from April to December 1973.

7. See Li Xinzhi and Wang Yuezong, eds., *Weida de shijian, guanghui de sixiang,* p. 111; also Salisbury, *The New Emperors,* pp. 344–46.

8. Lee, *Deng Xiaoping,* p. 163; Franz, *Deng Xiaoping,* p. 228; Bonavia, *Deng,* p. 205; Evans, *Deng Xiaoping and the Making of Modern China,* p. 195. How far and how fast a rumor spreads!

9. Deng Xiaoping, *Speech by the Chairman of the Delegation of the People's Republic of China at the Special Session of the UN General Assembly,* April 10, 1974.

10. For Deng's activities soon after his return from the UN General Assembly session, see *Renmin ribao*'s news reports from May to December 1974.

11. For Beijing politics and the dispute over the cruiser *Fengqing* in October 1974, see Yang Shengqun, ed., *Zhonggong zhongda shijian,* pp. 284–85.

12. This might be called the second Zhou–Deng collaboration. They needed each other, politically as well as personally.

13. Zhang Tuosheng, "The general readjustment in 1975," in Tan Zongji et al., *Shinianhou de pingshuo,* pp. 102–40.

14. Deng Xiaoping, "The army must have readjustment," January 25, 1975, *Deng Xiaoping wenxuan,* pp. 2:1–3; "The party needs a general strategy to push the national economy forward," March 5, 1975, *Deng Xiaoping wenxuan,* pp. 2:4–7; "Several urgent problems need to be solved for the iron and steel industry," May 29, 1975, *Deng Xiaoping wenxuan,* pp. 2:8–11; "Strengthen the party leadership, readjust the party style," July 4, 1975, *Deng Xiaoping wenxuan,* pp. 2:12–14.

15. Zhang Tuosheng, "The general readjustment in 1975"; also Han Shanbi, *Deng Xiaoping pingzhuan,* p. 2:255.

16. An Jianshe, ed., *Zhou Enlai de zuihou suiyue,* p. 381; Gao Wenqian, "Final days of Zhou Enlai," *Renmin ribao,* January 8, 1986.

17. Mao Yuanxin and Zhang Yufeng differed in the nature of their impact on Mao, the former's influences being political and the latter's being personal.

18. Wang Nianyi, *Da dongluan de niandai,* pp. 551–56.

19. The conference was called by Mao Yuanxin at Mao's suggestion. Besides Deng, there were only three other participants: Mao Yuanxin, Wang Dongxing, and Chen Xilian.

20. Franz, *Deng Xiaoping,* p. 250.

21. An Jianshe, ed., *Zhou Enlai de zuihou suiyue,* pp. 338–54.

Notes to Chapter 16

1. See Terrill, *Mao,* pp. 400–403. For this entire chapter, see Li Zhisui, *The Private Life of Chairman Mao,* parts 1, 4. Despite this book's various questionable points, at least its author is authentic.

2. Deng Xiaoping, "Speech at memorial meeting for Comrade Zhou Enlai," *Deng Xiaoping wenxuan*, pp. 2:102–106; Zhang Yufeng's reminiscences, *Wenhui bao*, Hong Kong, July 23–25, 1988.

3. Yang Shengqun, ed., *Zhonggong zhongda shijian*, pp. 268–88.

4. Ibid.

5. Party History Research Institute, comp., *Zhonggong dashi nianbiao*, p. 208.

6. See "The Capitalist Roader is Still on the Road," *Wenhui bao*, March 22, 1976.

7. Party History Research Institute, *Zhonggong dashi nianbiao*, pp. 209–10.

8. Deng seemed quite stubborn this time. Although he admitted some mistakes, he kept his admissions to a minimum and also addressed them only to Mao, not to Jiang Qing and her peers.

9. Regarding the April 5 incident, see Party History Research Institute, comp., *Zhonggong dashi nianbiao*, pp. 210–11.

10. Based on my knowledge at that time; also Han Shanbi, *Deng Xiaoping pingzhuan*, pp. 2:317–19. As far as I can tell, nobody died in that Tiananmen incident, and Ye Jianying's speech, referred to by Han and Evans, is a fabrication.

11. See Gao Gao and Yan Jiaqi, *Wenge shinian shi*, vol. 3, chapter 7.

12. For a vivid discussion of Mao, sick and weak, meeting foreign visitors, see Terrill, *Mao*, pp. 416–17.

13. Liang Xiao, "Further comments on Confucius," in *Hongqi*, June 1976. Here Liang Xiao represents the Criticism Group of Beijing University and Qinghua University.

14. Regarding the Tangshan earthquake and its aftermath, see Fang Weizhong, ed., *Zhonghua renmin gongheguo jingji dashiji*, pp. 568–69.

15. Ibid.

16. For the conflicts between Hua and Jiang, see Terrill, *Madame Mao*, pp. 369–73; Ye Yonglie, *Jiang Qing zhuan* (Biography of Jiang Qing) (Shenyang: Spring Wind Press, 1994), pp. 566–82.

17. Fan Shuo, *Ye Jianying zai 1976*, p. 222.

18. Franz, *Deng Xiaoping*, pp. 252–53, and Evans, *Deng Xiaoping and the Making of Modern China*, pp. 212–14. Neither Deng nor Zhao Ziyang took part in the arrest of the "Gang of Four." In reality, neither of them, especially Zhao, could possibly have attempted to do so at that time and under those conditions.

19. See *Renmin ribao*, news report, October 20, 1976.

Notes to Chapter 17

1. Lee, *Deng Xiaoping*, p. 187; Franz, *Deng Xiaoping*, p. 252; Evans, *Deng Xiaoping and the Making of Modern China*, p. 212. It is preposterous even to think of Xu Shiyou or Wei Guoqing having smuggled Deng out of Beijing to Canton in 1976. Xu and Wei, by the way, had nothing to do with Deng in the Second Field Army, and Zhang Pinghua's speech, referred to by Lee and Evans, is another fabrication.

2. Deng Xiaoping, "A letter for Comrade Wang Dongxing to pass on to Comrade Hua Guofeng," Guofangbu zhongzhengzhi zuozhanwei, ed., *Deng Xiaoping yanlunji*, p. 108.

3. Hua's directives were carried in "Party Center Document No. 15, 1977," according to my own knowledge; also see Party History Research Institute, comp., *Zhonggong dashi nianbiao,* pp. 215–16.

4. Deng, "A letter to Comrade Hua Guofeng and Comrade Ye Jianying," Guofangbu zhongzhengzhi zuozhanwei, ed., *Deng Xiaoping yanlunji,* pp. 109–10.

5. See Fan Shuo, *Ye Jianying zai 1976,* p. 315.

6. Zhou Xun et al., *Deng Xiaoping,* pp. 22–33.

7. See "Practice is the Sole Criterion for Truth," *Guangming ribao,* May 11, 1978. In my own knowledge, Deng himself defined the debate as "less a theoretical issue than a political issue" and "a face to face political competition."

8. See Deng's speech, "Emancipate the mind, seek truth from facts and unite as one to look forward," December 13, 1978, *Deng Xiaoping wenxuan,* pp. 2:13–43.

9. According to my own knowledge at that time, Wei Jingsheng put up a big-character poster on the "democratic wall" in downtown Beijing in November 1978, asking the government for political freedom and democracy or "the fifth modernization" as he put it.

10. Ruan Ming, *Deng Xiaoping diguo,* pp. 40–50. Although it is good to look at this event from a domestic political perspective, as Ruan does, it may be too much to say that "the war to punish Vietnam lay the foundation for Deng's power."

11. Deng Xiaoping, "Uphold the four cardinal principles," March 30, 1979, *Deng Xiaoping wenxuan,* pp. 2:144–70.

12. Ryosei Kokubun, *Political Process and Democratization in China,* pp. 36–76. Kokubun offers a very credible survey of social and economic developments during 1979–80, while I attempt here to emphasize their relations to Deng's political purposes.

13. Fang Weizhong, ed., *Zhonghua renmin gongheguo jingji dashiji,* pp. 614–23.

14. See Harding, *China's Second Revolution,* pp. 71–74; Bachman, *Chen Yun and the Chinese Political System,* pp. 157–65.

15. Fang Weizhong, ed., *Zhonghua renmin gongheguo jingji dashiji,* p. 625. In Chinese, by the way, "east and west" also means "thing."

16. Chen Yun, "Uphold the principle of proportional growth, readjust the national economy," March 21, 1979, *Chen Yun wenxuan 1956–1985,* pp. 226–31; Deng Xiaoping, "Implement the policy of readjustment, ensure stability and solidarity," December 25, 1980, *Deng Xiaoping wenxuan,* pp. 2:313–33.

17. Zhao Wei, *Zhao Ziyang zhuan,* pp. 233–35; Shambaugh, *The Making of a Premier,* chap. 6.

18. See Party History Institute, comp., *Zhonggong dashi nianbiao,* pp. 228–30.

19. Deng Xiaoping, "Remarks on successive drafts of the resolution on certain questions in the history of our party since the founding of the People's Republic," March 1980–June 1981, *Deng Xiaoping wenxuan,* pp. 2:255–74.

Notes to Chapter 18

1. See news report of *Mingbao yuekan* (Mingbao Monthly), Hong Kong, July 18, 1981; also Li Hongfeng, *Deng Xiaoping zhongyao huodong,* pp. 162–63.

2. Terrill, *Madame Mao,* prologue and last chapter, p. 374.

3. Deng Xiaoping, "One heart and one mind for economic reconstruction," September 18, 1982, *Deng Xiaoping wenxuan*, pp. 3:9–11.

4. For Deng's comparison between the Seventh and Twelfth Congresses, see Lee, *Deng Xiaoping*, p. 211.

5. Regarding Ye's grudge against Deng, see Franz, *Deng Xiaoping*, p. 278; Goodman, *Deng Xiaoping and the Chinese Revolution*, pp. 103–4.

6. For Chen Yun's historical background and political position, see Bachman, *Chen Yun and the Chinese Political System*, 1905–1949, pp. 1–27; 1949–1984, pp. 28–93.

7. There was a popular rhyme at the time, "Ask Zhao Ziyang if you want grain, and ask Wan Li if you want rice." After Zhao and Wan left for the central leadership, the agricultural output proved not to be as good as had previously been announced in either Sichuan or Anhui. But it did not matter much anymore, as both had already been promoted to Beijing.

8. Deng Xiaoping, "Improve economic zones, develop openness to the world," February 24, 1984, *Deng Xiaoping wenxuan*, pp. 3:51–52.

9. Deng Xiaoping, "Build up socialism with material as well as spiritual civilizations," April 29, 1983, *Deng Xiaoping wenxuan*, pp. 3:27–28.

10. Deng Xiaoping, "Ensure severe punishment for criminal activities," July 19, 1983, *Deng Xiaoping wenxuan*, pp. 3:33–34.

11. Few, including Deng himself, really regarded Deng as a theoretician type. Besides his "black cat or white cat" remarks, another of Deng's famous sayings was "Feel the rocks to wade across the river." Therefore, many in China would sum up Deng's philosophy as "kitten theory" plus "rocky river theory."

12. Deng Xiaoping, "An idea for peaceful reunification of the Mainland and Taiwan," June 26, 1983, *Deng Xiaoping wenxuan*, pp. 3:30–31.

13. Evans, *Deng Xiaoping and the Making of Modern China*, pp. 222–44. According to Evans, the British side raised the Hong Kong issue first in 1980, and China was just responding in 1982.

14. See "Deng's dirty swear shocks the whole world!" *Baixing*, Hong Kong, June 1984.

15. Deng Xiaoping, "Be a bit more far-sighted for developing Sino-Japanese relations," April 25, 1984; *Deng Xiaoping wenxuan*, pp. 3:53–55.

16. Deng's talks with Reagan were not included in *Deng Xiaoping wenxuan* and were reported only briefly in *Renmin ribao*, May 1, 1984.

17. See *Renmin ribao*, news report, August 23, 1984.

18. Central China TV broadcast, October 1, 1984; also Deng Xiaoping, "Zai Zhonghua renmin gongheguo chengli sanshiwu zhounian qingzhu dianlishang de jianghua," October 1, 1984, *Deng Xiaoping wenxuan*, pp. 3:69–71.

Notes to Chapter 19

1. See Deng's talks with Lee on September 20, 1985, in Li Hongfeng, *Deng Xiaoping zhongyao huodong*, pp. 321–22.

2. For the emerging problems of rural reforms in 1985, see Chen Yizi, *Zhongguo shinian gaige yu bajiu minyun*, pp. 45–47.

3. Harding, *China's Second Revolution*, pp. 163–71. For Chen's and Hu's criticism of the SEZs, see Franz, *Deng Xiaoping*, p. 291.

4. For Deng's remarks about his being a "layman," see Evans, *Deng Xiaoping and the Making of Modern China*, p. 256.

5. Deng Xiaoping, "Strengthen the people's sense of legality," June 28, 1986. *Deng Xiaoping wenxuan*, pp. 3:163–64.

6. Deng Xiaoping, "On questions of reform of the political system," September–November 1986, *Deng Xiaoping wenxuan*, pp. 3:176–80.

7. Yang Zhongmei, *Hu Yaobang: A Chinese Biography*, pp. 113–15. There is no evidence to support the commonly held claim that Hu was a student of Deng's at Kangda (Anti-Japanese University) in Yan'an in 1937.

8. See Lu Keng, *Hu Yaobang fangwenji*.

9. See *Renmin ribao*, editorial and news report, January 2, 1987.

10. Deng Xiaoping, "Take a clear-cut stand against bourgeois liberalization," December 30, 1986, *Deng Xiaoping wenxuan*, pp. 3:195–97.

11. Ruan Ming, *Deng Xiaoping diguo*, pp. 133–46. It should particularly be noted that Zhao wrote to Deng and other party veterans to criticize Hu, obviously to curry political favor for himself.

12. Zhao Wei, *Zhao Ziyang zhuan*, p. 275. Deng and Zhao first met in the Jin-Ji-Yu Base Area in the late 1930s, but they did not establish a close relationship in an intraparty factional sense until around 1979–80.

13. Ibid.; also Shambaugh, *The Making of a Premier*, p. 55.

14. Deng Xiaoping, "Reform and openness bring to China a new life," May 12, 1987, *Deng Xiaoping wenxuan*, pp. 3:232–35; "Quicken the pace of reform," June 12, 1987, *Deng Xiaoping wenxuan*, pp. 3:236–43.

15. See the communiqué of the CCP 13th congress, published in *Renmin ribao*, November 12, 1987.

16. For Zhao's reference to Deng's status as paramount leader, decided at the party's Thirteenth Congress, see "Zhao Ziyang's confession," *Zhongguo zhi chun*, New York, July 1994; also Zhao Wei, *Zhao Ziyang zhuan*, p. 121.

17. For the price reform, panic purchasing, and their bearing upon Zhao-Li relations, see Zhao Ziyang, "Zhao Ziyang's confession"; also Chen Yizi, *Zhongguo shinian gaige yu bajiu minyun*, pp. 124–28, 145–46. The common tendency to connect the 1988 price reform directly with the 1989 Tiananmen incident was not entirely wrong but was somewhat lacking in insight.

18. For Deng's pushing for price reforms in early 1988, see Deng Xiaoping, "Rectify price, speed reform," May 19, 1988, *Deng Xiaoping wenxuan*, pp. 3:262–63; "The more the mind is liberated, the faster the pace of reform," May 25, 1988, *Deng Xiaoping wenxuan*, pp. 3:264–65; "Current situations urge us for more reform and openness," June 22, 1988, *Deng Xiaoping wenxuan*, pp. 3:269–70.

19. For the change in Deng's attitude toward price reforms in late 1988, see "The central government must have authority," September 12, 1988, *Deng Xiaoping wenxuan*, pp. 3:277–78, and his talks to Shultz and other foreign visitors.

20. Zhao Wei, *Zhao Ziyang zhuan*, pp. 275–77.

21. See *Renmin ribao*, September 22, 1988; Chen Yizi, *Zhongguo shinian gaige yu bajiu minyun*, pp. 128–29.

Notes to Chapter 20

1. Deng Xiaoping, "Stability is above everthing else," February 26, 1989, *Deng Xiaoping wenxuan,* pp. 3:284–85. For Deng's meeting with George Bush, see *Renmin ribao* and *New York Times,* February 27, 1989.

2. Deng Xiaoping, "Uphold the tradition of hard struggle," March 23, 1989, *Deng Xiaoping wenxuan,* pp. 3:288–90; Li Hongfeng, *Deng Xiaoping zhongyao huodong,* pp. 439–40.

3. Chen Yizi, *Zhongguo shinian gaige yu bajiu minyun,* pp. 150–60; also Wu Mouren et al., eds., *Bajiu Zhongguo minyun jishi,* vol. 1, pp. 5–35.

4. *Renmin ribao,* editorial, April 26, 1989.

5. See Wu Mouren et al., eds., *Bajiu Zhongguo minyun jishi,* vol. 1, pp. 39–41.

6. *Renmin ribao,* editorial, May 4, 1989.

7. Chen Yizi, *Zhongguo shinian gaige yu bajiu minyun.*

8. Regarding the Deng–Gorbachev summit, see *Renmin ribao,* news report, May 16, 1989; also Deng Xiaoping, "Close the past, open up the future," May 16, 1989, *Deng Xiaoping wenxuan,* pp. 3:291–95.

9. Yan Jiaqi, "May 17 announcement" in Wu Mouren et al., eds., *Bajiu Zhongguo minyun jishi,* pp. 1:248–49.

10. Zhao Ziyang, "Zhao Ziyang's confession." Thanks to this uniquely valuable document, all the major points regarding relations and decisions in the central leadership of the Chinese Communist Party can be clarified, at least up until May 20, 1989.

11. Chen Yizi, *Zhongguo shinian gaige yu bajiu minyun,* pp. 160–62; Evans, *Deng Xiaoping and the Making of Modern China,* pp. 295–96.

12. See Yang Shangkun's speech to the military commanders, May 25, 1989, in Yi and Thompson, *Crisis at Tiananmen,* pp. 182–84. There were various rumors regarding Deng's whereabouts in late May and early June 1989. I tend to believe that Deng remained in his suburban residence in the Western Hills, communicating from there with Yang at the Military Council headquarters.

13. Deng Xiaoping, "Organize a reforming and hopeful leadership," May 31, 1989, *Deng Xiaoping wenxuan,* pp. 3:296–301.

14. See Wu Mouren et al., eds., *Bajiu Zhongguo minyun jishi,* vol. 1, pp. 566–96; vol. 2, pp. 598–745.

15. Deng Xiaoping, "Speech at the meeting with cadres from Beijing's martial law troops," June 9, 1989, *Deng Xiaoping wenxuan,* pp. 3:302–8.

16. Deng Xiaoping, "The pressing need for the third generation of leadership," June 16, 1989, *Deng Xiaoping wenxuan,* pp. 3:309–14.

17. Goodman, *Deng Xiaoping and the Chinese Revolution,* pp. 110–11; Evans, *Deng Xiaoping and the Making of Modern China,* pp. 301–2; "Zhao Ziyang's confession."

18. Deng Xiaoping, "Letter to the Political Bureau of the CCP Central Committee," September 4, 1989, *Deng Xiaoping wenxuan,* pp. 3:322–23.

19. It should be noted that in China, and other nations as well, political outcomes sometimes seem uncertain and unpredictable—either because the outcomes themselves are inherently uncertain and unpredictable or because we as political observers are ignorant or mistaken.

Notes to Chapter 21

1. Deng Rong, *Wode fuqin Deng Xiaoping,* pp. 2–6; Ruan Ming, *Deng Xiaoping diguo,* pp. 194–211.

2. Georg Hegel, *Philosophy of History,* chaps. 1, 2. The myth as well as the reality of China is that six hundred million people participated in the "Great Leap Forward" in the 1950s; thirty million people died in the "three bitter years" in the 1960s; twenty million youngsters rose up as "red rebels," and one million citizens got killed as "black bandits" during the "Cultural Revolution"; ten million confronted the government for "democracy and freedom" over the years; and one billion follow the government to become "rich and wealthy" now. What next? Despite all the ostensibly conflicting phenomena, there should be something consistent and coherent.

3. For Deng's talk with Ceausescu on October 17, 1988, see *Renmin ribao,* October 18, 1988; see also Li Hongfeng, *Deng Xiaoping zhongyao huodong,* pp. 432–33.

4. Deng and his colleagues' watching videotapes of the Romanian coup is based on information I obtained from unofficial sources in Beijing.

5. The CCP and Deng's reflections on the Soviet coup, in *Zhongguo zhishi fenzi,* New York, January 1993.

6. Deng's talk about Western sanctions, January 9, 1990, in Li Hongfeng, *Deng Xiaoping zhongyao huodong,* p. 458.

7. Evans, *Deng Xiaoping and the Making of Modern China,* p. 305 and also *Zhongguo zhishi fenzi,* December 1992. It is called the twenty-four-character policy because its name consists of twenty-four Chinese characters. In a refined form, this policy was summed up in three points: observe calmly; stick to our foothold; and act properly. Among the practical applications of this diplomatic policy or strategy, China's vote in the United Nations on the Gulf War in 1991 could be taken as a major one and its handling of the Yin He incident in 1993 as a minor one.

8. For Deng's boosting of Jiang's image and authority, see *Deng Xiaoping wenxuan,* p. 3:334; also Li Hongfeng, *Deng Xiaoping zhongyao huodong,* p. 466.

9. See Jiang Zemin, "Speech at the celebration meeting for the Chinese Communist Party's 70th anniversary," *Renmin ribao,* July 2, 1991.

10. See "China must go all for the reform and openness policy," *Renmin ribao,* September 1, 1991, and the CCTV news broadcast the previous night.

11. The *Renmin ribao* story is based on information I obtained from an unofficial source in Beijing.

12. Deng Xiaoping, "Key points of talks in Wuchang, Shenzhen, Zhuhai, and Shanghai," January 18–February 21, 1992, *Deng Xiaoping wenxuan,* pp. 3:370–83.

13. See *Zhengming,* Hong Kong, June 1992.

14. Regarding Deng's visit to the Capital Steel and Iron Plant, see *Zhongguo shibao,* New York, August 1992.

15. See Chen Yun's speeches in *Renmin ribao* on May 1 and July 12, 1992, respectively. The shift in tone is subtle but clear.

16. See *Kaifang,* Hong Kong, November 1992. Although Deng dismissed the Yang brothers, he simultaneously comforted them and warned army veterans against pursuing the case any further.

17. Ibid.

18. I was told by some unofficial sources that, in organizing the central leadership of the Fourteenth Congress, Bo Yibo headed a special group to draft a preliminary list and report, for review by Chen Yun and others, with the final decision made by Deng himself, and that at one point Deng thought of changing Jiang Zemin as his successor and then was dissuaded by Bo Yibo.

19. See State Statistical Bureau, *Zhongguo tongji nianjian* (Chinese Statistical Yearbook), 1985–1994 (Beijing: Chinese Statistical Press, 1985–1994).

Notes to Chapter 22

1. For Deng Pufang's remarks, see *Shijie ribao*, May 25, 1993.

2. *Renmin ribao,* February 5, 1994.

3. *New York Times,* March 13, 1994.

4. Ibid.

5. As far as the public knows, Kim's and Deng's latest meeting was in December 1992. Kim took numerous unpublished trips to China, mostly by train from Pyongyang to Beijing, just a 10 hour ride.

6. *New York Times,* March 20, 1994.

7. It was top secret at the time, but becomes public knowledge now that the Chinese troops of 180,000 secretly moved into North Korea on October 19, 1950, while General Macarthur still regarded such as an absolute impossibility before the first campaign started the next month. Even then, they were still regarded as some small number of intelligence squads until the massive second campaign took place in November-January 1951. See Cai Chenwen, *Kangmei yuanchao jishi,* pp. 60–66.

8. *Renmin ribao*, August 23 and October 1, 1994.

9. See National Statistic Bureau, *Zhongguo tongji nianjian,* 1995.

10. Ibid. For various political factors leading to or then caused by economic reforms, see Shirk, *The Political Logic of Economic Reform in China.*

11. *New York Times,* January 14, 1995.

12. CCTV news report, February 15, 1996.

13. During and since the 1989 Tiananmen incident, there have been numerous irresponsible reports from BBC, ABC, CNN, Hong Kong and Taiwan media, on Deng's death or fatal illness.

14. See *Shijie ribao,* January 15, 1996.

15. See *Jingbao Monthly,* Hong Kong, April 1994.

16. One of Deng's ideas was for China to avoid international tensions in order concentrate on its own economic growth; another was for China to enhance its national integrity and make progresses into world politics. More discussions about these conflicting ideas will be given in the next chapter.

17. *New York Times,* March 9, 1996. Has the Chinese army ever made any hostile plans against Taiwan? Yes, probably far more than once or twice, but information about any of them was unlikely to fall into the hands of *New York Times* editors.

Notes to Chapter 23

1. Li Xinzhi and Wang Yuezong, eds., *Weida de shijian, guanghui de sixiang,* p. 221.

2. This author's personal experience and knowledge. Salisbury established relations with the Beijing authorities in 1984 through a few Chinese students in the United States. He wished to interview Deng in person for a nice biography in 1988, as Snow did with Mao in 1936. Deng refused to meet him at the last moment, despite President Yang and Foreign Minister Huang's recommendations. The source materials Salisbury had prepared for a Deng biography were eventually turned into *The New Emperors,* with a sharp change in approach.

3. On politics, see Yang, *From Revolution to Politics,* pp. 258–61.

4. See Lucian Pye, "An Introductory Profile: Deng Xiaoping and China's Political Culture," in David Shambaugh, ed., *Deng Xiaoping: Portrait of a Chinese Statesman,* pp. 32–33.

5. For Deng's talks with U.S. Secretary of State Shultz on March 3, 1987 and with U.S. President Bush on February 26, 1989, see *Deng Xiaoping wenxuan,* pp. 3:207–209, 3:284–285.

6. We may take Japan in the 1960s and Taiwan and South Korea in the 1970s as practical instances of this "bottleneck" phenomenon.

7. There are different standards for calculation with different results. This current year of 1997, China's GNP should be in the range of $2 trillion–$3 trillion, and its per capita income $800–$1,500. By the year 2000, the respective figures should be $3 trillion–$5 trillion and $1,000–$2,000. If Hong Kong and Taiwan were also drawn into the picture, China should soon overtake the United States as the world's largest economy with its annual GNP of about $8 trillion.

8. For quite opposite viewpoints, see Jack Goldstone, "The Coming China Collapse," *Foreign Policy,* Summer 1995, and Charles Krauthammer, "Why We Must Contain China," *Time,* July 1995.

Here I do not mean that Americans cannot do anything with China. Of course, they can and they will. Among the most necessary and least expensive things they can do, as I stress again, is to improve their approach to and knowledge of China. Anything or everything practical should start with simply that!

Bibliography

Sources in English:

Bachman, David. *Bureaucracy, Economy and Leadership in China*. London: Cambridge University Press, 1991.

_____. *Chen Yun and the Chinese Political System*. Berkeley: Institute of East Asian Studies, 1985.

Bonavia, David. *Deng*. Hong Kong: Longman Group, 1989.

Bowie, Robert and John K. Fairbank. *Communist China 1955–1959: Policy Documents with Analysis*. Cambridge, MA: Harvard University Press, 1962.

Central Committee, Department for Party Literature Research. *Deng Xiaoping: A Photo-biography*. Beijing: Central Party Literature Press, 1991.

Chang, David. *Zhou Enlai and Deng Xiaoping in the Chinese Leadership Succession Crisis*. Lanham, MD: University Press of America, 1984.

Chi Hsin. *Teng Hsiao-ping: A Political Biography*. Hong Kong: Cosmos Books, 1978.

Deng Maomao. *My Father Deng Xiaoping*. New York: Basic Books, 1995.

Deng Xiaoping. *Speech by the Chairman of the Delegation of the People's Republic of China at the Special Session of the UN General Assembly, April 10, 1974*. Beijing: Foreign Languages Press, 1974.

Erbaugh, Mary. "The Secret History of the Hakkas: The Chinese Revolution as a Hakka Enterprise." *China Quarterly*. No. 132, December 1992.

Evans, Richard. *Deng Xiaoping and the Making of Modern China*. New York: Viking, 1994.

Fairbank, John. *The Great Chinese Revolution, 1800–1985*. New York: Harper & Row, 1986.

Franz, Uli. *Deng Xiaoping*. Boston: Harcourt Brace Jovanvich, 1988.

Goodman, David. *Deng Xiaoping and the Chinese Revolution*. London and New York: Routledge, 1994.

Griffith, William. *The Sino-Soviet Rift*. Cambridge, MA: The MIT Press, 1964.

Hamrin, Carol. *China and the Challenge of the Future*. Boulder: Westview Press, 1990.

Harding, Harry. *China's Second Revolution: Reform After Mao*. Washington, DC: Brookings Institution, 1987.

Harrison, James. *The Long March to Power*. New York: Praeger Publisher, 1972.

Hegel, Georg. *The Philosophy of History*. New York: Dover Publications, 1956.

Kampen, Thomas. "The Zunyi Conference and Further Steps in Mao's Rise to Power. *China Quarterly*. No. 117, March 1989, pp. 118–34.

Khrushchev, Nikita. *Khrushchev Remembers*. Boston: Little, Brown & Co., 1970.

Klein, Donald and Anne Clark. *Biographic Dictionary of Chinese Communism*. Cambridge, MA: Harvard University Press, 1971.

Kuo, Warren. *Analytical History of the Chinese Communist Party*. 4 vols. Taipei: Institute of International Relations, 1968–1971.

Lardy, Nicholas. *China in the World Economy*. Washington, DC: Institute for International Economics, 1994.

Lee Ching-Hua. *Deng Xiaoping: The Marxist Road to the Forbidden City*. Princeton: Kingston Press, 1985.

Li Zhisui. *The Private Life of Chairman Mao*. New York: Random House, 1994.

MacFarqhuar, Roderick. *The Origins of the Cultural Revolution*. 2 vols. London: Oxford University Press, 1974, 1983.

MacFarquhar, Roderick and John Fairbank, eds. *The Cambridge History of China*. vols. 14, 15, New York: Cambridge University Press, 1987, 1991.

Pye, Lucian. *Mao Tse-tung: The Man in the Leader*. New York: Basic Books, 1976.

———. "An Introductory Profile: Deng Xiaoping and China's Political Culture." in Shambaugh, ed. *Deng Xiaoping: Portrait of a Chinese Statesman*.

Saich, Tony. *The Rise to Power of the Chinese Communist Party*. Armonk, NY: M.E. Sharpe, 1996.

Salisbury, Harrison. *The Long March: The Untold Story*. New York: Harper and Row, 1985.

———. *The New Emperors: China in the Eras of Mao and Deng*. Boston: Little, Brown & Co., 1992.

Schram, Stuart. *Mao Tse-tung*. New York: Penguin Books, 1966.

Schwartz, Benjamin. *Chinese Communism and the Rise of Mao*. Cambridge, MA: Harvard University Press, 1951.

Shambaugh, David, ed. *Deng Xiaoping: Portrait of a Chinese Statesman*. London: Clarendon Press, 1995.

———. *The Making of a Premier: Zhao Ziyang's Provincial Career*. Boulder: Westview Press, 1984.

Sheng Yue. *Sun Yat-sen University in Moscow and the Chinese Revolution*. Lawrence: Center for Asian Studies, University of Kansas Press, 1971.

Sheridan, James. *Chinese Warlord: The Career of Feng Yu-hsiang*. Stanford: Stanford University Press, 1966.

Shinn, James, ed. *Weaving the Net*. New York: Council on Foreign Relations, 1996.

Shirk, Susan. *The Political Logic of Economic Reform in China*. Berkeley: University of California Press, 1993.

Snow, Edgar. *Red Star over China*. New York: Grove Press, 1961.

———. *Random Notes on Red China, 1936–1945*. Cambridge, MA: Harvard University Press, 1957.

———. *The Long Revolution*. New York: Random House, 1972.

Solinger, Dorophy. *Regional Government and Political Integration in Southwest China, 1949–1954. Berkeley: University of California Press, 1977.*

Swaine, Michael. *The Military and Political Succession in China*. Santa Monica, CA: RAND Corporation, 1992.

Teiwes, Frederick. *Politics at Mao's Court: Gao Gang and Party Factionalism in the Early 1950s*. Armonk, NY: M.E. Sharpe, 1990.

————. *Politics and Purges in China*. Armonk, NY: M.E. Sharpe, 1993.

Terrill, Ross. *Mao*. New York: Harper & Row, 1980.

————. *Madame Mao: The White Boned Demon*. New York: Simon & Schuster, 1992.

Wakeman, Frederic. *History and Will*. Berkeley: University of California Press, 1973.

Wang, Nora. "Deng Xiaoping: The Years in France." *China Quarterly*. No. 92, December 1982.

Yang, Benjamin. *From Revolution to Politics: Chinese Communists on the Long March*. Boulder: Westview Press, 1990.

————. "Complexity and Reasonability: Reassessment of the Li Lisan Adventure." *Australian Journal of Chinese Affairs*. No. 21, January 1989.

————. "The Zunyi Conference as One Step in Mao's Rise to Power." *China Quarterly*. No. 106, June 1986.

Yang Zhongmei. *Hu Yaobang: A Chinese Biography*. Armonk, NY: M.E. Sharpe, 1988.

Yi, Mu, and Mark Thompson. *Crisis at Tiananmen*. San Francisco: China Books, 1990.

Sources in Chinese:

Academy of Military Science, ed. *Zhongguo renmin jiefangjun dashiji* (Big Events of the Chinese People's Liberation Army). Beijing: Military Science Press, 1983.

An Jianshe, ed. *Zhou Enlai de zuihou suiyue* (The Last Years of Zhou Enlai). Beijing: Central Documentary Press, 1995.

Ban Yang and Zhuo Xiaowei, "Black cat or white cat: review of Han Shanbi's biography of Deng Xiaoping." *Tansuo*. Nos. 55, 56, 57, January, February, March 1986.

Ban Yang, "Verifications of Deng Xiaoping's relations with the Seventh Red Army." *Tansuo*. Nos. 104, 105, August and September 1992.

————, "Verifications of the timings of Deng Xiaoping's joining the Communist Youth League and the Communist Party." *Tansuo*. No. 110, March 1993.

Bo Yibo. *Ruogan zhongda juece yu shijian de huigu* (Reminiscences of Some Important Events and Decisions). Beijing: Central Party School Press, 1991.

Bureau of Political Struggle of the Ministry of Defense, comp. *Deng Xiaoping yanlun, 1957–1980* (Deng Xiaoping's Speeches, 1957–1980). Taipei: Ministry of Defense, 1982.

Chen Yizi. *Zhongguo shinian gaige yu bajiu minyun* (Ten Years' Reforms and the 1989 Democratic Movement in China). Taipei: Lianjing Press, 1990.

Chen Yun. *Chen Yun wenxuan* (Selected Works of Chen Yun). Beijing: People's Press, 1986.

Deng Rong. *Wode fuqin Deng Xiaoping* (My Father Deng Xiaoping). Beijing: Central Documentary Press, 1993.

————, "My father's days in Jiangxi." *Renmin ribao*, August 22, 1984.

Deng Xiaoping. *Deng Xiaoping wenxuan* (Selected Works of Deng Xiaoping), 1937–1965, vol. 1. Beijing: People's Press, 1989.

———. *Deng Xiaoping wenxuan* (Selected Works of Deng Xiaoping), 1975–1982, vol. 2. Beijing: People's Press, 1983.

———. *Deng Xiaoping wenxuan* (Selected Works of Deng Xiaoping), vol. 3. Beijing: People's Press, 1993.

———. *Deng Xiaoping tongzhi lun gaige kaifang* (Comrade Deng Xiaoping on Reform and Openness). Beijing: People's Press, 1989.

———. *Deng Xiaoping tongzhi lun minzhu yu fazhi* (Comrade Deng Xiaoping on Democracy and the Legal System). Beijing: Legal Press, 1990.

———. *Deng Xiaoping tongzhi lun guofang yu jundui jianshe* (Comrade Deng Xiaoping on National Defense and Military Development). Beijing: Military Science Press, 1992.

Fan Shuo. *Ye Jianying zai 1976* (Ye Jianying in 1976). Beijing: Central Party School Press, 1990.

Fang Weizhong et al., eds. *Zhonghua renmin gongheguo jingji dashiji* (Big Economic Events of the People's Republic of China). Beijing: Chinese Social Sciences Press, 1984.

Feng Yuxiang. *Feng Yuxiang riji* (Diary of Feng Yuxiang). Beijing: National History Press, 1932.

Gao Gao and Yan Jiaqi. *Wenge shinian shi, 1966–1976* (A Ten Year History of the Cultural Revolution, 1966–1976). Tianjin: Tianjin People's Press, 1986.

Guofangbu zhongzhengzhi zuozhanwei, ed., *Gongfei yuanshi ziliao hubian: Deng Xiaoping yanlunji 1957–1980* (Collection of CCP Materials: Deng Xiaoping's Speeches 1957–1980) Taipei: Guofangbu, 1983.

Han Shanbi. *Deng Xiaoping pingzhuan* (A Critical Biography of Deng Xiaoping), 2 volumes. Hong Kong: East and West Cultures Company, 1984.

Hu Hua, ed. *Zhonggong dangshi renwu zhuan* (Biographies of People in CCP History), 50 vols. Xi'an: Shaanxi People's Press, 1980–1991.

Jiang Zemin, "Reminiscences of diligent work and thrifty study in Belgium and France." *Tianjun wenshi ziliao xuanbian* (Historical Materials of Tianjin), vol. 14, 1982.

Li Hongfeng. *Deng Xiaoping xinshiqi zhongyao huodong jiyao* (Deng Xiaoping's Important Activities in the New Epoch). Beijing: Overseas Chinese Press, 1994.

Li Huang. *Xuedun shi huiyilu* (Memoirs from an Ignorant Scholar's Studio). Taipei: Biographic Press, 1973.

Li Weihan. *Huiyi yu yanjiu* (Reminiscences and Studies). Beijing: Party History Materials Press, 1986.

Li Xinzhi and Wang Yuezong, eds. *Weida de shijian, guanghui de sixiang* (Great Practice and Glorious Thought). Beijing: Hualing Press, 1990.

Liu Shaotang. *Minguo dashi rizhi* (Daily Records of Big Events of the Republic of China), 2 volumes. Taipei: Biographic Literatures Press, 1973.

Lu Keng. *Hu Yaobang fangwenji* (Interview with Hu Yaobang). Hong Kong: Baixing Monthly, 1985.

Mao Zedong. *Mao Zedong xuanji* (Selected Works of Mao Zedong), five volumes. Beijing: People's Press, 1978.

———. *Jianguo yilai Mao Zedong wengao* (Writings of Mao Zedong after 1949), 11 volumes. Beijing: Central Documentary Press, 1987–1996.

————. *Mao Zedong wenji, 1921–1976* (Writings of Mao Zedong, 1921–1976), 5 volumes. Beijing: People's Press, 1993.

————. *Mao Zedong sixiang wansui* (Long Live Mao Zedong Thought), 2 volumes. Beijing: n.p., 1967.

Nie Rongzhen. *Nie Rongzhen huiyilu* (Memoirs of Nie Rongzhen), 3 volumes. Beijing: Soldier's Press, 1983–1985.

Party History Research Committee of the Guangxi Region. *Zuo'you jiang geming genjudi* (The Revolutionary Base Area of the Left and Right Rivers), 2 volumes. Beijing: CCP History Press, 1989.

Party History Research Group of Qinghua University. *Pufa qingong jianxue yundong shiliao* (Historical Materials on the Work-Study Movement in France), 3 volumes. Beijing: Beijing People's Press, 1981.

Party History Research Institute of the CCP Central Committee. *Zhonggong dashi nianbiao* (Annual Records of CCP Major Events). Beijing: People's Press, 1981.

Party School of the CCP Central Committee. *Zhonggong dangshi gao* (A Draft History of the CCP), 4 volumes. Beijing: People's Press, 1983.

Peng Dehuai. *Peng Dehuai zishu* (Peng Dehuai's Autobiography). Beijing: People's Press, 1981.

Ruan Ming. *Deng Xiaoping diguo* (The Deng Empire). Taipei: Shibao Publishing Co., 1992.

Secretariat of CCP Central Committee, ed. *Liuda yilai: dangnei mimi wenjian* (Since the Sixth Party Congress: Secret Documents within the Party), 2 volumes. Beijing: People's Press, 1980.

Shi Zhe. *Zai lishi juren shenbian* (Beside the Historical Giants). Beijing: Central Documentary Press, 1991.

Tan Zongji et al. *Shinianhou de pingshuo* (Comment after Ten Years). Beijing: Materials of Party History Press, 1987.

Tong Xiaopeng. *Fengyun sishi nian* (My Forty Stormy Years), 2 volumes. Beijing: Central Documentary Press, 1994.

Wang Jianying, comp. *Zhongguo gongchandang zuzhi shi ziliao huibian* (Historical Materials of CCP Organizations). Beijing: Red Flag Press, 1982.

Wang Li. *Xianchang lishi* (My Eyewitness of History). Hong Kong: Oxford University Press, 1993.

Wang Nianyi. *Dadongluan de niandai* (The Chaotic Years). Zhengzhou: Henan People's Press, 1989.

Wang Yongxiang et al. *Zhongguo gongchandang lu'ou zhibu shihua* (History of the European Branch of the Chinese Communist Party). Beijing: Chinese Youth Press, 1985.

Wu Lengxi. *Yi Mao zhuxi* (Reminiscences of Chairman Mao). Beijing: New China Press, 1995.

Wu Mouren et al., comp. *Bajiu Zhongguo minyun jishi* (Records of the 1989 Democratic Movement in China), 2 volumes. New York: n.p., 1989.

Wu Xiuquan. *Wode licheng, 1908–1949* (My Life Experiences, 1908–1949). Beijing: People's Liberation Army Press, 1984.

Yang Guoyu. *Liu Deng huixia shisannian* (Thirteen Years under the Liu-Deng Command). Beijing: People's Press, 1986.

Yang Shengqun, ed. *Zhonggong dangshi zhongda shijian shushi* (Discussions of Important Events in CCP History). Beijing: People's Press, 1993.

Zhang Guotao. *Wode huiyi* (My Memoirs), 3 volumes. Hong Kong: Mingbao Monthly Press, 1973.

Zhao Cong, comp. *Wenhua dageming ziliao huibian* (Collections of Documentary Materials of the Great Cultural Revolution), 4 volumes. Hong Kong, 1977.

Zhao Wei. *Zhao Ziyang zhuan* (A Biography of Zhao Ziyang). Beijing: Chinese News Press, 1989.

Zhou Enlai. *Zhou Enlai xuanji* (Selected Works of Zhou Enlai). Beijing: People's Press, 1980.

Zhou Xun. *Deng Xiaoping*. Hong Kong, Crystal Glass Press, 1979.

Sources in Japanese:

Hatano, Kenichi. *History of the Chinese Communist Party*. Tokyo: Jiji Tsushin, 1961.

Kokubun, Ryosei. *Political Process and Democratization in China*. Tokyo: Simul Press, 1992.

Takagi, Keizo. *An Authentic Biography of Deng Xiaoping*. Tokyo: Elite Press, 1978.

Shibata, Minoru. *Deng Xiaoping: The Pathfinder for China's Modernization*. Tokyo: Yamaten Press, 1978.

Wada, Takeshi, and Tanaka Shinichi. *Deng Xiaoping: An Indomitable Revolutionary*. Tokyo: Tokuken Bookshop, 1977.

Yuasa Makoto. *Deng Xiaoping*. Tokyo: Japanese Literature Press, 1978.

Index

Benjamin Yang came in 1981 from Beijing University to Harvard, where he earned his Ph.D. in 1986. Since then he has until recently worked with Harvard's John King Fairbank Center for East Asian Research and distinguished himself as a serious scholar and author of several influential academic writings. Yang is currently professor of international politics at the Chinese People's University in Beijing.